CALVIN COOLIDGE

The Quiet President

CALVIN COOLIDGE

The Quiet President

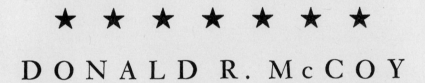

DONALD R. McCOY

The Macmillan Company : NEW YORK

Collier-Macmillan Limited : LONDON

TO ROMA

for her love and patience

E
792
.M 117

First Printing

The Macmillan Company, New York
Collier-Macmillan Canada Ltd., Toronto, Ontario

Printed in the United States of America

CONTENTS

PREFACE

H<small>E STOOD FIVE FEET, NINE INCHES TALL.</small> He had blue eyes and sandy hair. The features of his head were delicate, and included finely chiseled nose and ears, a thin line of a mouth, and smooth skin, which remained smooth because of lack of exercise in either frowning or smiling. He had adequate hair for a man in his fifties. His figure was slender and well proportioned, and his clothes fitted him well. In short, he looked the model of equanimity. He was the thirtieth President of the United States, Calvin Coolidge.

Knowing all that, however, one still does not know much about Coolidge. Consulting earlier biographies will not help greatly, for most of them are the recounting of apocryphal anecdotes held together by a glue of fact and blather that too often passes for biography. Even Claude M. Fuess and William Allen White, the two serious biographers of Coolidge, were restricted by their political predilections and by the limited amount of material available to them when they wrote over a quarter of a century ago. Yet whatever understanding of Coolidge White and Fuess added has been offset by the many historians, journalists, and political scientists who have pictured him simply as a cunning office seeker who became a know-nothing, do-nothing Chief Executive.

Because the Yankee President has become something of a national scapegoat for the coming of the Great Depression and World

War II, and because so much information about him has become available during the last twenty-five years, it is desirable to take a new look at Calvin Coolidge. That I have done in this inquiry. The result of my work, I believe, is a broader based, more fully developed biography of a politician who was less than crafty, of a President who deserves some praise and much understanding along with criticism.

The list of people to whom I am indebted is long. I might start by mentioning some of my colleagues at the University of Kansas who helped: W. Clarke Wescoe, M.D., Mrs. Janet Russell of the Department of Psychology, and George Caldwell and Mrs. Rita Lucas of the University Libraries. I am grateful to Mrs. Reuben B. Hills of Haydenville, Massachusetts, for permission to use and quote from letters sent her by Mrs. Calvin Coolidge. Special thanks are due Bernard Rogers of Henry Ford Community College for his critical reading of the manuscript of this biography. Among the many other people who gave generously of their time to help me were Newton F. McKeon, Amherst College Library; Lawrence E. Wikander, Forbes Library of Northampton; James Mahoney, Holy Cross College Library; Joseph Snell, Kansas State Historical Society; David C. Mearns, Manuscript Division, Library of Congress; I. Albert Matkov, Massachusetts State Library; Miss Jane F. Smith and W. Neil Franklin, National Archives; Mrs. Elizabeth Martin and Allen Price, Ohio State Historical Society; Louis M. Starr, Oral History Research Office, Columbia University; and James J. Rowley and Jack Warner, United States Secret Service.

Donald R. McCoy

March 15, 1966

I

Born on the Fourth of July

CALVIN COOLIDGE came into the world on July 4, 1872. He was born and raised in one of the backwaters of America. A rural Yankee, he was untouched by the cultural majesty and hauteur of most of the Boston aristocrats or of their kin in smaller cities like Hartford, Providence, Portland, or Worcester, who were less cultured but quite as haughty. He was also untouched by the immigrants and their children who served in the mansions, toiled in the mill towns, and slaved in the fields to make the wealth that supported the culture and splendor of the first families of New England. Calvin Coolidge was of another New England, that which bent its back in the stony fields and in the small crossroads stores it could call its own. Coolidge was of the yeoman New Englanders, a diminishing class even by the time of his birth. He came from among those who were content to make do with what they had, those who held to high moral standards, those of low metabolism who had little interest in seeing what lay beyond the nearest ridge, those whose prosaic thoughts often seemed profoundly expressed and who had little truck with ideas that were not prosaic.

Coolidge was born in Vermont, a rugged and out-of-the-way state. Packed into its 9,609 square miles were 921 heights of 2,000 feet or more. Climate, though bracing and healthful, contributed to the isolation of the state and its communities. Winter gripped Ver-

1

mont from late October to late April, with the average January temperature running eighteen degrees and the approximate yearly snowfall mounting to ninety inches. The state's soils, mainly sand and clay loam, further bound most of its citizens, who were well advised to give great attention to their crops in order to make ends meet. Manufacturing was of little importance in Coolidge's day, and Vermont, because of its location, was not destined to become a significant path of trade. The population of the state in 1870 was only 330,000, not much under its present population of about 400,-000. It was not cosmopolitan; over 80 percent of its people were native-born Vermonters.

Plymouth, one of the state's most isolated townships, was first settled in 1777. Four years later Captain John Coolidge, Calvin's great-great-grandfather, came from Lancaster, Massachusetts, to locate a farm in the township on the heights overlooking the Black River. Part of the lands accumulated by Captain Coolidge lay about Plymouth Notch, which was situated in a small valley about 1,400 feet above sea level to the east of the township's chief community, Plymouth Union. The Notch was where Calvin Coolidge was born and is the location of the Coolidge family cemetery. At its peak the Notch included a store, a school, a parsonless church, and seven farmhouses with their outbuildings and sheds. It was the crossroads trading and gossiping center for the farmers of the vicinity when they lacked the time to go to the area's chief marketing towns, Ludlow, some dozen miles south, or Woodstock, eleven miles east. To those towns the people of Plymouth had to go by horse, for the railroad had not and was not to come any closer.

By the time of Coolidge's birth in 1872 whatever prosperity the township could expect had passed. Its limestone, most of its marble, and its little gold had been exploited. Its largest population had been 1,400 in 1850, was down to 1,285 by 1870, and by 1940 had dipped to less than 400. It was in this declining community that Coolidge was raised. Life was not easy. A boy in the Notch was up before dawn, dressing in his chill room and then going to the kitchen to wash in cold water. He was bound to his parents and was expected to do their bidding without question. When very young, a boy's duties were to keep the woodbox filled, lead the cattle to and from the pasture, feed the chickens and hogs, plant potatoes, and even drive the mower and horse rake. By age fourteen he usually joined the men in more strenuous chores. It was a healthful but monotonous existence, one with little margin for error. Out of that life came men who were rugged, lean, and self-reliant. They were rugged because physical exertion was essential to survival; they were lean because there was rarely more than enough food available for a basic diet and essential trading; they were self-reliant because whatever they gained, they gained solely by their own efforts.

They were also proud and unimaginative: proud because they asked no man for quarter; unimaginative because the ambitious moved away and those who remained were worn down by the rigors of labor and climate and were rarely challenged by outsiders, who had little reason to come into their midst. The rural Vermonters were also conservative because they possessed so little—and could get so little more—that they were not prepared to risk losing what they had. They were throwbacks who celebrated virtues of preceding generations. Their education did not push them ahead. They possessed few books, most of which could not prepare them for the world's emerging industrial society. Their newspapers, like the Ludlow and Woodstock weeklies and the daily Rutland *Herald*, were out-of-date when they arrived and were turned out by people who were scarcely more sophisticated than the rural folk who read them.

As a matter of course, the Vermonters did not seek much more than they had. Politically they voted and acted conservatively, expecting little if any change from their leaders. Their conservatism was even carried forward into the twentieth century, for Vermont was one of the two states that voted for William Howard Taft in 1912 and for Alf Landon in 1936. As Claude M. Fuess has written of Vermonters, "In accordance with the Puritan tradition brought by the original settlers from Massachusetts, they regarded frivolity as a misdemeanor and idleness as a sin, and stressed the virtues of thrift, industry, and honesty."[1] These conservative virtues were deserving of perpetuation in the nation, but only in combination with attributes found outside Vermont. No nation has risen to heights of culture, spirituality, and material accomplishment based only on the virtues of soberness, thrift, industry, and honesty. This can be said also of individual men, and particularly of Calvin Coolidge.

That Vermonters usually sought little was seen also in other ways. They were uncommunicative and unbending with strangers and even among themselves. They did not need outsiders to survive and in fact often feared that they might be tempted by the devil. They sought no great cultural gains because their culture and beauty had been created by God in the loveliness of the surrounding hills, woodlands, and brooks and in the sturdiness of men. This concept of beauty was well stated by Coolidge when as President he said: "Vermont is my birthright. Here, one gets close to nature, in the mountains, in the brooks, the waters of which hurry to the sea; in the lakes, shining like silver in their green setting; fields tilled, not by machinery but by the brain and hand of man. My folks are happy and contented. They belong to themselves, live within their income, and fear no man."[2] Coolidge could express what Vermonters felt, but though bound to many of their values, he was among those who had the ambition and energy to leave. That should never be forgotten about Calvin Coolidge.

His family came from early Puritan stock. One John Coolidge, at about age twenty-six, sailed from England to New England probably in 1630. He settled in Watertown, Massachusetts, and became a man of some property and the founder of a family of distinction in America, though ironically the most prominent Coolidge, Calvin, came from the least promising branch. Other lines of the family brought forth historian Archibald C. Coolidge, architect Charles A. Coolidge, Massachusetts Senate Clerk Henry D. Coolidge, diplomat John Gardner Coolidge, Harvard academician Julian Lowell Coolidge, author and public servant Louis A. Coolidge, and United States Senator Marcus Coolidge. Coolidges were people of substance and prominence from the family's earliest days in America, except for the mavericks who relocated in Vermont. The most that could be said of the Green Mountain State Coolidges was that they were hardworking farmers and storekeepers, who took their turns at community tasks, paid their bills on time, and were never convicted of a crime.

The first Coolidge in Vermont, Captain John, had long and honorable service in the Revolutionary forces, beginning as a private soldier at Lexington and winding up in Rhode Island as a captain toward the war's end. John Coolidge gave the farm at Plymouth Notch to one of his sons, Calvin, who in turn gave the property to his only surviving son, Calvin Galusha Coolidge. "Galoosh," as he was known, was popular in Plymouth, perhaps because of his fondness for practical jokes or perhaps in spite of it. He served as town agent, constable, justice of the peace, and state representative. It was from this farmer-politician grandfather that Calvin Coolidge received his first substance, forty acres of land, Lime Kiln lot, in the hope that it would bind him to the soil. It was also by his paternal grandfather that Calvin came by his trace of Indian blood, as Galoosh's wife, Sarah Almeda Brewer, had acquired redman's blood somewhere in her background. Galoosh and Sarah Coolidge gave a great deal of attention to Calvin, their only grandson. Galoosh sparked the lad's interest in land and people, and Sarah, who was the person closest to being a church leader in the Notch, superintended most of the boy's religious training and much of his behavior.

The future President's father, John Calvin Coolidge, was Galoosh's only surviving son, a brother, Julius Caesar Coolidge, having died in 1870 at age twenty. John was born in 1845 and was educated at the school in the Notch and spent a few terms in Ludlow at the Black River Academy. Afterward he served as the Notch's wheelwright, did chores on Galoosh's farm, and even kept school for a while at the Pinney Hollow District School. John married in 1868 and settled down to the life of a storekeeper in the Notch.

His bride, Victoria Josephine Moor, was a year younger than he and was the daughter of the owner of the large farm situated across the road from the Coolidge store. Victoria Coolidge was a handsome woman. As her son later recounted, "She was of a very light and fair complexion with a rich growth of brown hair that had a glint of gold in it."[3] Her delicate facial features were inherited by her son. But she was not made of the stuff that could endure life in the Notch. Fastidious, a lover of poetry and natural beauty, she had a dash of mysticism and a strong strain of sentiment that were unlikely to be rewarded by the grinding routine of crossroads Vermont life. Her health cracked soon after her marriage and she became a chronic invalid, probably suffering from tuberculosis. She died when Calvin was twelve but passed on to him some of the idealism that marked his thinking and the veiled sentimentality that sometimes gripped him. The son, knowing that he was missing something from life in his mother's long illness and death, and perhaps blaming himself for them, revered her memory throughout his life.

John Calvin Coolidge was a jack-of-all-trades, well adapted by constitution to the life that his mate could not endure. He was a man of considerable ability and character. If anything had to be done around the Notch, he could do it. More importantly, if he promised to do something, it was as good as done. He was a good businessman in a precarious and limited market. He rented the store building in the Notch for forty dollars a month and made a profit of some twelve hundred dollars a year. He did well enough that in 1876 he was able to buy a house across the road, the one in which almost a half century later he was to swear in his son as President of the United States. The house was set on a couple of acres of land and the reported purchase price of $375 also bought several sheds and barns as well as a blacksmith shop.

When Galoosh died in 1878 John Coolidge inherited enough of his father's property that he felt able to sell the Notch store to his brother-in-law, Franklin C. Moor. Thereafter, John lived on his accumulated wealth, such as it was, and the proceeds from work on his farm properties. He had considerable time in which to seek public office. His offices were many and poorly paying. He served as the township's superintendent of schools, three terms in the state house of representatives, and one in the state senate. He was also at one time or another selectman, tax collector, road commissioner, constable, deputy sheriff, notary public, and school commissioner in the township. From his appointment to Governor William W. Stickney's staff in 1900 derived the title colonel, which John Coolidge, a warrior who took up no arms, enjoyed for the rest of his life.

From his father's political life, Calvin Coolidge received both valuable training in how the shrewd and discreet politician acts in search of office and a feeling of civic responsibility. Added to the sense of looking for something greater than could be found in the Notch, or indeed in all of Vermont, that he probably got from his mother, Calvin was a good bet to move on to test his mettle. The irony was that he was only half-molded, half-prepared for his destiny. He was armed with political skills and a sense of responsibility that fitted rural Vermont well but not necessarily bigger things, and he was looking for a mission and a glory that he perceived only hazily. He was very much as Harold J. Laski later described him, "a natural churchwarden in a rural parish who has by accident strayed into great affairs."[4] Some of the things with which he left home he would develop well; others would not grow well or at all. The result was that when he possessed the thing he had thought he wanted, he found that he wanted something else more. Whether at home or in traveling abroad to seek his fortune, he never was able to define the glory he was seeking. But he was searching for something better than that to which he had been heir.

The search began with his birth in a small, drab room in the family quarters that adjoined his father's store. The baby was named John Calvin Coolidge after his father, but he was called Calvin or Cal by his parents in order to eliminate confusion in the use of names at home. After he settled in Northampton, Massachusetts, over twenty years later, he dropped his first given name and thereafter was known only as Calvin Coolidge. Before he entered school the memorable incidents of his life were few. When he was three he broke his arm in a fall from a horse and earlier that year his sister, Abigail Gratia Coolidge, was born. During the same year, 1875, Galoosh took him and his mother to the state capital, Montpelier, to tour it and to see John Coolidge, who was then serving in the legislature.

Calvin was brought up in as much luxury as could be expected in Plymouth township. Not only was his father a prominent figure locally, but he had prospered. The new home into which the Coolidges moved in 1876 had, in the parlor and sitting room, pieces of black walnut furniture brought all the way from Boston. A piazza, almost a novelty for the time and place, was later added to the house. When John Coolidge was not engaged in farm work, he dressed like a gentleman in "store clothes." The Coolidges could also afford to have both a hired man and a hired girl, though they were treated, as was their right in down-to-earth Vermont, almost as members of the family. Indeed, Calvin recalled that often he had to take second place to them. Certainly Calvin was treated like a hired hand in many respects. He had chores to do: sugaring off in April, mending fences, spring planting, piling up wood for winter, plucking the fruit of the fields and of the trees, and even ploughing by himself by the time he became twelve. He also engaged in salesmanship, selling apples and popcorn balls at town meetings, as many Coolidges had done before him. If any specific boyish ambition came out of all this, it was to be, as he said later, a storekeeper as his father had been.

Though he did not become a storekeeper like his father, he did acquire many things from John Coolidge, including interest in politics, tightness with a dollar, and economy of words, the last of which was notable even among Vermonters. Calvin was to capitalize upon those characteristics after he left the Notch.

His boyhood activities were many. He did some fishing and scouting in the woods, played checkers and backgammon, engaged in candy pulls, singing, and husking bees and went bobsledding, skating, and hayriding. He recited, acted in plays and minstrel shows, played pranks, and showed occasional signs of orneriness. Yet he was different from other children. The red-haired boy was frail and occasionally was seized with sneezing and coughing, which came from a variety of minor allergies. Those allergies contributed to congestion of his nasal passages that produced an unusual quacking quality in his voice, a voice that would forever set him apart.

He was also shy, perhaps because of sensitivity to his voice and ailments and probably because his father by example and his grandmother outspokenly made it clear that he was allowed to make few mistakes. As Calvin Coolidge told his friend of later years Frank W. Stearns:

> Do you know, I've never really grown up? It's a hard thing for me to play this game. In politics, one must meet people, and that's not easy for me.... When I was a little fellow, as long ago as I can remember, I would go into a panic if I heard stranger voices in the house. I felt I just couldn't meet the people and shake hands with them. Most of the visitors would sit with Mother and Father in the kitchen and the hardest thing in the world was to have to go through the kitchen door and give them a greeting. I was almost ten before I realized I couldn't go on that way. And by fighting hard I used to manage to get through that door. I'm all right with old friends, but every time I meet a stranger, I've got to go through the old kitchen door, back home, and it's not easy.[5]

Not only was young Coolidge shy, but he was comparatively uninvolved with his fellows. He was a boy who was discouraged from dancing and who had neither a childhood sweetheart, an adolescent romance, nor played kissing games. No one even suggests that these things were for him. An earlier biographer wrote that Calvin's life at Plymouth was "simple, wholesome, and unfurtive."[6] It might have been all those things, but it was also somewhat abnormal for a boy. Young Coolidge was unusually attached to his mother, and after she was taken from him he was left with a father who could communicate only sparingly. The lad was not often punished, but when he was, the penalty, meted out by his grandmother, was frightening: he was shut up in a dark, cobwebby attic. It was little wonder, as a result of his upbringing, that he was shy.

Calvin's school days began in December, 1877. The school, which was ungraded, was held in a small stone building only paces away from his doorstep. It was crude in many ways. It met only so long as its scholars could be spared from farm work, and its teachers, who were poorly paid and often deservedly so, seldom taught for more than one school year. Its crude spruceboard seats were situated around a wood-burning box stove. The school was attended in 1877 by twenty-three children, who were between five and eighteen years of age. Sooner or later the students were escorted through spelling, reading, writing, arithmetic, algebra, geography, government, and state and national history. Calvin was rather regularly in attendance and his deportment was considered good.

The quiet Coolidge boy did nothing to make himself outstanding in school to either his teachers or schoolmates. He was studious enough to pass a teacher's examination when he was thirteen, though the edge was taken off the accomplishment when his sister Abbie passed it when she was twelve. Whatever serious reading he did came from the home. Under his mother's direction he read some Tennyson and Scott. His grandmother gave him a set of Shakespeare's works, which he took with him when he went to college. She also read to him daily a chapter from the Bible and introduced him to history and biography. Yet he never had a bookish turn of mind, for to him books were largely tools to be used in his craft. As Coolidge would decades later say to Bruce Barton, "I have little time to read books and magazines, except those that bear on problems that are before me for solution."[7]

By 1886 Calvin had acquired all that the Notch school could reasonably be expected to give and plans were made for him to go on to higher things. On a cold, snowy November day John Coolidge and his son arose, washed, dressed, and breakfasted as usual. The day was not, however, to be an ordinary one in their lives. Calvin was going away to Black River Academy, in Ludlow, where Grandmother Coolidge and John and Victoria Coolidge had gone to school. After breakfast John and his son got into the family's horse-drawn sleigh, into which had already been placed the lad's two small handbags and a calf being taken to market. They glided and slid the twelve miles over hilly, ice-covered roads to Ludlow. When the four-teen-year-old boy got off in Ludlow, his father said something like, "Calvin, if you study hard and are a good boy, maybe some time you'll go to Boston too." Then he added drily, "But the calf will get there first."[8]

Black River Academy dated back to 1835. It was a Baptist-sponsored "finishing school" for the children of the better-off country folk of southern Vermont. The classrooms, offices, tiny library, and great hall of the academy were housed in an ugly building which stood on a bluff above the Black River. The school was supervised by twenty-four trustees, one of whom was John Coolidge. Its approximately 125 students were taught by the principal and his two assistants. The cost of tuition was seven dollars a term. Room and board in the town—the academy had no dormitories—could be had for about three dollars a week. During his first year there, Calvin studied English grammar, Latin, and more algebra and became familiar with the national Constitution in a course in government. In 1887–88 he began the study of Greek, of which he became an acceptable scholar. He also studied French, ancient history, geometry, rhetoric, and American literature. He proved to be an average student, though he experienced considerable difficulty with mathematics. His early letters from Ludlow show that he needed further instruction in his native language. As he wrote his sister Abbie: "I am going to a set of 4 lectures commenceing next friday. I got a half ticket which cost 50 cts they are illustrated by the magic lantern including scenes in all the wonderland of the world."[9] It can be said, however, that his handwriting was good and clear.

Calvin did more than study and take advantage of the cultural offerings of Ludlow. He worked when he could, sometimes making toys and baby buggies in the town's carriage shop. Of course, during the long summer vacations he labored in his father's fields back in the Notch. One can presume that in Ludlow, a small trading center, Calvin observed some of the niceties of middle-class life and the necessities of commercial existence. Perhaps he came in contact with people a bit more sophisticated than those back home. Fun and pranks were also part of his life in Ludlow. Playing ball, swimming, skating, sledding, and walking along the banks of the Black River were enjoyments open to him. He could occasionally spend a weekend with Mrs. Sarah Pollard, his mother's elder sister, in Proctorsville, which was three miles away.

Sadness also intruded at Ludlow. Probably from loneliness, certainly from affection, Calvin often raised the question of when his sister would join him at the academy. The energetic and attractive redheaded girl would be a splendid companion for him. Abbie left home to enter the academy in the fall of 1888, when Calvin was a junior. She was wonderful to have around and was an outstanding student. In March, 1890, however, she was stricken ill, apparently with appendicitis, and died within a week. Calvin was with her at her deathbed. With Abbie's passing, John and Calvin Coolidge were left alone to care for each other. From the academy in April Calvin wrote his father, in what was for a Coolidge an outpouring of emotion, "It is lonesome here without Abbie."[10]

It was lonesome at Ludlow without Abbie, but Calvin was soon caught up in the whirl of activities attendant upon his graduation from the academy. Five boys and four girls were all who had stayed on to earn diplomas. The baccalaureate sermon was given on Sunday, May 16, and the commencement ceremony was held the following Friday. Young Coolidge was secretary of the class of 1890 and delivered one of the many addresses, which was an appreciation of the role of oratory in molding public opinion and pushing forward great movements in history. He also heard one of the academy's trustees, G. L. Armington, remark that "the end of education is attainment,"[11] an idea that might well have been adopted by Calvin as his motto.

Yet education, not attainment, was still uppermost in the young man's mind. Black River's principal, George Sherman, had encouraged him to consider going to college, particularly to Sherman's alma mater, Amherst. After some discussion, John Coolidge finally consented to have his son seek admission to the Massachusetts college. Admission was not automatic because the academy did not have the right to grant a college entrance certificate. Therefore, after a summer of working days on the farm and reading during the evenings, Calvin set off for Amherst to sit for the college's entrance examinations in English, Greek, Latin, and mathematics. He made the trip alone, marking his first journey by train and his first trip outside his native state. On the way down he developed a bad cold, or perhaps influenza, from which he suffered so much that he was unable to complete his examinations satisfactorily. He was forced to return to the Notch and did not recuperate for a couple of months. The story of his failure is incomplete and vague, and many interpretations can be given to what is known. The fact is, however, that Calvin was not then admitted to Amherst and that he felt it necessary to prepare further for admission.

Late in the winter he returned to Ludlow for postgraduate study, and while there was persuaded by Principal Sherman to attend St. Johnsbury Academy, which was Vermont's best preparatory school. The plan was for the young man to spend the spring term of 1891 at St. Johnsbury and receive a college entrance certificate, which that academy had the privilege of granting, at the end of the term. Calvin applied himself well during his two months at St. Johnsbury and the principal there, Dr. Charles E. Putney, agreed to give him a certificate. With that the doors of Amherst College were opened to Calvin Coolidge, as indeed were the doors of the world beyond Vermont.

2

On to Amherst

Nᴏɴᴇ ᴏꜰ ᴛʜᴇ Cᴏᴏʟɪᴅɢᴇꜱ of Plymouth had gone to college. Indeed, college men were scarce in southern Vermont, so Calvin's step to Amherst was a giant one. Amherst College by 1891 had acquired a reputation as a sound, conservative educational institution. For Calvin Coolidge it had the additional advantages of being neither too expensive nor too distant from home. The college was also a splendid transitional step from the isolation of Plymouth and Ludlow. Amherst was located in a rustic part of Massachusetts, but it was a section that had developed a modicum of culture and sophistication. The college was small enough that a lad from Vermont would not feel lost. It was also a bit cosmopolitan with about a third of its 336 students coming from beyond New England's boundaries. Yet most of Amherst's students came from rural and small-town backgrounds so that the impact of meeting young men from other areas was not overwhelming to the son of Vermont's stony fields and pastures. Most of the undergraduates were also sons of lawyers, ministers, teachers, and physicians, which perhaps turned Calvin's inclinations toward entering a profession.

Amherst College was a closely knit community, where the students, without the distractions of speedy methods of transportation, not only studied together but stayed together as well. The undergraduate company was gay. At this western Massachusetts Heidelberg gathered some of the better young prospects of rural and small-town New England, most of them off on their first big adventure in the world. They gathered in intimate little groups for discussions about the nature of the universe and its problems, for sprightly gossip, for close-harmony singing, for athletic contests, for felicitous use of the many spare hours that a leisurely age allowed its college students. They were of a time and of the social classes that, as John Chamberlain has said, "enjoyed themselves with the enjoyment of a blessed naïveté."[1]

Young Coolidge had spent the summer of 1891 on the farm. It was a momentous summer for him. Not only was there the excitement of knowing that he would soon be on his way to Amherst, but his father took him to Bennington to observe the ceremonies attendant upon the dedication of the 300-foot-high Battle Monument. There he also heard an address by President Benjamin Harrison and wondered, as he was to recall, "how it felt to bear so much responsibility and little thought I should ever know."[2] Later that summer the young man witnessed the marriage of his father to a spinster Plymouth schoolteacher, Carrie A. Brown. The problems that often accompany the coming of a stepmother were absent in this instance. The new Mrs. Coolidge was to fill a void in John Coolidge's life left by the passing of his wife and daughter and his son's going away to college. That in itself was enough, but Carrie Coolidge was also a cultivated and lovable woman, one who treated Calvin like her own. She could never take the place of Calvin's mother in his heart, but she was able to carve for herself there a place of esteem and affection.

In September Calvin went down to Amherst. He was duly enrolled as a freshman, thanks to his certificate from St. Johnsbury. He had arrived at the intimate college. He was to find, however, that he was not to be readily enveloped in its intimacy. Because the two Amherst dormitories, dating back to the 1820s, had fallen into disrepair, most of the undergraduates lived in private dwellings or in fraternity houses. Calvin took a room in a comfortable brick house, "Mr. Trott's," on South Pleasant Street. There he lived with one other student, Alfred Turner of Rutland, Vermont. Calvin's room cost him sixty dollars a year and twenty-five cents a week for service. He also was expected to provide oil for his lamp and his own wood.

He boarded down the street for three and a half dollars weekly, and among his fellow boarders was Dwight W. Morrow.

As Amherst as early as the 1890s was a strong fraternity school, Coolidge endeavored to be pledged. The quiet, redheaded country boy was unsuccessful, partly because he was unsponsored and partly because he had none of the superficial qualities which were attractive even in the days when campus Greeks knew Greek. On a campus where most of the apples remained in the barrel, he was a cull, an "Ouden," a "Barbarian." This rejection was aggravated by his inability to mix well and caused him numerous attacks of homesickness. This was reflected in his letters home. In mid-October, 1891, he wrote, "I don't seem to get acquainted very fast," and after the Christmas holidays he complained, "Every time I get home I hate to go away worse than before."[3] Yet he settled down to his studies, probably better than he would have had he been pledged, and enjoyed what he could of the activities around the college. He regularly attended the events sponsored by the Amherst College Lecture Association. He also took great interest in the mock Republican National Convention held at the college in March, 1892. At the end of the 1891–92 school year he returned for the summer to the farm. At home he got some of the recognition he had missed at Amherst when he was invited to give the Independence Day speech at Plymouth. And a good representative nineteenth-century Fourth of July oration it was, with a florid twisting of the British lion's tail and fervent exaltation of America's past revolutionaries. It was a flaming introduction of Calvin Coolidge to the business of public oratory.

September, 1892, saw the young man back at Amherst and at Mr. Trott's. His boarding place had changed, as it did again many times during his college days. And with the changes came more acquaintances. Yet because of his quietness he remained inconspicuous. Even in the classroom he was little more than just a body filling a seat. Outside of class he did not pay calls on his professors as Amherst students frequently did. He did not join his fellows in close harmony and certainly did not accompany them on the mandolin. He took no apparent interest in girls. He joined neither the YMCA nor the church. As for athletics, he was almost always a spectator. The most he could confess to later was that he did "hold the stakes" bet on various contests. He was not an undergraduate actor or journalist. He was, in the best New England backwoods tradition, "getting by." And getting by was of importance, for he sorely felt the inadequacy of his educational background. In his freshman and sophomore years he was able to make up some of this lack because of his isolation from his classmates. He was no greasy grind, but he had to work hard to get by academically.

During his junior year, 1893–94, Coolidge began to bud. The first step out of obscurity came, ironically, because he was a loser. The junior class celebrated its growth to social maturity in a "Plug Hat Race." In the contest the juniors, each wearing a silk hat and carrying a walking stick, ran the length of the college's athletic field. The seven young men who crossed the finish line last were duty-bound to stand their classmates to supper. The unathletic and unaggressive Coolidge was among the seven losers. At the oyster stew and beer banquet thrown by the losers on November 23, Coolidge was assigned to speak on the topic "Why I Got Stuck." He carried his assignment off in good fashion, explaining that pitching hay was poor preparation for successful sprinting. He ended saying, "Remember, boys, the Good Book says that the first shall be last and the last shall be first."[4] The prophecy of this struck no one, including the speaker, at the time, but Coolidge did win the reputation of being a good sport and laid the foundation for being considered something of an undergraduate wit.

During his last academic year Coolidge finally became affiliated with a social fraternity. He had maintained his interest in joining throughout his college years. In spring, 1892, there was some discussion of starting at Amherst a chapter of a prominent national fraternity, Phi Gamma Delta. Coolidge was asked whether he was interested in membership, and he allowed that he was. The chapter was not established though, and he continued as a Barbarian. One of his few close friends, John P. Deering, was asked in the fall of 1893 to join one of the better Amherst societies, but consented to do so only if Coolidge too were invited to join. The result was that both young men were left to remain outside the fraternity. In December, 1894, another movement was begun to start a Phi Gamma Delta chapter at Amherst. Harry O. Rhodes, who had been a "Fiji" at Wittenberg College before transferring to Amherst, succeeded in the undertaking and among the ten charter members of the Alpha Chi chapter at Amherst was John Deering. Probably at Deering's instigation, Coolidge was invited to join, and he accepted the invitation with a simple "Yes."

Coolidge, as could be anticipated, did not indulge in the minor sins so dear to the young—smoking, dancing, beer drinking, and card playing. However, he faithfully attended business meetings, was always on hand for formal social functions, and spent a good deal of time hanging around the house, though like most of the brothers he did not lodge there. His few months as a fraternity member were important, at least to him, for they gave him the sense of acceptance which he so much desired. He was to be actively interested in "Fiji" affairs the rest of his life. In fact, it was one of the few organizations with which he ever had close ties.

Coolidge's training at Amherst was of the rigorously classical turn required in good American colleges toward the end of the nineteenth century. The study of language dominated his work during the six terms of his freshman and sophomore years. He took French, German, and Italian each for three terms, Latin for four, and Greek for five, including three terms under Levi Elwell, who had cultivated his beard in order to enhance his resemblance to what he supposed Socrates looked like. Coolidge was enrolled in five terms of mathematics, including differential and integral calculus, and was particularly impressed by the brisk, imaginative instruction of George D. Olds, who in the 1920s became Amherst's president. Declamation, rhetoric, and physics each were studied for two terms. Although Coolidge studied hard during his first two years at Amherst—indeed, he had the time to do so—his grades were those of the gentlemanly pass, with an A in rhetoric and in two terms of French, and in physics a D, the lowest grade he received.

His scholastic performance improved greatly during his junior and senior years, when he concentrated on work in history and philosophy. For five terms the young man studied history under the direction of Anson D. Morse, a teacher of national repute whose demand for factual accuracy and judiciousness in interpretation left a mark on the many of his students who later became prominent in political and academic life. As this tall, almost emaciated-looking man paced restlessly back and forth on his lecture platform, he also tried to imbue his students with a sense of responsibility for civic leadership. Coolidge later wrote that those who took his course "came to a clearer comprehension not only of their rights and liberties but of their duties and responsibilities."[5] Morse, who was at the peak of his powers in the 1890s, not only impressed Coolidge, but left a strong stamp on two other students, Dwight W. Morrow and Harlan F. Stone, whose lives were to become closely involved with Coolidge's.

The dynamic lessons of Morse were, however, second to those taught Coolidge by the most famous Amherst professor of the time, the philosopher Charles E. Garman. Like Morse, Garman was convinced that education's basic aim was to heighten the student's sense of morality and to develop his desire to serve society. This aim the philosopher tried to advance at every turn. Professor Garman cut an unusual figure on campus. His sparkling white teeth and piercing black eyes were set in a pale face. He wore the habit of a minister, a black frock coat and a bow tie. He lived a secluded life, and, a frail man, he avoided physical exercise and lived under hothouse conditions, even keeping his throat wrapped in a muffler on warm days of spring. The texts that students studied in his course were contained in pamphlets which he, assisted by a servant, ran off on a hand press in his cellar. These he circulated among his students, after pledging them to return the pamphlets to him and not to let anybody outside the class see them. During the four terms of his course, he set various philosophies before his pupils, and using a distorted version of the Socratic method, he exploded each theory until Christianity and particularly Garman's interpretation of Congregationalism emerged triumphant.

Garman's Socratic game may have allowed the students to work cynicism out of their systems. It may have given their Christian morality a sturdier foundation and provided them with the essentials of other philosophies. Certainly his injunctions to "weigh the evidence" and to "carry all questions back to fundamental principles"[6] were worthy precepts. His method was, however, neither a sound approach to philosophy nor the technique of one who was pursuing truth. Garman abused some of the best traditions of the academy in his attempt to produce true believers. The philosophy professor's impact on the future President was reflected in the comment in Coolidge's autobiography, "We looked upon Garman as a man who walked with God."[7] Garman encouraged the young Vermonter's leaning toward serving the public. He also taught him well to appreciate social stability and to "weigh the evidence" and to "carry all questions back to fundamental principles." The problem was that the principles taught by Garman and learned by Coolidge were circumscribed. They were not broad enough to cover the complexities of the society over which Coolidge was later to reign as President.

Literature and especially rhetoric also had their impact on Coolidge, though the impact was to shape, not his principles, but his expression of them. He took three terms of public speaking, from which he developed considerable skill as a debater and even emerged at the end of his junior year with half of the J. Wesley Ladd Prize for his oration "The Story of the Cid and Its Meaning." Literature had some appeal for him in Amherst. He read, for class or for pleasure, Shakespeare, Milton, Scott, Longfellow, Whittier, Kipling, Riley, and Field. He also wrote, for publication in the college's *Literary Monthly*, an imitation of romantic literature entitled "Margaret's Mist." This story, published in October, 1894, was based on a New York State legend, which Coolidge had probably heard on a visit to Ausable Chasm the preceding summer. It concerned a fair country girl who discovered that her lover was a highwayman. In the climactic passage, where the lass confronts the miscreant with his misdeeds, Coolidge wrote:

> "Waldo Martin," said the emotionless Margaret, "I need no explanation. I know now. How I have loved you! How I've trusted you! Robber! Murderer! Betrayer! Yet I cannot expose you. I love you still. Go over the earth in freedom. Expiate your crime. I plead for you before a Higher Tribunal."
>
> While speaking, she had moved towards the pool, and, with her eyes still fixed upon the man she had loved, she plunged beneath its eddies. The black water closing over her buried the sorrowing maiden forever beneath its bosom.[8]

Fortunately for American literature, Coolidge did not attempt further fictional publication.

Coolidge's greatest prominence as a student came during his senior year. It would be stretching the facts to say that he was a popular member of the class of 1895 or a leader in college affairs. Indeed, had he dropped out along the way he would have been missed by few. He had some close friends like Deering and had acquired a small reputation as a result of his dry wit and his ability to be a good listener. As a scholar, he came out with a four-year grade average of 78.71, which was enough for him to be graduated *cum laude*.

Coolidge also won the Sons of the American Revolution silver medal awarded to the Amherst senior who in the judgment of the college's history department had written the best essay on the topic "The Principles Fought for in the American Revolution." This honor apparently was not announced publicly and the young man was closemouthed about it. His paper was automatically entered in competition for the national SAR essay prize. The fall following his graduation Coolidge won that award, which was a gold medal worth $150. He was quiet about that recognition too. After news of it was carried in the Springfield *Republican*, Henry P. Field, with whom he was reading law, asked him, "Is this item true?"

"Yes, here's the medal," Coolidge said, pulling it out of a desk drawer. Field asked Coolidge whether he had told his father about it. "No," replied the reserved young man, "do you think I'd better?"[9]

Calvin Coolidge liked, even craved, recognition but he was never one to spread news of himself.

Whatever eminence the young Vermonter enjoyed among his Amherst fellows came, however, from his ability as a speaker. In September, 1894, when his class began making preparations for the activities surrounding the commencement the following spring, Coolidge was elected Grove Orator, the only time he was elected to anything while at Amherst. His task would be to address and amuse his classmates and the alumni at the Class Day exercises. The job was conferred upon him because he was a satisfactory speaker and something of a wit. He also probably was elected because he was considered an amusing figure—the quiet, frail country lad who is found in any college class and who frequently is the butt of jokes made by his more urbane classmates. Yet it was an honor, one he sought, and successfully, for he was elected on the first ballot, 53 to 18, against one of his classmates from Brooklyn. It also was an opportunity to step out of the shadows of the class and into the limelight, however briefly.

The commencement activities began Sunday, June 23, 1895, with the baccalaureate sermon by the Reverend Mr. Henry A. Stimson. It continued with the competition of eight men for the Hardy Prize Debate, and of six for the Hyde Speaking Prize. Coolidge was not among the competitors, perhaps because he believed he had already won his prize by his election as Grove Orator. Class Day came on Tuesday. During the morning Edwin J. Bishop gave the Ivy Oration, and William J. Boardman the Ivy Poem. After lunch the member of the class considered most outstanding, Dwight Morrow, delivered the Class Oration, followed by Charles T. Burnett, who read the Class Poem. Later the seniors and their guests went to the College Grove where, as tradition pleasantly required, the members of the graduating class lay back on the grass, smoked corncob pipes, and listened to the Grove Oration and Grove Poem.

Coolidge's address fitted the occasion well. It was humorous, of the order of humor that undergraduates like: it was packed with puns and wisecracks, particularly with sarcastic observations on the faculty and Amherst life. As was customary, Coolidge was heckled by his classmates, and he handled them well, condescendingly tolerating some and answering others with mock scolding. It revealed not only that Coolidge had wit but also the thick skin necessary for the out-of-the-mold type to survive and triumph.

The next day, Wednesday, June 26, the seventy-six members of the Amherst class of 1895 marched into College Hall to hear a surfeit of speeches and to receive their bachelor's diplomas from President Merrill E. Gates. They then marched out into life and among them marched Calvin Coolidge, who though not last among them in college was far from being first. As so often happens, some of the top members of the class were to disappear into the jungles of life and a number of the obscure were to become worthies in their communities, businesses, and professions. Calvin Coolidge, marching to his own tune, was to surpass them all.

3

Settling Down in Northampton

THE CLASSES OF '95 all over the nation had been graduated as the depression of 1893 was beginning to lift. For those graduates whose families were well off, the depression was of little moment, but for those who had modest means and few connections, the depression was important to their considerations of the future. Calvin Coolidge, though not poor, was one of those affected by the depression. In January, 1895, he wrote his father that he was unsure of what he would do after leaving Amherst, though he thought he probably would work in the Plymouth Notch store or go to a Boston or New York law school. "That is about as far as I can get, and think you will have to decide which I shall do. I do not see as I have much of any preference now but may have later." He also declared that his goal was to "be of some use to the world," not just to "get a few dollars together."[1] One can discount his interest in being a storekeeper for he was already recorded among the members of his class who had decided to study law. Yet because that required further support from his father during a time of financial distress, young Coolidge had to face the fact that he might be forced to return to the Notch.

During the summer of 1895, Calvin worked on the family farm and pondered his future with his father. If he had to convince John Coolidge that his education would be thrown away should he remain in Plymouth as a storekeeper or a farmer, he did a good job. During the summer he discarded the idea of attending law school, because of the expense involved. Instead he and his father agreed that he should become a lawyer in the customary Vermont way by reading law in an established firm and being admitted to the bar on examination. That seemed the most practical and the least expensive method of acquiring the advocate's art.

Calvin therefore sought an office in which to read law. On August 30 he wrote an acquaintance of his father, William P. Dillingham, a former Vermont governor and future United States senator, asking whether he might study under him in Montpelier. Before Dillingham, who had been out of town, could send his reply offering a place in his office, another situation developed. One of Coolidge's Amherst classmates, Ernest W. Hardy, who was reading law with Richard W. Irwin in Northampton, invited him down to seek a position in that Massachusetts city. Hardy took Coolidge to the offices of John C. Hammond and Henry P. Field, where he introduced him with fulsome praise to Field, the firm's junior partner. After saying only "Good morning," Coolidge stood impassively listening to Hardy and then to Field. The lawyer explained that though he would be unable to give much time to a student, Coolidge could sit in the office and read and learn what he could. That arrangement the Vermonter accepted.

Hammond and Field were both Amherst graduates, the classes of '65 and '80, respectively. That and the fact that Hammond had heard and liked Coolidge's Grove Oration probably explained his acceptance by the firm. The joining of the firm and the young Vermonter was almost accidental, but it certainly was not unfortunate for those concerned. Hammond and Field were to find their new clerk a good one, and the clerk was to find that he had been apprenticed to two very capable men. Not only were they able practitioners of their profession, but also were men of substance and influence in Northampton, with Hammond a bulwark of community enterprises, later receiving an honorary doctor of laws degree from Amherst, and Field a force in local and area politics, who later was to become Hampshire county's probate judge.

In 1895 Northampton was a trading center for west-central Massachusetts and an outpost of the burgeoning industrialism of the state. The city was spread out over several gently rolling hills, and its

invested $800 from his savings and his inheritance from Grandfather
Moor in necessary books and furniture, and on February 1, 1898,
opened his own law office in two rooms on the second floor of the
new Masonic Building. Although not remarkably successful during
his first year of practice, he did earn over $500, which almost consti-
tuted financial independence for him. He prospered his second year,
earning some $1,400, part of which was derived from his appoint-
ment as counsel for the recently established Nonotuck Savings Bank.
More easily than most young lawyers in that era he had bridged the
chasm between dependence on family and financial independence.

His practice was never to be exciting or the kind that would lead
him to eminence at the bar. It was to be more along the lines of a
solicitor in the English tradition instead of a barrister. Coolidge
would infrequently be seen in court, partly because of his conviction
that the greatest service a lawyer could render was to arrange settlement out of court, partly because of his ability to do so, and
largely because most of the business that came his way called for the
solicitor's talents. He busied himself with drawing up legal documents, doing mortgage and title work for the bank, managing real
estate, settling estates, taking on some collection work, and giving
whatever legal advice was called for. He was in his office as much as
possible. Usually anyone looking for him would find him there, his
feet resting on the writing surface of his shiny oak roll-top desk
while he read, wrote, or looked down on the activities of Main Street
from his window. He did his work ably, with a minimum of fuss and
talk. He was representative of a young man striving to become a
respectable and worthy small-town lawyer. He would be available
when needed because he felt it his duty to his clients and because he
was not going to miss a chance to fatten his bank balance.

Yet he had derived from his association with Hammond and
Field a start in a second profession, politics, that was to become his
main pursuit in life. Politics came naturally to Calvin Coolidge. His
grandfather Galusha had dabbled in it and his father John had been
as close to being a professional politician as one could come in rural
Vermont. Calvin's chief interest in reading was along the lines of
political history and oratory, and in Northampton the one topic of
conversation that could open his mouth was politics. He had no
hobbies or romances to occupy his spare time, and he was not so
dedicated to the law that he had no spare time. Politics also prob-

ably drew him because almost any person is welcome in it and no true politician can afford to avoid or ignore anyone who shows interest in what he does. More than most lines of endeavor, and as much as any, politics overlooks background and status. It is the truest democracy in a democracy.

Henry P. Field opened the doors of Northampton politics for the young Vermonter. Within weeks after Coolidge began sitting in Hammond and Field's outer office, Field was nominated by the Republicans to run for mayor of Northampton. Coolidge enlisted in his mentor's campaign, handing out ballots for him in Ward Six. Field won the election and at the same time John Hammond was chosen district attorney. In 1896 the legal apprentice went to Chester as an alternate delegate to a Republican convention called to nominate a state senator. He participated during the summer in a minor way in the campaign to prevent William Jennings Bryan's election as President of the United States. While visiting home, Calvin debated in defense of the gold standard at Plymouth Union. On August 5, at Field's urging, the young man contributed an article to the Northampton *Daily Hampshire Gazette* in answer to a defense of Bryan's position on the silver question by the former Democratic mayor of Northampton, John B. O'Donnell. In the article Coolidge displayed his debating skills. Pointing out the fallacies of O'Donnell's arguments, he wrote:

> William J. Bryan is accused of financial heresy and we are told that his morals are orthodox. He is censured for an attempt to debauch the monetary system of America and the defense is "a personal character as pure as a woman." He is charged with desiring to pollute the sacred shrine of the public credit, and we are calmly informed that he says his prayers every night.[2]

This kind of activity, and support from Field and Hammond, led to Coolidge's recruitment into the lower ranks of Northampton's Republican hierarchy. In 1897, when he was graduating from his legal apprenticeship, he was one of the five men chosen from Ward Two to serve on the Republican city committee, the thirty-five members of which were responsible for selecting their party's nominees for municipal offices. The following year, in October, he represented Ward Two as a delegate to the Republican convention that nominated John Hammond for re-election as district attorney. Coolidge himself became more than a nominator when he was nominated for city councilman from his ward. He was elected to that post in December, 1898, and it represented his first election to government office.

The unpaid post was insignificant. At the time each of Northampton's seven wards elected one alderman and three councilmen annually. That meant that Coolidge was a junior member of the lower chamber of the city legislature. As such, little was expected of him, and he lived up to the expectation. Only two of his acts on the council are noteworthy. One was his work in behalf of the construction of an armory for use by the local soldiery, which could be seen as a gesture toward the veterans of the Spanish-American War. The other was that after the death of an Irish-American Democratic councilman he presented a resolution of respect. It was another gesture, but one that was sincere and that was well received by Irish-Americans and Democrats.

As unimportant as the office of councilman was, Coolidge made it pay off. He had won enough respect in less than a year to believe that he could persuade a majority of the aldermen and councilmen to support him for city solicitor. With that in mind, he declined renomination for councilman. Coolidge had judged his strength correctly as the city council elected him solicitor early in 1900. The position was desirable for a young lawyer and politician. The duties required were not burdensome and he was paid $600 a year for his work. The post afforded him additional experience as a lawyer and additional knowledge of the workings of government. Moreover, it gave him increased prestige and prominence as a politician. It put him in a position to seek better things later on.

With the solicitorship under his belt, Coolidge was able to keep his financial independence. The advice he had to give the city council, the documents he had to draft or review, and the few cases he had to take to court left him sufficient time to expand his private practice. Money was not pouring into his hands, but he was making a decent living. His earning capacity was not, however, coming up to his expectations. As he wrote his father a few weeks after his re-election as city solicitor in 1901, "If I ever get a woman some one will have to support her."[3] That was all the more true when in January, 1902, he was defeated in his effort to gain a third term as solicitor. A Democratic opponent, Theobald M. Connor, was chosen by the city council over Coolidge, perhaps on the issue of rotation in office and more likely because of Connor's outgoing personality.

Coolidge, however, was not long out of public office. During spring, 1903, he was appointed clerk of the courts for Hampshire county to fill the term of William H. Clapp, who had died. It was a coveted position, paying $2,300 a year and existing almost as a sinecure. Plum or no plum, Coolidge decided soon after his appointment not to seek election to the post the following fall. As clerk of the courts, he was barred from legal practice and that barrier, he concluded, blocked his possibilities for both political and financial advancement.

Soon after his retirement from the clerkship, he took his next step in politics. He was chosen chairman of the Republican city committee, a job made all the more burdensome, though important, because it came in 1904, a presidential election year. The national Republican ticket triumphed in Northampton and over the country, but the Republican nominee for mayor of the city was defeated and, for the first time in years, the Democrats elected a governor in Massachusetts. The Republicans, it seemed to Coolidge, "made the mistake of talking too much about the deficiencies of our opponents and not enough about the merits of our own candidates."[4] This was discouraging enough, but the next year Coolidge met his only defeat as a candidate before the people when he lost out in a three-cornered race with a Democrat and another Republican for a place on the school committee. When a neighbor later said that he had voted for the Democrat instead of Coolidge because he thought school committeemen should be parents of public-school children, Coolidge replied, "Might give me time!"[5]

It was just as well that he had been defeated for school committeeman. He had in 1905 come to a turning point vastly more important than election to a petty office. Except for politics and whatever stimulation he got from the law, his life was pedestrian. He took an occasional glass of beer in Northampton's beer gardens and sometimes loafed in Jim Lucey's shoeshop on Gothic Street while, as William Allen White has written, "the loafers' parliament babbled through an evening."[6] Coolidge continued to take most of his meals at Rahar's Inn, a three-story brick building on a side street, and he had quarters on Round Hill in the house of Rob Weir, the steward of the Clarke Institute for the Deaf. The young lawyer spent most of his nights in his rooms reading biographies, history, and law. He had not learned to dance and knew little of card playing. He had been persuaded to join the Warner Meadow Golf Club, but succeeded only in making work out of the game. He was still an odd stick around town. Although he was a neat dresser, one's eyes were drawn to his figure instead of his clothes. As an acquaintance of the period wrote: "In appearance he was splendidly null, apparently deficient in red corpuscles, with a peaked, wire-drawn expression. . . . As he walked there was no motion of the body above the waist. The arms hung immobile."[7] Perhaps Coolidge's greatest excitement was to return to Plymouth, where his most newsworthy adventure was hunting woodchucks.

He had in his loneliness thought of women. The Smith College girls never attracted him and their female mentors were too blue-stockinged and smart for him. Now that he was established, he did occasionally surmount his shyness and go out with town girls, but if he attempted any kind of courtship, it was well concealed. He became interested enough in one redhead to propose marriage, but she spurned his offer. It was at this point, in 1904, that he met Grace Goodhue. Miss Goodhue, who was descended from old New England stock, was the daughter of a Burlington, Vermont, mechanical engineer and steamboat inspector. She had been graduated with a bachelor of arts degree from the University of Vermont in 1902 and had come to Northampton to teach in the Clarke School.

Propinquity was the key to bringing together the vivacious, black-haired schoolteacher and the odd-stick lawyer. She lived in Baker Hall, a residence for Clarke teachers, which was located down the hill from Rob Weir's house. One day as she was sprinkling the flowers around Baker Hall, she happened to glance up at Weir's place. There she saw a strange sight. At the window stood Coolidge, shaving, wearing a hat, and apparently in his long underwear. Grace laughed spontaneously, and then, partly in embarrassment and partly to control her laughter, she quickly turned back to watering the flowers. Coolidge heard her laughter and inquired about her. Weir arranged for the two of them to meet. When they were introduced Coolidge explained that he had an undisciplined lock of hair that got in the way while he washed and shaved. To solve the problem he had to anchor the lock with the hat.

After that meeting the Vermonters-away-from-home frequently got together. They made a strange pair. She was outgoing, with a marvelous sense of humor, and had a wide variety of interests. Skating, sailing, picnicking, buggy-riding, sleighing, conversation, musicals, plays, tobogganing, singing, dancing, and card playing all attracted her. She showed a great and genuine interest in people for their own sake. Everyone who knew Grace Goodhue liked her immensely; those who knew Calvin Coolidge never quite knew what to make of him. She did almost everything, and he did almost nothing. Yet for her sake he tried. One of his earliest attributable bon mots was a joke on himself and a tribute to her. That was his expressed hope "that having taught the deaf to hear, Miss Goodhue might perhaps cause the mute to speak."[8] She did, though her achievements in this area were confined largely to his conversations with her. She also got him to take trolley and buggy rides, to go to church socials, meetings, and picnics, which he hated. They also went on long walks in the wooded areas around Northampton, which he liked. For her sake, he tried skating and dancing, but was singularly unsuccessful at them. He also learned, thanks to Jim Lucey, to compliment her on her looks and dress, both of which well deserved his praise.

Despite their differences in personality and interests, Grace and Calvin got along well. She enjoyed his wry, unexpected wit as much as he was warmed by her infectious good humor. She must have been impressed by his conscientiousness and he must have perceived her understanding nature. In summer, 1905, they went to Plymouth to visit his folks. The Colonel and his wife and Grandmother Coolidge liked her.

Calvin's grandmother told him, "That's a likely gal. Why don't you marry her?"

"Mebbe I will, Grandma," Coolidge replied.[9]

That summer he made up his mind to have her as his wife. He turned up unexpectedly in Burlington one day. Her father, Captain Andrew I. Goodhue, asked him, "Up here on some law business, Mr. Coolidge?"

"No," he replied. "Up here to ask your permission to marry Grace."

The Captain inquired, "Does she know it?"

"No, but she soon will," was the answer.[10]

Goodhue was taken aback by this unusual approach to courtship and marriage, but later came to like Coolidge, though the Captain's rather aloof wife, Lemira, never cottoned to the lawyer.

Coolidge's proposal to Grace was straightforward. "I am going to be married to you," he said.[11]

That was enough for Mrs. Goodhue, who became intent on breaking up the romance. She urged Grace to spend a year at home in order to learn housewifely skills. Lemira Goodhue pointed out that Grace could not even bake bread. Coolidge's reply was that she could buy it. Coolidge fought for his wife, engaging in arguments with Mrs. Goodhue and winning them point by point. The most bitter was over the wedding date, which his future mother-in-law wanted deferred, apparently in the hope that it would never arrive.

Coolidge finally won her acceptance of an autumn date in 1905. On October 4 Grace and Calvin were married in the parlor of the pale yellow, green-shuttered Goodhue home in Burlington. On that rainy day, without attendants and with only fifteen of the couple's friends on hand, Coolidge acquired the most important thing in his life.

It has been said that Lemira Goodhue attributed Coolidge's political success to Grace. She may have been correct. Although few people were emotionally touched by Coolidge, no one could help but be impressed by Grace Coolidge's charm, good humor, and interest in people. She was a perfect helpmeet to a loving but often cranky husband, whose conception of marriage was one where the husband dominated his home and family. Where he was dull, she shone. Where he was rude, she displayed strikingly good manners. Where he irritated people, she ingratiated herself with them. Where he turned men sour, she made them smile. Where he chilled women, she warmed them. In short, where he needed help, she supplied it, and without being pushy. Coolidge said, "We thought we were made for each other."[12] It is difficult to speculate on what kind of woman he was made for, but the Goodhue girl was made for him.

4

The Less He Spoke, the More He Heard

AFTER THEIR MARRIAGE, Grace and Calvin Coolidge traveled to Montreal for a two-week honeymoon. Grace was soon bored with the Canadian city and Calvin became restless. After a week, he told her, "Grace, gotta be going back home." When she asked why, he replied, "Running for School Committee, gotta go back and make a speech."[1]

Whether because he sensed her boredom or was eager to return to political action, the honeymoon was cut short and the couple returned to Northampton. They lived in the Norwood Hotel for three weeks and then moved into a small furnished house owned by a professor at Smith. It was in this period that Grace became acquainted with some of the odd stick's oddities. Here was a man who during their courtship had been translating Dante's *Inferno* into English and continued to do so after their marriage. He liked to read in bed and kept *The Letters, Lectures and Addresses of Charles E. Garman* at the head of the bed. It appeared that he had the largest collection of stockings in western Massachusetts, all seemingly with holes in them. One day he came home with a bag containing fifty-two pairs of stockings to be darned. Grace asked him whether this

33

was why he had taken her for his wife. "No," he answered, "but I find it mighty handy."[2]

By spring, 1906, it had become clear that the couple could expect an addition to the family. With this in mind, Coolidge looked for a larger dwelling. During the summer he rented half of a duplex at 21 Massasoit Street for $28 a month. The Coolidges' part of the white frame house contained three bedrooms, bath, parlor, dining room, kitchen, and attic and was adorned with a small entry porch and shuttered windows. It was in this house that the Coolidges were to live until he went to Washington to be sworn in as Vice President and it was to this rented house that they were to return after living in the White House. The most prominent decoration in their home was an embroidered quotation over the white mantelpiece which bespoke Coolidge's cardinal tenet, his personality, and something of the quality of both:

> A wise old owl sat on an oak,
> The more he saw, the less he spoke;
> The less he spoke, the more he heard,
> Why can't we be like that old bird?[3]

It was in the Massasoit Street two-family house that Grace Coolidge gave birth in September to John, their first-born son. Calvin was proud, though outside the family he gave little sign of it.

It was also that fall that Coolidge was to take his next step up the ladder of politics. He had laid a good basis for political advancement. His mentors in Northampton, Hammond and Field, were men of standing among local politicians. Coolidge himself had served his party faithfully and well for a decade. Moreover, he had a reputation for dry wit and for using it effectively in political discussions. Through his officeholding and his attendance at party affairs, at Jim Lucey's shoeshop parliament, and at Rahar's Inn, he had become well known. His plain speech and unaffectedness made him understandable to the voters and gave him the advantage of being one Yankee who did not seem to look down upon those who were not Yankees. His taciturnity made him appear to be minding his own business and kept him from making promises he could not keep. Then, too, there were several men who served him faithfully in politics. Among them were the gregarious Ernest Hardy, who was his chief lieutenant, and Rob Weir, who had been elected Ward Two alderman through Coolidge's efforts. He had also ingratiated himself with a number of Democrats, including tavernkeeper Johnny Dewey, baker Jim Maloney, brickmason Ed Lynch, and innkeeper Dick Rahar, because there was much charity and no meanness in his partisanship.

As a lawyer, Coolidge had a reputation that further assisted him in politics. He was the kind of attorney who would go out late at night to draw up a dying Irish lady's will and charge her only five dollars instead of the usual twelve or fifteen. He did not disdain helping those who were in trouble with the law. He intervened in injury suits to see that the little fellow got a break. He represented drunks in court and also looked out for those barkeepers who occasionally violated regulations. William Allen White tells the story of Ed Harris' wife's aunt, who broke her hip in getting off a trolley car. The transit company offered to settle for $1,500. Harris asked Coolidge to look into the matter. Three days later the lawyer called to say that the company would pay $2,000 and medical and legal expenses. When Harris and the aunt came around to collect the check, which included the lawyer's fee, Harris gave Coolidge a personal check for $50. The attorney handed it back to him, saying: "You got most of the evidence. Here's something for you!"[4] Such acts were not forgotten.

In 1906 Coolidge was nominated by the local Republicans for the state house of representatives, and he was elected in November by a margin of 264 votes. He arrived in Boston the following January to begin his service in the Massachusetts legislature, the General Court. The General Court was buffeted by political waves which were to affect the young Northampton lawmaker. Usually the influence of corporations at the time is emphasized, but there were other factors as well. The Republican majority could not help but be affected by tides of progressivism which emanated from Washington during the Presidency of Theodore Roosevelt. Moreover, the Boston reform elements which had been gathering strength for a generation were a considerable power and the young western Massachusetts legislator had to cope with them. They included the movement of Louis D. Brandeis and organized labor to secure legislation authorizing savings banks to issue life insurance and old-age annuities in an attempt to force down the rates of the big life insurance companies.

As important to the state, and even more important to Coolidge, was the character of the contemporary Republican leadership in Massachusetts. The governor was Curtis Guild, Jr., who had recaptured the executive post from the Democrats in the 1905 elections. Guild was a good choice. Aristocratic in background, but democratic in person, he espoused programs that met many of the reformers' objections. He called for civil service reform, regulation of telephone and telegraph operations, further state supervision of insurance companies, a limit on campaign expenditures, and a prohibition of corporate political contributions. He also favored a graduated inheritance tax, protection of bank savings, and enforcement of factory laws, and he warned the railways, the Commonwealth's most troublesome corporations, to give better service or be forced to do so by the state. Governor Guild struck a note deep in Coolidge's heart with his fervent pleas for economy in government and reduction of the state debt.

The leading figure in Massachusetts Republican politics at the time was National Committeeman Winthrop Murray Crane. This thin, mustachioed, tight-lipped man in his mid-fifties was one of the Cranes of Dalton, who were paper manufacturers and had long been influential in western Massachusetts. Murray Crane had served as governor from 1900 to 1903 and had been known for his emphasis on governmental economy and efficiency. As noted by one observer, Crane's "three inaugural addresses were more of the nature of business documents than political harangues or reviews."[5] Crane was proud of the state's industry, which stood at about a billion dollars in value and was manned by a half-million employees at the century's turn. His pride also led him to be well aware that the Commonwealth was no longer a state of just fishermen, farmers, traders, and tinkers. It was a state that had to cope with the complicated problems that grew out of an industrial society. Under Crane the state had not dealt dynamically with those problems but it had not ignored them either. Balance and stability had been his economic and political goals. Under Governor Crane pure-food laws had been strengthened, savings banks divorced from national banks, vaccinations made compulsory, blue laws loosened, the number of hours worked by women and children limited, and the teamsters and rail-

road strikes of 1902 settled diplomatically. Crane had done we
enough for the state and for himself that he was sent to the United
States Senate in 1904.

Crane's record is important in connection with Calvin Coolidge's
career, for he was considered one of Crane's men from his first day
in the General Court until his election as Vice President of the
United States. To Crane he was loyal, not only because it was smart
in Massachusetts politics, particularly for a man from western Massachusetts, but also because Crane's belief in economy and efficiency
and his seeking of balance and stability impressed Coolidge. Something for everybody so long as it did not cost much was a creed to
which Calvin Coolidge could subscribe. It was the key to justice for
all elements of society. Coolidge could also respect Crane because he
was an easy boss. He was not one to give orders, demand appointments for his men, or force or obstruct legislation. His influence
came from his judgment, decency, knowledge, philanthropy, widespread contacts, and willingness to be consulted. "Mr. Crane," his
biographer wrote, "had no henchmen in politics in the ordinary
acceptance of the word, but of willing friends a multitude."[6]

High behind the desks of the state representatives of Massachusetts hangs the sacred codfish, the symbol of prosperity. In the
ornate chamber of representatives, Calvin Coolidge was to sit for
two years looking, to outward appearances, as though he could smell
the fish and did not like it. He arrived in the General Court a
countryman low in the pecking order. His bag of tricks was so small
that he was to remain that way during his two terms. Nothing about
him indicated that he was a man who would rise in the world. His
clothes though neat were cheap. He was unknown and because of his
introversion was a good bet to remain unknown. He lived in low
style, having hired a dollar-a-day room at the Adams House overlooking the inner court. His first year in the house of representatives
he was appointed to two minor committees, those on mercantile
affairs and constitutional amendments. During the day he worked on
his committees and in the house. At night he read, picked the lint off
his two suits, daydreamed, and on rare occasions sipped tea or drank
beer with his harder drinking political acquaintances. On weekends
he traveled home by train to be with his family and to catch up on
his law business. He was probably one of the few legislators who
lived within his daily pay of five dollars.

Because of the reform currents of the time, the waves of which gently splashed even as far away as Northampton, Coolidge's record in the house was progressive. Moreover, he had to be responsive to the labor vote in his district. During his two terms in the house he voted for a six-day week for workers, limitation of the working hours of women and children, direct election of United States senators, female suffrage, pensions to firemen's families, half fares for school children on streetcars, and the equipment of factories with basic surgical instruments. During his second term he was given some recognition by appointment to the judiciary committee, where he helped to draft an unsuccessful bill that would have prevented the issuance of injunctions in labor disputes. He also served on the banks and banking committee and there he worked to codify the state's banking laws, a task that badly needed doing.

The 1907 General Court was adjourned on June 28 and Coolidge went home to his family and law practice. That fall he again was nominated and elected to the house of representatives. Things were not, however, that cut and dried on the state level, where there was a new political movement under way. The yellow journalist William Randolph Hearst was grasping for political power in the nation under the banner of reform. As part of his move to force the Democratic party to nominate him for President in 1908 or, failing that, to develop his own political vehicle, he encouraged the formation of the Independence League in Massachusetts. The League's 1907 candidate for governor in Massachusetts was forty-nine-year-old Thomas L. Hisgen, whose chief issue was opposition to the use of price-cutting by corporations in order to force competitors out of business. In this Hisgen had a deep personal interest. He was one of four brothers who ran an axle-grease business in West Springfield. Standard Oil, the colossus of the petroleum industry, reputedly offered to buy out the Hisgens for $600,000. When they refused to sell, the company resorted to price-cutting in order to ruin them. Somehow the Hisgens survived that attack and even increased their sales. Thomas Hisgen was so angered by Standard's tactics that he launched a crusade to prevent their use in the future. His anger and conviction fitted in well with Hearst's plans.

Governor Guild was renominated by the Republicans and met not only the opposition of Hisgen and Democrat Henry M. Whitney but also that of Charles W. Bartlett, who was campaigning to prevent the merger of the Boston and Maine and the New Haven railroads. The result of the election was a smashing victory for Guild. He polled 188,000 votes to 84,000 for Whitney, 75,000 for Hisgen, 11,000 for Bartlett, and a total of 11,000 for three other candidates. Yet it was significant that Hisgen, who was colorless personally and lacking in organizational support, could draw over 20 percent of the vote. That he was a western Massachusetts man and that the chief issue of his campaign had been opposition to monopolies were not lost on Coolidge. It was also clear that the Independence League would try to follow up its 1907 showing and that Hearst would one way or another be involved in both the presidential and gubernatorial campaigns of the next year. It would pay a young politician whose ambitions went beyond the state house of representatives to be aware of this movement.

In his messages to the 1908 General Court, Governor Guild showed his awareness of the forces demanding greater regulation of capital. He called for further safeguards on the savings of citizens, division of the private control of trolley, express, railroad, and steamship companies, stricter regulation of public service corporations, and medical certification of the health of minors before they could be permitted to work. Unfortunately for the regulatory movement Guild was ill during most of the legislative session. Yet there were others who were willing to fill the gap, and indeed, like Calvin Coolidge, not only to meet the objections of the Hearst-Hisgen forces, but to climb into bed with them.

Hisgen had since 1906 been trying to obtain a law to prohibit the practices of undercutting competitors by charging less than cost and of charging higher than par prices when there was no competition. In 1907 and 1908 the representative from Northampton sponsored a bill incorporating Hisgen's ideas and was successful in guiding it through the house, though it met defeat in the senate. Even after he had left the house, Coolidge appeared before the judiciary committee as Hisgen's counsel to argue for the bill. It was work of that kind that finally resulted in the adoption by Massachusetts of antimonopolistic pricing legislation. Coolidge's efforts, whether purely political or partly sympathetic in motivation, were not to be completely forgotten by the assortment of reformers and small businessmen who had backed Hisgen's bill.[7]

The 1908 legislature was adjourned June 13 and Coolidge retired from the house of representatives, probably wary of violating his district's convention against running for a third term. He had had two years of valuable experience and had made some contacts and a reputation for loyalty to the party and Murray Crane. The Northampton lawyer would later return to the General Court, and his reputation, experience, and contacts would do him some good. But at the time he left the house, few cared much and no one predicted that he would some day be a power in the General Court and the state.

Coolidge came home to Northampton to a newly enlarged family. In April, 1908, a second son, Calvin, had been born. That helped draw the lawyer home from the General Court because now he had to bolster his income, which had sagged during his two terms in Boston. The Coolidges lived frugally. They had to on an income that ran about $1,500 a year. Although with the arrival of the second son Grace Coolidge had the help of a maid, she still did many of the family chores. Moreover, the Coolidges used a party-line telephone and rarely entertained or went out socially. Coolidge was far from being the model husband. In the early days of their marriage, he nagged about Grace's shortcomings. He was a finicky eater and most of his complaints stemmed from her food. Occasionally he would drop one of her biscuits and then stamp his foot to emphasize the clump it made when it hit the floor. He was also apt to observe before guests that her piecrust resembled cement.

Yet she usually had her way with him. She became adept at joking about his nasal twang, clipped speech, and terseness of expression. Even though the townfolks called him Cal behind his back, she always addressed him as Calvin. In return he always signed his letters to her, from out of town, with his full name. He did have one extravagance, one that lasted throughout his life. That was to encourage Grace to buy pretty clothes. In his eyes the only real sin she could commit was to appear at public functions twice in the same gown. He was so interested in her wearing apparel that he took the time to pick things out for her, especially hats. All this was an extravagance that she appreciated. Yet it was the only extravagance he had, because Coolidge, until he became governor, probably never earned much more than $2,000 annually and of that he usually managed to save something. His family would have to share his interest in political honors, for there was little money to enjoy.

After leaving the state house of representatives, Coolidge worked to shore up his law practice. It was a small business and little changed in character from that which he had had ten years before. He still served the Nonotuck Savings Bank, drew up legal documents, mediated disputes, made collections, and settled estates. As a newer line of work, he represented a few small corporations, including the Springfield Brewery's business in Northampton. In the community he regularly attended Edwards Congregational Church, though, reflecting his formless church background, he was neither a church member nor leader. He was not, and never was to become, a civic booster, a leader of community betterment projects, or a chamber of commerce worthy. If he remained a lawyer with small income and was lacking in Main Street boosterism, it was largely because of his dry personality and his addictedness to politics and government service. He had neither the time nor the interest to spread himself all over the community. Although some, like William Allen White, have looked down on Coolidge for that, the Yankee was a man who knew what he wanted and would not be diverted from it. Calvin Coolidge was much like an artist dedicated to his art. He concentrated his efforts on law and politics in order to make a living and to fulfill his desire for public service and honor.

Coolidge's fulfillment was slow in coming. He was a plodder. He was not the type to flash into the political skies. Neither by temperament nor by his location in a small city could he do anything except take advantage one by one of the opportunities that came. The year 1908 offered him no opportunity for public service. As he practiced law, though, he also kept his hand in politics. He talked it when he could and kept up his contacts. It was clear that he was available at any time to help his party and to run for office.

He did not have to wait long. In 1909 the Republicans needed a nominee who could retake the mayorship from the Democrats. That Coolidge knew, and his closest friends knew that he was not averse to running for the office. He had, of course, several advantages. As a former councilman and city solicitor, he knew Northampton government. As Ward Two leader and a former city Republican chairman, he knew Northampton politics. And as the latest retired state representative, he had some prominence and even some claim to preference. The mayor's office attracted Coolidge. It would give him the most important local honor. It would allow him to stay at home and continue his law practice on a year-round basis, something this frugal Yankee appreciated. It would also permit him to remain with his family while he rendered public service.

When the time came in fall, 1909, to nominate someone for mayor, there was no leading candidate. At the meeting of the city Republican committee, it was suggested that Alexander McCallum, the head of the McCallum Hosiery Company, be nominated. Mc-Callum was an attractive figure who had the confidence of local businessmen and was noted among workers for the high wages he paid. The McCallum movement was, however, quickly deflated by George Spear, one of Coolidge's neighbors, who said that the manufacturer could not accept the nomination because he was too busy. No one was on hand to contest Spear's contention, so he was able to place Coolidge in candidacy. The Ward Two leader was endorsed unanimously.

The lawyer's campaign was based on hard work. He campaigned with letters and by going from door to door to tell Northampton's voters that he wanted to be mayor. He avoided issues and concentrated instead on general principles of government like honesty, economy, and efficiency. He never gave his Democratic opponent, Harry E. Bicknell, free publicity by referring to him. Coolidge's was largely a campaign of saying: "I want your vote. I need it. I shall appreciate it."[8]

Of course, there was more to the campaign than that. Harry Bicknell, a merchant, had been nominated on the assumption that he would carry the usual Democratic vote and, because of his position as a merchant, his speaking ability, his reputation as a good sport, and his Congregational affiliation, would appeal to many Republican voters. Those were logical assumptions, but as it turned out they were invalid. It worked the other way around, for it was Coolidge who kept his party's votes and made inroads on the opposition's strength. Many workingman Democrats were leary of a businessman and were impressed by Coolidge's ability to meet people of all classes as equals.

Coolidge missed few opportunities to gain votes. The Democrats were betting two-to-one that they would carry Ward Seven over

Coolidge. The Republican nominee gave a janitor friend of his $100, instructing him to bet half of it on Coolidge and to use the other half to buy drinks and cigars around the ward. The Seventh went for Coolidge, who saved his $50 bet, and with his winnings covered his investment in drinks and smokes, and gave the remaining $50 to the janitor for his help.

Bicknell also got himself tangled up in one of the key local issues. The drys and wets had been at each other furiously since the turn of the century. In a church debate Bicknell had, for the fun of it, taken the side of the temperance forces. The wets saw no fun in it at all and pressed the Democratic nominee to clarify his position during the campaign. In trying to explain the circumstances of the debate, Bicknell lost dry votes and gained no wets. Coolidge, by keeping his mouth closed, offended no drys and found that his legal services for the Springfield Brewery and Northampton's barkeeps had enhanced his reputation among the wets. The result of the campaign was that Coolidge was elected, though by the slender margin of 187 votes.

Calvin Coolidge served two terms as mayor of Northampton, beginning his continuous service in public office until he left the White House twenty years later. His administration was not dynamic, but it benefited the city. He gained expansion and improvement of the fire and police departments and secured an increase in teachers' pay. Sidewalks and streets were improved and a planning project for a growing, prettier Northampton was started. He intervened to stop the city council from approving an electric lighting contract that would lose the city money. By shrewd and efficient administration, he lowered the tax rate and even reduced the town's debt almost by half. He also sold the Smith's Ferry area owned by the city to Holyoke for $45,000, a good price, and had it invested to earn money for Northampton. It was Coolidge's endowment of his city. His administration was honest and he made sure that no scandal attached to those who surrounded him in government. His municipal improvements were appreciated by many Democrats and yet his fiscal administration appealed to the frugal instincts of most Republicans. He also kept his own ward organization intact and extended his influence over the rest of the city's Republican organization. He had, in brief, served Northampton well and strengthened himself politically during his two years as mayor.[9]

5

Senator Coolidge

C OOLIDGE HAD TIMED things well for political advancement. In 1911 it was the turn of Hampshire County's Republicans to vie for the state senate seat for Hampshire, Hampden, and Berkshire. Mayor Coolidge was a logical nominee. He was his county's most prominent political figure, one whose background included municipal, county, and state public service. He had made friends in Hampden County by his sponsorship of Hisgen's antimonopoly bill and his legal services to the Springfield Brewery. Moreover, National Committeeman Murray Crane, who came from Berkshire County, found him acceptable. In any event, Coolidge sought and received endorsement for state senator from the Republican organizations of the three counties. In the November election he easily won the seat for the predominantly Republican senatorial district.

When Coolidge arrived in Boston in 1912 it was clear that his approach to the General Court had changed little from his days of service in the house of representatives. Again he rented an inexpensive room at the Adams House. He rarely missed sessions of the senate and of his committees, and he just as rarely spoke in public. His intelligence and tough fiber were well guarded by his taciturnity, and he was as much a Murray Crane man as before. Yet things had changed for him and for the state. For him, entering the senate was less exciting than when he had first spread his wings in the General

Court in 1907. He was lonesome because most of his close friends in the house of representatives had departed. Moreover, his assignments to the committees on agriculture, cities, and legal affairs were not of great interest to him.

For the state, things were even more politically unsettled than they had been five years before. The governor, Eugene N. Foss, was in his second term. He was a Democrat who had come over from the Republican party. He gave all the appearances of a progressive reformer, calling for initiative, referendum, recall, workmen's compensation, direct election of United States senators, and equable redistricting of congressional seats. Foss, who was nicknamed the Old Boy, had been at loggerheads with the 1911 legislature and was determined to force his program on the 1912 legislature. Actually his prospects seemed dim since the senate contained 36 Republicans to 14 Democrats and the house 142 Republicans to 97 Democrats. Yet the Old Boy kept the state and the General Court in an uproar, especially with his fight to prevent the New Haven Railroad from dominating the Commonwealth's street railways.

Coolidge was pitched against Governor Foss on the railroad issue. The General Court had passed a bill authorizing the New Haven to build a trolley system that would serve Northampton and much of the rest of Coolidge's district. Coolidge's constituents and therefore the freshman state senator were much interested in that legislation, but his general unhappiness in the session was crowned when Foss vetoed the bill and was upheld in the General Court.

The highlight of Coolidge's first year in the senate was his service as chairman of the special legislative committee on conciliation, which was formed to deal with the great textile strike in Lawrence. The strike had started as a result of the cutting of wages of some of the city's 30,000 mill workers. Most of the laborers, all of whom were overworked and underpaid, walked out when the cut came in January. Immediately the radical Industrial Workers of the World jumped in to guide the efforts of the largely unorganized mill hands. The situation soon became ugly, with the companies meeting the passive resistance of the strikers with police force and even violence. The workers held out, however, and in February the General Court stepped in to conciliate the dispute, which had already attracted national attention and was widely viewed as a crucial confrontation between capital and labor. Coolidge was probably appointed head of the committee, not only because he was on good terms with both labor and management, but also because as a rookie senator he could not refuse the assignment. His committee stepped in at a good time. The Lawrence mills were pessimistic about winning the strike and the workers had become eager to listen to terms. After a month of negotiations, a settlement was arrived at. It provided for increases in wages ranging from 5 to 25 percent, time and a quarter for overtime work, and no discrimination in rehiring the mill hands. Coolidge had handled his part tactfully and, though his solution did not meet all the strikers' demands, it was generally conceded that he had been fair and dispassionate.

Peace had been restored to Lawrence and the textile industry, but it was vanishing in Coolidge's party. In Massachusetts as elsewhere in 1912 the Republican party was splitting into two irreconcilable groups. In the preferential presidential primary election William Howard Taft narrowly carried the state's Republicans over Theodore Roosevelt. The delegates, when selected, were evenly divided at eighteen each for the President and the former President. After Taft was renominated for President by the Republican National Convention, Roosevelt refused to accept the decision. He formed a new party, the Progressive party, and several million Republicans flocked to stand with him at Armageddon against Taft and the Democratic nominee, Woodrow Wilson. The Massachusetts Republican party was split all the way down the line. On the state level, former Speaker of the House Joseph Walker and Charles Sumner Bird were nominated respectively by the Republicans and Progressives for governor. Foss was named for a third term by the Democrats in a race accurately described by Oklahoma's Thomas P. Gore as one in which "no Walker could walk fast enough or Bird fly swift enough to pass Governor Foss."[1] Foss and Woodrow Wilson carried Massachusetts, but Calvin Coolidge, who had remained loyal to Taft and Walker, won his three-cornered contest for re-election to the state senate.

Although the Republicans managed to retain control of the General Court, things looked dark for them as the 1913 session began. Governor Foss asked for more reforms than the Republicans thought wise, but his policies met with some success as the amendments for a federal income tax and popular election of United States senators were ratified. Further regulation of child labor, improvement of workmen's compensation, and salary raises for state employees were also approved. Yet Foss' program was not completed, partly because he was critical of his party's low tariff ideas. Coolidge was able to take advantage of the resulting animosities among the Democrats.

He had, of course, been irritated by the governor's veto of the western Massachusetts trolley bill and had set out during the summer of 1912 to do something about it. Appointed chairman of a recess committee on the matter, he worked hard to gather the information, arguments, and support necessary to get the legislation passed, even, if necessary, over a second veto. He was helped by his appointment early in 1913 as chairman of the senate committee on railroads. That meant that he was now in a position to gain favorable action on the establishment of a trolley system west of the Connecticut River.

The bill which the railroad committee reported out provided that the New Haven line might construct trolleys between Northampton and neighboring cities. Coolidge steered the trolley bill through the senate and it was also passed by the house. Governor Foss vetoed it but was overridden by the General Court. That was a victory which Coolidge savored all his days. Indeed he was to write years later in his autobiography that the 1913 General Court was "the most enjoyable session I ever spent with any legislative body."[2] Coolidge's committee also reported out legislation opposed by Foss that would transform the railroad commission into a public service board that could, among other things, restrict the borrowing powers of railroads. As it was amended on its passage through the two houses of the legislature, the bill gave the roads more than enough favors to offset the financial restrictions. Again the governor used the veto only to be reversed by the legislators.

Coolidge was acting as a party regular in these matters and, on the trolley act, as the representative of his constituents. Yet he was also acting sympathetically to the railroad interests. Had that not been true, he would never have been appointed to chair the recess committee and the railroad committee. He had become acquainted with and supported by the New Haven's lobbyist, J. Otis Wardwell. Not only did they both want the trolley act, but in Wardwell's eyes Coolidge was a safe man, a regular of the tribe of Murray Crane. The state senator was also acquainted with Arthur P. Russell, a New

Haven vice president, and Charles Hiller Innes, the Republican leader of Boston, who was in the pay of the New Haven. Moreover, the Northampton man's political mentor in the General Court was Thomas White, who was reportedly on a retainer from the railroad. Coolidge was also acquainted with Guy Currier, who, while technically a Democrat, was a political leader whose influence knew no party boundaries. Currier served to perpetuate what William Allen White has called the "Hamiltonian plutocratic aristocracy"[3] by political push and pull. Coolidge was not personally close to Currier, but he was not unfriendly to his economic ideas.

Too much can be made of the two men's relations, but it is true that Currier offered Coolidge a position in an insurance company at twenty thousand dollars a year with splendid prospects of promotion. It is also true that Coolidge's response was, "No, that doesn't lie along my line of influence."[4] No evidence has been found that shows why Currier offered the senator the opportunity to become wealthy. It is possible that it was part of an unsuccessful attempt to keep Coolidge from going along with Louis Brandeis' drive for state insurance and banking regulation. But it could also have been offered as a reward for services already rendered to the railroads.

Robert Washburn, who had worked closely with Coolidge on railroad matters in the General Court, said of the Northampton senator, "He looked upon himself as a cog in the government, to do his part, to follow the leaders."[5] Representative Washburn described Coolidge well. He stepped on no toes within his party and on few outside it. He rarely stuck his neck out on issues. He never attacked men and seldom assailed ideas. He had been connected with some of the great controversies of his time in the state, but had incurred no personal enemies and few critics. He had remained true to Murray Crane's leadership without antagonizing other elements of the Republican party. He had even gotten himself in the good graces of a number of Democrats. He had given favors to fellow legislators and to lobbyists and had asked for little in return. He had been the friend of business, agriculture, and labor in his district, and was not considered the enemy of any of them elsewhere. He was well enough known to be effective as a state senator, but not well enough known to be anyone's target. He knew his party and who was who in it. And he liked public office, even the use of the title senator, though he wisely discouraged its use in order to maintain his picture as an unostentatious fellow. He was a regular Republican. No one doubted his loyalty to the party, yet he was not mean in his Republicanism. It was a comfortable vehicle, not a crusade, for a man of his views and ambitions.

Coolidge's legislative record was a bit on the progressive side, thanks to his faithfulness to his constituents and his quest for stability in society. He had, as chairman of the railroad committee, supported the "full crew" bill, which endeared him to train workers. He had backed a fair sales bill for ice and oil dealers and had endorsed female suffrage, which saved him from the attacks of Massachusetts' well-organized suffragettes. He was sympathetic to pensions for widows, a minimum wage for women workers, and aid to needy mothers. He also favored workmen's injury compensation. He voted for a state income tax, legalization of picketing, primary elections, and popular election of United States senators. Yet he always made it clear that he stood for economy and efficiency in government. Something for everybody so long as it did not cost much was decidedly his political creed.

Politics was not Coolidge's whole life. He loved his family even though it took second place to public service. His family life, matching his income, remained modest. The Coolidges continued to live in the Massasoit Street two-family house, and John attended public school as would young Calvin. Grace stayed out of politics, although she occasionally traveled to Boston to be with her husband and to shop. Senator Coolidge went home every weekend on the day train, as he had when a representative, to be with his family and to keep track of his law business. On the Saturday train he could usually be found silently smoking a cigar. His manner with strangers and even his family was curt though not unpleasant.

Calvin Coolidge's relations with his boys left something to be desired. The quiet, frail father was not easily a playmate or even a companion. Moreover, being away as often as he was, he could not be as close to his boys as most fathers were to theirs. He read to his sons when possible and took them skating and fishing. More often, he shared his favorite recreation, walking, with them. The walks were long and only seldom punctuated with talk. He encouraged his sons to save. One day, while walking past the bank where John and Calvin had small deposits, he said, "Boys, listen here a minute and maybe you can hear your money working for you."[6] Save, not spend, was Coolidge's prime precept for his sons. That others must spend the savings to make money work did not impress him greatly.

The Coolidges also continued to be stay-at-homes. Even when given free passes to Northampton's theater while he was mayor, Coolidge rarely went. Music and drama were not along his line of influence. He persisted in his practice, born as much of thriftiness as of shyness, of not going out much and of having few people in. Coolidge's reputation for taciturnity also continued. One of the Coolidge stories most often told is that of Grace asking him what a minister had said in a sermon about sin.

"He was against it," was Coolidge's reply. The story is apocryphal, but it conveys the flavor of the man.

Another story was true, according to his wife. The Coolidges had a Baptist minister as a dinner guest before he was to conduct a revival meeting. The preacher ate little, explaining that temperance in eating improved his ability to preach. After hearing the man do his preaching, Coolidge clucked to Grace, "Might as well have et."[7]

In 1913 Coolidge was, whether he knew it or not, at a turning point in his career. He was forty-one years old, a man with family responsibilities. Yet he was not overly successful in his chosen profession, the law. Nor, despite his string of local successes, did political lightning seem ready to strike him. He was a state senator in his second and apparently last term. What did he think and feel? It is implausible that he was plotting and scheming to advance himself in politics. He neither had the energy nor was of the nature to do so. And, as far as making a living was concerned, he probably preferred the relatively steady income from the law to the risks of politics. Yet he was, as he so often wrote in his autobiography, "ready" to grasp whatever political opportunities appeared.

His ventures in politics were somewhat motivated by the desire that any lawyer has to get ahead. Politics offered a way to make acquaintances, to acquire intimate knowledge of government, law, and the community, and to gain a reputation, hopefully deserved, for probity. Furthermore, his desire for public service was high by the time he came to Northampton. Not only was there his family's heritage of service, but also the lessons of Garman and Morse which he so esteemed. In Northampton he soon found that his sense of civic responsibility could pleasantly and effectively be expressed through politics. It also gave him excitement and action as nothing else had and brought him the recognition and honor that he obviously desired. As important was his belief that political service helped to build his law practice.

It must have been clear to Coolidge, though he never admitted it, that there was a limit to how far politics would help his law business. He was not much more prosperous in his practice in 1913 than he had been in 1905. He had no retainers and little corporation business. He had to count on the turnover of many small cases for his income. After his two terms in the house he returned to Northampton to wait for clients to crowd into his office and for some lucrative retainers. Neither the crowds nor the retainers came. When the opportunity arose to run for mayor, he accepted it believing that it would "advance me in my profession."[8] Although the position paid an annual salary of eight hundred dollars, Coolidge was worse off than before, so much so that he had to accept financial assistance from his father. His prospects certainly were not brightening at the law. Yet one can take him partly at his word when he wrote: "Remaining in one office long did not appeal to me, for I was not seeking a public career. My heart was in the law." He went on blandly to say, "I thought a couple of terms in the Massachusetts Senate would be helpful to me, so when our senator retired I sought his place."[9]

The senate seat might ultimately have advanced his law career. During his first two terms he doubtlessly made some impression on the state's political and business leaders. But by 1913 he was aboard the trolley to the political heavens. Opportunity was to come the way of the small-town lawyer, but it was an opportunity undreamed of.

6

Do the Day's Work

OPPORTUNITY CAME in the fall of 1913 for Calvin Coolidge, but it was a teasing one. The president of the Massachusetts senate, Levi Greenwood, had decided to run for the Republican nomination for lieutenant governor. His chances looked good because the Democratic incumbent in that office had set his cap for the governorship. Coolidge requested and received Republican endorsement for a third term as senator in the hope that he might be selected Greenwood's successor. After it was too late for Coolidge to withdraw gracefully, Greenwood, discouraged by the amount of competition for the lieutenant governorship, announced that he was seeking election only to the senate and its presidency. Opportunity had been extended to Coolidge only to be withdrawn. Yet it was unexpectedly to reappear.

Greenwood was a forceful opponent of female suffrage, and he was picked by the suffragettes as their prime target in the 1913 elections. Led by Margaret Foley, who was as full of political fight as any man in the state, the emancipationists helped to defeat Greenwood in his bid for re-election to the senate. The presidency was open after all. "Again I was ready," Coolidge has written.[1] After learning of Greenwood's defeat the morning after election day, Coolidge jumped on the first train to Boston and from there began to solicit support for himself as senate president. Within five days, he recalled, he had enough votes from his fellow senators to assure election. Another story is that the forces of Crane, Innes, and the fat cats of Boston, when Greenwood's defeat appeared certain, got together and decided on Coolidge for the post. Then they got in touch with him and worked with him to round up the votes necessary for his election as senate president.

Neither story has been proven completely true, but it is obvious that he could not have been elected without the leaders' approval. Too much was at stake. The Democrats had elected, not only the governor, David Walsh, but also the lieutenant governor. Moreover, the Republicans had lost their majority in the house of representatives, so control of the senate became all the more important. And in the senate, where there were 21 Republicans to 17 Democrats and 2 Progressives, it was essential for the Republicans to have a presiding officer who could hold them together. The bosses were not, under those circumstances, going to be indifferent to who was elected the third-ranking officer of the state. The man had to be experienced, hard-working, knowledgeable, moderate, and respected by both the senate and his party's organization. Coolidge worked for the senate presidency, but he could not have had it unless he had met those criteria and had the machine's backing.

When the General Court convened in January, 1914, Coolidge was unanimously nominated by the Republican caucus and then elected president of the senate. In fact, he was elected by ten votes more than those held by the senate Republicans. He later proudly wrote, "I had not only become an officer of the whole Commonwealth, but I had come into possession of an influence reaching beyond the confines of my own party which I was to retain so long as I remained in public life."[2] He was an officer of the whole state and indeed was second only to the governor in power. He had the right to name the senate's committees, to assign bills to committees, to determine who should sit on conference committees to iron out disagreements with the house, and to recognize members on the floor. That gave him tremendous influence in determining what legislation would or, especially, would not succeed.

Coolidge's pride in holding the presidency was reflected in the speech he made to the senate upon his election. Not only was his "Have Faith in Massachusetts" speech the finest he ever made, but it was also the best statement of his philosophy. After thanking his colleagues for the honor and obligations bestowed upon him, Coolidge said:

This Commonwealth is one. We are all members of one body. The welfare of the weakest and the welfare of the most powerful are inseparably bound together. Industry cannot flourish if labor languish. Transportation cannot prosper if manufactures decline. The general welfare cannot be provided for in any one act, but it is well to remember that the benefit of one is the benefit of all, and the neglect of one is the neglect of all....

Men do not make laws. They do but discover them. Laws must be justified by something more than the will of the majority. They must rest on the eternal foundation of righteousness. That state is most fortunate in its form of government which has the aptest instruments for the discovery of laws. The latest, most modern, and nearest perfect system that statesmanship has devised is representative government. Its weakness is the weakness of us imperfect human beings who administer it. Its strength is that even such administration secures to the people more blessings than any other system ever produced. No nation has discarded it and retained liberty....

The people cannot look to legislation generally for success. Industry, thrift, character, are not conferred by act or resolve. Government cannot relieve from toil. It can provide no substitute for the rewards of service. It can, of course, care for the defective and recognize distinguished merit. The normal must care for themselves. Self-government means self-support....

Ultimately, property rights and personal rights are the same thing. The one cannot be preserved if the other be violated. Each man is entitled to his rights and the rewards of his service be they never so large or never so small.

History reveals no civilized people among whom there were not a highly educated class, and large aggregations of wealth, represented usually by the clergy and the nobility. Inspiration has always come from above. Diffusion of learning has come down from the university to the common school....

It may be that the diffusion of wealth works in an analagous way. As the little red schoolhouse is builded in the college, it may be that the fostering and protection of large aggregations of wealth are the only foundation on which to build the prosperity of the whole people. Large profits mean large pay rolls. But profits must be the result of service performed. . . .

Do the day's work. If it be to protect the rights of the weak, whoever objects, do it. If it be to help a powerful corporation better to serve the people, whatever the opposition, do that. Expect to be called a stand-patter, but don't be a stand-patter. Expect to be called a demagogue, but don't be a demagogue. Don't hesitate to be as revolutionary as science. Don't hesitate to be as reactionary as the multiplication table. Don't expect to build up the weak by pulling down the strong. Don't hurry to legislate. Give administration a chance to catch up with legislation.

We need a broader, firmer, deeper faith in the people —a faith that men desire to do right, that the Commonwealth is founded upon a righteousness which will endure, a reconstructed faith that the final approval of the people is given not to demagogues, slavishly pandering to their selfishness, merchandising with the clamor of the hour, but to statesmen, ministering to their welfare, representing their deep, silent, abiding convictions.[3]

Charles Garman would have been satisfied with his erstwhile student, just as satisfied as Coolidge was with himself as he stood before the venerable Commonwealth's senate acting the role of statesman. He carried it off well, even though his address tended to be archaic in style and loose in structure. The "Have Faith in Massachusetts" speech is important for two reasons: first, for the circumstances under which it was given, and second, for its exposition of Coolidge's philosophy. Confronted by a governor, David Walsh, who was dynamic and popular and able to raise issue after issue skillfully, Coolidge had set a keynote that was not hostile, but that made clear that nothing was going to be hustled through under his eyes. Confronted by a senate which was almost split down the middle in partisan groupings, he tried to strike the higher notes in the senators' hearts and minds. He was warning conservatives and liberals alike that compromise was necessary, that through the middle path lay equanimity in the senate and progress. His speech bespoke his concern for stability, which could, he believed, be reached only through the consideration and balancing of the legitimate interests of all. That the interests were not all legitimate, that his principles did not always work, did not disturb Coolidge for he recognized that human beings are imperfect. Striving for legitimacy and workable laws was the important thing.

Yet there was more to Coolidge's philosophy, and it transcended partisan considerations. The key was the sentence in his address, "Inspiration has always come from above." The last word, "above," did not mean the head of state. It meant, in Coolidge's lexicon, man's spiritual nature and the laws of God and nature. And it was the task of the people's representatives to discover and of public administrators to implement them. "Above" must also be interpreted, in the economic sphere, as "large aggregations of wealth." To Coolidge those aggregations were not beyond criticism or restraint, but they had to be handled gingerly. He believed in the trickle-down theory: increased prosperity trickled all the way down the line from the operations of concentrated wealth on high. The problem was to know how to regulate the flow so that the prosperity-giving concentrations would not be destroyed. Those political and economic concepts must be understood if Coolidge in turn is to be understood, because he generally acted on them throughout his career. The flaws in his thought come not from the quality of his intentions, for he meant to do well by all people. The weaknesses come from the fact that his philosophy was too simple, too sketchy to fit the growing intricacies of American life. In addition, his faith in the perceptiveness of the people's representatives was too high, his view of the executive's role was too limited, and his concept of the desire of the wealthy to earn their profits was distorted. An equally great problem was that neither society nor Coolidge was able to be "as revolutionary as science" and "as reactionary as the multiplication table" in response to society's needs.

Coolidge did strive manfully to adapt his philosophy to Massachusetts when he was president of the state senate. He hoped that his "Have Faith in Massachusetts" speech would prevent enactment of measures destructive of property rights. His hope was, to his satisfaction, realized. He wrote in his autobiography: "Many people in the Commonwealth had been waiting for such a word, and the effect was beyond my expectation. Confusion of thought began to disappear, and unsound legislative proposals to diminish."[4] As important was that he sought to play down partisanship in the senate and to cooperate with Governor Walsh on a number of bills. Walsh's proposals were largely an accumulation of unfulfilled progressive demands. He urged financial and managerial reorganization of the Boston and Maine Railroad that would divorce it from the New Haven. He called for adoption of initiative, referendum, recall, biennial state elections, increased administrative discretion for the governor, female suffrage, tax revision, compulsory workmen's compensation, additional home rule for municipalities, establishment of a central state purchasing agency, and consolidation of certain governmental boards. Little of that could be called radical.

The list of legislative accomplishments during Walsh's first term is long. Granted in part or full were injury compensation, home rule, regulation of public service corporations, division of the Boston and Maine and the New Haven, a health department, reorganization of parts of state government, compulsory arbitration of labor disputes, taxes on out-of-state corporations, and the beginnings of tax reform. These and other accomplishments were proudly claimed by the Walsh administration. They were, however, also accomplishments for Calvin Coolidge, who had supported many of them, forced compromises on others, and prevented, sometimes to the governor's relief, more far-reaching measures from passing. Coolidge was not entirely pleased with the record of the General Court and administration for 1914, yet he could take satisfaction from the knowledge that the middle path had been followed and stability maintained. He had acquitted himself well as a politician and as an officer of state.

After the adjournment of the legislature, Coolidge took a hand in the work of pulling his party together. The Republican party had suffered for several years from divisions between the regulars and the progressives, with many of the latter going outside the party in 1912 to form their own. The results had been disastrous for Republicans. They had lost the governorship and even the lieutenant governorship. Their strength in the General Court had dwindled so that by 1914 they barely controlled the senate and organized the house only with the help of the Progressive party representatives. The Republicans were threatened with continued division in 1914. Coolidge and other moderates worked to reduce strife in their party's ranks and to bring back the Progressives. The Republican moderates were determined to start their party on the upgrade again. Their tactic was to woo the Progressives by reconciliation and program concessions.

Central to the Republican reorganization were the actions of the party's state convention of October, 1914. The nomination of liberal Congressman Samuel W. McCall for governor appealed to a large number of Progressives. Equally important was the convention's "social justice" platform, which was drafted by the resolutions committee chaired by Calvin Coolidge. The document has been called conservative by Coolidge, and so it was, compared with the Democratic and Progressive platforms. Yet the Republican platform of 1914 was more liberal and conciliatory than its predecessors. It bowed to Progressives and Republican liberals by considering the party as an organization encompassing a variety of viewpoints. It emphasized the positive aspects of the Republican party's record instead of engaging in criminations and recriminations. It pledged that the party would continue to seek positive benefits of government for all people, though conservatives were assured that it would not be done by disrupting the bases of prosperity or the confidence of the classes in each other. The Coolidge touch, stability through moderation, was evident throughout the document.

The work of the state convention paid off in the November elections. Although McCall lost to Governor Walsh, it was by the small margin of eleven thousand votes. Moreover, the Republicans captured the other statewide offices, regained a majority in the house of representatives, and increased their majority in the senate from two to twenty-six. Coolidge, returned for a fourth time from his western Massachusetts district, was in that majority. When the senate met on January 6, 1915, he also was re-elected its president.

Coolidge's address to the senate upon his re-election to the presidency was brief, a mere forty-two words, the shortest in the body's history:

> My sincerest thanks, I offer you. Conserve the firm foundations of our institutions. Do your work with the spirit of a soldier in the public service. Be loyal to the Commonwealth and to yourselves. And be brief; above all things,
> Be Brief.[5]

Governor Walsh in contrast the next day gave a long inaugural address in which he advocated establishment of a state budget system, further railroad reorganization, financial maintenance of the public service commission by the communications and transportation businesses it regulated, a constitutional convention to overhaul the state's unwieldy organic law, and work relief appropriations for the jobless. He renewed his requests for woman suffrage, initiative, referendum, and biennial state elections.

The General Court's response was far from progressive. Of the things requested by the governor, only work relief appropriations and reorganization of the Boston and Maine were granted. His failure to obtain more from the lawmakers can be ascribed to a number of factors. Acting out of conviction as well as partisanship, the Republicans, with their large legislative majorities, rarely went along with the governor. Moreover, Walsh's efforts in behalf of progressive proposals and the people's interest in them were wearing down. That was contributed to in considerable measure by the impact of the Great War in Europe and the new concerns that it had given both the American people and their elected officials.

Coolidge took it upon himself in the 1915 session of the General Court to be concerned chiefly with the dispatch of business. He no longer had to serve as the bulwark against the governor's liberalism now that the Republicans were again firmly in the legislative saddle. His concern with dispatch had, of course, been indicated in his opening address. "Be Brief" was his watchword throughout the session. He pressed the senate's committees to get out their reports. He kept down the length and number of the body's daily sessions. And he had a hand in limiting the volume of laws and resolves passed by the legislature. The result of his work was reflected in *The Blue Book of Acts and Resolves*, which was reduced in length from 1,423 pages for 1914, to 1,230 for 1915.

Coolidge did not accomplish dispatch of business by pettiness. Open-mindedness and even humor were established as his hallmarks in the 1915 session. Once while Coolidge was presiding in the senate, a member complained to him of being told in debate by another senator to go to hell. The senate president's reply was, "I've examined the Constitution and the Senate rules, and there's nothing in them that compels you to go."[6] Coolidge was conservative during the session, more so than he had been previously or was to be as lieutenant governor and governor, but he balanced his conservatism so that it did not offend his more liberal colleagues. Joseph Martin tells a story that explains the Coolidge touch. As a state senator, Martin opposed a bill supported by Coolidge that would extend the time necessary before an injured workingman could apply for benefits under the state's compensation law. The senate president took no offense. In fact, one afternoon after their disagreement Coolidge poked his head out of his office door and called Martin. He told him, "Joseph, go in and call the Senate to order and preside until I get there."[7] That Martin gladly did, for it gave him a sign of distinction, and it also incurred his good will for Coolidge.

The senate president was not completely conservative. Massachusetts' savings banks had been authorized to issue small life insurance policies. In 1915, however, the life insurance companies sought to discontinue the legislative appropriation supporting the savings bank insurance system. The system's legal representative, Judd Dewey, visited Coolidge the morning before the appropriation bill was to come up for a second reading in order to review it with him. After Dewey had given his arguments for the appropriation, Coolidge said only, "What you say sounds reasonable."

Dewey departed, dismayed with what appeared to be a brushoff. As he was walking along the corridor, a senator asked him what Coolidge had said.

"He didn't say anything, except 'it sounds reasonable,'" Dewey replied.

"My God, did he say that?" blurted the senator. "Then you're all right."

When the appropriation bill came up that afternoon, Coolidge was in the chair. He spoke, "Those in favor say aye."

Not a voice was heard.

When he called for an indication of opposition, nays rang out from all over the chamber.

Coolidge then solemnly intoned, "The yeas have it, and the bill is ordered to a third hearing."[8]

That was but one of the several occasions on which Coolidge as senate president and governor helped the savings bank insurance program, for which organized labor had been battling for years. What his motives were for such extraordinary action can only be guessed. Although he had had a long association as counsel of the Nonotuck Savings Bank, such institutions were lukewarm to the insurance program, and one can guess that he was too. Yet Coolidge would not want to see savings banks, as small institutions, dictated to by the great insurance companies and their allies among the national banks. Of course, he was not averse to keeping labor's respect and he did believe in competition. Whatever his motives, his action did him no harm with the reform forces of the state, which were still strong enough to tip the balance in statewide elections.

Coolidge ended the 1915 session of the General Court holding the confidence of conservatives and moderates and not having alienated liberals. He had had dealings with a variety of interests and even contacts with corrupt elements, but he had not been bought by the interests or corrupted by the elements. He emerged with a reputation for efficiency, humor, and open-mindedness. Should opportunity come again, he would be ready.

7

Lieutenant Governor

COOLIDGE HAS WRITTEN, "When I went home at the end of the 1915 session it was with the intention of remaining in private life and giving all my attention to the law."[1] This may have been true, but Coolidge was aware that his name was being talked about in connection with the lieutenant governorship.[2] Although he might, at last, have built a decent practice on the basis of his contacts with business and political leaders, his enjoyment of honor and position would be better served by a boost in office. Moreover, some of his friends said that with the lieutenant governor's salary of two thousand dollars and his law practice he would still increase his income.

An unusual situation existed in the Republican party. In 1914 Samuel W. McCall had been induced to leave a sure seat in Congress to run against Governor Walsh, with the understanding on the part of a number of Republican leaders that should he be defeated they would support him for renomination the following year. That understanding did not go unchallenged. The successful Republican candidate for lieutenant governor in 1914, Grafton Dulaney Cushing, demanded the customary privilege of being the next Republican nominee for governor. McCall refused to step aside, contending that because of his sacrifice he deserved a second chance to be elected governor. The result was a head-on clash between McCall and Cushing for the nomination.

The significance of all this for Coolidge was that it left the nomination for lieutenant governor open. He played his cards well. While the General Court was in session he stuck to business. As the state's second-ranking Republican officeholder, Coolidge was an obvious possibility for the nomination, but he was not a seeker of it, at least not prematurely. He let the situation develop, for he was wise enough not to become involved in the battle between McCall and Cushing. By summer Cushing had become so committed to contesting McCall that he could not gracefully back down and run for renomination as lieutenant governor.

It was also in 1915 that Frank Waterman Stearns, the man most identified with Coolidge's rise to the American Presidency, came into the life of the Northampton man. Stearns owned and managed R. H. Stearns and Company, one of Boston's leading dry goods stores. He had been graduated from Amherst and served not only as a trustee of the college but also as one of its chief boosters. One must, of course, understand the position of Amherst in the state's hierarchy. The western Massachusetts Heidelberg was the mother of many of the Commonwealth's leading citizens and, indeed, had sent her sons into positions of prominence all over the country. Her alumni were proud of her and with good reason. Yet in the political affairs of Massachusetts, Amherst was well down the ladder from the giant on the Charles, Harvard.

In the winter of 1914–15, at an alumni dinner, some of the sons of Amherst discussed their political insignificance in the Commonwealth and they concluded that they should organize to push some of their brothers to the fore. Judge Henry Field suggested that Calvin Coolidge, who was already well up in the state's hierarchy, deserved consideration. Few knew him, for while the senate president had never lost touch with his alma mater, he had not been outstanding in alumni affairs. Stearns had a reaction to Coolidge, and it was not pleasant. He pointed out that in 1913 he had approached Coolidge about a bill to enlarge the college's sewer facilities. The trustee had been greeted with a terse reply, "I'm sorry! It's too late,"[3] and then was quickly ushered out of Coolidge's room. Yet Stearns was willing to go along if some of the alumni wanted to back the senate president for higher office.

Stearns went out to work for Coolidge, using his broad contacts across the state in the senator's behalf. He also set out to become better acquainted with the Northampton lawmaker and found him more to his liking than he had earlier imagined. Of course, it helped that Coolidge had finally put the Amherst sewer bill through the legislature, though he probably did it at Judge Field's behest. Stearns worked for Coolidge, though he did not know exactly what the goal was. He contented himself with touting the senate president with Amherst alumni, business acquaintances, and advertising contacts. By spring it became obvious to Stearns that the lieutenant governorship was the best goal and this he pressed on Coolidge. The senator made no move toward the post, though he did not discourage Stearns' activities. The Boston business baron was a novice in politics, which in part explains his effectiveness in Coolidge's behalf because he seemed to represent disinterested forces behind the senate president. Stearns' amateur status probably also explains his growing affection for Coolidge. The businessman quickly became enamored of politics and of his identification with Coolidge, who he convinced himself would grow into a force in the state and then in the land. Frank Waterman Stearns had been bitten by the political bug and had gotten one of the worst cases of election fever on record. Coolidge tried to ameliorate Stearns' disease in 1915 by telling him, "I hope you will not take politics too seriously."[4] It had no effect on Stearns, who went so far that year as to tell some Boston politicians, much to their amusement, that Calvin Coolidge would some day become President of the United States.

Coolidge was not the only possibility for the Republican nomination for lieutenant governor. Openly seeking the endorsement was a member of the governor's council, Guy Ham. The councilor was an accomplished orator, a man of much service to the party, with a great deal of experience in the General Court. Ham's candidacy was both a threat and a help to Calvin Coolidge. On the one hand, Ham might, with his outgoing personality, win the nomination. On the other hand, he was considered unsafe by most party leaders. Not only did he have maverick tendencies, but even worse he was a temperance man, and temperance was a cause that most experienced Massachusetts Republicans tried to avoid. In a showdown between Ham and Coolidge, the Republican leaders and the business interests of the state had no choice. It had to be Coolidge, the stable, safe organization man. He was not the type to thrill and inspire the crowds, but where it counted, in the back rooms of government, he was one to be relied upon. Thus, stirred up by Stearns and somewhat obligated to Coolidge by his service over the years, the business interests and the Murray Crane organization turned to the Northampton senator.

Coolidge had to be induced to run. Stearns' urgings and enthusiasm had not moved him to enter the race. Yet it was becoming clear to Coolidge that he had an excellent chance to win the nomination and the election because of the turning of party regulars and business support to him. As he wrote Stearns, "I figured it out that it was worth while for me to be a candidate even if I do not get it. I want you to know you have done me a great benefit by encouraging me to run whatever the result—but I shall win."[5]

In his campaign for the lieutenant governor's nomination Coolidge relied chiefly on Frank Stearns' publicity operations, the work of the party regulars, and the efforts of business, particularly the breweries, to line up votes for him. He wisely made no attempt to slug it out on the stump with Ham. He tried through publicity, including widespread distribution of his "Have Faith in Massachusetts" address, letters to party leaders and workers, and his few speeches to stand in contrast to his vigorous, colorful primary election opponent. If the contest was one of the Republican progressives and temperance people against the regulars and business interests, it was also one of the maverick against the tried and true man of stability and common sense. It was also one of a few scattered leaders against the forces of the two chief Republican factions, as Coolidge was backed by Senator Henry Cabot Lodge's son-in-law, Congressman Augustus P. Gardner, whose speech was silver, as well as by Murray Crane, whose silence was golden. Coolidge, with the support of most conservatives, many moderates, and even some progressives, won by a comfortable margin, 75,000 to 50,000 votes, over Guy Ham. Now there was the much tougher general election campaign to win.

The head of the Republican ticket was Samuel W. McCall, who had won his fight for the gubernatorial nomination from Grafton Cushing. McCall had a rich and varied background. He had been chief editorial writer for the Boston *Daily Advertiser* and a practicing lawyer. He had served in the General Court and, for twenty years, in Congress. He was faithful to his party but was not a standpatter. He had written often and well of problems of government, which he approached from a scholarly, as well as a political, viewpoint. He was also one of the best orators in Massachusetts. After being renominated, he worked to draw progressives back into the Republican party, and he was one of the few men who could do so, for personally and politically he attracted the confidence of all Republicans. In the 1915 state convention McCall helped the progressives commit the Republican party to a constitutional convention and to reasonable working hours for employees of factories operating twenty-four hours a day.

McCall's opponent again was the popular and resourceful Governor David Walsh. Coolidge was more fortunate, running against Edward P. Barry, who had been defeated for re-election to the lieutenant governorship in 1914. McCall, by his conciliatory tactics, had attracted most of the old Progressives. In fact, their foremost leader in Massachusetts, Charles Sumner Bird, openly supported the McCall-Coolidge ticket. McCall had also shut the Republican temperance men out of the platform-making, and although that resulted in a stronger Prohibition party campaign for governor, it kept a large number of antiprohibitionist Republicans from shifting to Walsh. It was better that twenty thousand votes go to the Prohibitionists than fifty thousand to the Democrats. Furthermore, there was some truth to the charge of the Prohibitionist nominee, William Shaw, that the "organized liquor vote of Massachusetts knifed Governor Walsh to elect Samuel W. McCall, in a desperate effort to prevent the Republican party from adopting prohibition."[6] Yet it was true that neither McCall nor Coolidge was a prohibitionist and that they were well thought of by the liquor and beer trade. The irony was that Coolidge was to be the President most identified with national prohibition. The answer to the seeming paradox is simple. In both instances he went along with the effective majority sentiment.

In the 1915 general election campaign Coolidge did the hardest electioneering of his life. He accompanied McCall, who was a vigorous campaigner, and the two of them spoke from automobiles during the day and ended with outdoor rallies at night. For Coolidge it was stimulating and fascinating to be with McCall; for McCall it was restful being with a running mate who asked no questions and volunteered no advice. Coolidge did not become a dynamic speaker. Indeed, it was said that "McCall could fill any hall in Massachusetts and Coolidge could empty it."[7] Coolidge devoted his speeches to supporting McCall, who had by far the tougher campaign. Coolidge recognized that his own opponent would win or lose on Governor Walsh's coattails and that Walsh's defeat would insure his Democratic running mate's defeat.

Coolidge shared the chores equitably with McCall. As McCall was the liberal on the ticket, Coolidge's job was to supply a note of conservatism by emphasizing "the urgent necessity of preventing further increases in state and national expense and of a drastic reduction wherever possible."[8] McCall got the headlines, but his running mate kept the party conservatives happy. Coolidge, when requested, gave the head of the ticket information about state government, on which he was an expert compared with McCall. Their campaign was successful. McCall, faced with opposition, not only from Walsh but also from a rump Progressive ticket and the enraged Prohibitionists, won by some 6,000 votes. Coolidge sailed home to election by a 52,000-vote plurality.

In January, 1916, a new regime, Samuel McCall's, entered office in the Commonwealth of Massachusetts. In his inaugural address Governor McCall requested a constitutional convention, emphasizing the need for reform and regrouping among the more than one hundred boards, commissions, and departments that made up the expensive and overly complicated machinery of state. He also called for extension of civil service regulations to most state employees, curbing of moneylenders, establishment of reasonable working hours in various industries, including paper mills, tax reform to reduce the burden on real estate, and state insurance to guard workers against the financial hazards of illness, old age, and unemployment. McCall had made an interesting blend of progressivism and conservatism. He would have the state do dynamic things, but economically and efficiently. The General Court, in the shortest session in eleven years, put the question of a constitutional convention before the voters, reorganized some state agencies, set up a commission to study unemployment insurance, and limited work in around-the-clock paper mills to eight-hour shifts. Coolidge staunchly supported his chief, because it was in his faction's interest to do so and because of his personal admiration for McCall.

The lieutenant governor's job in Massachusetts differed from that in other states. He did not preside over the state senate. Instead he chaired the governor's council, which had the right of advice and even veto on pardons, finances, appointments to state offices, and affairs of penal and charitable institutions. Coolidge was also chairman of the council's committee on nominations to state offices and, at the governor's urging, made frequent inspection trips to public institutions. McCall further assigned to his lieutenant governor an unusually large number of speaking engagements over the state. The work load, which Coolidge had thought would leave him plenty of time, became so heavy that he was forced to add a partner, Ralph W. Hemenway, to attend to much of his law practice. Now that Coolidge was away from home most of the time and his wife was expected to attend more public functions than ever before, the family also had to employ a full-time housekeeper. Coolidge was earning more money, but he had more financial obligations.

Life had changed decidedly, as Coolidge became not only a considerable figure in the affairs of Massachusetts but, almost by profession, a public speaker as well. The 1915 campaign had allowed him the opportunity to develop a style. It was not that of the orator, the advocate, the professor, or the preacher. It could only be called Coolidgean. In his nasal, almost unmodulated voice, he quacked out facts in a well-organized manner, trying to enliven them with aphorisms. He drafted his speeches on yellow foolscap at night and then dictated them for typing the next morning. They were short, as were the sentences within them. Humor was absent, as were beauty and brilliance. His speeches did, however, express his basic philosophy of moderation, self-reliance, and social stability. And they had the virtue of giving his listeners a few quotable remarks to take away. The speeches buttressed the picture of Coolidge as a man of common sense and firmness, a man who could be trusted, and because of their frequency they gave him opportunities to become better known. His speechmaking trips contributed to the experience, knowledge, and publicity he needed to "be ready" to move up to the governorship when the time came.

Life had changed in other ways too. Although he did not have a personal organization, Coolidge now had large numbers of friends and acquaintances in the Commonwealth. Some he acquired just in the normal course of discharging his duties and others he acquired because of the possibility that he might some day be governor. He also carried along his old friends and acquaintances, for a man who was aiming at the governorship could afford to alienate no one.

Foremost among his friends was Frank Stearns, who was, by the consensus of all who knew him, the only man who ever worshiped Coolidge. The Boston merchant was a man approaching sixty, short and rotund, bespectacled, and prosperous-looking. Coolidge offered him the opportunity to rise to the stars, to become part of history, and Stearns seized it eagerly. Coolidge was also a man who did not tell him what to do, who did things efficiently, almost mysteriously. That Stearns liked and that he concluded made Coolidge the Lincoln of his times.

In turn, that Coolidge should like Stearns is understandable. The attention the businessman paid the politician was just short of idolatry and no man could help but find it appealing. Stearns also knew the right people and was of the class that Coolidge admired: those of wealth who gave service. Stearns was as close to being an alter ego as the Northampton man would ever have. He could be trusted to do almost instinctively what Coolidge wanted and needed. He respected Coolidge's need for silent companionship. When Stearns spoke, he did so deliberately. Furthermore, he was not self-seeking in terms of position, though he did see Coolidge as a man who would as a matter of course advance business interests.

Stearns also showered Coolidge with hospitality. Often the Coolidges were entertained at the merchant's Swampscott mansion and in his suite at the Touraine Hotel. This was the style of living Coolidge enjoyed, for although he did not have the grand manner, he liked it when it was forced upon him. Stearns also did favors for and gave gifts to Grace and the boys. He even gave Coolidge a check for five thousand dollars, which was returned. The lieutenant governor became embarrassed by Stearns' generosity and had to ask him to cut down on his favors to the family. He even commented, "I have often wondered why the greatest merchant in Boston was giving so much attention to my welfare."[9] The businessman saw to it, though, that Coolidge had no political expenses. He might insist on financial independence for himself and his family, but as Stearns wrote to Dwight Morrow, "I have not been able to discover that it frets him that I have assumed some of these bills."[10]

Stearns touted Coolidge as often as he could. He introduced and reintroduced him to countless editors and businessmen and made him an Amherst man of note. He entertained men from all over Massachusetts in Coolidge's behalf. He publicized whatever could be publicized about the lieutenant governor. And he took Coolidge on his first trip to Washington, in 1916, in the hope of meeting important political figures. It was then that Coolidge and Senator Henry Cabot Lodge, the state's most illustrious political leader, met. If they did not fall into each other's arms, they were at least not hostile. That was an accomplishment, for Coolidge was in the camp of Lodge's chief factional enemy, Murray Crane, and had supported Governor McCall against Lodge's lieutenants back home. Stearns also went to the 1916 Republican National Convention, not, as Murray Crane and William Allen White said, to get Coolidge the presidential nomination, but in order to get the wiry little lieutenant governor better known.

The year 1916 was the time of a national presidential election. Massachusetts' Republicans were split three ways in supporting contenders for the nomination, but Coolidge kept on good terms with all three groups by neither backing nor condemning anyone. After the convention had nominated New York's Charles Evans Hughes for President, Coolidge campaigned actively for the national ticket. He also had himself and Governor McCall to campaign for. They had both been renominated without opposition and, now that the Progressive party had completely folded camp, they were both re-elected by comfortable margins.

McCall's 1917 inaugural address was another summons for progressive action. He renewed his request for a state insurance program, asked for extension of old-age pensions, and demanded the abolition of capital punishment, which, had it been adopted, would have spared Massachusetts and the nation most of the turmoil resulting from the Sacco-Vanzetti case in the 1920s. The governor was rejected on all those requests and on many of his lesser ones. The General Court was more interested in America's involvement in the World War and in the rising war-borne tide of prosperity than it was in social welfare legislation.

One administration measure that did pass was connected with the lieutenant governor. During the previous summer Coolidge had headed a commission that was seeking to solve the scrambled finances of the Boston Elevated Street Railway. That was no small matter since the El's operations were vital to public transportation in the state capital and had for years been a center of sharp controversy. Once again, as in the Lawrence textile strike situation, Coolidge did not duck trouble and he acquitted himself well. The commission recommended the appointment of a board of trustees to control the El's property and fix fares that would provide stockholders with a fair return and yet keep passenger rates at a reasonable level. This plan was approved by the legislature, and though not greeted with unanimous praise, it did operate to strike a decent balance between the interests of the El's stockholders and passengers.

The coming of the war involved McCall and Coolidge in new tasks. The governor formed the nation's first state committee of public safety and authorized it to settle industrial disputes and keep the labor force up to levels required by war needs. Coolidge supported the national and state administrations' war efforts as an oratorical minuteman, going before the public to explain the country's needs for cash, men, and material. That and his participation in war loan and charity drives made him well known over Massachusetts as a patriot.

Coolidge also maintained his reputation for frugality and open-mindedness. When in 1917 the tenure of Joseph B. Eastman on the public service commission was coming to an end, McCall was tempted not to reappoint him. Eastman was an independent who had been appointed by a Democratic governor and it was thought that he might be a liability to a Republican administration. Coolidge assured Governor McCall that Eastman was both competent and unpartisan. The commissioner was reappointed. It is true that Eastman was an Amherst man, class of 1904, but that was not enough to compel Coolidge to put in a good word for him.

As for Coolidge's frugality, John Hays Hammond tells a story about the lieutenant governor which, whether apocryphal or not, was widely circulated. Three reporters were scheduled to interview Coolidge one day. It turned out to be a chill, stormy day. One reporter arrived a few minutes ahead of the others. Mrs. Coolidge noticed that he was cold and wet.

She thoughtfully said, "Calvin, I think Bill needs a drink of whiskey."

"All right! Give him one," answered Coolidge.

When the other two reporters came in, Bill's glass was empty. Mrs. Coolidge poured drinks for the newcomers and was going to fill Bill's glass again when Coolidge quacked, "Oh, no! Bill's already had his."[11]

When the McCall-Coolidge ticket went before the people for the third time, in fall, 1917, it was again victorious. It benefited from a good record, good publicity, and its patriotic spirit. McCall polled a plurality of some 90,000 votes and Coolidge was returned with a margin of slightly over 100,000. McCall's third term was largely devoted to war work, though he also urged the General Court to strengthen the workmen's compensation law, explore ways to protect workers against shop injuries, and enact health insurance and a state budget system. He got little from the legislators, but he continued the pressure for social welfare and efficiency measures to which his successor was to respond. McCall had built up public confidence in his party and he had given Calvin Coolidge a good apprenticeship in state administration. The lieutenant governor was ready for promotion.

8

We Must Steadily Advance

IT WAS NO SECRET that Calvin Coolidge wanted to be governor. As he later wrote, "Under the custom of promotion in Massachusetts a man who did not expect to be advanced would scarcely be willing to be lieutenant governor."[1] It was almost ironical that a man like Calvin Coolidge would become governor of Massachusetts. He was not much of a joiner and he was the antithesis of a gladhander. He resided in the western, predominantly rural part of the state. He was a Yankee, but not of the aristocracy. Except for the Republican party, he did not belong to anything that was popular or strong in Massachusetts. Yet he rose to become first man of the state. And the state was one that belied most of what he represented. It was populous, with over 3,500,000 people. It was highly industrialized, with the value of its manufactured output running fortyfold over that of its agricultural products. It had 700,000 wage earners, but only 120,000 people lived on its farms. It was crowded, with its population density of 479 people to the square mile ranking second only to Rhode Island in the nation. Massachusetts was urban, with one-fifth of its people living in Boston and four-fifths in communities of 10,000 or more. It was alien to the old America, with two-thirds of its inhabitants being immigrants or children of immigrants. It was cosmopolitan, with heavy settlements of recent comers from Britain, Denmark, Germany, Greece, Ireland, Italy, Norway, Portugal,

Sweden, Syria, and with sprinklings of Armenians, French Canadians, Jews, Lithuanians, and Poles.

Nevertheless, Calvin Coolidge, who had few of the characteristics of his fellow citizens or politicians, became Massachusetts' governor. There were numerous reasons for his election. He was riding a trend of Republican successes in the state. In particular, he was walking in the footsteps of the respected and statesmanlike Samuel W. McCall. Yet Coolidge had an appeal of his own. He represented experience, stability, and common sense. Although he was not closely identified with any of the significant voting blocs or economic interests of the state, he benefited because he was viewed as a man who was not in league with anybody's enemies. He was a member in good standing in Murray Crane's tribe, but his factional activity was not such that it antagonized the leaders of other Republican factions. He had the enthusiastic support of Frank Stearns, but that appeared so innocent that if offended no one. In brief, Coolidge was in the position that a loner occasionally and enviably gets in: he was not disliked as much as other contenders for the post he sought, and he was trusted more than any of them. He was seen as a technician of government, one who would administer it honestly and efficiently, meeting those situations that justice and order required him to meet but not dashing out to find trouble. He was the picture of a man who could be counted on to do his job, neither hindered by corruption nor overstimulated by brilliance.

Although it was known that Coolidge wanted the Republican gubernatorial nomination, he personally did little to capture it. He assumed the position of letting the office seek the man. He could afford to, for circumstance, his political friends, and the custom of the lieutenant governor succeeding to the governorship carried the nomination to him. McCall decided to quit after the usual three terms and seek a seat in the United States Senate. He told Coolidge to stand for the gubernatorial nomination. Although McCall later decided not to run for the Senate, he did not renege on his support of Coolidge for governor. Coolidge had no trouble getting the Republican nomination. Stearns and his contacts provided money and publicity, Crane and his forces had early lined up behind Coolidge, McCall encouraged him, and Henry Cabot Lodge's men decided that he was no threat to them. Coolidge was nominated without opposition in the primary election.

The Democratic nominee for governor was Richard H. Long, a political amateur from Framingham, whose chief asset was that he was wealthy. His record, what there was of it, was unclear. He previously had been defeated for the nomination for lieutenant governor. As a manufacturer of shoes and shoemaking machinery, his chief political motivation seemed to be to settle a grievance against the United Shoe Machinery Company for alleged infringements of patents. The Democrats were apparently drawn to Long because all their funds were committed to David Walsh's campaign for the Senate against John Weeks, the Republican incumbent. When Long made it clear that he would finance his own campaign as well as conduct it vigorously, the Democrats, who had no other comers in sight, gave him their endorsement.

Coolidge had more difficulty in his campaign than he had anticipated. The Republican party organization suffered from a feud between Governor McCall and Senator Weeks. Moreover, Weeks was even a duller campaigner than Coolidge, and that was bound to hurt them in contrast to the vigor of Walsh and Long. There were additional problems. Meetings were disrupted by the great influenza epidemic of 1918, which even forced the Republicans to call off their state convention. The party also divided over the conduct of the campaign, with some Republicans like Coolidge urging support of the Wilson Administration's war effort and others instead ferociously attacking the record of the President. Coolidge's strategy was to appear the patriot. He talked little of himself or his party, and instead spent most of his time making war speeches. When he did get down to state issues, he did no more than stand on the record of the McCall administration. Weeks was a campaign liability because of his antifeminist and antilabor outlooks, his involvement in the prohibition question, and his vulnerability to charges that he had opposed preparedness and had attempted to reduce the amount of soldier's war risk insurance. As for the highly charged issue of war profiteering, it is difficult to say who was hurt most politically, for while many Republicans were vulnerable, so was Richard Long, who was said to have cleaned up on government contracts. Nevertheless, the contest was tight, in fact, so close that former Presidents Theodore Roosevelt and William Howard Taft were called upon for assistance. Coolidge was not sanguine about the results of the campaign. He felt the need to prepare Frank Stearns for defeat, writing that "It is the process that is important, let the result be what it may."[2] Coolidge's dim outlook was somewhat justified. Weeks was defeated by Walsh for United States senator. Coolidge squeaked by Long by sixteen thousand votes and trailed the rest of the state Republican ticket. Yet Coolidge had been elected. He was to be the first man of the Commonwealth.

The Friday after election Governor-elect and Mrs. Coolidge went to Maine for some rest. There was little of it, though, for Sunday night Coolidge was routed out of bed by news that the war had ended. Although it was a false report, by the time the Coolidges arrived back in Boston the real armistice had been signed. Enthused by victory and relieved by the end of the carnage, Coolidge happily participated in Massachusetts' celebrations of the armistice. Whatever rest he was to get between then and his inauguration, he had to find nights in Boston or on the few days he was able to steal away to Northampton. He launched into a series of conferences to plan what he would do as governor. He studied further the apparatus of state government. Because of illness suffered by Samuel McCall, Coolidge spent a good deal of time as acting governor. He worked on his inaugural address. He met and corresponded with a wide range of people. He attended Frank Stearns' social functions.

Grace Coolidge was drawn into the preparations leading up to her husband's inauguration, as Mrs. Stearns arranged a luncheon to introduce her properly to the prominent ladies of Boston. Stearns, who had taken on the task of being Coolidge's mentor in social matters, pressed him to rent a house, preferably an historic one on Beacon Hill, and to employ a lady to care for the boys and to help with social correspondence. That Coolidge rejected. If the Commonwealth did not provide its governors with housing, there was no need for the governor to engage a house. The family would stay in Northampton. Coolidge's only concession was to take a second room at the Adams House.

At noon on New Year's Day, 1919, cannon on the Boston Common boomed out a salute of twenty-one guns. In that traditional way notice was given that Calvin Coolidge, the forty-fifth governor under the Constitution, had taken his oath of office. On Beacon Hill, amid the splendor of a Bay State inaugural ceremony, surrounded by formally garbed citizens of rank and quaintly clad soldiery, the new governor delivered his inaugural address to a packed audience in the chamber of the house of representatives. Coolidge in very general terms urged the state to further public health and education and to enlarge opportunities for employment of its citizens at fair pay. Those and assistance to returning veterans had to be accomplished, though with attention being paid to economy and efficiency. He also proclaimed the possibility of a new era:

> You are beholding the fulfilment of the age-old promise, man coming into his own. You are to have the opportunity and responsibility of reflecting this new spirit in the laws of the most enlightened of Commonwealths. We must steadily advance. Each individual must have the rewards and opportunities worthy of the character of our citizenship, a broader recognition of his worth and a larger liberty, protected by order—and always under the law. In the promotion of human welfare Massachusetts happily may not need much reconstruction, but, like all living organizations, forever needs continuing construction....
>
> Whether we are to enter a new era in Massachusetts depends upon you. The lessons of the war are plain. Can we carry them on into peace? Can we still act on the principle that there is no sacrifice too great to maintain the right? Shall we continue to advocate and practise thrift and industry? Shall we require unswerving loyalty to our country? These are the foundations of all greatness....
>
> Let there be a purpose in all your legislation to recognize the right of man to be well born, well nurtured, well educated, well employed, and well paid. This is no gospel of ease and selfishness, or class distinction, but a gospel of effort and service, of universal application.[3]

For those who looked for more than generalizations, the meaning of the message became clearer as the new governor acted. Coolidge was to adhere to the moderate social justice program that he had written into the Republican state platform of 1914. He was to try to keep faith with Samuel McCall, whose record he had taken for his own in the 1918 election campaign. He was to do his duty. He would maintain law and order, and he would provide honest and efficient government. He would urge legislators to abide by their consciences. He would encourage them to seek a balance between the interests of the community and those of individuals. He would urge the qualities of patriotism, self-reliance, and service upon his fellow citizens. He would be the kind of governor to suggest generally to the people and the legislature what was right and then to look to them to tell him specifically what to do. In 1919 and 1920 that was satisfactory because the Commonwealth was willing to respond, to search for balance and fairness in society, and having found them, to rely on the governor to implement them faithfully.

Coolidge was a busy governor. That was not, as it had been with his immediate predecessors, of his own volition, for Coolidge did not have much of a preconceived legislative program. His activity stemmed from his attempts to meet piecemeal the problems of the postwar period. The Commonwealth had to catch up with many of the normal programs that had been interrupted or slowed down during the war. It had to deal with pressing questions of readjustment of salaries and wages, prices and taxes, supply and demand. It had also to take cognizance of the new era of which Coolidge had spoken in his inaugural address.

The return of the veterans placed a number of burdens upon Coolidge and the state. This began with ceremonial functions. The first act of the General Court that he signed was an appropriation of ten thousand dollars to defray the expenses of welcoming home the Twenty-sixth Division. In April Coolidge stood for five hours under overcast skies in a chill wind with the other New England governors to review the homecoming parade of the Yankee Division. It was an occasion that, though it overjoyed New England's citizens, was not greatly appreciated by the troops or the six governors who were on display. More important was the demand of veterans for preference in appointment to Massachusetts' civil service. Such pressure had been exerted originally by Civil War soldiers, then was taken up by the Spanish-American War veterans, and now by the doughboys of the Great War. Earlier governors of the Commonwealth had resisted fairly well, but Coolidge was faced, not only by the huge numbers— some 200,000—of the returning veterans, but also by considerable public sentiment "to do something for the boys." The demand of many returning soldiers was to legalize, as the proposal went, "appointment of all veterans without examination and without regard to age, height, and weight limitations."[4] That was too extreme, for it obviously would have made a mockery of the idea of a civil service based on competence. Coolidge was able to gather enough support from the public and even veterans to force a compromise that gave preference in hiring to former soldiers when they had passed the appropriate entrance examinations.

The postwar period also saw the development of great inequities in purchasing power among the classes. This was to be the most vexatious issue confronting the governor, one which contributed to the Boston Police Strike and the rise of Coolidge as a national figure. Almost as bad were the problems created by landlords and other businessmen who tried to take advantage of shortages to gouge their tenants and customers. Coolidge worked assiduously to secure legislation to ease the situation. The General Court at his urging passed legislation designed to hold down profiteering by landlords. Municipalities were authorized to use the right of eminent domain to provide living space for people in times of emergency, courts were permitted to delay eviction proceedings for as long as six months, rent increases were limited to 25 percent annually, and penalties were enacted for landlords who failed to give tenants promised utilities. Coolidge also appointed a commission to study the problems of housing in the Commonwealth.

The work of another gubernatorial commission led to adoption of a law that made profiteering in the necessities of life a crime. Massachusetts' greatest commodity problem, both in terms of price and supply, was coal. The state seemed unlikely to procure enough fuel from its own resources or from elsewhere before the chill arms of winter embraced New England. Coolidge established the office of fuel administrator to attempt to increase the amount of fuel available to the state's people and businesses. He badgered officials of Massachusetts, other New England states, and the federal government to facilitate the supply of coal. His efforts were only partly successful, though they did result in the Interstate Commerce Commission shifting some transportation to carrying coal to New England.

Coolidge also sought to deal with the cost-of-living problem by encouraging increases in compensation for factory workers and public servants. He tried to bring workingmen's wages up to reasonable levels and to prevent long-drawn-out strikes by often mediating pay disputes between labor and management. Again success was only partial, though in most instances where the governor acted he was praised for his open-mindedness. Allowances under the workmen's compensation law were increased, however, and pay raises were voted for state employees. Governor Coolidge also took pains to point up the need for increases in teachers' salaries. He announced publicly: "It has become notorious that the pay for this most important function is much less than that which prevails in commercial life and business activities. . . . more money must be provided."[5]

Most of the other accomplishments of Coolidge and the General Court were extensions of drives for reform that antedated the war. The governor successfully urged ratification of the Nineteenth, or Women's Suffrage, Amendment to the United States Constitution. He approved a law reducing the maximum work week from fifty-four to forty-eight hours for women and children. Additional home rule was granted town governments, and municipalities were given power to operate their own street railways. In a special session, relief was afforded the financially ailing private trolley lines. The reforestation of 100,000 acres of waste land was authorized. Outdoor advertising, which was already growing into an eyesore, was placed under state regulation. To help the little fellow in the courts, small claims cases were made easier to file. A commission was appointed to study establishment of a pension system for public servants.

Coolidge also implemented two of the reforms authorized during the McCall administration. Governor McCall had been successful in securing legislative approval of a state budget system, but it was up to Coolidge to establish it. The work involved in doing so was worth while for it helped Coolidge to keep expenses down and secure the reputation of an efficient administrator. The other reform resulted from the efforts of the Massachusetts Constitutional Convention of 1917–18. Actually, the convention's work gave Coolidge many tasks. Most of them were minor, but there was one that was knotty both administratively and politically. That was the reorganization of the offices of state government. The new Article LXVI of the Massachusetts Constitution provided that the number of state agencies be reduced to twenty. Considering that they numbered well over a hundred, a huge pruning job, and one with political repercussions, was in order.

More than two years had been given to carry out the task, but Coolidge insisted that the legislature get on with it immediately. Although the 1919 General Court was pressed with piteous appeals from political appointees, the governor succeeded in getting action.

Shrieks and squeals were heard from all quarters as holdover Democrats and independents and Republicans lost their offices or were downgraded. Even more protests were heard when early in 1920 Coolidge made his selections of the heads and deputy heads of the twenty new agencies. Not only did Democrats complain of being ignored, but it was obvious that Republican bosses and hacks had not been consulted. The governor had two criteria for appointment: competence and political acceptability to him. The results were an improvement in the caliber of high-level public servants and a bolstering of the Crane men in the government, for Senator Lodge and lesser Republican leaders got control of only the less meaty appointments. Coolidge acted on the premise that if he was responsible for the administration of state government, he was going to have men under him who would follow his lead. If that strengthened his party and his faction within the party, it was good. If it also gave him a reputation for efficiency, so much the better. He was fortunate in that all three goals were achieved.

Coolidge's relations with the General Court were good and he seldom felt the necessity of vetoing its acts. The two outstanding instances of disagreement were evinced in his vetoes of a salary increase for lawmakers and of a bill authorizing the sale of 2.75 beer. The first came in June, 1919, when Coolidge rejected the General Court's salary raise, because legislative service is not "a profession or a means of livelihood. It is a voluntary public service.... Men do not serve here for pay."[6] The legislators, however, did not agree with the governor and overrode his veto. The following year, in May, Coolidge rejected the beer bill on the ground that it violated the federal Constitution. In that case he was sustained, though not happily, by the legislators. The beer veto was constitutionally correct and the pay raise veto certainly squared with Coolidge's personal beliefs, for he was never a salary grabber. Moreover, the vetoes were politically wise because the first reinforced the governor's image as a man of economy and civic responsibility and the second came when the prohibitionist forces, both in Massachusetts and the nation, were at the peak of their strength.

Although Coolidge's administration was as honest and clean as any in Massachusetts' history, he did have his brush with scandal, and he met it forthrightly. In August, 1920—fortunately after Coolidge's nomination for Vice President—a number of bankers charged the elected state treasurer, Fred J. Burrell, with pressing them to place their advertising with an agency in which he was financially interested. The penalty for not doing so apparently was to have been loss of state deposits from uncooperative banks. Coolidge and the General Court ordered investigations, and the governor announced that he would act against Burrell if evidence of malfeasance were found. The treasurer resigned and took his case to the people in the primary election. There, however, he was defeated by Coolidge's appointee by a 2-to-1 margin.

On the whole, Coolidge had acquitted himself well as governor. He had in fact been an effective, responsible, and conscientious executive, one well above the average of postwar governors in the various states. Yet his rise to national prominence and his nomination for Vice President of the United States were not founded on that. They were based on a dash of political organization, a jot of luck, and the tremendous leavening of the Boston Police Strike. The irony is that, although his administration deserved attention, prominence came to Coolidge largely from the strike, an affair in which he did little and from which he deserved little.

9

When Firmness Was Needed

COOLIDGE'S FIRST SEVEN months in office had been lively and full of accomplishment. By August the frail governor was tired from his labors and exhausted by the summer heat of Boston, which always bothered him. After the adjournment of the General Court, he and Mrs. Coolidge sought rest and relaxation in Vermont. New burdens of state were, however, to arise in his absence.

American labor in 1919 was making demands for higher wages and shorter hours which it had postponed during the war. It also pressed its drive to organize the nation's workers into trade unions. Labor's activity was bitterly resisted by much of management with the result that industrial disturbances became epidemic. This situation became increasingly alarming with the Seattle General Strike of February, and the walkouts of woolens workers in March, carpenters and machinists in May, building trades men in June, marine and tobacco laborers in July, and silk workers in August. Much of this had been connected in the public mind with international bolshevism by ambitious or hysterical politicians and editors.

Massachusetts under Coolidge had met the situation fairly well. Hysteria had been kept under control and the administration had worked to meet labor's legitimate grievances. A threatened strike of firemen had been headed off. In April a walkout of telephone workers in New England had been settled, thanks in part to the climate of reason maintained by Coolidge, although at one point he had asked the federal government for authority to take over telephone lines should the strike not soon be concluded. In midsummer a labor tie-up had struck the operations of the Boston Elevated Street Railway for several days. As it was paralyzing the city, Coolidge jumped in to help secure an agreement that sent the matter to arbitration while the men went back to work. The result of the arbitration was a substantial increase in wages.

Coolidge went off on his vacation in August not knowing that the worst labor crisis was yet to come. While the governor and his lady were resting in Vermont, a situation was brewing that would bring Massachusetts and Coolidge to the front pages of every newspaper in the land. It was a situation that would strike fear in the hearts of those Americans who had been persuaded that Reds were under every bed and anarchists in every closet. It was the Boston Police Strike.

The working conditions of the Boston police had become scandalous. They found themselves on duty for long hours, working out of dirty, shabby station houses and receiving admittedly low wages. During the war they had resented drawing pay that was half that received by warworkers. After the armistice, the police were pinched by trying to make do on low, fixed wages at a time when costs were rising rapidly. Disgruntlement increased as their requests for relief remained unmet. Governor Coolidge had tried to help, but he had been unable to persuade lawmakers to do anything for the policemen. Police Commissioner Edwin U. Curtis, who was a former mayor of Boston, was more successful. In May he had been able to induce the city to grant a two-hundred-dollar raise and to set the maximum annual salary at sixteen hundred dollars. Yet this did not go far in meeting either the requests or the needs of the policemen. Their hours remained long, their working conditions deplorable, and their pay raise fell short of the increases in the cost of living. Their demands for further relief were neglected.

With a deep sense of frustration, the police officers decided to take an unusual step to secure their goals. They had a local organization, the Boston Social Club, which became the vehicle for their efforts to get help. In June, 1919, the Club made tentative plans to affiliate with the American Federation of Labor, in the hope that a unionized police force, with organized labor's support, would be more successful in bargaining with public officials. Although the police in some other cities had joined the AFL and although there was no specific law or rule against affiliation in Boston, Commissioner Curtis' reaction was hostile. He was not going to deal with his men through a labor union. Curtis was an honest official and he tried to be fair. But as one of his admirers, Sherwin Cook, pointed out, he was "a stiff-necked executive."[1] The commissioner would do his best for his men, but they were not going to tell him what to do or how to do it. He told the policemen that "a police officer cannot consistently belong to a union and perform his sworn duty."[2] He subsequently issued orders banning membership in any state or national organization that might get involved in labor questions.

Irish-Americans composed the largest element in the Boston Police Force, and Commissioner Curtis' stand aroused their dander. Agitation increased in police ranks and the Boston Social Club announced on August 1 that they were proceeding with plans to affiliate with the AFL. They soon requested the union to grant them a local charter, which they received on August 15. Meanwhile, the Central Labor Union of Boston pledged the police "every atom of support that organized labor can bring to bear."[3] Curtis acted swiftly to meet the challenges to his authority. By the end of the month he had charged nineteen police union leaders with violating his orders. He found them guilty, but deferred sentencing as a lure for the leaders to dissolve their ties with the AFL.

Meanwhile, the young Democratic mayor of Boston, Andrew J. Peters, had appointed a committee of thirty-four citizens, headed by financier James J. Storrow, to seek a solution of the problem. The citizen's committee found, as Storrow said, that it had been "brought into opposition with a man [Curtis] who, maintaining rigidly the official point of view, dealt in ultimatums."[4] Moreover, the committee had been brought into a no man's land of jurisdiction.

To understand that no man's land, one must know the peculiar administrative organization for control of the Boston Police Force. The police commissioner, who supervised the work of the police, was a gubernatorial appointee, in this case McCall's, and under the law was responsible to no one. The city government controlled the fixing of police wages and working hours. It also provided station houses, though legally it had nothing to do with their maintenance. The city and the mayor could give no orders to the commissioner, and certainly an *ad hoc* committee could do no more than try to reason with him. The governor could at most only remove the commissioner from office, though the law was not clear on that point. Coolidge later wrote, "The governor . . . has no more jurisdiction over his acts than he has over the judges of the courts."[5] The situation had all the makings of a grand Mexican standoff, with a police force firmly opposed to a commissioner who could not be dictated to by either a concerned city administration or a governor who was keeping whatever distance he could.

Coolidge returned from his Vermont vacation to give a Labor Day address in Plymouth, Massachusetts, on September 1. In that talk he praised calmness as a rule in labor relations. He also showed his sensitivity to mass political influence, saying, "We have known that political power was with the people, because they have the votes." He also mentioned his usual themes of stability and endeavor. "All of us must work, and in that work there should be no interruption."[6] At the time his comments seemed like Coolidgean platitudes, but they were to be his guidelines when confronted by the Boston Police Strike. He would be guided by public pressure and the need for stability, though none too quickly.

Trouble was quickly developing. The policemen made it clear that they intended to have their union. Commissioner Curtis made it clear that he considered the mayor and the Storrow Committee to be interlopers who were intent on undermining his authority. Mayor Peters made it clear that he would try to head off a strike in order to keep his political supporters happy. The governor made nothing clear. He only, as he said, "kept carefully informed of conditions."[7]

The Storrow Committee was developing a plan which it hoped would bring a peaceful and reasonable solution of the problem. The plan called for the appointment of a committee of three citizens acceptable to the police commissioner, the mayor, and the Boston policemen. That committee would study and report publicly on police wages, hours, and conditions. As a concession to Curtis, questions of discipline would not be considered. Affiliation with the AFL and recognition of the right to strike were out of the question, though there would be no objection to the police officers having their own local organization. Curtis refused to consider the plan. Mayor Peters and Storrow sought Coolidge's support for it, even before their proposals were in final form, but he refused to get involved.

Peters correctly warned the governor that if the nineteen police union leaders were suspended from duty by Curtis, the police force would probably strike. Coolidge remained aloof, convinced he had neither the power nor reason to intervene.

The governor left Boston on Saturday, September 6, to fulfill engagements in Abington and Andover. On Sunday he motored to Northampton, where he spent the night. The following day he went to Greenfield to speak before the convention of the Massachusetts Federation of Labor. That Monday morning Commissioner Curtis announced that the nineteen union leaders had been suspended from the police force. Coolidge was back in Boston by four in the afternoon and was immediately besieged by alarmed representatives of the city. Peters and Storrow talked with him at length. They implored him to endorse the Storrow Committee's plan, but he refused. Then they urged him to have troops on hand in case the police left their posts. Again he refused, contending that Curtis could deal with the situation.

Storrow has written that the governor's only constructive suggestion was "that the mayor should forthwith call the City Council together and arrange immediately whatever additional compensation the city government felt the policemen ought to have, and also rearrange the hours and fix up the old police stations." The financier later commented, "To my mind, this looked much more like backing down than our arrangement."[8] Coolidge's idea, which pointed up the fact that the city had been penny-wise and pound-foolish, was at that point academic. The outraged Boston police had already voted 1,134 to 2 to leave their posts the next day, Tuesday, September 9, after the 5:45 afternoon roll call. Their goals were reinstatement of the nineteen union leaders to the force and recognition of the right of policemen to have an AFL-chartered union.

With the strike vote, the issues were clearly drawn. Would the police commissioner back down? Would the city government act effectively either to meet the policemen's demands or to deal with their strike if it occurred? Would the governor in any way intervene? The Storrow Committee and Mayor Peters, without success, begged Coolidge to act, and it was apparent that they did not know what to do. Coolidge would not act because he did not feel authorized to do so and perhaps, as his record during the episode suggests, because he felt it politically unwise with an election coming in November. As far as he was concerned it was the task of the mayor and the police commissioner to settle the situation.

Legally Coolidge's position was correct, but in a situation complicated by misunderstanding on all sides and by the hopelessly inadequate administrative arrangement governing the police force, the governor's aloofness was inexcusable. It was also inexcusable in view of his earlier vigor in helping to settle the telephone and elevated railway strikes. Moreover, what little he did in his public comments aggravated the Boston police crisis. One statement coming from his office said: "Understand that I do not approve of any strike. But can you blame the police for feeling as they do when they get less than a street car conductor?"[9] Another comment was contained in a telegram to the convention of the Massachusetts Federation of Labor, in which he said, "I earnestly hope circumstances may arise which will cause the police officers to be reinstated."[10] The police unionists could not help but gain some hope from his comments. Yet it was false hope, for in effect he backed Commissioner Curtis' intransigent position. Curtis took for a sign of confidence in his ability the governor's refusal to urge a change of direction upon him. And from the available evidence it seems apparent that that was Coolidge's intention. In any event the city officials seemed incompetent to act. The commissioner remained in authority. The governor remained uninvolved. And nothing was settled.

Boston became almost hysterical when confronted by the prospect of the police striking. The newspapers wrote of a defenseless city that would be looted and assaulted. They also expressed fear of a general strike in which all union men would leave their jobs in a gesture of labor solidarity with the police. Bolshevism was seen by many so-called solid citizens as contributing to the entire labor situation. A vigilante spirit was also abroad. An enlistment office for volunteer policemen was opened. Banks and other businesses recruited security guards from among their employees. American Legionnaires and other war veterans offered to help police the city. Harvard's President A. Lawrence Lowell announced that students who served as volunteer police would not be penalized academically. While the citizenry did what it could to prepare for the strike, city officials did little. The Metropolitan Police Force of slightly more than one hundred men was alerted for duty in Boston as was a forty-man contingent of State Police. More was not done because the mayor was unsure of his powers. Commissioner Curtis thought it sufficient to say, "I am ready for any crisis,"[11] which was only a mask for his conviction that the strike would not come off.

The police did strike, though. After the early evening roll call on Tuesday, 1,117 of Boston's 1,544 officers walked out. Those who stayed on were composed largely of supervisory personnel and older officers who could not be expected to jeopardize their pensions. Coolidge, his secretary Henry F. Long, Attorney General Henry A. Wyman, and Adjutant General Jesse F. Stevens kept watch in the Adams House until after 11 p.m. The governor made several unsuccessful efforts to get in touch with Mayor Peters. The situation, however, appeared to be fairly well in hand. To be sure, small incidents occurred before Coolidge retired before midnight. Rowdies stole spare tires from some parked cars and a few pedestrians had their hats knocked off. A trolley car was stoned and its passengers forced to get off. Yet the incidents were not of emergency proportions.

At midnight, though, real trouble began. Hoodlums looted stores. Riots occurred around Scollay Square and in Roxbury and South Boston. Numerous citizens were robbed on the streets. Windows were broken and fruit stands overturned. The Boston Common, which had become a gathering place for night-owl toughs, became one big dice parlor. Regular and volunteer police were insulted and became targets for whatever their tormentors could throw at them. There were just not enough regular police on hand to keep the peace and the untrained and inexperienced volunteers proved not to be very useful. The Provost Guard of the Boston Navy Yard was rushed into the city as the big disorders broke out, but it was too small to make any difference.

While law enforcement was breaking down over the city, Coolidge slept undisturbed in the Adams House. Peters gave every sign of not knowing what to do. Curtis did no more than try to sit on the lid, perhaps in the hope that matters would become so critical that he would have overwhelming public support, not only to suppress lawlessness, but to break the strike and the agitation for a police union.

Action was not taken until after dawn broke on September 10. Then Mayor Peters, who suddenly seemed aware of the powers he could exercise, called out the State Guard resident in Boston and asked Governor Coolidge for three thousand additional troops. Before nightfall guardsmen were patrolling the streets with rifles in hand and bayonets fixed. Peters also declared General Charles H. Cole in charge of the police and the mobilized Guard. Commissioner Curtis, who was supposed to have commanded both in an emergency, had been superseded.

Tension was high in Boston that Wednesday. Civic leaders, prominent businessmen, and the newspapers were freely labeling the police strikers as Bolsheviks and deserters. The press lovingly exaggerated the damage and outlawry that had occurred. Appeals went out from the authorities for more volunteer policemen and peace-loving citizens were advised to keep off the city's streets after dark. Hoodlums were warned of the consequences if they were caught defying the law. Tension was high among unionists too. Many labor leaders viewed the city's mobilization as primarily an attempt to suppress the union movement. The Central Labor Union of Boston had pledged its support of the striking police and after the bluecoats' walkout it had ordered a vote from its affiliates on the question of a general strike. Sentiment for walkouts increased among firemen and streetcar men. There was even talk of reviving the old telephone strike. When rumors of a strike among the workers at the Boston powerhouse circulated, a naval vessel loaded with electrician ratings was placed offshore ready to land the men to keep the plant going.

Pressures in the meantime mounted on Coolidge to intervene. Commissioner Curtis went to him in great distress. Both the commissioner and the governor were worried that the issue that had precipitated the strike would be lost. They feared that Mayor Peters, now that he was in command, would submit the police strikers' grievances to arbitration. That was unlikely as the mayor did not have the Storrow Committee's support. Yet no one knew or could predict what Peters might do under stress. Governor Coolidge did not care to find out. As he put it in his autobiography:

> I did not see how it was possible to arbitrate the question of the authority of the law, or of the necessity of obedience to the rules of the [Police] Department and the orders of the commissioner. These principles were the heart of the whole controversy and the only important questions at issue. It can

readily be seen how important they were and what the effect might have been if they had not been maintained. I decided to support them whatever the consequences might be. I fully expected it would result in my defeat in the coming campaign for reelection as governor.[12]

Yet Coolidge waited through another night of troubles before standing on his principles. Despite the fact that the volunteers and the metropolitan, state, and loyal city police had been supplemented by 4,800 guardsmen, disorders again broke out the evening of September 10. In South Boston the Guard fired on a disorderly crowd, killing two men and wounding several others. Another riot was dispersed in Scollay Square when cavalry with sabers drawn charged a mob, with one death resulting. Again there were looting and assaults, but the efforts of lawmen and military forces broke the back of lawlessness in Boston. By Thursday morning, September 11, the situation was under control, and more men were being recruited and federal assistance had been assured if needed.[13]

Although the authority of the law had been restored, the calm of the city and the state had not. The governor was pressed all the more to do something, from civic leaders, from Curtis, and now from Murray Crane. William M. Butler, Crane's graying, iron-jawed envoy extraordinary, was dispatched to confer with Coolidge. Crane was upset both by the disorders of Tuesday and Wednesday nights and by the probability that he would be held responsible for what his protégé in the state house was—or, more accurately, was not—doing.

Butler and the governor, along with Curtis' legal adviser, former Attorney General Herbert Parker, discussed the matter over lunch at the Union Club on Thursday. Coolidge, who had now concluded that he should act, asked what ought to be done. Butler later recalled, "I said that the governor should take over the situation, call out the militia and also take charge of the police affairs of Boston."[14] Parker, seeing a return of Curtis to power, enthusiastically approved.

Later at the state house Coolidge drew up a proclamation and an executive order. In the proclamation he turned out the entire State Guard, called upon all loyal policemen to obey him, and asked them and all citizens "to aid me in the maintenance of law and order." In his executive order he directed Edwin Curtis "to proceed in the performance of your duties as police commissioner of the city of Boston under my command and in obedience to such orders as I shall issue from time to time."[15]

After Coolidge had finished preparing the two documents he turned to Butler and asked, "What further damage can I do?"[16] There was no damage to be done. The situation was already in control by the time the governor's proclamation and executive order were issued, and now Coolidge controlled those who were in control. It was, from Mayor Peters' viewpoint, a *coup d'état*. For Coolidge it was a stroke of luck. The governor, not the mayor, would receive credit for restoring order in Boston. The governor, not the police commissioner, would receive most of the credit for upholding the principle that the sole allegiance of policemen should be to the public.

Coolidge did not know what he had done when he issued his proclamation and executive order. The situation appeared to be in hand because of his action. Equally important, he had dramatized the question of what to do when police strike, at a time when a nationwide audience was interested in the drama. By not acting to settle the strike before it started, by not crushing disorder at the first signs of it, Coolidge had unwittingly allowed a situation to develop that took hold of the country's imagination and diverted it to ponder the question. By supporting Curtis' authority, passively at first and later through timid action, the governor had provided an answer. Maintenance of public authority comes before anything.[17] Even the labor elements of Boston saw that, for on the evening of September 11 they defeated the proposal to launch a general strike.

The Boston Police Strike commanded the nation's attention. All over the land Wednesday's newspapers had carried stories of it and of the subsequent disorders as front-page news. The Thursday morning papers were full of the work of the troops and the loyal police in crushing the South Boston and Scollay Square riots, and the evening papers carried the story that Coolidge had taken command. After that peace reigned, as the press indicated, and the conclusion was obvious: by taking charge, the governor had put an end to disorder and had maintained law in Boston. Since many editors could not keep themselves from seeing bolshevism at every turn, they linked the strike and the disorders with left-wing radicalism. Coolidge was not responsible for that nonsense. He knew better. But much of the public got the impression that the nation had been saved, by Coolidge, in a second battle of Boston, this time from the Reds instead of from the Redcoats.

The impression of Coolidge as an outstanding governor was fortified with every passing hour. Not only did the press keep it up, but public officials did their bit. Democrats as well as Republicans viewed the police strike as an assault on the American way of life. President Woodrow Wilson, touring the country for ratification of the Treaty of Versailles, took time out at Helena, Montana, to denounce the strike as "a crime against civilization."[18] Democratic Senator Charles S. Thomas of Colorado went further. He told the United States Senate of Coolidge, "It is to such men that we must look for the preservation of American institutions."[19]

There were those, however, who did not see it that way. On Friday, September 12, Samuel Gompers urged the police to return to work and hope for mediation of their grievances. Then the American Federation of Labor chieftain started an exchange of telegrams that made Coolidge, not just an outstanding governor, but a national hero. Gompers wired Coolidge and Mayor Peters requesting reinstatement for the strikers and arbitration "to honorably adjust a mutually unsatisfactory situation."[20] The press across the land howled for no compromise. On Saturday Commissioner Curtis announced that the strikers would not be reinstated. Coolidge telegraphed Gompers:

> Under the law the suggestions contained in your telegram are not within the authority of the governor of Massachusetts but only of the commissioner of police of the city of Boston. With the maintenance of discipline in his department I have no authority to interfere. He has decided that the men here abandoned their sworn duty and has accordingly declared their places vacant. I shall support the commissioner in the execution of law and the maintenance of order.[21]

That was hardly the stuff of which heroes are made, and it did not stop the dean of American unionism from communicating further. Gompers pressed Coolidge, citing a situation where President Wilson had suggested that the police of the national capital be allowed to have some collective bargaining rights.

This time, Sunday, September 14, Coolidge came back with full force. He pointed out that in Washington the police had not deserted their posts. "Here the Policeman's Union left their duty, an action which President Wilson characterized as a crime against civilization. Your assertion that the commissioner was wrong cannot justify the wrong of leaving the city unguarded." Then came the sentence that would make Calvin Coolidge unforgettable: "There is no right to strike against the public safety by anybody, anywhere, any time."[22]

The reaction was astounding. Coolidge received as much newspaper space as had the police strike. His September 14 telegram to Gompers was reprinted throughout the land. His photograph was published on the front pages of papers all over the country and editorial writers exhausted their lexicons finding words of praise for the Massachusetts governor. His telephone was jammed by calls of thanks. Tens of thousands of wires and letters of congratulations were stacked in his office.

Thus Coolidge, who was no rabble-rouser, had become the uncrowned king of the rabble-rousers and the Saint George of the innocently frightened. He who had given little thought to Marxism had become the champion of the anti-Marxists. He who had often been labor's friend had become a hero of antilabor forces. He who had not wanted to become involved had become deeply involved. He who had been the last in acting had become the first in receiving credit.

IO

The Most Popular Figure

in the State

T HE LAW . . . should be supreme."[1] If anything, that was the
issue on which Calvin Coolidge's 1919 campaign for re-election was based. His supporters urged him to stand on it and it appeared that the nation expected him to do so. But he had qualms
about supremacy of the law as an issue. There was the labor vote to
be thought of. Also to be considered was that Richard H. Long was
again the Democratic nominee for governor. A man who had been
elected by only sixteen thousand votes when his party had been
sweeping the country had to be careful. Moreover, that man, Calvin
Coolidge, whose heart was in stability and decency, did not want
to seem to be a rabble-rouser.

The sandy-haired, blue-eyed Coolidge was the reluctant hero of
law and order. Only with great caution did he recognize the issue
that had been forced on him by the Boston Police Strike. On September 24, the day after his renomination for governor, he released
a proclamation in which he said:

> There appears to be a misapprehension as to the position
> of the police of Boston. In the deliberate intention to intimidate and coerce the government of this Commonwealth a

large body of policemen, urging all others to join them, deserted their posts of duty, letting in the enemy. This act of theirs was voluntary, against the advice of their well wishers, long discussed and premeditated, and with the purpose of obstructing the power of the government to protect its citizens or even to maintain its own existence. Its success meant anarchy. . . .

The authority of the Commonwealth cannot be intimidated or coerced. It cannot be compromised. To place the maintenance of the public security in the hands of a body of men who have attempted to destroy it would be to flout the sovereignty of the laws the people have made. It is my duty to resist any such proposal.[2]

Once again the American press wrote rapturously of the Massachusetts strong man. Yet they had misinterpreted him. He had made the statement, not for their joy, but because he feared that sentiment in Massachusetts was beginning to react unfavorably to his position in the police strike. What the press of the nation skipped over lightly was the opening sentence of his proclamation: "There appears to be a misapprehension as to the position of the police of Boston." That sentence was the key to why he discussed the issue. Coolidge was trying to justify himself to his constituents against the charges of critics that he had been a tyrant. He was trying to dampen down the issue, for it could not contribute to stability and it could, he thought, lead to his defeat at the polls.

Only once in a political speech did he dwell on the subject of supremacy of law. After his renomination he appeared before the Republican State Convention in Boston. He explained at length his view that the police unionists had violated departmental rules and orders, that he could not interfere with the works of the police commissioner, that once the policemen had struck he could give no "aid and comfort . . . to support their evil doing." His speech was one of justification, not attack. "The government of Massachusetts," he said, "is not seeking to resist the lawful action or sound policy of organized labor." In support of that, he went so far as to say that his administration had more than any other in the state's history "passed laws for the protection and encouragement of trade unions." Coolidge promised that it would continue to assist labor. Although he criticized bolshevism, he went out of his way to observe: "Wholesale criticism of everybody and everything does not necessarily exhibit statesmanlike qualities, and may not be true. Not all those who are working to better the condition of the people are Bolsheviki or enemies of society."[3] His was the speech of a cautious politician, not that of a rabble-rouser.

Richard H. Long's campaign for governor drew the backing of the police strikers and their sympathizers. The Democratic platform had neither condemned nor condoned the strike. Long, however, charged Coolidge with hiding during the crucial stages of the affair and with using Prussian methods in dealing with it when he did act. The governor's proclamation and speech to the Republican State Convention were replies to Long's kind of criticism, but they did not dispose of the issue. Coolidge's strategy during the rest of the campaign was to speak little and in that he was helped by a bout with influenza. When he did speak, it was to emphasize the development of moral character. Only occasionally did he mention law and order, as when the Saturday before election, in an obvious reference to Long, he talked about "a rash man . . . seeking to gain the honor of office by trafficking with disorder."[4] In a sense Coolidge too trafficked with disorder, for he extended help to the discharged policemen in their efforts to gain employment in other fields of work. One will never know what went through his mind during the 1919 election campaign. His actions bespoke, however, the thoughts of a man who, though he believed deeply in law and order, felt that he had not done all he could to head off a crisis and that when the crisis came he had not acted decisively to meet it. He certainly had reason to feel that way.

Although Coolidge played down the issue of supremacy of the law, other Republicans raised it for him. Widely published newspaper advertisements told voters, "Remember September the 9th." Attorney General Henry A. Wyman, who had been connected with the governor on strike matters, had his own campaign to run and he took his stand on law and order. Newspaper editors also pressed it. Some of them pressed Coolidge, too, asking why he had not really campaigned on the issue when he felt the election to be so close. The governor replied to Edwin A. Grozier of the Boston *Post*:

The outcome of the present election is, of course, uncertain. The people must be aroused to the exact meaning of it.

I have already said it was a campaign not for a candidate but a cause—the supremacy of the law, which is above all parties.[5]

Yet Coolidge did little to arouse the people. One Republican did, though. That was Chairman Herman Hormel of the Republican City Committee of Boston, who wrote Richard Long asking whether he would reinstate the police strikers should he be elected. Hormel did this, it has been said, against the wishes of Coolidge. Whether that was true or not, the Boston Republican leader pushed the issue and finally Long indicated that he would reinstate the policemen.

Thus, during the 1919 campaign Coolidge became wed to an incident and an issue he would gladly have played down. The election results were stunning: he was returned to office in a landslide. Leading the Republican ticket, Coolidge polled 317,774 votes to 192,673 for Long. He was, as one Massachusetts Democrat has written, "easily the most popular public figure in the state."[6] And the conclusion could not be avoided, even by Coolidge, that the Boston Police Strike was largely responsible for it.

Coolidge could look back on his first year as governor with considerable satisfaction. Although he was least satisfied with the affair for which he was best known, he had been a good governor by his and most people's criteria. And his administration had been overwhelmingly approved by the voters. Although the governorship was a giant step forward in his political career, it marked no great changes in his way of living. He was, by his standards, making a small fortune as governor. The post carried an annual salary of ten thousand dollars and of that he saved a good deal.[7]

During his gubernatorial years he rented two ordinary rooms in the Adams House at $3.50 a day, which were somewhat beautified by Mrs. Coolidge, who put books, pictures, a tea table, and some of her own handiwork about. She and the boys stayed in Northampton in the duplex, saying, with her husband's full approval, "Mr. Coolidge may be governor of Massachusetts but I shall be first of all the mother of my sons."[8] His wardrobe remained a blue business suit, a gray traveling suit, and an outfit of formal clothes. His only extravagances were a housekeeper in Northampton, a Ford automobile—his first car—and Grace's clothes, which were more attractive than ever. The Boston Brahmins and their imitators over the state, however much they approved Coolidge's policies, were condescending toward the quiet, frugal governor. That condescension the Coolidges never forgot. As Grace later, in Washington, bitterly remarked: "I don't know what they expect me to do. Hang my wash in the East Room like Abigail Adams?"[9]

Coolidge's personality was not changed by power or popularity. He was as quiet as ever. His family ties remained close to his heart, but he was undemonstrative about them. Gamaliel Bradford described Calvin Coolidge's relations with Colonel Coolidge: "They loved each other, they trusted each other, they admired each other. They expressed these things by little more than the 'ugh! ugh!' of the Indian."[10]

The governor himself put it succinctly when with pride he said, "The Coolidges never slop over."

That puzzled many people who looked for emotion in their public figures. Coolidge's public emotions could rarely be discerned, because he rarely let them get out of control. A Boston *Globe* reporter said that one could never tell how deeply involved the governor felt himself to be with pieces of legislation, for "wild Indians could not have tortured a groan or a grin from him."[11] The closest Coolidge came to public displays of emotion was on the occasions when he could not restrain himself from making a joke. Even his jokes were delivered with a straight face, only occasionally relieved afterward by a hint of a smile and a gathering of crow's-feet at the corners of his eyes.

Coolidge had, of course, grown in prestige and prominence while governor. And as a consequence he was constantly on display. There were people to be greeted and ceremonies to be attended. There were many speeches to be given, for he rarely refused an invitation to speak. All those things he did manfully, but the stress, he felt, affected his health. He often appeared tired. He felt too cold in winter and too warm in summer. He coughed to such an extent that he feared that, like his mother, he was a victim of tuberculosis. His nostrils and throat bothered him, and, with the reaction of a mild hypochondriac, he became addicted to taking pills of all sorts to relieve them. He understandably often felt tense, but there were no pills for that, only the welcome trips home to Northampton and Vermont.

He got some relief in his magnificent office in the state house.

There he sat at a mahogany desk which was protected by a smooth glass top. The desk was never cluttered, and its dignity was crowned by a picture of his mother, which he had set upon it. There he would work in a well-organized fashion, assisted when needed by his secretary, Henry F. Long. The governor spent a great deal of time in his office, probably because it was more appealing to his sense of dignity and self-importance than his rooms in the Adams House. In his state house office he could better handle visitors, reinforced as he was by the room's stateliness and the portraits on the wall of governors long past.

The one disadvantage of the room was that it was considered something of a museum and special guests occasionally were ushered in to see it while he was working alone. The story has been told of when Mrs. John D. Long went to the state house to see the portrait in the executive chamber of her husband, who had been governor in the 1880s. She was escorted to the room by a minor official. When they got there, Governor Coolidge was at his desk, and the escort told him that Mrs. Long wished to see her husband's picture. Without rising, Coolidge aimed his thumb at the portrait and quacked, "Well, there it is."[12] Those begrudged four words summed up Coolidge's dislike of the unexpected, his taciturnity, and the veil he kept over his emotions.

He was a man who stuck to his work. When in the capital he seldom did anything but work, except when Mrs. Coolidge was in town. His big treat and his only form of physical exercise was walking, which he accomplished daily in the company of his bodyguard, Edward Horrigan. Even those were silent walks, and one never knew whether Coolidge was thinking of the day's work, daydreaming of what would come after the governorship, or just enjoying the air. Occasionally, his few Boston friends would drop in and divert his attention from the work before him.

His most likely caller was Frank Stearns. Sometimes the merchant would drop in and sometimes he was summoned by the governor. Those were rarely business or political calls. They were social, for Stearns had discovered that he could seldom elicit replies from Coolidge through conversation. The governor's taciturnity and penchant for thinking things through made it necessary for his chief backer and admirer to write him in order to get a response.

When the time came for a social call, the thin, hatchet-faced governor and the bespectacled, plump, and pleasant-looking merchant would light up cigars and sit in silence. Occasionally Coolidge would work and other times he would just stare off into space. Stearns had little choice but to stare too, usually out the window. Then, after they had finished their cigars, a few remarks about the weather or some other casual subject would pass between them. That was it. But Coolidge, who disliked being left alone, was satisfied. And Stearns was happy because he had been of assistance to his twentieth-century Lincoln. He had given him solace.

II

Nomination to Some
Other Office?

Frank Waterman Stearns gave Coolidge more than solace. He
gave drive and direction to his political daydreams. Even before
Coolidge became governor, Stearns had considered him of presidential timber, and with Coolidge's election as Massachusetts' chief
executive, Stearns began to make earnest efforts to put him in the
White House. On January 8, 1919, the Boston merchant wrote to
Dwight Morrow, by then a partner in the gigantic Wall Street firm of
J. P. Morgan and Company, to recruit him for a Coolidge-for-President campaign. Coolidge's Amherst classmate enlisted with Stearns,
and soon the two of them were working with Thomas Cochran,
another Morgan partner, and Republican National Committee Secretary James R. Reynolds to boom Governor Coolidge for President.

Stearns' motives were clear. He now craved the excitement of
politics and desired immortality by bringing onto the national scene
a man who, he believed, would rank with Lincoln as a statesman.
But Stearns also wanted something more tangible. As he wrote Morrow, "I do not know of anything better that can be done to help
human beings and help business than to make Calvin Coolidge the
one great leader in the country."[1]

Morrow's reasons for supporting Coolidge were somewhat diffcrent. He had tasted public service while on wartime duty with the Allied Maritime Transportation Council and he wanted more of it. He also sought to combat what he regarded as the selfish, monopolistic thinking of the Republican party and America's monied classes. His ammunition was nineteenth-century liberalism and free trade, and Coolidge could be his weapon. He wrote Stearns:

> I should like to see him "as revolutionary as science." I should like to see him get the real facts with reference to some of the things that are wrong in the world and take a bold stand in making them right.... I have come to the conclusion that the division of the people of the world is not really between conservative and radical, but between people that are real people and people that are not. Calvin is one of the fellows who is real. He really wants to make things better, not to pretend to make them better.[2]

While Stearns was touting Coolidge, Morrow was trying to tutor him. In an attempt to make his old classmate more critical of the businessman's protectionist principles, Morrow sent him four volumes by William Graham Sumner as a lesson in free trade. In March, 1920, Coolidge responded:

> I have read most of the four volumes of Sumner. I regard his arguments, on the whole, as sound. I do not think that human existence is quite so much on the basis of dollars and cents as he puts it. He argues in one place that the enunciation of great principles has had little to do with human development; that America became democratic through economic reasons rather than the reasons that came from the teachings of philosophy and religion. He nowhere enunciates the principle of service.
> That principle so far as I know has never been applied to protection. My observation of protection is that it has been successful in practice, however unsound it may appear to be in theory. That must mean that the theories have not taken account of all the facts. If I am poor and need the assistance of a protective tariff, why does not the law of service require others to furnish it for me? Or, if I am powerful, why is it not my duty to use my power for the protection of less

fortunate industries or people? There must have been something in our country besides an abundance of land to draw the population of Europe here for there was an abundance of land in Russia and in Africa, less convenient of access and so of use.[3]

It seems that the governor had ideas of his own and was up to trying to educate Morrow in return.

Morrow was not discouraged, however. He jumped with gusto into the campaign to build up Coolidge. Indeed, he showed so much enthusiasm that Stearns had trouble concentrating the financier's efforts on the 1919 Massachusetts election, because Morrow "was so much interested in the future."[4] Morrow and Thomas Cochran, because of their House of Morgan connections, stayed behind the scenes, raising funds and working eagerly to spread word of the Good News of Calvin Coolidge.

That word spread slowly by voice and letter and print. Stearns made the most tangible contribution by subsidizing publication in 1919 of a number of Coolidge's speeches and pronouncements. The volume, which was entitled *Have Faith in Massachusetts,* was sold to anyone who would buy it and given away free to editors and politicians across the country. Later each delegate and alternate to the 1920 Republican National Convention was sent a second-edition copy of the book. Other tactics were used in Coolidge's behalf. Of course, Amherst alumni were appealed to for support, as were the friends of Cochran, Morrow, Reynolds, and Stearns. Businessmen, editors, and lawyers were sent articles on the governor as well as copies of his speeches and public statements. Stearns and his associates sought honorary degrees for Coolidge, and he received them, from Amherst, Tufts, and Williams, in 1919.

Coolidge kept aloof from all this maneuvering for political advantage. The governor's position was well stated by Frank Stearns: "He feels that nothing queers a man in public life more than to have folks feel that [he] is using one very high office merely as a stepping stone to get another . . . . he does not intend to make that mistake."[5] One of Coolidge's supporter's bolder efforts to find publicity almost did involve him. That came after Theodore Roosevelt's death in 1919. Then a Bostonian suggested to Henry J. Whigham, the editor of *Metropolitan Magazine,* that the Massachusetts governor take the late President's place in writing a column for the magazine. Some of Coolidge's writings were given to Whigham. After paging through them, he decided against the idea, saying, "This is just a lot of platitudes." Then the Bostonian replied that the governor's material would be ghost-written. The answer was still No.[6] General Leonard Wood, one of Coolidge's competitors for the nation's favor, was chosen to replace Roosevelt.

As much as Stearns and Morrow worked for Coolidge, nothing resembling a respectable campaign developed until after the Boston Police Strike and the governor's landslide re-election. The reasons were obvious. Coolidge was not known outside Massachusetts and Vermont, and because of his taciturnity he was unlikely to become known. Until fall, 1919, most politicians considered him to be little more than a Crane organization man who had been tapped for the governorship because of his loyalty and respectability. He controlled neither his faction nor his party. There was no Coolidge clique in the legislature and only a very small one among the Bay State's citizens. It took the police strike to make him well known and his overwhelming re-election to get people talking about him for higher things. From then on some people began to respond to Stearns' and Morrow's publicity efforts.

One of the biggest problems Coolidge and his supporters faced in seeking the presidential nomination was the division of the Massachusetts Republican party. Coolidge had, despite his identification with Murray Crane, kept out of factional battles and made few, if any, enemies. Consequently, he had received both the support of the Crane men and the acceptance of the Lodge men. In 1919, however, an issue came up that threatened to split the state party so far apart that even Coolidge could not span the gap. That was the struggle over the ratification of the Treaty of Versailles and particularly its provision for a League of Nations. Murray Crane ardently advocated the League idea and Senator Henry Cabot Lodge ferociously opposed it.

President Wilson's handling of the war had irritated Lodge. He had been opposed to signing an armistice, wanting instead complete victory over the Germans and their allies. He also had been irritated by Wilson's call for the election of a Democratic Congress in 1918, with the imputation that Republicans had not been patriotic. For a superpatriot like Lodge that was the supreme insult. Injury was added to insult when the President prepared for the peace conference at Versailles without consulting the leaders of either the Republican party or the Senate, particularly Lodge, who would be the next chairman of the Senate Foreign Relations Committee.

Crane, by contrast to Lodge, was a man who believed deeply that vengeance had no role in bringing and maintaining peace and that the peace must be safeguarded through international cooperation. Though failing in health, he enlisted in the fight for what he regarded as a sane approach to solving international problems. Coolidge was caught in the middle. He had thought little about the world problems and issues that stirred his seniors in the party in Massachusetts. That hurt his position. On the one hand, he had given the impression that he sympathized with Lodge's nationalistic ideas.[7] On the other hand, Coolidge favored Crane's approach, partly out of loyalty and partly out of a vague conviction that it would serve best to restore the stability he believed essential to progress.

The problem first touched Coolidge in February, 1919, when President Wilson returned to the United States from France to try to combat the rising criticism of his peace efforts. He chose Boston as his point of arrival. That further irritated Senator Lodge, who regarded it as an attempt to embarrass him in his own back yard. Coolidge became slightly involved in the issue of whether the President's critics should keep silent until Wilson returned. Before his departure from France, Wilson had asked the members of the House and Senate committees on foreign relations not to discuss the League publicly until he could talk with them. Although some, like Senators Borah, Poindexter, and Reed, would not be stilled, Lodge and the others held their tongues. Coolidge congratulated the senior Massachusetts senator for that. Then on February 22 he wrote Lodge suggesting that he reduce his criticism of Wilson's League of Nations idea. "Let others take the lead," he said, for Massachusetts generally favored the world organization.[8] Coolidge's criterion of bowing to the people's sentiment had no influence on the strong-willed senator.

Coolidge became further involved when Wilson's ship arrived in Boston, February 24. His involvement was unavoidable because, as a matter of courtesy, the governor should welcome the President of the United States when he visits the state capital. And welcome the

President, Coolidge did (and along with him Assistant Secretary of the Navy Franklin D. Roosevelt, who was to be Coolidge's opponent for Vice President in 1920). Indeed the governor's greeting of Wilson was almost worshipful:

> We welcome him as the representative of a great people, as a great statesman, as one to whom we have entrusted our destinies, and one whom we are sure we will support in the future in the working out of that destiny, as Massachusetts has supported him in the past.[9]

Coolidge had not been caught up in the excitement of the moment, for his speech had been written well in advance. Although it represented an outcropping of his personal sentiments, it was based also on his awareness that a governor barely elected to office the year before could miss no bets to share the limelight. Yet those who agreed with Lodge, and they were increasing in numbers and influence, made it clear to Coolidge that he had gone too far in his remarks on that cold, gloomy day. He was not again to be so impolitic on the peace question.

When the governor was next involved, he maintained a lofty impartiality. That was on the occasion of a widely publicized debate on the League of Nations. The debaters were Senator Lodge and Harvard President A. Lawrence Lowell. Coolidge was the presiding officer. Seventy-two thousand people sought tickets to the debate, and when it was held, March 19, 3,500 persons crammed into Symphony Hall. The two debaters were eloquent, with Lodge the more passionate and Lowell the more logical. The presiding officer was courteous, perfunctory, and neutral, so much so that it was scarcely noticeable that he was there. Coolidge's only quotable remark came after the debate, when he said of the exercise, "They both won."[10]

Coolidge's striving for neutrality was again indicated some weeks later when he refused to preside over an anti-League meeting held in Boston by Albert Beveridge and Senators William E. Borah and Charles S. Thomas. His equivocation was illustrated when he wrote the pro-League Dwight Morrow in April:

> I do not think there is any reason for losing faith in the American people or their ability to govern themselves, pro-

tect themselves and stand alone. I think too, we are all in agreement that some sort of a treaty that would tend to prevent a resort to arms in the future should be made and adopted. It will make necessary giving up something if we receive any benefit. I am very clear, however, that such a treaty ought not to be as a substitute for our self-reliance and preparation for a strong France and a restricted Germany.[11]

Coolidge's ambiguousness kept Lodge and Crane in support of him as governor, though neither leader was noticeably warm toward him until after the Boston Police Strike.

The sudden rise of Coolidge to prominence as a result of the police strike and the following election seemed to warm up the aging senator. Lodge wanted desperately to get Woodrow Wilson and his supporters out of command of the federal government. An alliance with Coolidge might give him additional bargaining power in the Republican National Convention. Then too, should the governor somehow win the presidential nomination, Lodge might be able to control him on policy. If Coolidge failed to be nominated, it was probable that he would be a fixture in Massachusetts politics, and the senator, who was a mediocre campaigner, might keep him through obligation from making a Coolidge versus Lodge contest for the Senate in 1922.

More immediate concerns were Lodge's desire to secure the Massachusetts Republican party's opposition to the League of Nations and to get for himself, without trouble, a place on the state's delegation to the 1920 national convention. No one can say for sure what ran through Lodge's mind, but he was too much of a politician not to have considered those things. In any case, after Coolidge was renominated for governor in 1919, Lodge praised him highly for his actions during the police strike. He was particularly outspoken in his praise of Coolidge in the Republican State Convention, though Lodge did not persuade it to endorse his stand against the League.

After the governor's landslide victory in the November, 1919, elections, Lodge came over to the Coolidge-for-President movement. Some people had already urged the sixty-nine-year-old senator himself to run for the Republican presidential nomination, but he firmly rejected the idea. He explained to Coolidge December 15: "I am far too old. A man who takes the Presidency should be at least ten years younger than I am and it would be better if he were twenty years younger."[12]

Twenty years younger, of course, was in the neighborhood of Coolidge's age. In his December letter, Lodge offered to nominate Coolidge in the national convention as Massachusetts' favorite son, which the governor took only as a courteous gesture. Yet others thought it more than that, and with reason. At Thanksgiving time the senator had gone to Coolidge and told him that he wanted to present his name for President. Lodge had also told Frank Stearns he was "for the governor, not merely as a favorite son, but really for him for the nomination for the Presidency of the United States."[13] This interest was no secret, for on November 26 Lodge became the first leading Republican to endorse the governor when he told the Boston *Transcript* that Massachusetts should support Coolidge for President. It is doubtful that Senator Lodge thought Coolidge should be President, but it is apparent that he intended to be on the right side should lightning strike.

As winter came in 1919 things looked good to Stearns and Morrow. Not only did it appear that Coolidge would have the support of both the Crane and Lodge factions, but another development bolstered his candidacy. As Sherwin Cook has written: "In Massachusetts a Coolidge cult arose. It was not altogether opposed to the conservative machine, nor was the machine antagonistic to the circle of especial Coolidge admirers. Still they were distinct."[14] "Cult" is the best term for it because it was neither a faction nor a party. Neither was it organized nor greatly encouraged by the object of its admiration. Largely composed of, and led by, political amateurs, that cult worshiped stability and exalted the law-and-order governor as its prophet. The cult carried the Coolidge-for-President movement through the winter, for as much as Massachusetts' Republican leaders might talk about nominating Coolidge, they were not doing much about it.

Frank Stearns, of course, was the chief generator of sentiment for Coolidge. He huffed and he puffed. He hailed the governor as the greatest American of the time. He pushed law and order as the issue on which Coolidge could be nominated for President. And now, after the Boston Police Strike and the election, he had some material with which to work. Even Democrats could see something attractive in Coolidge. Woodrow Wilson had gone so far as to telegraph congratulations to Coolidge after his re-election. Of that Stearns kept reminding Republicans who were interested in drawing Democratic votes.

The press of New England, with which Stearns as a heavy advertiser had good contacts, generally rallied around the section's resident hero. Coolidge also was becoming the subject of articles in national magazines like *Forum*, *Independent*, and *Outlook*. The governor, now that he had been re-elected, began to emerge as a conservative. In November, 1919, he gave a widely reprinted interview in which he said, "We have curbed the cupidity of capital; we cannot yield to the cupidity of labor."[15] He was a convenient tool for those interests who wanted to combat labor's demands for a better standard of living.

The Coolidge movement grew slowly, but it grew. He was endorsed for President by the Republican Club of Massachusetts in November, and the following month the Massachusetts Republican State Committee urged that he be boomed for President. Murray Crane began to take an interest in the movement, as did the congressman from the governor's home district, Frederick Gillett, who held the exalted post of Speaker of the United States House of Representatives. From South Dakota, the Republican State Convention proposed Coolidge for Vice President. Congressman William A. Rodenberg, a leader of Illinois Governor Frank O. Lowden's campaign for President, declared that Lowden and Coolidge would make a marvelous Republican ticket. The New Bedford *Standard* asked, "Why not the other way around?" and the Boston *Transcript* haughtily viewed Rodenberg's suggestion as "characteristic of the central western bumptiousness."[16] It may have been bumptiousness, but other politicians over the land began talking of Coolidge for Vice President. In January, 1920, James B. Reynolds, who had been secretary of the Republican National Committee since 1912, resigned his post in order to manage the Coolidge movement. He immediately opened Coolidge-for-President offices in Chicago and Washington.

Then a curious thing happened. On January 26 Coolidge denied that he was a candidate for President and announced he would not enter his name in the presidential preference primaries in the various states. There is probably truth in Coolidge's explanation that the other candidates for the nomination were sinking large sums of money in the primaries and that he probably could not and did not want to match those investments. He also said that he did not wish to use his office as an instrument to campaign for nomination to another office. The headquarters Reynolds had opened for him were closed just as suddenly as they had been opened. Coolidge probably meant what he said, but his statement did not put an end to the Coolidge-for-President movement. Nor did it discourage people from thinking that he wanted to be President when the same month *Forum* magazine featured his article entitled "My Principles of Citizenship." After all, he had left the door wide open for a draft nomination and he had not forbade his followers to use informal methods of campaigning.

And less formal methods they used. Reynolds continued seeking publicity and raising political funds for Coolidge. The distribution of free copies of *Have Faith in Massachusetts* spurted and soon newspaper editors seized upon the book for serialization. The governor's idea of sticking to his day's work, while other candidates scurried about for delegates, also was found attractive by many editors. Bruce Barton was brought in to write an article to make that quality seem even more attractive and to make Coolidge appear more human. Barton also set about to play him up as a man who kept his own counsel, a novelty when most prominent politicians freely gave advice on everything. Stearns and Morrow continued making contacts. In letters the Wall Street man praised Coolidge for his character, knowledge, and tolerance. "I am sure Coolidge would make a *good* President; I think he would make a *great* one."[17] That Morrow was sincere was revealed in a letter to fellow financier Thomas Lamont, whom he knew well and who was nobody's fool. Morrow wrote: "I think it is a miracle that a man of Coolidge's type has been produced for this emergency. Moreover, I think he is going to be nominated and elected."[18]

As spring came Coolidge's position was that of a dark horse, and a fairly good one at that. He had been well publicized and he had a good deal of rank-and-file Republican support. He had embarrassed no one. He had not offended the people of his state, whom he might ask for re-election as governor. Massachusetts had another possible favorite son, General Leonard Wood, who was legally domiciled there and was also a close friend of Senator Lodge. Coolidge had told the state's Republican delegates that they could support other candidates if they wished, and the governor had wound up with the support of twenty-nine of the thirty-five delegates and yet created no ill feeling. By staying out of other state conventions and preferential primaries, he had offended none of the other candidates for the Republican nomination. Moreover, he had not gotten into the unusually frantic fund-raising and spending efforts of 1920. His $68,000 fund was puny compared with those of $173,000 for Herbert Hoover, $194,000 for Hiram Johnson, $415,000 for Frank O. Lowden, and a whopping $1,773,000 for Leonard Wood. No one could say of Coolidge that the big money was trying to buy him anything. His strategy was not really a bad one under the circumstances. Because he did command considerable sentiment among the rank-and-file Republicans and because it appeared that the convention was certain to be deadlocked among the leading candidates, his best bet was to be a dark horse.

The big problem was to keep Coolidge's home forces together. As the time of the convention drew closer, Murray Crane became more interested in his protégé. The reason was obvious. Crane refused to consider the League question settled by the Senate's rejection of the Treaty of Versailles in March, 1920. He had decided to work to get the Republican National Convention to endorse a League of Nations or, failing that, to keep it from endorsing the Senate's action. Now that he was no longer a senator or a national committeeman, he needed additional leverage. Neither House Speaker Gillett nor the governor of Massachusetts could supply enough prestige, especially with Lodge and General Wood in opposition. What Crane needed was a candidate for President of his own who would receive the attention and the courtesies normally extended to a candidate for nomination in a national convention. The only candidate Crane could have was Coolidge and the old leader determined to make what he could out of sour dough. So as the June convention neared, Murray Crane worked all the harder for Coolidge and his own internationalist convictions. The problem was that the harder Crane worked, the less happy Lodge and the Wood men in the Massachusetts delegation would be with Coolidge.

Lodge continued to be for Coolidge at least as late as April, when he publicly announced that he would place the governor's name before the convention. Yet his interest was cooling. He had secured a place on the Massachusetts delegation without controversy and he was to be made the temporary chairman of the convention and later even its permanent chairman. Differing interpretations can and have been placed on what happened to his alliance with Coolidge. One Lodge biographer, Karl Schriftgiesser, argues that the senator's sympathies really belonged to the sometime Massachusetts man, Leonard Wood, who saw almost eye to eye with him on policies. Drawn to Wood and discouraged by Coolidge's lack of aggressiveness in seeking the nomination, Lodge used his supposed need to be impartial as convention chairman to excuse himself from placing Coolidge in nomination. John Garraty, another biographer, writes that Lodge, had he not been chairman, would have nominated Coolidge. Neither interpretation is convincing given Lodge's political astuteness and the fact that behind the scenes of the convention he deserted both Coolidge and Wood.

Poisonous feelings had developed between the Crane men and the Lodge men as the former threatened to debate the League of Nations question before the convention. It is possible that Lodge made use of Coolidge to get a delegate's seat and the convention chairmanship and, once having used the governor, was willing to abandon him. That is all the more plausible because it soon became clear to Lodge at the convention that the Coolidge movement was not advancing. A man who intended to use the convention, as the senator did, as a scoring board against Woodrow Wilson and the League of Nations could not afford to be closely identified with a losing cause. Lodge was glad to help first Leonard Wood and then a dark-horse contender from Ohio, Warren G. Harding, in order to maintain his influence on party policy. It can further be argued that Lodge must have been relieved to slip out of his commitment to Coolidge, who thanks to Murray Crane's efforts was becoming identified with the pro-League Republicans. Lodge would have looked ridiculous prosecuting his anti-League case from a pro-League shelter. Whatever his reasons, Lodge finally made it clear that he would not nominate Coolidge for President, and at the last moment the governor's team found itself without its star player.

12

"Coolidge! Coolidge!"

COOLIDGE REMAINED AT HIS job up to the opening of the Republican National Convention in June, 1920. As the convention neared he seemed less and less interested in the nomination. That was, however, attributable certainly to his mourning for his stepmother, who had died in May, and probably to a feeling that the presidential nomination was beyond his grasp.

Despite his apparent aloofness, Coolidge's men were working harder than ever in his behalf. James Reynolds and a few others went to Chicago several days before the convention opened in order to boost the governor. When the Massachusetts delegation arrived, others set to work, including Lieutenant Governor Channing Cox, Massachusetts House Speaker Joseph E. Warner, Supervisor of Administration Thomas W. White, drugstore magnate Louis K. Liggett, and manufacturer William F. Whiting. One of the chief contributions of the Coolidge delegates was to publish and to distribute among their fellow conventioneers a collection of Coolidge speeches entitled *Law and Order*. Dwight Morrow and Thomas Cochran also came, from Wall Street, to labor for the Massachusetts governor. In fact, Morrow's hotel room became a center of lobbying. From early in the morning until midnight he would usher politicians in and out to talk with them excitedly about how it was essential to the nation's soul that Calvin Coolidge be nominated for President. From time to time he would enter the corridor, go to other men's rooms, even descend to the hotel lobby and dining rooms in search of fresh prospects. Congressmen, governors, judges, state legislators, mayors, ward heelers, anyone who was a delegate or could influence one, were fair game to the financier.

Yet the small band of dedicated amateurs and professional politicians was working for Coolidge against great odds. It helped their morale when just before the convention began columnist Mark Sullivan put the Massachusetts governor toward the head of the dark-horse class of 1920. Yet when the Coolidge men arrived in Chicago they must have been impressed with the high power of the well-financed campaigns of Wood, Johnson, and Lowden. They must also have been impressed with the number of other dark horses, including former Food Administrator Herbert Hoover, Columbia University President Nicholas Murray Butler, Senator Warren G. Harding, and Governors Henry J. Allen of Kansas and William C. Sproul of Pennsylvania. The Coolidge men certainly were disturbed by signs that Henry Cabot Lodge would bolt their camp and bolster the Wood group in the Massachusetts delegation. Despite what they heard and saw, Coolidge's supporters worked fervently, hoping that by some miracle of politics their dark horse would sprint across the finish line ahead of the favorites and the field.

The convention opened Tuesday, June 8, in the huge central chamber of the Chicago Coliseum. Hearing routine business for hours on end, the delegates sat or strolled about under a canopy of American flags which hung down like cirro-cumulus clouds from the rafters. The first great excitement came when Senator Lodge, in his hour-and-twenty-minute keynote address, passionately urged the convention to make Woodrow Wilson and the League of Nations the main issues of the campaign of 1920. Meanwhile, in the Resolutions Committee, Murray Crane fought for Republican endorsement of a League with reservations. His struggle seemed to be on the verge of success when Senators William Borah, Frank Brandegee, and Medill McCormick threatened to denounce the party if it gave approval to the League of Nations. Finally a plank that was called a compromise was adopted by the Republicans. It damned the League as unjust and un-American but proposed an "international association" that would "secure instant and general international conference whenever peace shall be threatened."[1]

Although the plank was claimed as a victory by both the anti- and the pro-League forces, the Springfield *Republican*, speaking from Crane's home territory, labeled it correctly, "Bitter-Enders Score Complete Victory."[2] Crane himself, who had been treated abusively before the Resolutions Committee, could only see in the plank the possibility that it might be favorably interpreted by the party's national nominees. With that in mind, his interest turned to trying to influence any candidate who would listen to his views. Coolidge, seeing both Lodge and Crane slip away from him, roused himself to try to keep the nominal backing of Lodge and the active support of Crane. After the international plank had been drawn, the governor publicly stated, "They have met and solved the treaty and League questions in a way that will insure party solidarity."[3] He spoke in vain, for neither Lodge nor Crane was greatly interested in Republican solidarity.

After suffering through seemingly interminable speeches and announcements and the approval of the platform, the convention delegates took up the business of nominating a candidate for President on Friday, June 11. Then came more speeches. Governor Allen of Kansas, in effect removing himself from contention, gave a ponderous speech in favor of Leonard Wood. Representative William A. Rodenberg presented Frank O. Lowden to the convention. In what humorist Irvin S. Cobb called "the worst speech that ever was," Charles Stetson Wheeler offered Senator Hiram Johnson's name. Herbert Hoover was put in nomination by Judge Nathan L. Miller of New York. In an effective speech, Ohio Governor Frank B. Willis told the delegates about a "safe and sane" senator, Warren G. Harding. Other men came forward to urge the candidacies of Judge Jeter Pritchard of North Carolina, Nicholas Murray Butler of New York, Governor Sproul of Pennsylvania, Senator Miles Poindexter of Washington, and Senator Howard Sutherland of West Virginia.

In the middle of the nominating proceedings came the effort in behalf of Coolidge. Frederick Gillett had been persuaded to take Lodge's place in putting Coolidge in candidacy for the nomination. The House speaker's speech was brief, as Coolidge and, by then, the delegates would appreciate. It also was well constructed and enthusiastically delivered. The governor of Massachusetts was portrayed as a man for a time of crisis. This man, Gillett said, was "patient as Lincoln, silent as Grant, diplomatic as McKinley, with the political instinct of Roosevelt. His character is as firm as the mountains of his native state. Like them his head is above the clouds and he stands unshaken amid the tumult and the storm."⁴ The delegates were not affected by Gillett's enthusiasm; they were at best polite. Coolidge's nomination drew only a one-minute demonstration, which chilled the ardor of his workers after seeing Governor Lowden pull forty-six minutes of response, Wood forty-two, and Johnson thirty-seven.

The voting for a presidential nominee began directly after the candidates had been offered to the delegates. The initial ballots became a test of strength between General Wood's forces and those of the other candidates who were trying to destroy him before settling the nomination among themselves. Wood proved to have more delegates than anyone else, but considerably less than enough to nominate. Coolidge ranked well down the list on the first ballot, with thirty-four votes including twenty-eight from Massachusetts and six scattered from four other states. That represented his peak strength, as his votes declined to thirty-two on the second ballot, twenty-seven on the third, and twenty-five on the fourth. At that point no substantial change had been made in the positions of the three leading candidates, Wood, Lowden, and Johnson. The convention was adjourned and the reason was well stated by Senator Reed Smoot of Utah, who said, "There's going to be a deadlock, and we'll have to work out some solution."⁵

It was that night, Friday, June 11, that the so-called smoke-filled-room decision was made. After the convention's adjournment the Wood and Johnson forces worked frantically to form coalitions that would put their men over the top, and the Lowden men struggled desperately to keep their delegate strength intact. Yet others were working just as hard to push dark horses or to find a candidate who could appeal to a majority of delegates. Bargaining went on throughout the night. The old guard, composed largely of Republican senators and their friends and aides, met in rooms all over the Blackstone Hotel. Their main gathering place was in a thirteenth-floor suite rented by Republican National Committee Chairman Will Hays. There the editor of the *North American Review*, George Harvey, presided over meetings of shifting groups of leaders that extended into the early morning hours of Saturday, June 12.

At the beginning of the meetings Lodge offered Warren G. Harding as the best compromise candidate. In support of the Ohio senator it was said that Wood's and Lowden's reputations had been soiled by exposure of their huge campaign funds. It was contended also that Ohio was necessary to a national election victory. Because the Democrats would probably nominate the state's governor for President, the Republicans could best fight for Ohio and victory by nominating Harding. During the night the informal caucus returned to that idea, though never arriving at a clear-cut decision. If there was agreement, it was reached late by a small group. Yet the upshot was that a number of senators and their friends went out to work for Harding, though they also agreed to give Wood, Johnson, and Lowden several more ballots to try to break their deadlock.

The convention met again at ten Saturday morning. Four ballots went off, during which Harding gained slowly on the three leading contenders, who remained deadlocked. As that happened Coolidge's votes remained fairly steady with twenty-nine on the fifth ballot, twenty-eight on the sixth and seventh, and thirty on the eighth. After the eighth ballot was concluded at 1:40 p.m., a recess was taken.

For the next three hours Harding's men struggled to find a path to victory and the other candidates sought to block the senator from Ohio. Some of the old-guard senators who had agreed on Harding the night before now broke ranks in an effort to nominate National Committee Chairman Will Hays. Yet enough of the old guard stood by its earlier decision, and Harry Daugherty, the Ohioan's manager, deftly maneuvered to gain additional votes. The result was that on the ninth ballot Harding went into a substantial lead over the other candidates. Coolidge held on to twenty-eight votes, but on the tenth ballot the show was over. The Ohio senator swept easily to a majority, as ruined hopes littered the convention floor.

At the end Coolidge wound up with five votes, only one of which, Speaker Gillett's, came from Massachusetts. As Coolidge later said, "a coterie of United States senators"[6] had dominated the drafting of the platform and the selection of the Republican presidential nominee for 1920.

Coolidge, in the company of his wife, had followed the nominating proceedings from his rooms in the Adams House. When news of Harding's nomination came, the governor put on his hat and left the hotel. He walked across the Boston Common and down some of the streets leading off it. His walk was lonely. But it was a good way for

Coolidge to work off some of his disappointment at having failed, not only to be nominated, but to be a substantial contender. Had he known that Murray Crane and Henry Cabot Lodge had not even mentioned his name to the senatorial coterie, his disappointment might have been all the worse. In any case, the governor of Massachusetts had lost his interest in the convention. Satisfied with his exercise, Coolidge returned to the Adams House for a long talk with Grace.

While the governor was walking and talking in Boston, the convention in Chicago was winding up its business with the selection of a nominee for Vice President of the United States. As the tenth ballot for the presidential nomination was being completed, a group of leaders interested in the vice presidential selection met in a little room under the Coliseum's stage. Senator Medill McCormick of Illinois, Alvin T. Hert of Kentucky, Senator William Borah of Idaho, former Senator John Weeks of Massachusetts, and Harding's campaign manager, Harry M. Daugherty, all agreed that the ticket should be balanced by a liberal. McCormick suggested the name of Senator Irvine L. Lenroot of Wisconsin. Lenroot, a supporter of Theodore Roosevelt in 1912, a friend of Hiram Johnson, and an advocate of the League of Nations with reservations, would do the job, the little group agreed. Henry L. Stoddard, who covered the convention as a reporter, has said Harding wanted Johnson for his running mate but that the California senator had emphatically and even insultingly rejected the idea. With no one else in mind, the Harding men were willing to accept any other respectable candidate. Lenroot would do.

Other maneuverings, however, were occurring as the convention prepared to move to the vice presidential nomination. The Oregon delegates offered to place Henry Cabot Lodge in nomination, which the aristocratic senator declined almost haughtily. Then Oregon asked whether Coolidge could be put in candidacy as a substitute. It was all right with Lodge, for it could not make any difference since Lenroot would be nominated. Anyway, Coolidge's admirers might take it as a compliment.

Whatever was to be done by the convention had to be done fast. Many of the delegates were eager to leave Chicago as soon as possible in order to avoid paying another night's hotel charges and to avoid upsetting train reservations. In fact, several hundred delegates had already left and others were preparing to leave as soon as the vice presidential choice of the senatorial coterie became clear.

They did not have long to wait. Senator McCormick was recognized first by the chair and strode to the convention rostrum. On his way he passed through the press section. Newsman Henry Stoddard asked him, "What are you going to do, Medill?"

He answered, "We're going to put over Lenroot."

"The hell you are!" interjected another reporter.

Glaring at him, McCormick shot back, "Watch me and see."[7]

Senator McCormick had not spoken fifty words in nomination of Lenroot when a voice from the rear of the cavernous hall yelled, "Coolidge! Coolidge!"

The Illinois senator went on, but again came the shout, "Coolidge! Coolidge!" And this time it was echoed by individuals in several other delegations.

After McCormick finished his brief speech there was a small demonstration for Lenroot, but it had to compete with shouts from the floor and the gallery for "Coolidge! Coolidge!" Something was up, perhaps a protest against putting another senator and Midwesterner on the ticket. The convention leaders, however, were undisturbed. Lenroot was their choice and the convention would submit.

After Lenroot's nomination and several seconds had been given, a small, haggard-looking man named Wallace McCamant stood on a chair in the Oregon section, crying for recognition. Frank Willis, who was then presiding, apparently thought it was another request to second Lenroot and he recognized the Oregonian. Amid the noise of falling seats and shuffling feet, McCamant yelled:

When the Oregon delegation came here instructed by the people of our state to present to this convention as its candidate for the office of vice president a distinguished son of Massachusetts he requested that we refrain from presenting his name. But there is another son of Massachusetts who has been much in the public eye in the last year, a man who is sterling in his Americanism and stands for all that the Republican party holds dear, and on behalf of the Oregon delegation I name for the exalted office of vice president Governor Calvin Coolidge of Massachusetts.[8]

The man with the loud voice was greeted with a brief but powerful response of applause and cheers. McCamant had given the name of a man who did not belong to the clique that had been running the convention. Coolidge! He was the "law-and-order" man, the one who had sent out those books of speeches. Now the opportunity had come, thought many of the delegates, for them to do something on their own, as they had been sent to do. Spontaneously, seconds for Coolidge came from a dozen states. Other men were placed in candidacy, but the wave of Coolidge sentiment lost none of its force. When the names of the candidates for nomination were read by the clerk, a demonstration was launched for Coolidge. The Massachusetts delegates, who had been taken off guard by McCamant's unexpected action, were now ready. They led the demonstration, shouting "Coolidge! Coolidge!" and waving the "Law-and-Order" banners which they had tucked away after their presidential defeat. They had not even led a stroll the day before, but now the men from Massachusetts joined the Oregonians to head a genuine stampede.

When the balloting began, it was soon clear that for the first time since 1880, when James A. Garfield was nominated, the delegates had taken control of a Republican convention. Coolidge received 674½ votes to 146½ for Lenroot, with the rest scattered among five favorite sons. Coolidge's nomination was made unanimous on the motion of John G. Oglesby of Illinois. The convention which had already nominated one safe and sane man had also, in its moment of rebellion, nominated an even safer and saner one.

Calvin and Grace Coolidge had finished their long chat and were preparing to go to dinner when the telephone rang. The newspapers were calling about Wallace McCamant's speech. The governor perked up, and he and his wife waited alone in their rooms to see what would happen in Chicago. At one point the telephone rang and he picked it up, listened, and put it down again.

"Nominated for vice president," he said to Grace.

"You aren't going to take it, are you?" she asked.

The man who had been uninterested in the nomination answered, "I suppose I'll have to."[9]

13

Something More than a Landslide

COOLIDGE QUICKLY FELL into the spirit of being a vice presidential nominee. Friends had found him, later on the evening of
his nomination, sitting in his bedroom cross-legged, looking as satisfied as his reserve would allow. In his excitement, it is said, he even
had two cigars going at the same time. He loved the attention he was
receiving. Gladly he waited out questions from newspapermen,
though he did not usually chew off more than a sentence or two to
give them in reply. Only a few of Coolidge's comments made the
headlines, as when he affirmed that his rent on the Massasoit Street
house was only thirty-two dollars a month and then added that he
was afraid that it would be raised. Most of his sayings, like his
urging of saving and investment as paths to national economic reconstruction, were less interesting and commanded little space in the
press. Photographers were more fortunate. He happily performed for
them. His only adverse reaction came after he had been photographed in his blue Vermont farmer's smock. The remarks that it
was a stunt and that the garb looked silly, he took as mockery. He
never wore the smock again for cameramen.

He became a very busy man after his nomination. The following
week Coolidge arrived for his twenty-fifth class reunion at Amherst,

where he was treated like the biggest man ever on campus. Then he went on to Holy Cross College to give a speech. That was followed within a fortnight by speeches at Wesleyan, where he was given an honorary degree, at Harvard, where he was not given a degree, and at Bates and Vermont, which honored him as had Wesleyan. At the State University of Vermont he made the statement, appropriate for the 1920 campaign, that neither labor nor anyone else must be allowed to levy tribute on the country.

The governor then traveled to Washington, D.C., to make his debut in national politics. There, on June 30, he joined Harding in a waffle-and-chipped-beef breakfast at the senator's home. Coolidge was told that Harding would conduct a campaign that would "out McKinley McKinley."[1] After eating, the senator and the governor held a press conference in which Harding stressed that his running mate would have a big role in the campaign. Thinking perhaps of the comments in some newspapers that had favored Coolidge's nomination more than his own, Harding added:

> I think the vice president should be more than a mere substitute in waiting. In reestablishing coordination between the Executive Office and the Senate, the vice president can and ought to play a big part, and I have been telling Governor Coolidge how much I wish him to be not only a participant in the campaign, but how much I wish him to be a helpful part of a Republican administration. The country needs the counsel and the becoming participation in government of such men as Governor Coolidge.[2]

Whatever Senator Harding had in mind, his statement was well received. It was almost revolutionary, for no previous presidential nominee had suggested using a Vice President for anything besides presiding over the Senate. After the press conference came time for the photographers. The two Republican nominees—one, handsome and strapping, looking like a President, and the other, of slight build, looking somewhat like a country boy on his first trip to the city—posed for pictures. Then Harding, for luck, searched the grass for a four-leaf clover and he found one, which he pinned to his running mate's lapel. Harding should have kept that lucky clover, in view of what the future brought.

After returning to Boston for a couple of days' work, Coolidge went to his father's farm, where he spent the next three weeks doing political and farm chores. Coolidge Day was held at Plymouth on July 17. Vermont's leading Republicans turned up, partly out of courtesy and partly to make amends for having supported Leonard Wood for President instead of Coolidge. Several thousand of the state's citizens also jammed the little settlement to greet the man who was Vermont's most illustrious native since Charles Ira Hood, the sarsaparilla man. While in Plymouth, Coolidge also worked on preparations for an even bigger celebration, Notification Day, which was to be held in Northampton on July 27. He wrote his acceptance speech and kept in touch with affairs in Boston and Washington.

When July 27 came Northampton was all dressed up. Red, white, and blue bunting was draped all along Main Street and American flags appeared everywhere. Pictures of Coolidge inscribed with the slogans "Law and Order" and "Have Faith in Massachusetts" were prominent. Bells rang in the city's churches, and crowds of home folks and visitors swarmed over the town. The man of the day was readying himself for the acceptance ritual in his half of the only duplex house on Massasoit Street. The governor's secretary, Henry F. Long, and Senator Lodge came that afternoon to the green-shuttered dwelling in order to escort Coolidge to Smith College's Allen Field for the ceremonies. The college's former president, Dr. L. Clark Seelye, presided and Governor Edwin P. Morrow of Kentucky served as chairman of the committee that notified Coolidge that he had been nominated for Vice President of the United States.

Coolidge accepted the nomination in a speech that gave a preview of the 1920 Republican campaign and considerable insight into the Massachusetts statesman's ideas on government and the recurrent issues of the following decade. After praising the party and its leader, Warren G. Harding, Coolidge mounted an elaborate and sometimes ambiguous explanation of the Republican platform. The first issue he mentioned was the one with which he was most connected, opposition to "the organized efforts to undermine the faith of our people in their government." "Repression" and "discussion" were confusingly offered by him as cures for those efforts.

The governor then passed on to his chief issue, a full conversion from the necessary wartime "autocratic method of government" to the repossession by "the people of their government and their property." In government, he said, that required a return to a situation where "the three coordinate branches, executive, legislative, judicial, are separate and distinct and neither one directly or indirectly exercises any of the functions of either of the others." That was basic Coolidge, the foundation upon which he later operated as President. The reduction of taxes, based on cutting public expenditures, was the way people could prevent the government from unnecessarily taking their property. The Republicans were pledged to cutting federal taxes and expenses to the bone. Yet, Coolidge warned, property was also threatened by two other factors: profiteering and inflation. Those could, and would under a Republican administration, be controlled by encouraging increased production, lowering taxes, and reducing the amount of money in circulation. The governor had made it clear that his economics was classical.

Coolidge's acceptance address was peppered with homilies on character, understanding, and stability. "All true Americans are working for each other, exchanging the results of the efforts of hand and brain wrought through the unconsumed efforts of yesterday, which we call capital, all paying and being paid by each other, serving and being served." This interdependence had to be comprehended in order to achieve stability.

Moreover, solutions of the country's difficulties depended "for final solution on the character and moral force of the nation." The coming of peace called for greater national character than ever before. "In all things a return to a peace basis does not mean the basis of 1914. That day is gone. It means a peace basis of the present, higher, nobler, because of the sacrifices made and the duties assumed. It is not a retreat, it is a new summons to advance."

After that the vice presidential nominee nodded in deference to special groups: conservationists, war veterans, the economically weak, women, labor, and farmers. Only when he discussed the situation of Negroes was he clear and to the point. He said that the goals to be achieved for them were "to be relieved from all imposition, to be defended from lynching, and to be freely granted equal opportunities."

He discussed his last issue, international cooperation, in a curious turn of language. Most of his lengthy address had been given in the first person, but when he came to the League of Nations he spoke of the positions of "our party," "the Republican senators," and the "platform." In those terms he defended the defeat of the

Treaty of Versailles as presented by President Wilson but stressed that the Republican party "approves the principle of agreement among nations to preserve peace, and pledges itself to the making of such an agreement, preserving American independence and rights, as will meet every duty America owes humanity."

In closing his acceptance address, he said: "We shall search in vain in legislative halls, executive mansions, and the chambers of the judiciary for the greatness of the government of our country. We shall behold there but a reflection, not a reality, successful in proportion to its accuracy."[3]

The question to be asked after the 1920s was whether government in that decade had failed to reflect the nation's greatness or whether the nation's greatness was insufficient to meet the problems of the time.

The national political campaign of 1920 had already begun before Coolidge's speech. Senator Harding had given his acceptance address in Marion, Ohio, on July 22, in what Mark Sullivan called "an exalted and moving ceremony" that created "an atmosphere usually associated with churches."[4] Afterward the Republican presidential nominee settled down on his spacious front porch in Marion to conduct a solemn and dignified at-home campaign, or so he thought. In the meantime, the Democrats had met in convention and after an exhausting forty-three ballots had nominated Governor James M. Cox of Ohio for President. The young, energetic assistant secretary of the navy, Franklin D. Roosevelt, had been accorded the second place on the Democratic ticket.

After Cox's notification, August 7, plans were laid for a strenuous campaign that would take him 22,000 miles into 36 states to give almost 400 speeches before some 2,000,000 people. Roosevelt was to travel 18,000 miles from coast to coast, averaging 10 speeches a day. Cox began his campaign chiding the Republicans for the huge amount of money available to them. That "corruption fund," he charged, was part of an attempt to buy the election for big business. That issue did not draw the response that the Ohio governor wanted, so he changed to accusing Harding of "wobbling" on the League of Nations issue. Cox increasingly emphasized that issue as the campaign went on. By Election Day it seemed as though his campaign was based only on getting the United States into the

League, with treaty reservations if necessary, and on his own impressive personality.

As for Franklin D. Roosevelt, he backed Cox's crusade for the League and his contentions that progressivism was not dead. Conservation, education, rural communications, female and child labor, and conditions of work were, Roosevelt said, of great concern to the Democratic party and the country. Roosevelt seldom recognized the existence of his counterpart on the Republican ticket. One exception came in September when the Democrat said that Coolidge thought "the great accomplishments of our history are due to the preponderating wisdom and power of the Congress of the United States."[5] He followed it up by saying that Coolidge believed the President was a high clerk chosen by the people to implement the policies determined by insiders in the nation's Senate.

Although Harding began his campaign on his front porch, he ended it on the stump. He was pressed from all sides to come to the help of local Republican tickets, and there were those who, thrown into a panic every time Cox or Roosevelt spoke, implored him to go out into the field to answer the Democrats' charges. Surrendering to such pleas, Harding traveled to Minneapolis, August 8, to make the first of the many speeches he gave, not only in the Middle West, but also in the Border States and the East. Much of the Republican nominee's time was spent in defensive action. He called the Democratic charges of trying to buy the election "ridiculous and wholly without foundation,"[6] and apparently he was able to make his answer stick. More difficult was Harding's problem with the League of Nations. Here he endeavored to find a way to appease Republicans who favored the League and yet placate those who opposed it. His formula was to condemn "Wilson's League" and to propose a new association of nations to achieve international cooperation. The impression he gave was what James Cox called "wobbling," but it was sufficient to satisfy both the anti- and pro-League Republicans.

Harding also tried to appease the progressives in Republican ranks and to offset Democratic charges that he was an instrument of big business. He proposed easier credits for farmers and cooperatives. He pledged himself to ease tensions between management and labor without injury to the interests of either. He called for a federal public welfare department and government efforts to solve the problem of housing. Yet he did not ignore business, for he promised tax reduction, extension of foreign markets, and "more business in government and less government in business." For all Americans, he opposed "Reds" and endorsed a protective tariff.

It was against that background that Calvin Coolidge did his bit in the 1920 campaign, a bit that turned out to be less than that of Harding, Cox, or Roosevelt. Coolidge opened his campaign in New England, speaking before the Republican Club of Massachusetts on August 12. Indeed, whatever campaigning he did in August and September was spoken in Yankee accents to Yankees. He later appeared before the Associated Republican Clubs of Massachusetts and the state's Republican League. In September he ventured outside the Bay State to speak in Portland, Maine, where he called upon the United States to associate with other nations in improving the human condition. At Manchester, New Hampshire, he promised that Republicans would give government by party instead of government dominated by one man. The rest of September he contented himself with giving four speeches, all in Massachusetts. He did not venture beyond New England until October, when he spoke in Philadelphia to urge a return to the commonplace in American life.

In October the Republican National Committee ordered him to make an eight-day tour of the South with Governor Lowden of Illinois and Governor Morrow of Kentucky. Coolidge protested the order to both Harding and National Chairman Hays, "because I ought not to be away so long from Massachusetts and because my abilities do not lie in that direction."[7] Despite his protest, the National Committee's command stood. To the Yankee had fallen the task of conducting his party's campaign in the South and particularly to support the efforts of John J. Parker and Alf Taylor to win the governorships, respectively, of North Carolina and Tennessee. During the day Coolidge usually spoke from his train's observation platform and at night he starred at indoor rallies. He devoted himself to praising common sense, calling for its return to the federal government, and urging patriotism. "Thrift and industry," "work and save" were Coolidge's stock phrases. After the southern tour, he arrived in New York City, October 28, to urge the establishment of an association of nations and to lead a night parade up Fifth Avenue. He then went to Massachusetts, where he closed his campaign with a couple of speeches in Boston.

Coolidge's campaign had been neither extensive, eloquent, nor news shattering. He had been on the Republican ticket as ballast. He had done what he had been told. He had supported the head of the ticket as best he could. Murray Crane had hoped that the governor would help commit the party to ratification of the Versailles Treaty with minor reservations. In fact, Crane had told a newsman at Coolidge's Notification Day, "More will be heard about the League of Nations from now on."[8]

The old gentleman should have known better. Coolidge was a party man. As he later wrote of 1920, "Not being the head of the ticket, of course, it was not my place to raise issues or create policies."[9] Moreover, Coolidge was as tight-lipped as Crane himself, the kind of man unlikely to amend Harding's statements subtly. Yet Crane had hopes that Coolidge would do something. The Massachusetts governor tried to gratify his mentor. He spoke favorably of the general idea of the League in his acceptance speech and again at Portland. At Crane's urging, Coolidge, while visiting Marion, tried to steer the head of the Republican ticket in the "right" direction. Coolidge did deplore "Wilson's League," but he also went out of his way to approve international cooperation to preserve peace. The Harding-Coolidge position was, the governor said, to eliminate "what is bad" in the League and to adopt "what is good."[10] Coolidge's efforts, a wisp of Murray Crane's convictions, were insufficient to smoke Harding out on the issue.

Crane had been failing in health for some time and in fact had collapsed at Coolidge's notification ceremonies. Death came to the old leader on October 2. Without Crane to urge him on, Coolidge soon slipped to simple endorsement of Harding's ambiguities on the League. Coolidge was to inherit W. Murray Crane's organization but not the courage of his convictions on international affairs.

Of course, Coolidge was to delve into other issues during the campaign. James Cox's aggressiveness was labeled by the Massachuetts governor as being characterized by "coarser and coarser methods, wilder and wilder charges."[11] Coolidge's campaign generally was hinged on the idea that it was time for a change in national government. That change was to be from a government pictured as being run by an arrogant, visionary commander in chief to a sound, conservative administration guided by traditional Americanism and fair play. Coolidge also tried to get across the idea that the Republicans offered the best chance of implementing the League idea. Wilsonian intransigence could not succeed in doing it, but Harding's equanimity could. That idea was well stated by Speaker Gillett when he said, ". . . under President Harding an agreement will be reached between the Senate and the President which will preserve for us the features of the treaty which will make for permanent peace."[12]

November 2 was Warren Gamaliel Harding's birthday. It was also the day when 25 million Americans went to the polls. Harding was given a stupendous birthday present, overwhelming election as President of the United States. The man who looked like a President would now become President and along with him Calvin Coolidge would become Vice President. It was not unexpected. Coolidge had already written a friend that the ticket would be flooded into office on "something more than a landslide."[13] The Harding-Coolidge ticket received almost twice as many votes as did Cox and Roosevelt, and the Electoral College vote was even more lopsided, 404 to 127. Thirty-seven states went Republican, and Democratic strongholds like Boston and New York City succumbed.

Harding and Coolidge had benefited from the calming images they had projected to the American public. More importantly, they had also been the beneficiaries of adverse reaction to the coldness and stubbornness of Woodrow Wilson, the identification of the Democrats with liquor at a time of high dry sentiment, the outrage of nationalists and of hyphenate groups like Irish-Americans at Wilson's foreign policies, and what Arthur S. Link has called "the fragmentation of the progressive movement."[14] The combination of first inflation and then recession after the war had further spurred people to seek a change. It is also probable that women, voting for the first time in 1920, found Harding more attractive than Cox and that labor was willing to punish the Democrats for their lack of sympathy even if it meant voting for a man, Harding, who consorted with business leaders. Moreover, the dependence of many hyphenate groups on manufacturing for a livelihood pushed them toward trying the Republican party's high tariff and sound money panaceas. Their lot could not be worse, many of them believed, than it had been during the immediate postwar period. In short, the Republicans owed their great victory to Wilson's failure to achieve the better nation and better world of which he had so often talked.

14

A Capital Character

CALVIN COOLIDGE WAS now Vice President-elect of the United States and retiring governor of the Commonwealth of Massachusetts. As the latter there was little left for him to do. He had to tidy up the few remaining affairs of state, attend to the few ceremonial tasks expected of him, and sit tight until his successor, Lieutenant Governor Channing Cox, was inaugurated in January. As Vice President-elect there was much for Coolidge to do. He was his state's man of the hour and as such received a good deal of attention. Northampton held a great celebration in his honor, Boston feted and fed him at a number of luncheons and dinners, and he was even invited to New York City to speak.

While he was in the limelight in the Northeast, he made a few headline-grabbing pronouncements. He told a group of Boston businessmen that the election results had to be considered a rebuke to organized labor, and in New York, perhaps to even the score, he condemned what he saw as loosened morality in business affairs. His swan song in the affairs of New England was a plea toward the end of December to merge the region's railways for the sake of efficiency.

In December Coolidge also was extended the courtesy of hospitality and briefing on plans for the new Administration by Senator Harding. Calvin and Grace Coolidge traveled to Marion, Ohio, to be received by President-elect and Mrs. Harding. There Coolidge was casually informed of Harding's plans to reduce taxes and revise the tariff. More specifically the New Englander was told of deliberations about appointments to the Cabinet and, in an unprecedented move, was invited to sit in on Cabinet meetings, an invitation which he accepted.[1]

On the day of Channing Cox's inauguration as governor in January, 1921, Coolidge checked his office to make sure he had left nothing behind, and then, as was customary for a departing governor, he left before the ceremonies began. As the artillery pieces on the Boston Common were saluting the new governor, the Coolidges were preparing to board the day coach that would take them home to Northampton. For the next three weeks Coolidge occupied himself with seeing friends, answering correspondence, and boning up on what a Vice President does. Then he and Mrs. Coolidge traveled south to Atlanta, where he addressed the Southern Tariff Association on the need for tariff revisions. Afterward they spent two weeks in Asheville, North Carolina, vacationing and enjoying the southern sunshine. Back in Northampton the middle of February, the family devoted itself to straightening up affairs there and preparing for the trip to the national capital. Coolidge appointed Edward Taylor Clark, formerly Senator Lodge's aide, to be his secretary. At the end of the month the family left, receiving a rousing send-off from a crowd of neighbors and friends.

The Coolidges had faced some agonizing moments about moving to Washington. There was even a question whether the entire family would leave Northampton. Housing posed the chief problem. Coolidge's salary was to be twelve thousand dollars a year, an attempt to increase it to fifteen thousand dollars having been defeated in December. Also quickly scuttled had been a move to furnish the Vice President with an official residence. After looking over the housing situation in Washington, Coolidge decided that on the Vice President's salary he could not afford to rent or buy a suitable house, and when Frank Stearns offered to lease one for him, he spurned the proposal. Instead he sent his sons away to school at Mercersburg Academy in Pennsylvania and took over the eight-dollar-a-day suite of the retiring Vice President, Thomas Marshall, in the New Willard Hotel. In that suite of two bedrooms, a dining room, and a reception room, Grace and Calvin Coolidge were to live during his days as

Vice President. There they could live comfortably at a somewhat fashionable address and could entertain as was necessary, with the help of the hotel's catering service.

When the Coolidges arrived in Washington they were met at the train by Vice President and Mrs. Marshall. The incoming and outgoing Vice Presidents visited together and Marshall, the soul of nineteenth-century courtesy, tried to brief Coolidge on the rigors and rewards of the job. When later the Hardings arrived at Union Station, the Coolidges met them and then the two couples rode in a White House automobile, placed at Harding's disposal by President Wilson, to the Willard to wait for Inauguration Day.

The morning of March 4 the Coolidges were escorted to the White House by a committee of members of Congress. The presidential and vice presidential parties then motored to the Capitol. There Woodrow Wilson, whose health was too poor for him to take part in the ceremonies, went out of his way to bid Coolidge a personal goodby. Then came time for the inaugural ceremonies, with first the new Vice President being sworn in, in the Senate chamber, and a while later the new President being inducted at the East Portico.

The Senate was in an uproar, trying to finish its business before the inaugurals began and hampered by the chatter of visitors in the galleries. The gallery noise became so bothersome that at one point Senator Lodge had to ask the president pro tempore to admonish the guests of the Senate to stop their conversations. At 11:45 a.m. Speaker Gillett and the other members of the House of Representatives arrived to take their places. When the speaker took his seat to the left of Vice President Marshall, who had meanwhile assumed his duties as presiding officer, the ambassadors, ministers, and chargés d'affaires accredited to Washington filed in to be seated. Then announced were General of the Army John J. Pershing, the Chief of Naval Operations, the Army Chief of Staff, and the Major-General Commandant of the Marine Corps, who were immediately shown to their places. Then came the Chief Justice of the United States and the associate justices of the Supreme Court. Finally, the sergeant at arms, David J. Barry, announced the entrance of Calvin Coolidge and his congressional escort. The Vice President-elect was shown to a seat at the right of Vice President Marshall. Then, breaking precedent, the President-elect and his official party entered to observe the ceremony of the inauguration of a new Vice President. Marshall and

Coolidge rose and faced each other and the retiring Vice President gave the oath of office to his successor. Marshall then delivered a short address of farewell to the outgoing Sixty-sixth Congress before adjourning it.

No sooner had the old Congress been closed when new Vice President Coolidge convened the Sixty-seventh Congress. After calling the Senate chamber to order and after the prayer, Coolidge gave the traditional address, in this case a rather brief and unimpressive one. He began with a sentence clumsily patterned after the opening of Abraham Lincoln's Gettysburg Address: "Senators, five generations ago there was revealed to the people of this nation a new relationship between man and man, which they declared and proclaimed in the American Constitution."[2] The burden of the Vice President's message was that a legislative body was an important bulwark of America's liberties. At the conclusion of Coolidge's address, the assembled company trooped out to the East Portico, where President Harding was inaugurated and gave an address that, though not outstanding among inaugural speeches, easily outstripped his Vice President's address.

Coolidge's big day had come and gone. He was now duly installed in the second office of the land. His perquisites were few. He had an official automobile, a Cadillac inherited from Vice President Marshall. He also had a chauffeur, a secretary, a clerk, and an assistant clerk. The question of an official residence for the Vice President soon came up again, but Congress failed to act on it.

Coolidge's constitutional duties as Vice President were light, and he carried them out in a singularly undistinguished and, with one exception, uncontroversial manner. He cast no vote to break a tie. Unlike most of his predecessors and successors, he made no remarks on Senate policy and therefore did not stamp his personality on the office either as a wit, as had Thomas Marshall, or as a political force, as was Charles Dawes. Indeed, Coolidge rarely made any remarks not strictly called for by his duty and whatever he said was spoken as succinctly as possible. His comments were almost entirely of the nature of "The Senate will be in order," "The amendment will be read," "The bill will be passed over," and "Does the senator from ――――yield to the senator from――――?"

Once when the members of the Senate were yelling at one another, a senior senator called upon Coolidge to pound his gavel to restore order. Amid the confusion the Vice President answered, "I will if they become really excited."[3] His unwillingness to get involved was partly natural and partly because he felt intimidated by what he later called the "one fixed rule" of the Senate, "that the Senate would do anything it wanted to do whenever it wanted to do it."[4]

He who had been such a success as presiding officer of the senate of a major state was almost a nonentity in the world's greatest deliberative body. Composed as it was of ninety-six personalities who were awed neither by each other nor by a mere Vice President, the Senate overshadowed and overawed Coolidge. Duff Gilfond put it well:

A reverer of silence, he was here subjected to an oratorical cannonade from noon to nightfall that must have tickled the devil; a deliberative man, he was in a position where quick decisions are vital; a self-sufficient man, he was obliged to bask in the simpers and smirks of official society.[5]

Coolidge did his job as best he could, but he did not fall into the spirit of it. He has said that he "did not waste much time on the . . . rules."[6] For that he relied on the assistant to the secretary of the Senate. He used his power to recognize speakers in a way that he thought would most benefit his party's regulars and leaders. In the business of the Senate he assumed responsibility for assigning petitions from the territories to committees. He also on occasion wound up with a "hot potato," for example, when he, for lack of other sponsors, presented the petition of "sundry citizens" for legislation to release those accused or convicted of sedition.

He twice encountered trouble. Soon after the Congress met in April, 1921, Coolidge was chided by Senator Oscar Underwood for not fully stating a pending question, a mistake the Vice President never again made. More important was his one controversial action in the Senate. One of the great issues of the 1920s was that of providing relief to the American farmer. The conversion from war to peace was painful to farmers, most of whom saw their purchasing power dwindle rapidly. Senator George W. Norris of Nebraska had introduced a bill to ease marketing of American agricultural surpluses abroad. This had been countered in late July, 1921, by an

Administration bill designed to facilitate domestic marketing. Senator Frank B. Kellogg of Minnesota was to introduce that measure at a key point in the debate of Norris' bill. Forewarned, the Nebraska lawmaker went to Coolidge to ask him to recognize Senator Joseph E. Ransdell first in the debate, which the Vice President agreed to do.

When the time came, however, Coolidge left the Senate, installing the most regular of regular Republicans, Senator Charles G. Curtis, in the chair. Ransdell jumped to his feet, shouting for recognition, but Curtis announced, "The chair recognizes the senator from Minnesota." Kellogg, taken off guard, had not yet asked for recognition. While Ransdell was shouting, Curtis had to call out three times that Kellogg was recognized before the Minnesotan rose to introduce the Administration's farm measure. Coolidge then strolled back into the chamber.[7]

The effect of the incident was to kill the chances for adoption of Norris' bill, and the progressive Republicans and their Democratic allies were infuriated with the Vice President for having reneged on his promise. He had decided to be an instrument of the Administration, but it was at the cost of his integrity as far as many senators were concerned. The episode may have doomed Coolidge to be an outsider for the rest of his time as Vice President and even have contributed to his troubles with Congress while he was President. He was now distrusted by the progressives and perhaps even disliked by the regulars for violating one of the unwritten rules of the Senate.

As Vice President, Coolidge had other incidental duties. Ceremonial occasions placed demands upon him as the Senate and the President assigned him to lay wreaths and unveil statues. That he did not particularly like because it intruded on his time, but he could carry it off well, being able to look as solemn and as dignified as an owl. He also frequently made speeches, some of which he gave as a representative of the Administration and others he delivered in order to supplement his pay as Vice President.

Most of his speeches were reviews of the glory of America's history, interspersed with injunctions to follow the moral right and with defenses of the Administration. In these talks Coolidge revealed himself to be a master of platitudes. He said at the unveiling of a bust of President Harding at Niles, Ohio, in June, 1921:

To such a leader, granted again by Providence, giving such wise counsel, inspiring such great confidence, accomplishing such results, holding the promise of such future benefits, we dedicate this day a memorial made in his likeness. But in what spirit do we dedicate it? How can we worthily consecrate it? How can we approach to that high standard here so nobly represented? There is but one method, already indicated, the price of continuing sacrifice.[8]

Coolidge was platitudinous, but he gave full support to the President in his speeches around the nation. And the solemn Yankee lent respectability to Harding's government and its policies.

Coolidge could also unbend on occasion and enjoy his speaking chores. Speaking at the Plymouth, Massachusetts, Tercentenary, he followed Senator Lodge, who had said that although he had addressed the Plymouth Society at length before, he had not "fully covered the subject, so I am coming back to discuss the further historical significance of Plymouth." When Coolidge's turn came to speak, he said with some relish, "I likewise was present on the occasion the senior senator so eloquently refers to and I also spoke on that occasion, but unlike him, I exhausted the subject."[9] Although he only occasionally liked his speaking duties, Coolidge recognized that they conferred personal benefits on him. His speaking, as he pointed out, "took me about the country in travels that reached from Maine to California, from the Twin Cities to Charleston. I was getting acquainted."[10]

Coolidge had one other duty and that was to be a helpmeet to the President. Harding had promised the Vice President a role in the Administration and, true to his word, he had Coolidge sit with the Cabinet. As it turned out, however, Coolidge was not the "real, vital contact between the executive and legislative branches"[11] that the President and his alter ego, Harry M. Daugherty, had envisioned. At Cabinet meetings the Vice President sat at the far end of the table, looking like a spectator. Harding always gave him the opportunity to speak after the others had done so, but his comments were unenlightening. A typical one was, "Well, I don't see anything we can do about the railroad situation."[12] Although one can be sure that he let none of the Cabinet's doings escape him, Coolidge was not a force in its deliberations.

Nor was the Vice President a force in the Harding Administration. He did what he could on Capitol Hill to support the government's proposals. But that was unimportant, for he had little influence among the senators and after his experience with the Norris farm bill he was most cautious in using his power of recognition. Outside the Senate he spoke frequently to support the Harding Administration, but not in words and accents that thrilled his audiences or caused reverberations over the country. He was rarely consulted by Harding, perhaps because he was so unassertive that he was easily overlooked, perhaps because of Mrs. Harding's condescending attitude toward him, but probably because he was not the kind to warm to the President or to warm the President to him. About the only record of his influence at the White House concerned Massachusetts, for which he was able to get some patronage, though his influence was not as great as Senator Lodge's.[13]

Coolidge's public work gives only limited insight to the man while he served as Vice President. He had a private life and attitudes that help round out the story. During 1921, 1922, and 1923 he gathered a small reputation for being a man who attended to his business calmly and with little fanfare. He also got the reputation of a capital character, the reputation of Silent Cal. It has been said that he cultivated it for political reasons, that by being silent and withdrawn in a city of halcyon oratory and breast-beating he could draw attention to himself. There is no evidence to support that view. On the contrary, his reserve was part of his nature. He also wanted to remain his own man. He wanted little involvement unless he had responsibility. Unlike his predecessors, he craved the right to decide what part of his life was public and what part was private. His insistence on a certain amount of privacy was no pose. He never had been one of the boys and he was not now. And yet becoming one of the boys would have been almost essential for his advancement in national politics, especially when he was overshadowed in Congress by two other Massachusetts men, House Speaker Frederick Gillett and Senator Henry Cabot Lodge.

The Vice President's life was simple. Here was a man who dwelled in four rooms in a hotel. He entertained only when it was imperative. He joined clubs, but seldom appeared. He refused to dash around Capitol Hill or Washington to make political contacts. If Coolidge were wanted, he could be found during working hours on the rostrum of the Senate or in his office, behind a large desk ornamented with his mother's photograph. After hours Coolidge made the necessary rounds of parties and dinners, in fact a large number of them because the Vice President's attendance, even that of an introverted Vice President, was *de rigueur*. At least in the beginning, he liked the parties, for as Grace Coolidge wrote Frank Stearns in 1921, "He is becoming quite a 'social butterfly.' "[14] Once when asked why he attended so many luncheons and dinners, Coolidge's wit came out. "Got to eat somewhere," was his reply.[15] Grace Coolidge also did her part, frequently accompanying her husband on his rounds and taking with grace and courtesy the many social calls made upon her. Moreover, she did not hide behind the prerogative of the Vice President's wife not to return them. Call she did in return, several hundred times a year. If Coolidge became known for his reserve, his wife established a reputation for manners and charm.

The Coolidges were rarely the center of attraction even where he was the highest ranking official present. It was easy to overlook a small Puritan among so many tall Cavaliers. The one time that he figured in gossip it was connected only with his office. That was early in 1923 when Mrs. John B. Henderson, the wife of a former senator from Missouri, offered her stately home and grounds as a residence for the Vice President on the condition that Congress accept it and appropriate funds for its maintenance. Mrs. Henderson's gracious offer was greeted with rage in one quarter. President Nicholas Murray Butler of Columbia University has recorded Mrs. Harding's reaction. When the question came up, she responded, almost shouting at the Butlers: "Not a bit of it, not a bit of it. I am going to have that bill defeated. Do you think I am going to have those Coolidges living in a house like that? An hotel apartment is plenty good enough for them."[16] Whether or not the First Lady was involved, the bill was defeated.

In all, Coolidge's was only a moderately busy life. He had a good deal of time on his hands and he did not use it to build a Coolidge clique either in the capital or in the national Republican party. He dipped into his spare time to maintain his rather high level of sleep, ten hours a night. Even then he had time to write, read, and even daydream. Most of his writing was invested in his many speeches, but he occasionally wrote articles. Most notable among them was the series of three pieces, entitled "Enemies of the Republic," which he wrote in 1921 for *The Delineator*. Those articles showed how far he had come since the Boston Police Strike, when he rarely mentioned radicalism. Now he felt called upon to warn the nation of Red proselyting on college campuses and elsewhere. It was a phase that was soon to pass for him. The Library of Congress had a regular customer in Coolidge, especially in books on history which he read, not only for enlightenment, but for use in his speeches, which almost always had an historical angle.

He rarely patronized the theater, and music, serious or otherwise, was beyond his ken. Literature, aside from history and biography, largely escaped him, as he read at most only three novels a year, mostly of low grade, and no poetry. He did follow current magazines and newspapers, such as the *Times* and the *Herald Tribune* of New York, the Baltimore *Sun,* and the Washington *Post.* He may not have been interested in the arts or inventive in ideas, but he probably was in those days one of the best informed men in the national government.

Coolidge had few friends or even close acquaintances. His aides were treated like employees, not junior colleagues, and his wife rarely shared his secrets and never was asked for advice. Frank Stearns wrote and visited often, and some Massachusetts acquaintances received generous treatment from the Vice President. Joseph Martin tells of the time he came as a tourist to Washington and Coolidge offered him his official car and chauffeur for sightseeing. Such spontaneous tokens of affection came seldom because few in Washington could call Coolidge friend and rarely did his old friends from either Massachusetts or Vermont come visiting. When they did, the Vice President in his own reserved way celebrated the occasion.

Coolidge seemed to feel better during his early vice presidential days, although his concern for his health continued to be high. Grace Coolidge wrote during the summer of 1921, "He hasn't looked fagged as he always did when it was hot in Boston."[17] It is probable that, released from the worries of the governorship and the problem of dividing his time between his work in Boston and his family in Northampton, he felt under less physical pressure. Yet he worried constantly about becoming tubercular and continued, as his wife said, to take "various sorts of pills upon slight provocation."[18]

He also prospered during his years in the capital. His income rose and he saved large amounts of it. His bank interest and stock dividends increased steadily, from $1,194 in 1921 to $10,483 in 1928, which would indicate cash investments of between $25,000 and $30,000 in 1921 and between $200,000 and $250,000 in 1928. Most of his capital was earned from his vice presidential and presidential salaries with the remainder coming from his small income from speeches, writings, and lands. One item of interest is that when he came to Washington in 1921 he borrowed money from the First National Bank and Hampshire County Trust Company in Northampton. Apparently he did that to finance his move to the capital on the principle that he would be further ahead paying a small amount of bank interest than by disturbing funds already comfortably invested.[19]

Coolidge was not a social delight, a party power, or a preeminent Vice President, but during his years in that office he became a minor legend. That legend was of a man who wore out capital hostesses who tried to make him talk, of a thrifty, even penurious man, of a man who did and said little because he believed in being as thrifty with his genius as with his money. He was different and it was noted all over town. Yet whatever people thought or said of Calvin Coolidge, they considered him only part of the passing scene. It was agreed that because of his difference he was not a coming force in national politics.

15

★ ★ ★ ★ ★

Vice President of What?

CALVIN COOLIDGE MAY NOT have had a fixed place in the nation's capital, but he did in Massachusetts. Several things contributed to that. Often a man who leaves his state to serve as Vice President of the United States fades as a political influence at home. The myth of the Coolidge luck helped him avoid that fate. Here was the man who should not have become the president of the Massachusetts senate, but through a stroke of fortune he did. Here was the man who should not have become lieutenant governor, at least not when he did, but luck again intervened. And here was the man who received the Republican vice presidential nomination by happenstance. His luck, many were certain, would hold up. In Northampton it was said, "I wouldn't give two cents for Warren Harding's life."[1] Fred Sterling, one of Frank O. Lowden's closest associates, wrote the Illinois statesman after a trip East in 1921, "Up in Boston Coolidge's friends seem to all think that Harding will not live his term out and that Cal's luck will pursue him into the White House."[2] After Coolidge's run of good fortune it would not do for anyone in Massachusetts to count him out of the state or national political scene.

There was another factor. After Murray Crane's death, the old boss' lieutenants needed a leader of state fame and national prominence through whom they could work. The trustworthy and lucky

Coolidge was the man to whom they looked to become their titular if not actual head. In the name of the Vice President the Crane men could and did demand a bigger voice in the affairs of the Massachusetts Republican party. In that they were immediately successful. When John Weeks resigned his post as national committeeman in 1921 to become secretary of war, they were able to elect as his replacement Crane's henchman William M. Butler, who readily became Coolidge's henchman. The iron-jawed Butler invoked Coolidge's name like a natural resource when in seeking the committeeman's post he declared that he wanted it to protect the Vice President's political future. It is also probable that Coolidge's name was used in matters with which he had nothing to do. When Frank Stearns wrote of grumbling against him in Boston, he replied: "I do not understand the attitude of certain persons in Boston. I supposed I was here keeping quiet and doing what I could do without harming anyone."[3] Whether or not the Vice President was keeping quiet in Washington, his name was used as a weapon in Massachusetts politics.

A third factor working in Coolidge's favor was that he was widely credited with giving Massachusetts' Republicans the greatest victory they had ever had. In 1920 the Harding-Coolidge ticket swept the state by 681,000 to 276,000 votes for the Cox-Roosevelt slate, with the result that Republican candidates for state offices were carried to victory by unusually large margins and that the party elected two additional representatives to give them fourteen of Massachusetts' sixteen congressional seats. Even those who were skeptical of Coolidge's political magic were unwilling to take chances. Therefore most Republicans deferred to the Vice President on state matters. Coolidge made it easy for them to do so, for compared with Lodge, the head of the opposing faction, he was almost jolly.

The final and most important factor in keeping Coolidge alive as a political force in Massachusetts was the power of his faction. The Crane machine controlled not only the Vice Presidency, the speakership of the United States House of Representatives, and the national committeeman's place, but also the state administration under Governor Channing Cox. The Crane protégés, out of common sense and out of habit, stuck together, and Coolidge as the top-ranking factional leader benefited from their cohesiveness and their power.

Coolidge responded to the requests of his faction for help. Because he had gone to Washington, and perhaps into political limbo, did not mean that he no longer felt obligations to those with whom he had worked for so many years. When the faction called, he answered. That meant that he would return to Massachusetts in 1922 to be identified with his fellow heirs of Uncle Murray and to campaign for them. Moreover, when they called for crowding Henry Cabot Lodge out of power over the state party machinery, Coolidge went along, no matter how friendly he and the senator had become. It was, however, not something that would split the party. Most of the adherents of Coolidge and Lodge were sensible enough to keep their differences in the Republican family. When Lodge was renominated for senator in 1922 he knew that he faced a tough campaign for re-election and he called upon the Vice President for help. He came and contributed to Lodge's re-election. Coolidge was, after all, a party regular and, as Frank Stearns told him, it never hurt him to get out to see the people.

The Vice President got a kick out of going back to Massachusetts to campaign and to visit with old friends in the fall of 1922. It was a welcome break from Washington life. Congress had been in session almost continuously since April, 1921, and after the election would soon reconvene. At first Coolidge had enjoyed presiding over the Senate and even liked the pageantry connected with official life in Washington, but as time went by he gave the appearance of being bored. Certainly life in the nation's capital was less challenging for him than it had been in Massachusetts. Although he was seldom treated discourteously, he was not an insider and his nature and position were not such to push him into the forefront of either administrative or legislative affairs.

His routine was to preside unobtrusively over the Senate, to sit almost silently in Cabinet meetings, and to make the social rounds in the capital. That was punctuated by his travels over the country to make speeches or to be present on ceremonial occasions. He had no escape valve for the frustrations he must have felt, for he had few, if any, friends with whom he could talk and certainly he would never dream of discussing such things with Grace. He continued to worry about his health. He suffered from hay fever and perhaps bronchial asthma. For years he had been bothered by frequent attacks of indigestion. His eating habits were not to be recommended to anyone. A regular attender of banquets and one who craved indigestible foods like peanuts, pancakes, and crackers dripping with preserves would have trouble. His ailments must have been added to by nervous tension, for the reserved and unathletic New Englander could not release his frustrations in any healthy way. Whatever release he got came in the form of tantrums, the brunt of which his wife bore. Anything that was unexpected could lead him to prolonged moods of sulking and even to fits of yelling.

Coolidge's ill temper probably was an indication that life was not going the way he had hoped. For a man who craved honor and service, the Vice Presidency was turning out to be a mockery. He might have derived some satisfaction from comparing himself favorably with the President and with some of the members of the Senate. But that was not enough to satisfy him. The stories circulating that he was keen and sly must have pleased him except that they were countered by other stories that he was shallow and obvious. Most frustrating was that he was not the kingpin, the center of power in the United States Senate as he had been in the Massachusetts senate. Indeed he appeared in the federal Senate as though he had never before had legislative experience. Moreover, he did not have the magnetism to draw senators toward him, and his prior acquaintances in the Senate, like Lodge of Massachusetts and Dillingham of Vermont, did little to make friends for the Vice President.

Duff Gilfond tells a story that, though a bit exaggerated, strikes toward the truth of Coolidge's position in the Senate:

> In the senators' restaurant where the great consolidator, the table, wipes out the dissension and division of the floor, Mr. Coolidge appeared timidly, slipped off into a corner and ate, facing the wall. Nobody in that scene of clatter and chatter joined him.
>
> "Is that how you treat your presiding officer?" asked a Representative of Senator Ladd.
>
> "Nobody has anything to do with him," said the Senator in a mournful tone. "After this, of course, he's through."[4]

That that was not completely the invention of an imaginative journalist is testified to by Senator Henry F. Ashurst, the soul of integrity. Early in 1923 the Arizonan confided to his diary that the Senate Republicans were looking for someone else to nominate for Vice President the following year.

Even with the public, at least outside of Massachusetts, Coolidge was a cipher. Another story, told by Coolidge himself, indicates that. There was a small fire at the New Willard Hotel and, for safety's sake, all the guests were ordered down from their rooms. After it appeared that the danger had passed, Coolidge started up to his suite.

A fire marshal challenged him, "Who are you?"

"I'm the vice president," responded Coolidge.

"All right, go ahead," he was told.

Before taking more than a few steps upstairs, Coolidge was again challenged by the marshal. "What are you vice president of?"

The answer was, "I am vice president of the United States."

"Come right down," declared the fire official. "I thought you were the vice president of the hotel."[5]

The winter of 1922–23 was the season of Coolidge's political despair. The winding up of the Sixty-seventh Congress had not been any more joyful to the Vice President than had been the previous sessions. It is true that Harding, during an illness, had shown enough confidence in Coolidge to have him deliver the President's address at the annual budget meeting. But that was only momentarily satisfying. More appealing was that the end of Congress in early March, 1923, meant a long respite for Coolidge. Perhaps when he returned in December he could summon new energy and zest for his job.

After bidding President Harding good-by on March 4, Coolidge and Grace took a few days' vacation at Hot Springs, Virginia, and then went to Northampton to the humble duplex on Massasoit Street, which now seemed large after the long confinement to Suite 328–332 at the Willard. They remained in Northampton for several months, with the Vice President leaving only to fulfill some speaking engagements. In July the Coolidges went to Vermont to vacation and to help Colonel John with the farm. The boys, John and Calvin, were set to work at hire in the area. The Vice President's sons were not to be pampered. That July, Coolidge began to feel better, braced by contacts with the homefolks and by work out-of-doors. Things would look better, he believed, when he returned to Washington.

16

★ ★ ★ ★ ★

To Wake Up a President

O N AUGUST 2, 1923, Calvin Coolidge was out haying with a
neighbor. He had set himself to operating a horse rake to finish
the chore. After a hearty meal and a little conversation, the Coolidge
family retired at 9 p.m. Soon the Vice President, tired from a day in
the fields, sank into a deep sleep. Across the continent, in San Francisco, the President of the United States was sinking into the deepest
of sleeps, never again to awake.

Warren G. Harding had left Washington in June to combine
business with pleasure in a sweep across the country. Upon his
return from a visit to Alaska in late July Harding came down ill,
reportedly from eating bad sea food. His speaking engagements in
Portland, Oregon, were canceled and his train went through to San
Francisco, where the ailing President was treated for a cardiac condition. Newsmen were sent to be near Coolidge just in case the
President died. Harding seemed to improve in San Francisco, so
much so that by the afternoon of August 2 he was considered to be
out of danger. That evening, however, he suffered a relapse and died
within a few minutes.

The news spread quickly. A reporter called Henry Cabot Lodge
to ask for a comment. The newspaperman told the senator of Harding's death, but before he could put his question Lodge exclaimed:
"My God! That means Coolidge is President!"[1]

Plymouth Notch was one of the last places in the land to receive the news. Colonel John Coolidge had refused to have a telephone and the nearest one was in Miss Florence Cilley's store across the road. When word of President Harding's death arrived at the telegraph office in Bridgewater, the station nearest to Plymouth, attempts were made to reach Miss Cilley, but the jangling telephone failed to arouse her. The Bridgewater telegrapher, Winfred A. Perkins, put on his clothes, grabbed the message of Harding's death, and sought out Coolidge's staff, which was staying in the small town. Erwin C. Geisser, the Vice President's stenographer, and Joseph N. McInerney, his chauffeur, accompanied by newspaperman William H. Crawford, raced over the bumpy country roads in Coolidge's official car to take the telegram to Plymouth Notch. They pulled up in front of John Coolidge's place and went up to rap on the door. The noise awakened the Colonel, who slept in a downstairs room. Upon finding out who was knocking, he opened the door. Then Colonel Coolidge learned that Harding was dead. He climbed upstairs, calling in a trembling voice, "Calvin! Calvin!"

Coolidge woke up immediately. His father handed him the telegram and, addressing him as "Mr. President," told him that Harding had passed away. Calvin and Grace Coolidge dressed. Tears came to Mrs. Coolidge's eyes as she did so. Coolidge's first thought, and not a flip one, was "I believe I can swing it."[2] Before going downstairs the Coolidges knelt. The new President asked God's blessing on the nation's people and for the strength to serve them, a prayer he was frequently to repeat during his years in the White House.

When he came downstairs he sent a message of sympathy to Mrs. Harding and dictated a public statement. By then the house was lit up with the illumination of oil lamps and became a beacon over the countryside. Reporters who had stayed near Coolidge during Harding's illness had already arrived in the Notch. They were told of Coolidge's telegram to Mrs. Harding and were given his statement in which he expressed his mourning for his "Chief and friend" and declared his wish to continue Harding's appointees in office.

Coolidge had been urged in a telegram from Attorney General Daugherty to take the oath of office as soon as possible. He examined the Constitution to determine what qualifications were necessary to receive the oath. He concluded that he filled the bill and that the presidential oath was the same as that he had taken as Vice President. Most of the reporters had left to rush word to their newspapers of Coolidge's first reactions to becoming President and in doing so they missed the biggest story of the new day.

After they had left, Coolidge, in the company of the young editor of the Springfield *Reporter,* Joseph H. Fountain, Congressman Porter H. Dale, and his political associate L. L. Lane, walked across the road to Miss Cilley's store. There he was put on the telephone with Secretary of State Charles Evans Hughes who urged him to take the oath of office immediately. "It should be taken before a notary," said the secretary.

Coolidge replied, "Father is a notary."

"That's fine," Hughes said.[3]

The ceremony took place in the sitting room. There gathered Representative Dale, Lane, Fountain, Geisser, McInerney, and Crawford. The three Coolidges joined them. It was a memorable scene. The fourteen-by-seventeen-foot room was the essence of rural America. Under its eight-foot ceiling the assembled company stood on a worn Wilton rug amid the furnishings of a wood stove, with its pipe running along the ceiling, a rocker, two straight chairs, a marble-topped table, and a desk. The oil lamp on the table cast its pale light onto the faded wallpaper.

Standing to his full height of five feet, nine inches, Coolidge raised his right hand. Then his father, dressed in his black Sunday clothes, gave the oath, phrase by phrase, which his son repeated after him. "I, Calvin Coolidge," it began, and finished when the new President intoned, "So help me God!" Coolidge then signed the typewritten form of the oath, as the rococo clock on the mantel showed 2:47 a.m., and John Coolidge affixed his notary's seal. Calvin Coolidge then retired to salvage what he could of his night's rest.

While the President slept, soundly he said the next morning, Lane and several others kept guard. Only Lane, a railway mail official, was armed. Representative Dale had gone off to make arrangements for Coolidge's return to Washington. Secret Service operative Alphonso L. McCormack sped through the night by car from Boston to take up the protection of the new President. Often there were stirrings about the house as reporters came again, as the curious arrived to look at the President's home, and as telephone linemen worked to put a phone into the Coolidge place.

The oil lamps again lit the house, before six, as Coolidge arose to prepare for the trip to the national capital. In his shirtsleeves he shaved and then put on his shoes, collar, tie, and coat. After breakfast he and Grace opened the door to leave. Coolidge observed that a stone step up to the porch had been knocked askew and turned to his father, saying "Better have that fixed."[4] The President and his lady entered an awaiting car and drove off. They had not gone a hundred yards when Coolidge ordered the automobile stopped by the family cemetery. There he got out and walked to his mother's grave, where he stood silently and reverently for a while. "Some way, that morning, she seemed very near to me," he later wrote.[5]

The presidential party boarded a day coach at Rutland, later switching to a private Pullman car at Albany, New York. Frank Stearns and Edward T. Clark joined the party at New York City. At every stop the President went out to wave to the crowds that had assembled, to give them assurance. He arrived in Washington that night at nine, to be met by the pastor of the First Congregational Church, Dr. Jason Noble Pierce, whom he had requested to be at the station. The following Sunday, without fuss or publicity, he joined a church for the first time in his life.

Meanwhile, another presidential train started its journey. Harding's special had been converted into a funeral train and was making its way across the continent. Crowds of people stood silently at every crossroad and station. Mourning filled the land and grief was displayed for the popular Harding. Time after time his favorite hymn, "My Redeemer Liveth," was played and sung along the route of the train. He was on his way, for the last time, to Washington, where his body would lie in state before being removed to Marion, Ohio, for burial.

When Coolidge arrived in Washington, he and Secretary of State Hughes began making plans for Harding's funeral. The new President issued, in his first state action, a proclamation of national mourning for Harding. The days that followed were busy. Coolidge found that his father, as a state official, was probably ineligible to administer the oath of office to a federal officer. Attorney General Daugherty therefore advised the President to take another oath. That was given by Judge A. A. Hoehling of the District of Columbia Supreme Court at Coolidge's rooms in the Willard. No publicity was given the event, probably for fear that it would take the edge off the impression of the first oath-taking, the simplicity of which, as Senator Ashurst said, had "fired the public imagination."[6]

Coolidge soon received the press in his hotel suite, telling them: "I am glad to meet you. I want you to know the executive offices will be open as far as possible, so that you may get any information your readers may be interested to have. This is your government. You can be very helpful in the administration of it."[7] He promised to hold news conferences twice weekly. Although Coolidge was not to be a great favorite of the press, he showed that he knew its importance and intended to make full use of it.

The new Chief Executive acted immediately to fortify himself politically. When he arrived in Washington, he summoned Speaker Gillett and Senate Whip Charles Curtis, telling them he wanted a secretary who comprehended the political work of the President's office and knew Congress and its members. Whom would they recommend? Gillett and Curtis along with Secretary of War John Weeks chose C. Bascom Slemp, a veteran Virginia congressman and southern Republican leader. Slemp accepted appointment with the understanding that his work would concern Coolidge's nomination and election as President. The Brooklyn *Daily Eagle* observed that "Washington today knows that Calvin Coolidge is a candidate." The ironies of the appointment were as interesting as its significance. As Bascom Slemp was a millionaire it was a case of a poor President being served by a rich secretary. It was also a case of two taciturn men being thrown together. As the New York *Times* commented: "One can imagine each of them waiting for the other to speak. There should be eloquent long silences."[8]

Coolidge also worked to organize the new Administration. He soon got in touch with the members of the Cabinet and their deputies. Except for Secretary of War Weeks they knew very little of the new President. That was mirrored in the diary of Assistant Secretary of the Navy Theodore Roosevelt, Jr., who wrote: "Coolidge becomes President. In so far as I am concerned, he is a sealed book. I know nothing of him. I have no personal relationship with him at all. I don't believe he has any personal relationship with anyone in the Cabinet. I do not know his policies. Though I sat for more than two months in the Cabinet with him I have never heard him express his opinion on major questions."[9]

Coolidge moved swiftly to get into working relations with the executive officers, not only to take advantage of their knowledge of government affairs, but also because he felt under obligation to keep Harding's appointees on at least until the end of the term. The new Chief Executive made it clear that he wanted them to remain in office. When the secretary of the treasury, Andrew Mellon, came to present his resignation in order to give the President freedom in selecting his subordinates, Coolidge turned him aside adroitly. He greeted Mellon cordially and then plunged into a discussion of the government's financial system. The Secretary became so engrossed in it that he left without having offered his resignation. Flustered, he re-entered Coolidge's office saying, "Mr. President, I neglected to tell you that I had come to resign."

"Forget it," replied the President.[10]

Advice was needed by Coolidge and to gain it he saw a large number of people, Cabinet members and others, to discuss government and political affairs. One of the most interesting of those conferences was with George H. Harvey, who was on leave from his post as ambassador to Great Britain. Seeing Harvey was a wise move because he was an astute, effective, and even dangerous politician. That both men were Vermonters helped the President in enlisting the ambassador's aid. Coolidge asked him for his estimate of the general political situation, and Harvey told the President that he was in a fortunate position, for he would inherit whatever credit Harding had earned for his government's accomplishments but would not be held responsible for any cause of resentment against the Administration. Coolidge also asked him for information on the World Court. Harvey, who was no friend of the Court, advised Coolidge to delay taking a stand because it was a lively issue in the Republican party. About Europe generally, the ambassador said that affairs there were fluid. There was no reason for the United States "to inject itself into the situation."[11] Coolidge followed Harvey's advice for the time being.

Of course, of immediate attention to Coolidge were the ceremonies connected with the burial of President Harding. Funeral services were conducted in Washington on August 7 and then the body was transported to Marion for burial. Coolidge and most of the high officials of the government accompanied Harding on his last journey and attended the burial services in Ohio. On the way back Coolidge was the target of a scramble of politicians for favor and

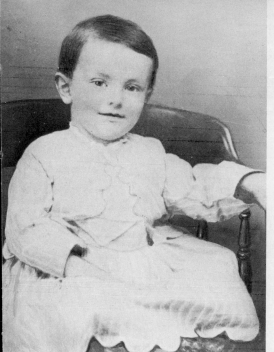

Calvin Coolidge at age three seems to look upon the world with equanimity and optimism.
Calvin Coolidge Memorial Room, Forbes Library, Northampton, Mass.

Colonel John C. Coolidge was a jack-of-all-trades. He was also, like his son, Calvin, a man of much character and little speech.
Calvin Coolidge Memorial Room, Forbes Library, Northampton, Mass.

In his teens Calvin Coolidge was very much the solemn and quiet lad shown here.

Calvin Coolidge Memorial Room,
Forbes Library, Northampton, Mass.

A dashing-looking Coolidge is seen in this photograph taken when he was an undergraduate at Amherst. The college opened the door to the world for the young man from rural Vermont.

Calvin Coolidge Memorial Room,
Forbes Library, Northampton, Mass.

Calvin Coolidge, as Vice President, with Grace and their two sons, John and Calvin, Jr. His love of family was deep, but his teasing was exasperating.

Calvin Coolidge Memorial Room,
Forbes Library, Northampton, Mass.

The Coolidge men never got too much hay down.
The Vice President is shown here, in his Vermont
farmer's smock, with his sons and his father.

Calvin Coolidge Memorial Room,
Forbes Library, Northampton, Mass.

Vice President-elect and Mrs. Coolidge greet the next
President, Warren G. Harding, and Mrs. Harding
upon their arrival at Washington's Union Station
before the inaugural ceremonies of March, 1921.

The Bettmann Archive

Harvey Firestone, Henry Ford, and
Thomas A. Edison, three symbols of technological progress, visit President Coolidge
in Vermont during the 1924 campaign.
Coolidge holds a sap bucket which he will
present to Ford.

Calvin Coolidge Memorial Room,
Forbes Library, Northampton, Mass.

The President and the Cabinet, 1923. Throughout his Presidency, Coolidge relied heavily on the department heads for advice and assistance.

Culver Pictures, Inc.

Attorney General Harry M. Daugherty. Public reaction to the exposure of his questionable actions and transactions in office, and his inability to explain them, led Coolidge to ask for his resignation in March, 1924.

Culver Pictures, Inc.

Calvin and Grace Coolidge out for a walk in Northampton, after retirement from the White House. Because of her vivacity, gentleness, patience, and tact, Mrs. Coolidge was an outstanding First Lady.

Calvin Coolidge Memorial Room,
Forbes Library,
Northampton, Mass.

Coolidge, in 1929, sitting with his dogs on the porch of 21 Massasoit Street in Northampton. He was soon to leave his old residence for the greater privacy and comfort of an estate called The Beeches.

Calvin Coolidge Memorial Room,
Forbes Library,
Northampton, Mass.

attention. Talk of patronage and of the 1924 national convention and election was unceasingly heard on the train. Chief Justice William Howard Taft was not so dignified that he did not participate in the scramble to talk with Coolidge. He passed on the news that Secretary of State Hughes, a former Republican nominee, had told him that under no circumstances would he run for President in 1924. Taft warned the new Chief Executive not to yield to pressures to make political patronage out of judicial appointments. The rotund Chief Justice and former President was, it would seem, only too willing to control judicial appointments himself and, at least intellectually, to be Coolidge's Warwick.

During this time the new Head of State was remarkably solicitous of the widowed Mrs. Harding. He personally arranged automobile transportation for her when aides had neglected to do so. When she returned from Ohio on August 11 Coolidge dined with her. She was assured that there was no hurry for her to leave the White House. In fact, as if to make certain, Coolidge allowed the executive mansion to stand vacant for almost four days between her departure and his family's moving in. It was a magnificent performance for the taciturn Yankee and for a man who knew how little Mrs. Harding had thought of him.

The Coolidges moved into the White House at 3 p.m., August 21. A new regime had begun. What did it portend?

17

★ ★ ★ ★ ★

═══════════

Different from the Rest

S OME OF THE NEW Administration's portents could be found in the man who had just become President. He was decidedly "not like the run of the herd," as William Allen White said in 1925.[1] Many of both his better and worse qualities were disguised by his reserve at a time when bonhomie and extroversion were prized. Feeling was, to him, something to be hidden. He would have agreed with fellow Vermonter Dorothy Canfield Fisher that "We are brought up on the old adage, 'Praise to the face / Is open disgrace.' "[2] And that went in both giving and receiving praise and in all emotions. Coolidge was and would continue to be silent in his relations with most people, sometimes rudely so. Yet under the cover of public silence he could be talkative and loving with his family and close friends. He could be kind and even spontaneously generous.

The new President was a man of extreme caution. He resisted making moves that might lead to trouble and he avoided making snap decisions. He kept his business, as well as his family life, confidential as long as possible. That secrecy extended even to some of his attainments, for example, his ability still to read Latin. Coolidge was also frugal with his money, though he was not so close that he did not contribute decently to church, Amherst, Republican, and other appeals. He was sparing in his activities. He had almost no pastimes when he assumed the presidential office, for those squandered time and energy. Moreover, he was not good at recreation of any kind and probably avoided them because he feared embarrassment.

Coolidge's thrift and caution were complete, encompassing his speech, money, activity, and ideas. His upbringing, his conservative nature, and his fear of intruding on other people dictated that nothing was to be wasted. As much as possible should be saved for a rainy day. That was related to his suspicious nature. The chief White House usher, Irwin "Ike" Hoover, was right when he wrote: "President Coolidge was different from all the rest. He seemed always to be watching, rather suspicious lest something be 'put over' on him."[3] He had to watch if he were to conserve himself and his substance.

It has been said that Calvin Coolidge had no political philosophy. That is far from the truth. His may not have been a sophisticated philosophy, but he had one. He had not been raised under the influence of Puritanism or studied under Anson Morse and Charles Garman without results. The foundation of Coolidge's philosophy was that the citizen had an obligation to serve, to do good works. Although Coolidge enjoyed political service and obviously prospered from it, he saw it as an example of a man performing his duty to God and society. He could conceive of men doing their duty in many ways, but for him the most important area of service was politics because that was the cement that held society together. And politics had to be democratic in order that the greatest opportunities for individual development and service be given and that the bidding of the people be done. There was a form that democracy had to take. The job of the legislators was to seek the people's will and put it into law. The people and their representatives had the task of expressing their will in accordance with the highest virtues. The job of the executive was to implement their will as expressed in the laws.

Coolidge's task as President was not to sound alarms, to make trouble, or to tell the people what to do. His was to follow their instructions as indicated in the Constitution and by the laws of Congress. Stability, unity, and harmony were the goals he was to strive to achieve for the nation. The economic corollary of that had been stated by Coolidge in 1919 when he said:

> We are reaching and maintaining the position . . . where the property class and the employed class are not separate, but

identical. There is a relationship of interdependence which makes their interests the same in the long run. . . . This is the ideal economic condition.[4]

Although he believed in encouraging business, it was not so much because he idolized big business as because he thought that it was the instrument most likely to lead Americans to economic interdependence, prosperity, social stability, and general individual development. That was the spirit that led him in January, 1924, to say that "the chief business of the American people is business."[5]

In a society of individual enterprise the role of the government was to encourage the right always and to act positively only if things went drastically wrong. Its role was not to run things but to help them run themselves. "Don't hurry to legislate" was the advice Coolidge had given the Massachusetts senate and it was a precept to which he still adhered. Do not speak, spend, or act unless absolutely necessary. That Coolidge believed in. When he did act, it was usually enough to do what was needed, and when he did speak, it was, as Frank B. Kellogg said, "without flourishes but in clear, distinct terms."[6] All that gave a forecast of what government under Coolidge would be. Despite its consequences, it was, after Presidents Wilson and Harding, the kind of government most of the American people wanted.

Calvin Coolidge made clear to the country and to official Washington that things were to be different. He may have disliked the bombast and pomposity of Harding, the vulgarity and the tinny gaiety that had surrounded him, but it was Coolidge's nature, not a calculated reaction to his predecessor, that caused a change in the tone of the Presidency. He had not assumed new personalities upon becoming mayor, senate president, lieutenant governor, governor, or Vice President. He would not change now and what was remarkable was that the public happily accepted his acting the way he did. Just by being himself, he made a contrast with Harding.

The change was immediate. Coolidge told Chief Usher Ike Hoover: "I don't want the public in our family rooms on the second floor so much as they have been. . . . I want things as they used to be—before!"[7] Here was a man who could naturally take the presidential façade back to the way it had been, dignified and solemn, under Wilson and McKinley. And back it went in short order. Alice

Roosevelt Longworth recalls that the first time she "went to the White House after the Coolidges were there, the atmosphere was as different as a New England front parlor is from a back room in a speakeasy."[8]

In Coolidge the White House had also gained a sentimentalist. On his first morning in the executive offices he placed his mother's portrait on his desk. He remembered his friends of long standing, writing them notes, such as the one he sent to James Luccy on August 6:

> Not often do I see you or write you but I want you to know that if it were not for you I should not be here and I want to tell you how much I love you. Do not work too much now and try to enjoy yourself in your well-earned hours of age.[9]

The President's first guest in the White House was no party leader or state potentate, but one of his early Northampton friends, Richard W. Irwin. A later friend and Coolidge's only worshiper, Frank Stearns, came and went at the White House as a member of the family. Stearns was not there for political purposes—heaven help him should he suggest policies or appointments—but for the President to chat or to commune with. Coolidge did not forget those who had helped him even if they were not in his circle of friends. Wallace McCamant, the man with the loud voice who had nominated Coolidge for Vice President in 1920, was appointed to a federal appeals judgeship despite considerable opposition. As could have been predicted at the time, the Senate refused to confirm him. Harding's secretary, George B. Christian, had for a while remained at the White House to help the new President. Months after leaving, Christian, without even being consulted, was nominated by Coolidge to membership on the Federal Trade Commission, which he declined. Even the bighearted Harding had not let sentiment lead him to that kind of embarrassment.

Things were to be different in the White House in other ways. Early in his Presidency Coolidge rocked on the front porch of the mansion but gave it up because of the crowds that gathered to watch him. Yet the White House, as confining as it can be, provided some release for Coolidge. He became a prankster. During his first weeks there, he would ring the doorbell at the front of the mansion. He bestowed nicknames, not always flattering ones, on some of the White House staff. A doorman, John May, was called The Mink and a butler, Thomas Roach, was called Bug. The Chief Executive would occasionally, for the fun of it, ring all the bells on his desk to bring the staff running. Colonel Edmund W. Starling, the Secret Service man detailed as the President's personal bodyguard, tells of one joke Coolidge played from his office: "If the mood suited him he would press the buzzer which notified everyone that he was on his way to the White House. Then, while ushers, policemen, doormen, and elevator operators were rushing about getting things ready and snapping to attention, we would stroll out West Executive Avenue and leave them."[10]

Coolidge liked the White House and its grandeur. He would mince grandly from the East Room down the long corridor to the State Dining Room at the other end of the building. He enjoyed eating in the State Dining Room with his family and often the Stearnses, all dressed formally to do justice to the huge room, its English oak walls, and the Cogswell painting of Abraham Lincoln. His interest in the mansion was evidenced in his remodeling of the third floor, which had been used mainly for storage, into a habitable area. He also took pleasure in acting as boss of the White House. This was seen in the large additions he made to the civilian, Secret Service, and military staffs.

He spent an unusual amount of time looking into the management of his establishment. He reviewed the guest list, vetoed invitations to the mansion, prowled through the kitchen, poked into all the mail, including his wife's, and inspected the many gifts that came, especially those that were edible. He particularly gave his attention to things that were to be bought with his salary, keeping tabs on food purchases and plans, and reviewing and initialing household bills. Economy was the watchword, though his personal financial records indicate that he purchased foods, not from Piggly Wiggly and Sanitary Grocery stores as gossips said, but largely from suppliers like Cudahy's for meat and Anselmo's for fruit and vegetables. He considered the White House his personal domain, every bit of it, and everything and everybody in it. Everyone knew who the boss was when he was President, even if they detested him and his interference. Although he served as representative of the people in carrying out his presidential duties, he often acted like an absolute monarch in his own home.

The President's mastery of the White House compensated him for his inability, the inability of every American Chief Executive, to act freely beyond its walls. With others he would dicker, but not with those who were his family and servants. He demanded their conformity to his wishes. Whatever frustrations he felt would eventually be released in the White House in a storm of abuse and shouting or in a long frost of silence and nasty looks. That was the price of the public reserve that made Coolidge appear to be the rock of stability. He did not vent his feelings on the people and, with few exceptions, on his opponents, for that would have done violence to his ideals of unity and harmony. And he did not forget the people, from whom he had come to his high station. It may have been partly a political gesture, but he liked to go out among the people by making speeches and on his lengthy summer vacations. He might appear shy, aloof, or occasionally sharp with ordinary folk, but he went out of his way so that they might see and even shake hands with him. He even instructed his office staff to give special attention to letters from those citizens who had grievances against their government. When he was snobbish it was only toward snobs. "I come from Boston," a gushing woman once announced to Coolidge.

"Yes, and you'll never get over it," he replied tartly.[11]

Coolidge's life in the White House was like clockwork. He arose early in the morning, about quarter past six, dressed, took a walk, and then breakfasted at eight, reading the newspapers as he did so. He worked from nine to half past twelve, then had a light lunch, and usually a stroll or a nap. He was back at work by three, quitting about six. He avoided working after dinner if at all possible. At ten he went to bed. Indeed, his early bedtime became a natural mark for comedians. One evening Coolidge took one of his infrequent excursions to the theater to see the comedy *Animal Crackers*. The star of the show, Groucho Marx, gazed at the President at one point and chortled, "Isn't it past your bedtime, Calvin?"[12]

Although Coolidge did not put in the long hours at work that most of his immediate predecessors and all of his successors have, he worked in a well-organized way. He relied on his office staff and the executive departments to dispose of the routine business of government which occasionally has bogged down other Presidents.

He made maximum use of his subordinates in getting information and policy suggestions and was agile at drawing facts and ideas from his visitors. He was as studious as a scholar at his paper work, though doing only what he considered essential. He worked things out in his mind, slowly and deliberately, if not brilliantly. In order to avoid personal factors and pressure he asked that, when possible, discussions of policies be submitted to him on paper.

He was not one to share his ideas until and unless action was required. Even his family and Frank Stearns knew nothing of what was going on in the official compartments of the President's mind until he had made a public announcement. His White House staff often knew little more until he dictated a statement. When Coolidge was not picking other people's brains or doing his paper work or reading or attending to ceremonial duties, he was "morning, noon, and night," as C. Bascom Slemp said, "thinking, thinking."[13] About what he was thinking was seldom clear because he could concentrate his thoughts on the trivial as well as the exalted. He was a man who was a notable daydreamer: of his childhood, his mother, his home, his past successes and failures, his future—and of fantasies which the world will never know.

The sharp edges that the Yankee President often showed to the world were softened by his wife, Grace. If he was naturally introverted and suspicious, she was outgoing and friendly to all. Vera Bloom, one of the belles of congressional society, cites Grace Coolidge's "genuine interest in you, which shone out through her warm, dark eyes, and her *kindness* [which] seemed to cast a sort of glow around her wherever she went."[14] Coolidge was fortunate because Grace's charm made up for much of his lack of it. She enjoyed repartee, the kind that did not cut. She was an excellent conversationalist and could make the preceding week's weather reports seem interesting. She loved baseball, music, novels, and the theater. She was a good dancer, though Calvin forbade her dancing in public. She fitted in well with any person or crowd in official circles, and she rarely forgot names and faces. She had to be good at mixing with people to fill in for the President's long periods of silence at social events.

She even used his idiosyncrasies to contribute to the Silent Cal myth and particularly liked to tell the story of the hostess who said to him: "Oh, Mr. Coolidge, you are so silent. But you must talk to me. I made a bet today that I could get more than two words out of you."

"You lose," retorted Coolidge.[15]

Only Grace Coolidge could tell stories about the President that amused others, played up his wit, and yet did not anger him. Much of the credit for making Calvin Coolidge a capital character belongs to her.

Life with Coolidge had never been easy and it was less so now that he strove to be a most dignified President. In August, 1923, Grace Coolidge wrote her old Northampton friend, Mrs. Reuben B. Hills, "I must not forget that I am to be guided now by circumstances beyond my control."[16] And she was. Coolidge in effect superseded his wife as housekeeper in her own home. She could do little that the President did not check and often alter. He carefully restricted her personal life, forbidding her from driving, horseback riding, or being flown. She was commanded to express no political views. She could not bob her hair or wear slacks. She was seldom given adequate notice about the functions she was to hold or attend, against which she rebelled unsuccessfully.

One morning at breakfast while Coolidge was hidden behind his newspaper, she said: "Calvin, look at me. I find myself facing everyday a large number of engagements about which I know nothing, and I wish you'd have your Secret Service prepare for me each day a list of the engagements for the coming week, so that I can follow it."

He peeked around the edge of his newspaper and replied, "Grace, we don't give out that information promiscuously."[17]

When she was on her own, her husband had to know her whereabouts every minute. She was instructed never to hold a tea or be out to tea beyond six in the evening. Once when he thought she was abroad too late, he called her saying: "Grace, I've come home. You come home, too."[18] She bore the brunt of his tantrums, sulking, and teasing, and he was a dreadful tease both with her and the boys, John and Calvin, Jr. She bore his occasional jealousy, but she took that, however annoying, as evidence of his deep love. She took it all in stride and turned whatever irritation she felt into harmless jokes. As she so well put it, "Being wife to a government worker is a very confining position."[19]

Calvin Coolidge gave the impression that he did not care

whether people liked him or not. That may have been true with some people, but not with all. He liked flattery and attention as much as anyone and deeply resented being snubbed. His seeking of revenge for snubs of the past led him occasionally to refuse invitations, to cross certain people off the White House invitation lists, and to downgrade others by changing their positions in seating. Colonel Starling recounts an expression of this.

One day while the two men were on a walk, Coolidge muttered, "I'm not going." The Secret Service officer did not reply.

After a few blocks the President quacked, "I'm not going, and I'm not going to let that wife of mine go."

Starling thought he ought to reply and said, "You certainly ought to follow your own judgment."

A few blocks on, Coolidge poured out his feelings. "When I lived at the Willard and was vice president they didn't know I was in town. Now that I am President they want to drag me up to their house for one of their suppers and show me off to a lot of people, and I'm not going."

Starling now remembered the invitation. It had come from the capital's leader of smart society. Coolidge again muttered in resolution, "I'm not going, and I'm not going to let that wife of mine go."

In telling the story the colonel noted, "He didn't, either."[20]

The President was a lean man. Yet his figure belied his diet. He was an incurable nibbler. Fruits, candies, and especially nuts were always on hand in the White House. He liked to make cheese sandwiches and to smear preserves on crackers for eating between his ample meals. He often borrowed nickels from Starling to buy nuts from a vendor outside the White House grounds. Coolidge was also one for sleep. The metabolism that kept him from showing much excess weight required him to sleep ten hours a day in order to store up enough energy for the next day's work.

He got little exercise. During his early days in the White House Coolidge took to riding a gentle creature called General, but soon gave it up because he believed himself allergic to horse dander. The President obtained some exercise from his early morning walks around Washington, which he took in the company of Colonel Starling. Sometimes the strolls started off like a game with Coolidge trying playfully and unsuccessfully to escape the White House without his guard. On the walks Coolidge was "thinking, thinking" and window-shopping, which leads one to believe that exercise was not the President's object in strolling. One morning he said to Starling: "Guess you wonder why I like to window shop. It takes me away from my work and rests my mind."[21]

Coolidge often took to the presidential yacht, the *Mayflower*, on weekends to get away from the pressures of his work. He did not always take well to the water, but he enjoyed the isolation that sailing gave him from official life. He also liked being decked out in his mock ship captain's uniform. Perhaps the daydreaming President could compete with Walter Mitty in adventures of the imagination.

He could also smoke cigars with the best of them and his cigars were good ones. He enjoyed gifts of the finest cigars and in case they ran low he had his own stock of Fonesca Corona Fines de Luxe which he purchased at twenty-one dollars per hundred. Those and even better gift cigars he usually kept to himself, doling out three-cent stogies to his guests. The mining millionaire John Hays Hammond tells the story of the President sucking on one of the expensive cigars Hammond had given him, while offering the other a stogy out of his desk drawer. All of a sudden Coolidge realized what he was doing and clucked: "Come to think of it, you sent me these. Try one."[22]

This was the new President. What he lacked in charm, he made up in character and idiosyncrasies. He certainly was different from his predecessor, and the public liked it. As George Mayer has written, "From the outset, the shy, parsimonious Coolidge was lionized by his free-spending, pleasure-loving contemporaries in the way that the homespun Ben Franklin had been lionized by the jaded aristocrats of eighteenth-century France."[23] But just as his contemporaries were not aristocrats, neither was Coolidge another Benjamin Franklin.

18

A Man Among Men

ONE DAY WHILE Alice Roosevelt Longworth was at her physician's office, the doctor came in grinning. He told her: "Mrs. Longworth, the patient who has just left said something that I am sure will make you laugh. We were discussing the President, and he remarked, 'Though I yield to no one in my admiration for Mr. Coolidge, I do wish he did not look as if he had been weaned on a pickle.' "[1] That story made the daughter of Theodore Roosevelt laugh, as it did most of Washington when she circulated it.

Calvin Coolidge did look as if he had been weaned on a pickle, and many people thought he had a personality to match his appearance. Yet he could be and was pleasant with a large number of persons. That was not only because of his basic kindliness, but also as a matter of political necessity. To carry out the duties of his office he needed aides, contacts, and sources of information and publicity. Yet his pleasantness was not readily apparent to the nation. The President held himself aloof from strangers, from people he had not come to trust, and from those who could not benefit the administration of the government. He represented something of a break from the past public availability of Presidents. Many people found that they were better off talking with one of Coolidge's secretaries than with him. "Order, simplicity, and quiet dignity were," Merlo Pusey has said, "to be the watchwords of the new regime."[2] Only those who could help or be trusted were to be admitted to President Coolidge's thoughts and conversation. He did not think that every self-important person in the country had a claim on his time.

This reserve was attributable to Coolidge's shyness, his love of order, and his dislike of snobs, name-droppers, know-it-alls, and Pooh-Bahs. From the outset of his Administration intrusion was usually discouraged. Even his friends were affected by it. Frank Stearns, as has been noted, soon discovered that although he was the President's personal confidant, he was not his adviser on matters of state and only rarely on political affairs. Dwight Morrow, within a few days after Coolidge took office, wrote to give the President advice. Release those convicted of sedition, replace George Harvey as ambassador to London with Elihu Root, consider an international conference on the reparations question, and seek a consistent Latin American policy, wrote the financier. By his coolness Coolidge made it clear that if help was wanted, he would ask for it. Morrow was to wait two years before his Amherst classmate asked him to do anything.

Yet Coolidge did reach out for assistance and information. He was cordial to many who gave it to him unsolicited, because they knew what they were talking about. He maintained good personal relations with his old foe Samuel Gompers, the AFL president. He consulted with leaders of business, educators, publishers, and lobbyists, as well as government officials. One of his early actions as President was to write personal letters to the editors of the multitude of national and state farm journals asking for views and information on the "agricultural crisis."[3] That he failed greatly to impress many of the men whom he consulted was because he did not follow their ideas or because he felt he could not open up with them. Most of them, however, got along fairly well with him. John Hays Hammond summed up a comment frequently made by those who got by Coolidge's secretaries and had real business to discuss. The President was, he said, "a most interesting conversationalist."[4]

Coolidge drew on a wide range of people for help, more than he is usually credited with. He invited an extreme critic of government policies, Hugh S. Johnson, to the White House to discuss farm problems. He called in Harry A. Slattery, the wheelhorse of the conservationist lobby, on a number of occasions and got along well with him. The President's party friends ranged from the Republican wildman,

Senator William E. Borah of Idaho, to the conservative boss of Connecticut, J. Henry Roraback. He went out of his way to cultivate the general president of the Carpenters' Union, William L. Hutcheson. The chairman of the Democratic National Committee, Cordell Hull, found Coolidge "talked freely and easily from the beginning to the end of a conversation, and was as affable as I could have wished."[5]

He also showed that he could handle the most delicate duties of the President in fine fashion. When Woodrow Wilson died early in 1924, President and Mrs. Coolidge showed up at the services in the Wilson home, where otherwise only close friends and pallbearers were present. The Coolidges' gesture and their solicitous conduct at the funeral touched everyone present. Another duty was that of entertaining distinguished visitors and Coolidge's first action in that regard was considered a success. That was the visit of the Prince of Wales at the end of August, 1924. A luncheon was scheduled and Coolidge himself selected the menu. The Prince, noted for his informality, was indulged as the President decreed informal dress all around and a loosening of protocol. When Wales came he was visibly nervous and Coolidge did all he could to put his royal visitor at ease, chatting with him genially, not only upon his arrival, but all through the luncheon and afterward too.

Relations with the press is one of the touchiest aspects of the Presidency. Although Coolidge was remarkably successful in dealing with the Washington newspaper correspondents, he did not escape their criticism. He irritated them by not answering all their written questions and by rarely answering them from the floor at press conferences. They were further annoyed by his rule that he could not be quoted directly. His remarks were usually attributed to the "White House spokesman." The newsmen were often dismayed because he would rarely engage in controversy on issues for their benefit. As he wrote in his autobiography:

> The words of the President have an enormous weight and ought not to be used indiscriminately. It would be exceedingly easy to set the country all by the ears and foment hatreds and jealousies, which, by destroying faith and confidence, would help nobody and harm everybody. The end would be the destruction of all progress.[6]

Although he went too far in avoiding questions and in guarding his utterances to the press, he had a point, one demonstrated by some of the less well considered press statements of Presidents Franklin D. Roosevelt and Harry S Truman.

Despite the restrictions he imposed, Coolidge did well by the newspapermen. He usually met with them twice weekly, on Tuesdays and Fridays. The President obviously managed the news in his press conferences, but he did it in such a way that he enlightened as well as propagandized his audience. His candidness in responding to the questions that he decided to answer was striking. When he lacked knowledge on a matter, he freely admitted it. When he had information to give, and wanted to give it, he did so generously. When he stated his position on an issue, he usually did it knowledgeably and sometimes perceptively. Coolidge's comments also revealed his dry humor, as was illustrated when he told the correspondents in April, 1924:

I think this report that I am to attend the Republican convention . . . and make an address there, you will see is exaggerated. There will be plenty of members at the convention prepared, I have no doubt, to make sufficient addresses without calling me and my assistance.[7]

He also maintained considerable rapport with the newspapermen. On occasion he had them in as guests at social affairs. Once he felt free to ask the newsmen for nominations for the secretaryship of the navy and another time he earnestly advised them to wear rubbers to keep their feet dry in the heavy morning dew. He was not one of the gang, like Harding, nor was he as openmouthed, but he did give them much of what they wanted and in return was treated kindly in the news. Indeed, Coolidge used the press more adroitly than it was able to use him, and he set a valuable precedent for the regularly scheduled press conference.

Crucial to Coolidge's activities during his early days as President was establishing rapport with the chiefs of the various federal agencies. In that he was successful. Of course, he had attended President Harding's Cabinet meetings and had learned a good deal of the operations and issues of the government. Yet if he measured the capabilities of the men he inherited from Harding, he did so imperfectly. Within six months after he had succeeded to the Presidency, it would become obvious that he had not detected the worst weaknesses of some of his subordinates.

The Cabinet that he received and kept on from Harding included the dignified and distinguished Secretary of State, Charles Evans Hughes; the agile juggler of figures and funds, Secretary of the Treasury Andrew W. Mellon; the plump, fatherly-looking Secretary of War, John W. Weeks, who worried for fear that his old Massachusetts opponent would remove him; the affable, none-too-bright Secretary of the Navy, Edwin Denby; the even more affable jack-of-all-trades, Attorney General Harry M. Daugherty; the stern-appearing Postmaster General, Harry S. New; the Secretary of the Interior, Hubert Work, who towered over the rest of the Cabinet in height; James J. Davis, the Secretary of Labor, whose goal was never to offend anyone; the small, courageous Secretary of Agriculture, Henry C. Wallace; and the master-of-all-trades, Secretary of Commerce Herbert C. Hoover.

Those men Coolidge set out to know well during his first month as President and upon them he would rely heavily in drawing up his program for presentation to Congress in December, 1923. Indeed, he was to rely heavily on them or their successors for information and advice throughout his Presidency.[8] The records of relations between the White House and the executive agencies show that little policy originated in the presidential office. Coolidge's actions and requests largely followed departmental recommendations. His role was to modify or occasionally to disapprove. He considered himself the coordinator, not the boss, of his subordinates.

Coolidge kept in close touch with the executive officers. He held short formal Cabinet meetings from time to time and met frequently with the secretaries for individual discussions. Relations were genial. Secretary Hoover wrote in his memoirs: "With his associates there was little of taciturnity. Many times over the five years he sent for men to come to the White House after dinner just to talk an hour or two. He had a fund of New England stories and a fine, dry wit."[9] Secretary Davis in January, 1929, looked back with obvious pleasure on his Cabinet associations, which had been "shaped and colored by [President Coolidge's] kindly personality."[10] No member of Coolidge's Cabinet felt left out or was unclear that the President expected him to do his job without running to the White House for approval of all decisions. All the executive officers got to know and like him personally, although some frequently disagreed with him on policy.

The Cabinet had a life all its own. Charles Evans Hughes towered above his colleagues in demeanor, accomplishment, and influence. The former New York governor, Supreme Court justice, and 1916 Republican presidential nominee went his own way, dominating no one but influencing and being respected by all. He was a man apart, even to Coolidge. Until 1925, though, he was to serve as the President's first minister, being an adviser on most of the important issues confronting the Administration. A gentleman of the old school, he got along well with the prudent, reserved Chief Executive. Unlike Harding, Coolidge gave everything careful consideration and generally stuck to his decisions once they were made. Like Harding, the new President gave Hughes virtually a free hand in running the Department of State, but he also showed that he comprehended the issues and could discuss them intelligently, sometimes making contributions. Of course, it did not hurt their relations for Coolidge to hail Hughes as "the greatest Secretary of State this country ever had." That flattering sentiment probably helped Hughes to conclude early, as he wrote a former aide, that Coolidge "will impress the country as a man of rare ability."[11]

Andrew Mellon, the shy, crafty Pittsburgh banker and industrialist, was another man apart. He had had no admiration for Harding, but soon came to esteem Coolidge, perhaps more because they saw eye to eye on fiscal matters than out of respect for the new President's ability. The Yankee and his secretary of the treasury worked as a pair. Their views on economic matters coincided; it was not a matter of Mellon influencing the President. What Mellon did was to give his chief the facts and schemes necessary to pursue the goals they both heartily favored. Coolidge also saw in Mellon and his ideas the key to his own success as President. He could not be all over the ball lot. He had to pin his Administration on some one thing, something that agreed with his own sentiments and would appeal to the people, something that would make the voters look to a rosy future instead of the troubled past. That something, tax reduction and debt-cutting, would also fit Coolidge's idea that "the chief business of the American people is business" and serve to divert public attention from the revelations of scandal in the Harding Administration. As time went by Coolidge and Mellon grew more intimate, as shy men might, and after Hughes left the Cabinet in 1925 the President relied on the Secretary of the Treasury as his first minister. Their relations grew so close that a private telephone wire was installed between their offices.

There were two other men of power in the Cabinet and one dissenter. One of the men of power was Attorney General Harry M. Daugherty, who dominated Denby and influenced many of the lesser executive officers, but his power was on the wane. The other power was Herbert Clark Hoover, a man of the world, of vision, and of amazing self-confidence, who used the Department of Commerce as a base to sway all other executive agencies. Hoover, with his drive, brilliance, and dedication, was able greatly to influence Secretaries Davis, Weeks, and Work, as he sought to establish cooperation between business, labor, and agriculture, and to revamp the countryside with public improvements. He also set up his own foreign affairs branch and reached out to make the Post Office Department more businesslike and Agriculture conform to his ideas of efficiency. He might have been Coolidge's first minister had he not overreached himself. And yet as it was Hoover had amazing success in his works, to the point that he was able to implement many programs that the President disliked.

The one real opponent Hoover had in the Cabinet was the dissenter, Secretary of Agriculture Henry C. Wallace. A veteran farm journal editor and agricultural experimentalist, Wallace had been at odds with Hoover since World War I, when the two of them disagreed over the policies of the wartime Food Administration headed by Hoover. Their relations did not improve when they became members of Harding's Cabinet and in fact deteriorated as the agricultural situation worsened. Starting in 1920 America's farmers experienced a series of economic setbacks. Hit by the recession of 1920–21, increases in state and local taxes, and rising transportation and storage prices, farmers did not regain their prewar purchasing power. Various remedies had been sought without success, including better credit, tariff increases to protect the home market, and additional spurs to cooperative marketing and purchasing.

By 1923 Secretary Wallace, getting too little, too late, from Congress, sought restoration of the prewar price-cost ratio through establishment of an export corporation that would facilitate marketing abroad. Hoover's remedy was to extend further credit and to

urge farmers to band together to improve their lot through cooperatives. Both secretaries were victims of the protective tariff syndrome
in the United States, a disease neither tried to conquer. Yet the
battle was joined between them and the issues involved in it became
one of the most unsettling problems of the 1920s and indeed for
generations to come.

Coolidge, although a man with a farm background, did little to
intervene in the struggle between his two subordinates. It was not for
lack of interest but because he was oriented toward the relatively
prosperous New England agriculture which feared the increases in
flour and feed prices which farmers elsewhere sought. Moreover, he
thought of the Western and Southern farmers as being like the lady
"who doth protest too much." They were overdoing it and had always done so. Even worse were the farmers' sharp disagreements on
remedies. Each section, each farm organization, each commodity
interest had its own favorite cure for agriculture's problems. A
plague on all their houses. Something would have to be done, of
course, but it would be done only in the public interest as Coolidge
interpreted it and only when necessary.

Meanwhile, the two secretaries would have to continue to battle
it out, and in order to retain support for the Administration from the
groups they represented, neither of them would be removed from
office. Even when Wallace spoke openly in contradiction of Coolidge's expressed policies, which had been borrowed from Hoover,
the President did not ask for his resignation. Even knowing that
Department of Agriculture officials had helped draft legislation
which the White House opposed, Coolidge did not act against them.
It was a case of the new President's conviction that he had an
obligation to keep Harding's men on, short of scandal or malfeasance, and of his wish to offend no one before the 1924 elections.
The dispute between Hoover and Wallace was resolved only with the
Agriculture Secretary's death in October, 1924. The issues between
them, however, were to continue to be in contention.

The President's refusal to act against Wallace also reflected his
belief that executive officers had the right to seek the public will and
express it. Consequently, Coolidge never used his Cabinet in a command sense to further his policies. If he agreed with his subordinates, splendid. If he could persuade or bully them, good. But if, like
Wallace and later Hoover himself, they pressed their own ideas, their

punishment was a glare, some muttering, and usually lack of support from the White House on the ideas involved. The executive officers were not required to agree with Coolidge or each other on policy proposals. They were required only to administer their agencies efficiently and according to law and not to betray the President's confidences. Fortunately for Coolidge the situation did not get out of hand, for Wallace died before the agricultural controversy reached its peak, Hoover was circumspect, and other Cabinet members rarely strayed off the reservation.

Coolidge also worked at making other subordinate government officials feel rapport with the White House. Although they could easily be cowed by his manner, they almost always found him willing to listen to them on business and socially kind. The daughter of Solicitor General James M. Beck was to be married and Beck did not think to invite the President to the wedding. That would have been presumptuous. But to Beck's surprise and delight one day he received a note from Coolidge saying that he would like to attend. Two men, William Phillips and Joseph Grew, who served as under secretary of state also testified to the President's kindly behavior toward lower officials in the Administration. If one of Coolidge's goals was to encourage harmony in his Administration, he did rather well.

The judiciary was another area of great interest to Coolidge. That interest stemmed from his constitutional responsibility to make appointments to the bench—a ticklish matter both politically and judicially—and from the aggressiveness of Chief Justice William Howard Taft in bringing judicial problems to his attention. Taft had had considerable influence on court appointments during the Harding days and used it to get competent though conservative judges on the federal bench. The Chief Justice's influence had lost its force as President Harding and Attorney General Daugherty became more sure of themselves. When Coolidge succeeded to the Presidency, Taft moved immediately to try to become his chief adviser on not only court but other affairs as well. Coolidge listened to the Chief Justice, for he needed advice, and the jovial, chubby Taft was full of it. The former President wrote on August 14, 1923:

My feeling of deep regret [at Harding's death] is somewhat mitigated by the confidence I have in the wisdom, conserva-

tism and courage of his successor. Of course, he lacks the
prestige and experience, but he is deeply imbued with a sense
of obligation to following Mr. Harding's policies, especially
Mr. Harding's purpose to defend the institutions of the
country against wild radicals.[12]

At first Coolidge relied heavily on Taft for advice on judicial
appointments, but within half a year the Chief Justice's influence on
him had slackened. By March, 1924, Taft wrote his son, Robert,
that he was "going to keep out of judicial selections hereafter" because Coolidge had made it clear that he thought him "too insistent
on having good men" on the bench and was not greatly impressed by
Taft's trials with politicians regarding appointments.[13] Yet Taft did
not cease his efforts to sway Coolidge nor did he become disillusioned with him politically, backing him to the hilt for the presidential nomination in 1924 and even for renomination in 1928.

In throwing off Chief Justice Taft's domination on judicial matters, Coolidge developed his own criteria for appointments to the
federal bench. He generally was guided by the degree of unanimity
of political and bar leaders in the court district or circuit involved,
the Justice Department's assessment of the candidates' professional
qualifications and experience, and, for circuit court selections, the
principle of representation from the states in the circuit. He often
resisted heavy political pressure on appointments. When in 1924
President Harding's widow and Ohio's political leaders pushed him
to nominate Harding's chum and personal lawyer, Hoke Donithen,
to the Sixth Circuit Court, Coolidge made the appointment from
Kentucky, which had had no judge on the court for a great while.
Another example was his resistance, during his second term, to pressure from the House Judiciary Committee and the Republican and
Democratic representatives and senators from Ohio to nominate
former Congressman Israel M. Foster to the Court of Claims. Another interesting case was Coolidge's refusal to heed the pleas of
Vice President Charles Dawes and his brother Rufus regarding the
filling of a circuit judgeship for Louisiana and Texas where the
Dawes family had financial interests to protect. The President's
record on judicial appointments was not above criticism, for he did
on occasion appoint hacks and yield to political pressures. Yet during the Coolidge Administration Harlan F. Stone began his distin-

guished career on the Supreme Court, and Dean Thomas W. Swan of the Yale Law School, John J. Parker, and the illustrious Hand brothers, Learned and Augustus, were elevated to circuit court judgeships.[14]

Calvin Coolidge became President at a fortuitous time. The Cabinet was stable and a half year away from being rocked by scandal. The convening of Congress was four months off. Only one crisis faced the country during the summer of 1923, the threat of a strike of miners. In 1921 disputes between miners and operators in Pennsylvania's great anthracite coal fields had been settled, but that contract was only for two years and was far from satisfactory to the miners. Agreement on a new contract had not been reached between the hardheaded mine owners and the aggressive United Mine Workers, which was asking for a 20 percent increase in wages and formal recognition of the union. Neither the State of Pennsylvania nor the United States Coal Commission had been able to bring the two parties together on terms, and a strike had been scheduled for September 1. Its consequences would be severe. Relying largely on anthracite for power, industry and rail transportation all over the nation would come almost to a standstill, and layoffs of workers would be widespread. Fuel for home consumption for the next winter could be in short supply, bringing on a nasty public reaction reminiscent of the coal-short days of the winters of 1919 and 1920.

When Coolidge had talked to Ambassador George Harvey a few days after Harding's death, he had asked his advice on the situation. Harvey had told him to indicate to both the operators and the miners that he might make a statement asking the public to buy only bituminous coal if the anthracite crisis was not settled. That action did not appeal to the President, so he looked further. He summoned Secretary Hoover, the members of the Coal Commission, and Interstate Commerce Commissioner Joseph Eastman and told them he expected that they would do all they could to prevent the strike. He also consulted the Attorney General as to what action the White House could take and Daugherty advised him that the President was not authorized to act before the coming of a strike.

With that, Coolidge was satisfied that he had taken all the precautions legally possible. He rang for George Christian, his temporary secretary. Christian found him in a characteristic posture, gazing out a window and puffing on a cigar.

"Mr. Christian," the President said, "it is about time for many people to begin to come to the White House to discuss different phases of the coal strike. When anybody comes, if his special problem concerns the state, refer him to the governor of Pennsylvania. If his problem has a national phase, refer him to the United States Coal Commission. In no event bring him to me."[15]

In a sense it was the Boston Police Strike all over again, except that this time Coolidge had a veteran progressive politician, Governor Gifford Pinchot of Pennsylvania, playing the role of concertmaster instead of Mayor Peters. Pinchot was to prove to be a superb concertmaster. He pressed Coolidge for action on August 15. The President sidestepped him, exuding only optimism that the flow of coal would not be stopped. Eight days later Pinchot called the White House to say that if Coolidge did not act in the coal situation, he would. The governor's tone was such that Coolidge decided that he should at least see him. Pinchot therefore was invited down to lunch for the following day. At the August 24 luncheon only the President, Governor Pinchot, and John Hays Hammond, the chairman of the Coal Commission, were present. What happened is not clear. Pinchot's understanding was that Coolidge and Hammond suggested only what the mine owners had, that is to use nonunion workers to keep the mines going during a strike. Hammond had another view of the meeting, reporting that Pinchot had been promised the federal government would mediate the strike if necessary and certainly would investigate conditions in the mines. It is probable that both men were correct in their reports, that Coolidge and Hammond would urge mediation and if the strike came might also urge that mining operations be continued with scab labor. Moreover, the federal government would investigate in order to publicize the deplorable conditions in the anthracite industry.

Governor Pinchot returned home, convinced that he was free to act by himself in the situation. He was enraged, however, to read of the White House press release that said he was acting in cooperation with federal officials, with the inference that he was Coolidge's agent in the matter. Nevertheless, Pinchot worked vigorously to compose the differences between the coal miners and the owners. By September 7 he had persuaded the two parties to accept his plan of a 10 percent wage increase and an eight-hour work day. The crisis was over and Coolidge's only contributions had been to indicate that he had backed Pinchot in his endeavors and to put a modicum of federal pressure on the operators and the workers to reach agreement.

The President did not fail to claim credit for his contributions. He made Pinchot fume with anger when he wrote him after the new contract had been negotiated, "It was a very difficult situation in which I invited your cooperation."[16] If Coolidge was not a master at settling strikes, he was one at claiming credit for their solution. Furthermore, he showed himself to be adroit politically by calming the fiery Pennsylvania governor's anger. He publicly praised Pinchot. He also extended his cordiality to the governor, inviting him and his wife to visit the White House. Pinchot would never forget Coolidge's undue credit-taking, and indeed it might have spurred the Pennsylvanian's poorly conceived attempt to gain the GOP presidential nomination, but he did not become so angry that he refused to support Coolidge for President the summer and fall of 1924 when so many progressives bolted the Republican party.

19

★ ★ ★ ★ ★

Man of the World

GOVERNMENT BY nondirective therapy seemed to be Coolidge's way of guiding the efforts of his administrative subordinates in domestic matters. That was less true of his supervision of international relations. He came to the Presidency with no experience in foreign affairs, only one week of travel out of the country—his honeymoon in Montreal—and only what scattered knowledge he had picked up in reading matter and in Cabinet meetings and the Senate. He did have some convictions and a sensitivity to public and congressional opinion, though, and a willingness to be guided by his strong secretary of state, Charles Evans Hughes. Coolidge's convictions for the most part paralleled those of Hughes, and those that did not could be set aside or negotiated between the two men.

What were Calvin Coolidge's convictions on foreign affairs? He was antiwar. It was not only a killing, wasteful thing, but one that was unsettling to all layers of society and their relationships. As bad, war was expensive, and for a President who believed in economy it was necessary that steps be taken to avert war and to scale down armaments wherever possible. Another unsettling thing was international debt. Debt had to be paid to maintain confidence among nations. Therefore the general goals of Coolidge's foreign policy— ones that could easily be continued from his predecessor's policy— were to seek international stability without getting involved in forceful measures, to encourage peace, to stimulate business, to extend good will, and to uplift the world, if only by example and exhortation. His government was to endeavor to follow those policies from its beginning in 1923 until it left office in 1929.

When Coolidge assumed the Presidency in August, 1923, he was faced with a number of international problems. France had agitated Europe by marching into the Ruhr to force German payment of World War I reparations. The White House was being pressed to extend diplomatic recognition to Soviet Russia and Mexico. And efforts were being made to revamp the League of Nations and to bring the United States into it and the World Court. Most of those problems did not demand immediate decisions from the new President. Yet there were two situations he had to deal with before he had spent a month in office.

The first concerned Mexico. The United States had not recognized its neighbor to the south since the forces of Álvaro Obregón had overturned Venustiano Carranza's government in 1920. The chief issues involved settlement of claims for compensation of damage and guarantees of Americans' rights in Mexico. Through negotiations American and Mexican representatives had reached agreement on ways to settle those questions, and the State Department recommended to Coolidge that that agreement was a sufficient basis upon which to restore formal diplomatic relations between the two nations. For him it was an easy decision because he just took the Department's advice on the matter.

Recognition of Mexico, however, did lead to a tougher decision later in 1923. Anti-American rebels were on the warpath and threatening the outgoing Obregón Administration and the duly elected incoming Administration under Plutarco Calles. The Mexican government called upon the United States to lift its embargo on arms and to encourage American bankers to lend money to help buy weapons. Coolidge did not want to take sides in a revolution, but the threat of anarchy in Mexico and the possibility of an unfriendly government to the south convinced him that he had to help Obregón and Calles. Both Secretary Hughes and Secretary of War Weeks were sympathetic and supported the President in coming to a decision. As Coolidge said privately: "We'll be the laughing stock of the world if we don't send guns to Mexico. Look what happened when

Wilson refused to support Huerta. If we allow Obregón to be over-thrown, we shall be put in a ridiculous position as we have already rendered him some aid and are committed to his cause."[1]

The embargo was lifted early in 1924 and American financiers helped the Mexican government to buy the arms it needed. President Coolidge publicly justified the purchasing of "a few muskets and a few rounds of ammunition" on the grounds of ordinary comity between nations and because it concerned a domestic crisis, not international war.[2] (One consequence was that later some of those weapons turned up in the civil war in Nicaragua in 1927 and were used against the government that the United States was supporting there.) Coolidge pursued his good will policy toward Mexico even further in February, 1924, when he renewed President Harding's request for an appropriation to settle claims arising from Woodrow Wilson's occupation of Vera Cruz in 1914. The United States seemed to be on the high road to settling the train of disagreements and vexations that had developed between itself and Mexico since 1913.

Another matter that came up during Coolidge's first month in office demanded and received quick action. It showed the President at his best. While Hughes was absent from the capital, news came September 1 of the disastrous effects of earthquake and typhoon in Japan. Directly upon receiving the first dispatches from Japan, Coolidge called Acting Secretary of State William Phillips away from a dinner. Phillips rushed to the President's side and then waited silently while Coolidge studied reports of the disaster. Finally the Acting Secretary dared to break the silence. Coolidge took notice of him and asked where the Asiatic fleet was. Phillips did not know, so the President called the Department of the Navy and learned that it was in Chinese waters. Then he quacked over the telephone, "You might tell it to go right away to Yokohama." Hanging up, he said to Phillips, "Don't think there is anything more we can do this evening." Phillips suggested, however, that a message of sympathy to the Japanese Emperor would be appropriate. The President responded: "You might send such a message for me. Good night."[3]

The United States Navy beat even the Japanese fleet in bringing assistance to the stricken areas and Coolidge's expression of sympathy was the first received from abroad by the Emperor. The President later called upon the Army and the Shipping Board to extend aid and by his public statements initiated the great efforts of the American people privately to help relieve distress in Japan.

Coolidge was fortunate in that he had only one important replacement to make in his diplomatic staff during his early months as President. That replacement was of George Harvey as ambassador to the United Kingdom in October, 1923. Harvey had decided to return to the publishing business. His resignation posed a considerable problem. Although the London embassy was regarded as second in prestige only to the secretaryship of state in America's diplomatic establishment, it also was demanding in energy, tact, and knowledge, and taxing of its occupant's finances. Not many men were considered eligible for appointment to the ambassadorship and of those, few would accept. Coolidge first offered it to the distinguished former Secretary of State Elihu Root, who declined it, and then to the polished Frank O. Lowden of Illinois (maybe a contender for the presidential nomination could thus be eliminated), who also said no.

One of the men the President consulted in securing recommendations for the post was Frank B. Kellogg, who was among the few senators with whom Coolidge had established rapport while Vice President. The former Minnesota senator and trust-busting attorney had suggested Root, Lowden, Solicitor General Beck, and President Lowell of Harvard. After Coolidge had been turned down by Root and Lowden, he called Kellogg to Washington and offered him the ambassadorship. Kellogg asked that another man be appointed, for he wanted to remain out of public service in order to devote himself to the law. Coolidge and Hughes persisted, and after a week of pressure Kellogg surrendered, though on the condition that he be relieved of the post in March, 1925. His appointment was well received both in the United States and in Britain, and Kellogg did well enough in London to become the prime nominee for secretary of state when Hughes retired.

Three other matters were to occupy most of Coolidge's attention on foreign affairs during his first fifteen months in the White House, and indeed, those three were to be problems for him until he left office in 1929. One concerned the question of recognizing Russia; the second dealt with international peace and organizations; and the third involved issues of war reparations and international debts.

Coolidge, like the vast majority of Americans, saw no serious problem in the rise of fascist governments in Italy and Spain.

The Russian question was the least complicated of the three. Relations between the United States and Russia had been severed as a result of the Communist overthrow of the democratic Kerensky government in October, 1917. From America's standpoint obstacle upon obstacle was piled up by the Bolsheviks to prevent restoration of diplomatic relations. The United States was first affronted that the Communists should remove Russia from the Allied side during World War I. The slaughters of people and destruction of property that accompanied the Red Revolution and the later Civil War, the signs that the Bolsheviks were trying to start world revolution, constant propaganda against the United States and capitalism, the loss of American lives during the occupation of Archangel and Vladivostok, confiscation of private property by the Red government, the early Bolshevik concept of free love and support of atheism, the general use of intrigue and indirection, and the Communist government's refusal to pay Russia's debts, all combined to make the American people and their government unwilling to restore diplomatic relations. The Russian Communists, if not the Russian people, were enemies to all the United States stood for. Yet there were those in America, like the powerful Senator William E. Borah of Idaho, who urged recognition, contending that there was no hope for a change of Russia's attitudes unless the United States indicated a willingness to compromise. The benefits of diplomatic recognition, its proponents said, would be a more stable and peaceful world and, in addition, expansion of trade.

In 1923 there was clearly a relaxation in the policies of the Soviet government. Its policies on free enterprise at home were altered to allow some small-fry capitalism to develop, it sought trade abroad, and it was less antagonistic in its relations with other nations. All this spurred efforts in the United States to persuade the government to consider the possibility of recognizing Soviet Russia. To some extent those efforts succeeded, for in 1923 President Harding authorized Raymond Robins to visit Moscow confidentially to explore the question. Robins, however, had not reached Russia when Harding died. He had to return home and advocates of recognition had to begin again to work for a change in policy.

Coolidge felt the pressure for recognition of Russia so early that in his August, 1923, press conference he spoke out on the question. He told the reporters:

> There is no change in the American policy . . . of awaiting evidence of the existence of a government there that, in accordance with our standards, would warrant recognition, one that has such a form and has adopted such policies that we should be warranted in saying to the American people—this is a government that meets these standards and these requirements and you will be justified in making commitments accordingly, and expecting, that when those commitments are made, the usual support from your own government.[4]

The irritations of the American government were more clearly spelled out in other ways. When Senator-elect Burton K. Wheeler of Montana came to Washington in the fall of 1923, Coolidge asked him to the White House to talk about a trip he had recently taken to, as the President intoned it, "Roosia." Wheeler related that Soviet Foreign Commissar Georg Tchitcherin had told him the claims of Russia and the United States against each other should be studied by a commission so that settlement might be reached. That was in response to the President's grumble, "But they don't pay their bills." Wheeler had no answer for Coolidge's probing about religion in Russia.[5] Another thing worrying the Administration was expressed by Secretary Hughes when he spoke of the "subversive and pernicious activities" of American Communists, who he considered were working under Moscow's orders.[6]

The President formally presented his ideas on the question in his initial message to Congress, December 6, 1923. He stressed the nation's friendship for the Russian people by referring to America's "enormous charity" among their destitute after the war. He also pointed out that American citizens were not barred from trading with the people of Russia.

> Our government does not propose, however, to enter into relations with another regime which refuses to recognize the sanctity of international obligations. I do not propose to barter away for the privilege of trade any of the cherished rights of humanity. I do not propose to make merchandise of any American principles.

After the applause Congress gave him for that statement Coolidge went on to list the conditions under which the United States would consider changing its course toward Russia:

Already encouraging evidences of returning to the ancient ways of society can be detected. But more are needed. Whenever there appears any disposition to compensate our citizens who were despoiled, and to recognize that debt contracted with our government, not by the Czar but by the newly formed Republic of Russia; whenever the active spirit of enmity to our institutions is abated; whenever there appear works meet for repentance, our country ought to be the first to go to the economic and moral rescue of Russia. . . . We hope the time is near at hand when we can act.[7]

Foreign Commissar Tchitcherin, who had been tipped off beforehand by Raymond Robins to expect an overture from the President, took the message to Congress as an indication that the United States was willing to negotiate the differences between the two nations. He promptly communicated to President Coolidge the desire of Russia to re-establish friendship with America. Secretary Hughes, who was more suspicious of the Soviet government than was the President, replied bluntly, "There would seem at this time no reason for negotiations." The Soviet leaders, he said, could follow the steps listed by the President without entering into negotiations. Hughes specified one action in particular that might relax tensions between the two powers: "Most serious is the continued propaganda to overthrow the institutions of this country. This government can enter into no negotiations until these efforts directed from Moscow are abandoned."[8]

It is true that the Coolidge Administration gave little attention to the fact that Russia had grievances against the United States that were just as substantial as some of America's against her, particularly American military occupation of parts of Russia from 1918 to 1920. Nevertheless Secretary Hughes was correct in asserting that Russia could act unilaterally in laying the groundwork for resumption of relations. That it did not do so confirmed his belief that its government was insincere, as was the Soviet Union's failure to abide by all of its agreements after it was finally recognized by the United States in 1933. Yet it must be observed that the intransigence of the two governments closed channels of communication that might have been used to prevent or ameliorate future disasters which were worse by far than any disagreements between the two countries during the 1920s. That that was a possibility was seen neither by Presidents Wilson, who had established the hard line toward Communist Russia, Harding, Coolidge, nor Hoover, nor by their secretaries of state.

The horrors that the extreme left and right were to steer the nations into during the following decades could not be imagined during the 1920s by the world's democratic leaders, who thought that World War I had been the ultimate catastrophe. Their inflexibility, particularly America's, toward bolshevism, and their accommodation of the growing force of fascism only made it less possible to siphon off the strength of either or to play one off against the other if necessary. The dangerous feeling of inferiority of Russia and communism was to build, while the equally dangerous feeling of superiority of fascist movements was to be fed by the shortsighted policies of the leaders of the United States and other democratic nations. The result was to be the terrific pounding given to standards of decency and self-government, first from the right during the 1930s and World War II, and then from the left during the Cold War era.

The greatest hope during the 1920s for dulling the forces of communism and fascism seemed to be international organization for peace. Yet the questions involved in such organization were vexatious for American leaders. President Coolidge was caught betwixt and between. On the one hand, he believed in the principle of cooperation of nations to maintain peace and in its corollary that such cooperation should be organized. On the other hand, he had come to believe that the League of Nations as then organized could neither keep the peace nor respect America's rights and principles. Of course, it did not matter much what he thought personally about the League, for his paramount belief was to follow the will of the people, a belief supported by his intention to continue the policies of the Harding government, at least until he became President in his own right. The people had spoken clearly, as Coolidge saw it, through their representatives and in their rejection of Wilsonian internationalism in the election of 1920, and what they had said then was to be reiterated in congressional and presidential elections until

1940. Yet he recognized that the rejection of the League of Nations Covenant, as historian Dexter Perkins has written, did not imply "that the withdrawal of the United States from world affairs was to be anything like total, or that there was not much devotion to the peace ideal as an abstraction."[9]

One thing was clear, though. No President should toy with bringing the United States into the League of Nations. As Cordell Hull said of the 1920s, "the League of Nations [was] almost a byword for ridicule with many millions."[10] Indeed, a President should not come anywhere close to the League. Although Coolidge was a bit more flexible on foreign relations than Harding, he obeyed that rule. Knowing that politics is the art of the possible, he feared the hair-trigger sensitivity of Congress and the public to any flirtation with the League. The strength of anti-internationalist forces had early been brought to bear on him. Even before Harding had been buried, a group of powerful men, including Senators Lodge, Charles Curtis, Frank Brandegee, George Moses, James Wadsworth, Ambassador Harvey, Republican National Committee Chairman John T. Adams, former National Chairman Will Hays, Assistant Navy Secretary Theodore Roosevelt, Jr., and James Williams of the Boston *Transcript*, got together to impress on Coolidge their implacable opposition to the League and the World Court.[11] The new President was impressed, at least with the need for extreme caution in approaching the question of international organization.

It has been contended that a President of courage would have tried to persuade the people to support American entry into the League, with reservations respecting America's rights, or at least closer cooperation with the organization. But that view overlooks the fact that, had he done so, two platoons of senators and a company of representatives would have set out to destroy him, great and articulate segments of public opinion would ferociously have challenged him, and, not of least importance, he could not have counted on being unembarrassed by the unsteady and shifting elements within the League and over a world which itself had not displayed much more confidence in the League than had the United States. The forces that had destroyed Wilson, intimidated Hughes, Stimson, and Hull, Harding, Hoover, and even Franklin D. Roosevelt, were not likely at the height of their strength to be ignored by Calvin Coolidge.

Nevertheless, as veteran diplomat William Phillips has pointed out, the new President pursued foreign policy goals "with somewhat more flexibility" than had Harding.[12] Coolidge often appointed unofficial American representatives as "observers" and as "experts" to organizations affiliated with the League and kept in touch with United States citizens in the service of international organizations. He also, though cautiously, considered plans for increasing America's cooperation with other nations in the pursuit of peace. He was especially interested in following up the work of the Washington Naval Limitation Conference of 1921–22. That came from his belief that peace could be maintained through arms reductions and that arms limitation would permit accomplishment of two other policy goals: reduced federal expenditures at home and easier payment of the debts other nations owed to the United States.

Coolidge did not move toward arms limitation immediately. That was not because he felt unready to move in that direction but because he thought the other nations were unprepared for it. They were talking of a general world arms conference, which as he knew was likely to break up in disagreement as had similar efforts by the League. He also knew that as far as land armaments were concerned the United States with its miniscule army had nothing with which to bargain. Reduction of navies was the thing that could protect the United States from aggression and should that be successful it might encourage land powers to limit their armies.

Yet President Coolidge did not discourage European discussions of general reduction of arms, for such talk might lead to formulation of a workable agenda for naval limitations and even eventually to agreements on scaling down European and Asiatic armies. In May, 1924, he said that a general arms conference would be acceptable to the United States after the reparations crisis between France and Germany was settled. He further indicated that his government would welcome a world meeting on questions of international law, especially on neutral rights and on rules for submarine warfare. When the reparations crisis had been overcome by August, 1924, the President told the press that it appeared European countries would soon reach "a stable condition so that they are not disturbed lest they be attacked by each other." Then it would be appropriate to call another arms limitation conference.[13] Although the European nations showed a willingness to explore arms questions, it was through the League of Nations, which made it difficult for the United States to participate. Coolidge would have to wait until 1927 before he could arrange an international arms limitation conference.

There were, however, other avenues that seemed to stretch out in the direction of peace and stability, and Coolidge explored some of those roads. One was the World Court and another was the Outlawry of War movement. Advocates of the Court, such as Hughes, Taft, and Nicholas Murray Butler, felt that the United States could join that body, thereby signifying its intention to submit certain conflicts between itself and other nations to adjudication. That would give the world peace movement a boost as well as settle more easily and fairly disputes in which the United States was involved. The great obstacle to bringing America into the Court was that membership in it could be potently opposed on the ground that it was a back door for American admission to the hated League of Nations.

The Outlawrists believed they could answer both the wishes of the internationalists and the objections of the League's opponents. Rejecting the concept of collective security, because it was based on the use of force, the Outlawrists saw the legal banning of force between and among nations as the surest way to achieve world peace. A real and comprehensive world law could be worked out on that basis, and an effective international court could be established to implement it. Law, not intrigue, war, and politics, had to be the recourse in disputes between states if mankind was to achieve peace.

The Outlawry idealists, led by Chicago businessman S. O. Levinson, constantly pressed Coolidge to espouse their cause, and he in turn evaded them. One of the best examples of evasion was his reply in November, 1923, to a statement explaining Outlawry of War by Colonel Raymond Robins, the movement's evangelist. The President wrote:

I trust that our country is in theoretical harmony with the position you are striving to reach. It is exceedingly difficult, in fact almost impossible, to get any consideration of international questions in Washington at the present time. It would be especially so just before the Presidential election. Some of the things that you mention I am trying to do, in so far as I can find them practicable. You noticed, however, that when we made as mild a suggestion as that we take an inventory of what Germany had, the result of which was to be binding upon no one, we could not secure any agreement to that end. You will recall also the obstacle that stood in our path at the Washington Conference. These things are not hopeless, but they require long and painful effort. I am very much pleased that men like you who have the public ear are thinking of them and talking of them. You have expressed an ideal towards which I believe the world is moving.

Robins observed to Levinson, ". . . if you can determine from Coolidge's letter whether he is coming or going you are a better man at interpreting dead languages than I am."[14]

The President continued to evade the Outlawrists. To their disappointment and that of the anti-internationalists, he recommended to Congress in December, 1923, the nation's adherence to the World Court with an anti-League reservation. In doing so, Coolidge kept faith with Secretary of State Hughes and with Harding, who had in February requested American membership in it. Optimists to the core, however, Levinson, Robins, and other Outlawrists thought that Coolidge was coming over to their cause. He had convinced them of that in conversation, even though he had committed himself to nothing. They had to have a champion and Coolidge was the strongest one available. The fact that the President asked the Senate to ratify a Court protocol and that he successfully pushed the 1924 Republican National Convention to endorse American adherence to the World Court did not disturb their dream that he was favorable to their ideas.

The Outlawrists were led on, not only by Coolidge's honey-coated evasions, but by their own conviction that he needed them for election to the Presidency in 1924. It may be that Coolidge's heart belonged to the Outlawry movement and that he nodded in the direction of the Court only to appease its advocates. It may also be that he was firmly in the camp of the World Court men and was leading the Outlawrists on. It is probable, though, that the President was trying to keep the political good will of both groups, pushing the Court as he felt obliged to do out of deference to Harding and Hughes, but keeping the Outlawry notion on tap in the event the Court failed. In any case there is no evidence that he was attached to either movement. His attachment was to doing whatever the majority would support.

If Coolidge was fond of any plan to achieve world peace it was not a panacea of the nature of either the League, the Court, or Outlawry of War. It was to do the day's work, seeking stability, arms limitation, and world prosperity when the opportunities came. His opportunity for reduction of armaments had vanished in 1924 when the League entered the picture, but he had found an opportunity to pursue stability and prosperity. That concerned the settlement of war reparations and debts.

The question of repayment of loans given to foreign states during and immediately after World War I was one that commanded an exorbitant amount of the time and energies of statesmen. The United States had lent over 10 billion dollars and expected it to be repaid with 5 percent interest. The old rule of "lend a dollar, lose a friend" set in quickly as foreign governments, burdened with postwar reconstruction and the problems caused by shifts in economic power and markets, wriggled on the hook. The issue was further complicated by the difficulty of repayment when tariff walls and American successes in selling abroad gave foreign nations few opportunities to earn surplus dollars or gold. Moreover, payment in kind was hard when many of the surplus products of foreign lands were those which the United States already had in abundance. That does not mean that repayment was impossible, but it was, for most nations, difficult. The problem was aggravated by the psychology of many countries, particularly France's, that the loans should be considered America's equivalent of the blood and treasure expended by its erstwhile allies in winning the war. It was sufficient repayment, it was often argued abroad, that the war had been won by the Allies and that America's prime foreign markets had been saved.

Despite the difficulties and the arguments of their debtors, the American people and their leaders expected repayment. Coolidge, for example, believed that international trade and political confidence could be maintained only when debtors paid their creditors. Moreover, for the United States to absorb the debts could shake the economic foundations of the republic. It would certainly destroy the government's program of seeking a balanced budget and of reducing taxes and the domestic public debt of 22 billion dollars. That program was not a selfish one, Administration leaders argued, for it was necessary in order to maintain the economic stability of the United States, which was after all the mooring post of the reconstruction and economic security of the world.

Coolidge made his position clear on the question of intergovernmental debts soon after he entered the White House. When in the fall of 1923 the president of the American Bankers Association indicated that he thought the debts should be canceled, Coolidge told the press bluntly that the Administration opposed the idea. He pointed out, however, that the government was sympathetic to the difficulties involved in the payment of intergovernmental debts, indicating that they were "open to negotiation as to terms and conditions and so on."[15] That was precisely the policy the American government followed, renegotiating interest charges and periods of repayment to fit the ability of foreign nations to pay. On the average the interest was cut to 2.135 percent, ranging from 3.3 percent for Britain down to 0.4 percent for Italy. The period of repayment was to extend over sixty-two years. Those instances of *noblesse oblige* were determined, Coolidge told Congress, by America's "direct interest in the economic recovery of Europe. They are enlarged by our desire for the stability of civilization and the welfare of humanity. That we are making sacrifices to that end none can deny. Our deferred interest alone amounts to a million dollars every day."[16]

Perhaps Calvin Coolidge did say, "They hired the money, didn't they?" He certainly was determined that America's debtors would meet their obligations. Yet it is fair to say that many foreign governments did all they could to avoid payment of their debts and interest despite America's generous terms of repayment. In the long run, though, Coolidge's policies were hollow, for the coming of the Great Depression of the 1930s gave reason for a collapse of the whole debt structure. The United States lost everything and in doing so had not contributed one whit to either its own or the world's stability. It is also true that the United States did not go far enough to make repayment easier or to give foreign states less excuse for not paying. The American people and government were on the whole blind to connecting the tariff with the debt issue. A lower American tariff would have allowed debtor states to earn more of the dollars and gold necessary to reduce their debts, assuming that they would have used those reserves to that end. Yet Coolidge and his secretaries of state, Hughes and Kellogg, showed little interest in the tariff question. As the President himself drily commented, the tariff "has accomplished its two main objects. It has secured an abundant revenue and been productive of an abounding prosperity."[17]

Related to intergovernmental debts was the issue of reparations which the former Allied nations expected the Central Powers and especially Germany to pay to them. If the United States could be considered *l'Oncle Shylock* on intergovernmental debts, then some of the powers seeking reparations from Germany were out to get two pounds of flesh. The United States, through its government and its banks, worked diligently to try to reduce tensions over reparations. America assumed the burden of most of the reparations it could claim from Germany, asking only for a small sum to cover the expenses of the postwar army of occupation and the liquidation of debts owed to individual American citizens. The United States made liberal arrangements for Germany to pay those and, unlike most Allied powers, fairly recognized German claims against it.

The reparations situation reached crisis stage during 1923, when France and Belgium occupied the Ruhr in retaliation for German nonpayment. Germany was undergoing a disastrous inflation and the possibility of conflict flared. Hughes, fully backed by Coolidge, endeavored to reduce the tension. The Secretary, along with British spokesmen, urged the French to participate in an international study of the situation so that reparations could be put on a basis fair to both Germany and the nations seeking payment. In October Hughes stated that conditions in Europe made it essential to act soon in order to forestall a collapse of the continent's economy. He suggested that the reparations problem be studied by a commission of experts who would fix the amount that Germany was to pay, which had been left indefinite by the Treaty of Versailles, and then would work to establish conditions for its payment.

That proposal was accepted in November by all the former Allies and soon experts were delegated to explore Germany's financial situation and to make recommendations that hopefully would settle the issues involved. The United States, to show its keen concern in solving the reparations problem, contributed to the leadership of the committee of experts. In December President Coolidge appointed three American financiers, Charles G. Dawes, Henry M. Robinson, and Owen D. Young, as experts attached to the study group. The study committee eventually took the name of one of the Americans, becoming known as the Dawes Committee. It did its work well, fixing a reasonable schedule of payments from Germany. Allied and particularly American bankers agreed to extend loans to Germany to speed her reconstruction and her ability to keep up with the Dawes Plan schedule.

Coolidge's role in the reparations crisis was to support Secretary Hughes and the American experts and, through his press conferences, to explain to the public what was happening. He followed the situation closely. His only direct connection came toward the end of the process, when representatives of the powers met in London and Paris to accept or reject the experts' proposals. Toward the close of July, 1924, it seemed that the conference was going to break up in disagreement. The President cabled Frank Kellogg, who was one of the American delegates: "In case conference deadlocks finally over declaring default announce in that event to conference the President has a proposal to make. Keep conference for that and notify Department at once."[18] Ambassador Kellogg was able to reply that there was no danger of the conference breaking up. After receiving that word the President told Acting Secretary of State Joseph Grew that, had the conferees not agreed on a way to declare Germany in default of payments, he would have suggested that any charges that Germany was in default be arbitrated by the Chief Justice of the United States. That idea he based on the precedent of Chief Justice Edward White's arbitration of the Costa Rican–Panamanian boundary dispute in 1914. Coolidge never told Kellogg what he had had in mind. After Kellogg became secretary of state he asked the President about it. Coolidge said, with a smile on his face, "The conference did not break up, did it?"[19]

Thus did Calvin Coolidge meet foreign problems during 1923 and 1924. He relied on his secretary of state, but when necessary he took action himself. He sought to pursue a foreign policy that would achieve peace, stability, and national financial security, without angering sentiment in the Senate or among the voters. It must be said, however, that he was more successful in soothing the senators and the public than he was in contributing to ultimate peace, stability, and prosperity.

20

A President Approaches Congress

IF YOU SEE ten troubles coming down the road," Calvin
Coolidge once said, "you can be sure that nine will run into
the ditch before they reach you and you have to battle with only one
of them."[1] That was not so much a jot of philosophy as it was a
description of Coolidge's method of dealing with Congress. The
problem for him was that standing at his end of the road he had to
battle with more than one out of each ten problems that came from
Capitol Hill. His Administration was to fight one battle after another
with the Congress and the result was to be, to a considerable extent,
stalemate.

There were a number of reasons for battle between the legislative branch and the White House during the postwar years. Congress
was in turmoil. It was neither the rubberstamp instrument of the first
four years of the New Deal nor the body dedicated to compromise of
the Eisenhower years. It was an institution filled with vigorously
combative men, both Republicans and Democrats, who felt that they
owed little allegiance to a national party and who had crusades to
fight or revenge to wreak. Such men were unlikely to be harnessed
by any President and certainly not by one as unaggressive as Calvin
Coolidge. Despite his many years in legislative chambers, Coolidge
showed no zest for participating in the legislative process. To him it
was something in which the Chief Executive played a minor part.

The President's role, as he saw it, was to recommend items for consideration of Congress, not to formulate the content of legislation or to push or block bills. One authority, Wilfred Binkley, has said that Coolidge's informing of Congress on affairs of state was "so formal and perfunctory that sometimes it was difficult or impossible for Congress to discover his views."[2]

Soon after the House and Senate convened in December, 1923, Coolidge told the press: "I learned a great while ago that a proposal for legislation, or even the introduction of a bill that was not in accordance with sound policy wouldn't need any active opposition from the executive, in order to prevent its adoption. . . . Congress will look after it." When asked about how he stood on pending legislation, the President explained: "I can't very well announce beforehand that I am going to veto a bill, or that I am going to sign it. I have to keep my mind open about those things until the proposal comes to me. Nobody knows what the bill may contain when it gets here, so that I have to wait and see."[3] Coolidge meant it. Unlike other Presidents he rarely held the veto power over the graying heads of Congress as a bludgeon. Representatives and senators often begged him to find out what he would do and he would not enlighten them, so with all good intentions they would pass a bill and run into a presidential veto. Of course, his attitude was clear on some matters, for example, expenditures that would cripple his budget. Yet he took seriously the magisterial powers of the Presidency: his job was to consider legislation on its merits and that could not be done until a bill had been passed by Congress.

Coolidge's tactics in dealing with congressmen seem amateurish. Actually his legislative tactics were extensions of his personality and of his conviction that the executive and legislative branches were equal, that the one should not poach on the preserves and prerogatives of the other. He tried to maintain friendly relations with members of Congress, but not to intimidate them. Far less than Harding did Coolidge hold personal conferences on legislation with representatives and senators, and when he did see them he was no more adroit than his predecessor in discussing legislative matters. He had little patronage and used it none too well. He made few attempts to have congressmen friendly to him placed on key committees.

His famous breakfasts with congressmen constituted one of the mysteries of Washington. He would call them in, often members of both parties, greet them, bid them eat a hearty breakfast, usually wait for them to talk, and then listen to the resulting desultory conversation. After eating he would tell them good-by, and that would be it. Ike Hoover said that guests, upon leaving, occasionally asked, "What did he have us here for?"[4] One can only guess, but it was probable that Coolidge's breakfasts served a number of purposes. The fact that he often invited the congressmen in alphabetical order suggests that he considered the breakfasts as part of his job as the nation's chief host. Scattered comments by men who spent early morning hours eating with the President indicate that he used the occasions to size up his guests, to glean information and attitudes from their conversation, to give them the opportunity to raise questions, and to show them his good will. Whatever his reasons, his guests rarely felt that the White House breakfasts served much of a purpose.

Coolidge was an easy boss. Although the Republican leaders in the House and the Senate might discipline recalcitrant party members, he rarely did. He might offer a man an attractive appointment to ease him out of Congress, but seldom more. If Congress did what he recommended, he would take the credit. If it did not, he was satisfied that the legislators would have to accept the blame when things went awry. The question arises: Why did he follow such a course? It was partly a matter of conviction about separation of the executive and legislative branches and partly a failing in him, one that he admitted. He wrote:

> Some of our presidents have appeared to lack comprehension of the political mind. Although I have been associated with it for many years, I always found difficulty in understanding it. It is a strange mixture of vanity and timidity, of an obsequious attitude at one time and a delusion of grandeur at another time, of the most selfish preferment combined with the most sacrificing patriotism. The political mind is the product of men in public life who have been twice spoiled. They have been spoiled with praise and they have been spoiled with abuse. With them nothing is natural, everything is artificial.[5]

Coolidge could describe the political mind well, but he was less successful in coping with it. His hope was that the political minds would understand him, that they would rise to responsibility, that they would accept the yoke of party discipline. Although his hope was gratified less often than not, a more vigorous approach might also have failed during the 1920s. It is difficult to imagine that Democrats like Thomas Heflin, Thad Caraway, and Thomas Walsh or Republicans like Robert La Follette, George Norris, or Henry Cabot Lodge would have responded favorably to an aggressive President. The Democrats were too partisan and the Republicans too unpartisan.

When Coolidge did act to sway Congress, out of habit and conviction he relied on the Republican leaders there. It appeared that he had inherited a favorable structure of leadership in Congress. In the House Frederick Gillett, the representative from the President's home district, was speaker, and in the Senate Henry Cabot Lodge was the floor leader. It was a unique situation, with Massachusetts Republicans holding the Presidency and the leadership in both houses of Congress. Yet it did not work well. Speaker Gillett was not a strong leader. His position and influence were based on his geniality and judicial temperament. He presided over the House of Representatives, he did not run it. He got along well with Coolidge as a friend, a neighbor, and a member of the same faction of Massachusetts Republicanism. The President and the speaker agreed on almost everything. Gillett willingly submitted to the President, but he was effective only as an errand boy, not as a straw boss. Perhaps it was with relief that Coolidge lost him to the Senate in 1925, when Gillett was succeeded as speaker by a strong believer in party regularity, Nicholas Longworth.

As for Senator Lodge, geniality and judicial temper were not his hallmarks. He could, when he wished, crack the whip as well as any man and match the Democrats in debate and rough-and-tumble political tactics. Personally the President and Lodge got along well together. They were courteous to each other, both in speech and correspondence. Lodge had worked strenuously for fulfillment of Coolidge's desire to receive an honorary degree from Harvard. Coolidge, almost sentimentally, sent seventy-four roses to the senator on his seventy-fourth birthday. Yet their courtesy toward one another betokened political respect more than friendship. That respect was, however, insufficient to make a Coolidge man of Lodge, for he was almost as recalcitrant on Administration policies as the Democrats.

He opposed the President on some of the keenest issues, including the World Court, the veterans' bonus, Japanese exclusion, and raises for postal workers. Lodge was a weak reed and increasingly Coolidge came to depend on the Republican whip, Senator Charles Curtis of Kansas, who was little more than a party hack, though a reliable one.

Coolidge also tried to use on Congress the methods he had employed as an official of Massachusetts. If you cannot persuade your opponents, win them through love. In December, 1923, he wrote each of the Republican senators soliciting suggestions for appointments to administrative offices. He tried especially to woo the most obstinate Republican senators. They were welcome guests in the White House, coming and going almost at will, a situation that continued for many of them until the end of Coolidge's years as President. Some congressmen were temporarily appeased by Coolidge's pardoning in 1923 of those who had been convicted under the Sedition Act during the Wilson Administration. That represented a streak of compassion in Coolidge, for the chief congressional advocates of releasing the thirty-one political prisoners had not yet pressed the matter on the President before he started the machinery, over the Attorney General's doubts, that led to the pardons. Nevertheless the pardoning also probably represented political wisdom because the senators and representatives who favored the releases were to hold a balance of power in the new Congress that convened in December, 1923.

Presidential affection for the purpose of encouraging Republican harmony was expressed in other ways. To the grizzled progressive senator from Wisconsin, Robert M. La Follette, Coolidge restored his state's federal patronage, which had been withdrawn by Harding. The new President's cordiality was disturbing to Peter Norbeck of South Dakota. Early in 1924 Senator Norbeck, who opposed Coolidge's nomination as the Republican standard-bearer, wrote that the President "has been and continues to be personally very friendly. In fact, both he and his good wife go out of their way in this line, greatly to my embarrassment."[6]

Good relations between the President and the powerful Senator William E. Borah of Idaho antedated Coolidge's move to the White House. They had somehow gotten to like each other while the Yankee served as Vice President. The unpredictable, dynamic Westerner was often summoned to the White House for conferences and for dinner and was a frequent guest on the presidential yacht, the *Mayflower*. The two men discussed not only foreign relations, which was Borah's forte, but also domestic matters. Coolidge's reasons for this courtship were fairly clear. He liked Borah because the senator, however much they might disagree, could be counted on to speak forthrightly. Moreover, Borah was useful on the issue closest to the President's heart, economy, on which the two men saw eye to eye.

Coolidge's cordiality was extended to a number of other independents and opponents. The Farm Bloc leader, Arthur Capper, became a White House favorite despite his transgressions in the Senate. Democrats could find the President likable, as Representative Cordell Hull and Senator Henry Ashurst have testified. Friendliness did not win legislative victories for Coolidge, but it did take some of the edge off the opposition to him. Capper can be cited as an example, for when the President vetoed the first McNary-Haugen farm bill, the Kansas senator wrote for his publishing empire blaming, not Coolidge, but the "interests" for the proposal's defeat. Charles L. McNary was on friendly terms with the President and was most kindly treated on patronage. In fact, his brother John was appointed a federal district court judge. Coolidge's good will did not lead to cessation of the Oregon senator's efforts to pass the McNary-Haugen bill, but McNary did revise the measure in an unsuccessful attempt to make it acceptable to the President. He also supported most other White House policies and led the fight for Wallace McCamant's confirmation as a circuit court judge.

The President's friendliness probably led many independent Republican members of Congress to compensate him for their opposition to so many of his recommendations. Thus Norbeck was willing to endorse the World Court. Borah devoted extra effort to support economy measures and even Lodge absorbed some of the criticism aimed at the White House in the debates over the Teapot Dome, when he did not have to. The President lost frequently in his battles with Congress, but he lost less often than he might have otherwise, thanks to his attention to personal courtesies.

Of course, Coolidge's lack of aggressiveness, his limited insight into programs, and the general truculence of Congress account for much of his failure on legislative matters. Other things, however, were involved. Some members of the Senate, such as George Norris, would never forget Coolidge's double cross on farm legislation while he was Vice President. Other legislators could not cotton to him because he was not, like them, garrulous and outspoken, willing to step down into the dust and fight with bare knuckles.

Another factor contributing to Coolidge's apparently poor record with Congress was that many of the things for which his Administration has been condemned were moot issues only. Some Democratic and Republican congressmen in the 1920s talked about better rights for organized labor. They were not, however, thinking of a Wagner Act or even a Norris-LaGuardia Act but, instead, of a coalition of labor and management in which labor would serve as management's handmaiden. There was also considerable talk in Congress about solving the complicated problems of transportation. The Transportation Act of 1920, passed with bipartisan support, had commanded the Interstate Commerce Commission to bring the nation's railways together into a number of consolidated but competitive systems. After hearings were held in 1922 and 1923 a plan was devised to reconstruct the nation's railroads into nineteen separate systems to give good public service and yet to solve the roads' recurrent financial troubles. Both Harding and Coolidge, as Presidents, favored the revision, but legislative approval was not given it. A spurt of prosperity for the railroads and opposition both from the advocates of laissez-faire ideas and of the old progressive-born laws led to lassitude in Congress and in the ICC. Congress would not move and the members of the ICC, both Republicans and Democrats, did little to press the new plan. Consequently, the transportation mess was passed on to the next generation, which incidentally did little to try to resolve it. The target for the blame in the 1920s was Coolidge, who had considered his duty done when he had endorsed the ICC's plan. Others then in a position to do something about transportation would later blame him for doing little when they had done less.

On December 6, 1923, the members of the Cabinet and the Senate trooped into the House chamber to join the representatives to hear Calvin Coolidge deliver his first message to Congress. This was a moment eagerly awaited by the politically minded citizens of the nation. Now the policies of the new Administration would be unveiled. The President's address sounded like a political party platform and contained even fewer surprises. He dealt first with foreign affairs. The United States would continue to stand apart from the

League of Nations, but it should join the World Court. Russia should make amends before hoping for diplomatic recognition from America. The debts of other countries to the United States would not be canceled, though arrangements for adjustment of terms would not be objectionable. America's Foreign Service should be improved.

Foreign relations disposed of, the President told Congress, "Our main problems are domestic problems." He made it clear that chief among those were the questions of tax reduction and economy in government. He would do his part by pursuing a reduction of government expenses; Congress should do its part by reducing taxes. Specifically recommended were abolition of wartime excise levies and a decrease in income taxes. The President proceeded to praise the operation of the protective tariff of 1922 and called for a "moderate" improvement of inland waters for the development of flood control, transportation, and electric power. He endorsed expansion of the number of judges and a clarification of court procedures and rules. More stringent measures to enforce prohibition were urged, as was "prevention and punishment against the hideous crime of lynching." Support was requested for agricultural and medical education of Negroes. Establishment of a biracial commission to seek harmony between Negroes and whites in industrial areas was also suggested. Coolidge asked for extension of classified civil service, especially in the Post Office Department, and better housing for government agencies. He called for increased regulation of Alaskan fisheries, coastal water pollution, radio, ships in port, and aviation.

The government, President Coolidge told Congress, should be concerned with character development, frugality, industry, and education among the people. He asked for a new Cabinet department to encourage such things. Also requested were a constitutional amendment to restrict child labor and a minimum wage law for women working in industries exclusively under federal jurisdiction. He strongly boosted the movement to restrict immigration, saying: "Those who do not want to be partakers of the American spirit ought not to settle in America. . . . America must be kept American."

Coolidge demanded free hospital care for veterans needing medical assistance and more aid to disabled veterans. He also asked for serious consideration of the many proposals of the American Legion, though he added, "I do not favor the granting of a bonus."

Showing sensitivity to the problems he faced during the 1923 coal crisis, the President requested power to appoint a commission that could in emergencies step in to help solve labor disputes. For agriculture he warned that "simple and direct methods put into operation by the farmer himself are the only real sources for restoration [of income]." Yet the federal government could help farmers through tax reduction, facilitation of railroad efficiency leading to lower freight rates, provision of cheaper fertilizer, encouragement of agricultural organization to reduce production and expand cooperative marketing, and provision of better credit.

He closed his recommendations by encouraging highway construction and reforestation. Then he came to his peroration, which summed up the beliefs, if not the practices, of the decade. "We want idealism," the President said. "We want that vision which lifts men and nations above themselves. These are virtues by reason of their own merit. But they must not be cloistered; they must not be impractical; they must not be ineffective."[7]

Calvin Coolidge had spoken. His message was not that of a progressive but neither was it that of a reactionary. It was the address of a man who sought to satisfy most people by picking up the things they want and carrying them so long as they cost little. It was the speech of a man who relied largely upon his Cabinet's recommendations. It was the statement of a man who wanted stability and believed that it would come only if the government seldom interfered in the people's activities. It was the word of a politician speaking to a coalition of businessmen, veterans, Negroes, and prohibitionists, without trying to irritate labor and agriculture. Lastly it was the pronouncement of an idealist who thought that if one enjoined people to do right, they would do it. As Calvin Coolidge would not do, so he hoped the people would not.

There was a second, more practical message which the President gave Congress. That was the budget message for the following fiscal year which he sent up to Capitol Hill a few days after he had delivered his State of the Union address. The budget message was an elaboration of Coolidge's plea for governmental economy and tax reduction. What he suggested was to cut taxes by some $300 million and still have almost $400 million left for paring the national debt. Everything in his proposed $3.3 billion budget, the lowest since before the war, was cut except appropriations for the Departments of Commerce and Justice and a few minor agencies. The Post Office Department would be set up on a self-sustaining basis, Agriculture's funds would be slashed from $85 million to $69.5 million, and the Shipping Board from $50 million to $30 million. According to Coolidge the result would be salutary. "I have in mind," he said, "that the taxpayers are the stockholders of the business corporation of the United States, and that if this business is showing a surplus of receipts the taxpayer should share therein in some material way that will be of immediate benefit."[8] That benefit, if he had his way, would come in the form of reduced taxes, which would increase the amount of private funds available to industrial development. His budget and his legislative recommendations, he firmly believed, would meet the people's needs and lead to national prosperity. He would discover that many members of Congress did not share his beliefs.

21

Troubles down the Road

THE COOLIDGE BUDGET, though it was controversial, was not to be the central issue of the Sixty-eighth Congress. Politics was to occupy center stage and it was clear from the beginning of the new Congress that the Administration was in for great trouble. The first battle was fought in the House of Representatives, where a score of progressive Republicans held up Frederick Gillett's re-election as speaker by casting their votes for Wisconsin's Henry Allen Cooper, a veteran of twenty-eight years service in Congress. The insurgents' goals were to have bills fairly considered by committees and to have representation on the powerful Rules Committee. On and on the ballots went, with Gillett and the Democratic candidate for speaker, Finis J. Garrett of Tennessee, each failing to get a majority. Finally after three days, and eight ballots, Majority Leader Nicholas Longworth agreed that the rules of the previous Congress would continue in effect for thirty days. During that month amendments to the rules could be proposed to the Rules Committee for consideration and report to the membership of the House for action. One of the progressive Republicans, John M. Nelson of Wisconsin, was elected to the Rules Committee. When the rules for the Sixty-eighth Congress were adopted the insurgents had gained little change in them, but they had made it evident that the majority party was in danger at any time of becoming a minority.

Dissension also erupted in the Senate. Wisconsin's Battle Bob La Follette declared war when he called for blocking the re-election of Senator Albert Cummins of Iowa as chairman of the Interstate Commerce Committee on the ground that the 1922 elections had constituted the voters' rejection of the allegedly pro-business Transportation Act of 1920, which Cummins had written. The struggle to keep the Iowan from the chairmanship and replace him with La Follette, who claimed the post because of committee seniority, went on for a month. The five progressive Republican senators supporting La Follette refused any compromise and in turn the Republican leadership refused to accept Battle Bob. After thirty-two ballots had been taken, the insurgents went over to the Democrats and elected Senator Ellison Smith as chairman of the Interstate Commerce Committee. That was not the clear-cut progressive victory La Follette claimed it to be, but again the fragility of the Administration's majority in Congress had been demonstrated.

Had insurgency on rules and committee assignments been President Coolidge's prime problem in Congress he would have had little about which to worry. He had, however, been left a legacy of scandal from the Harding Administration that would not only hamper enactment of his program and lead to passage of measures he opposed but also would develop poisonous feelings between the two major parties and between the executive and legislative branches. Even worse personally for Coolidge it would seem for a time to jeopardize his nomination and election as President in his own right. Even before the Sixty-eighth Congress convened, investigations had revealed corruption in the Veterans Administration. That scandal, the proportions of which grew as time went by, Coolidge could handle. But coming upon its heels was a scandal that was to be immensely more shocking and damaging. That was the Teapot Dome affair.

On a fine April day in 1922 Coolidge was presiding over the Senate when Robert La Follette rose to demand an investigation of leasing of the United States Naval Oil Reserve Number Three, located in Natrona County, Wyoming, and better known among oilmen as Teapot Dome. The next day, April 22, he amended his resolution to ask that the Senate Committee on Public Lands and Surveys investigate the entire subject of naval oil reserve leases to private interests. Although Republican regulars were certain that his resolution would not pass, Senator La Follette, with an amazing show of facts, indignation, and tongue-lashing, was able to persuade and goad the Senate to adopt it without a dissenting vote. Little did La Follette and even less did Vice President Coolidge know to what that resolution eventually would lead.

Action on the resolution came slowly. Hearings did not begin until October, 1923. Even then most of the representatives of both parties on the Public Lands Committee dragged their heels and the chief investigator, Senator Thomas J. Walsh of Montana, was not wrapped up in the work. Walsh, a Democrat, had to be pushed on looking into oil leases by his party's national committee headquarters and by conservation champion Harry Slattery. Nevertheless, by the end of 1923 the hearings yielded nothing.

Early in January, 1924, when the investigation was on the verge of collapse, a great contradiction in testimony appeared. Albert Fall, who had been secretary of the interior from 1921 to 1923, testified that in order to buy a ranch he had borrowed $100,000 from Washington newspaper publisher Edward B. McLean. The publisher, however, denied that the loan had been consummated. When Senator Walsh pressed Fall January 11 in Palm Beach, Florida, the former Cabinet member admitted that he had not used McLean's money but had borrowed funds from another source, which he refused to identify. The Palm Beach episode gave the investigation a shot of adrenalin. Fall had been the central figure in the leasing of the Teapot Dome oil reserve, having had it transferred from the Navy to the Interior Department for leasing purposes. The question arose whether it was possible that Albert Fall had been bribed by the lessee, Harry F. Sinclair's Mammoth Oil Company. The Democratic National Committee pounced on the issue, comparing it to the Ballinger affair of the Taft Administration. A number of newspapers began discussing the question and congressional interest was raised.

Calvin Coolidge had early been warned by Senator Borah to do something to offset the rumors of scandal in the Harding Administration. The President thought the Idahoan was overestimating their importance and that anyway it was bad business to act on the basis of gossip. When in October, 1923, the press had asked him about the Teapot Dome hearings, Coolidge had replied, ". . . there is no action that could be taken by the President relative to it." As Senator Walsh's investigations began to attract national press notice,

Coolidge again was questioned by the newsmen. On January 18, 1924, he said disarmingly of the oil reserve lease, "That is under investigation, I think, by a senatorial committee, and of course no action is contemplated by any other arm of the government so far as I know."[1]

The investigation received new impetus on January 21 when hearsay evidence was given indicating that money had passed from Harry Sinclair to Albert Fall. Information also was given that Sinclair was hurriedly making plans to leave the country. The President was now becoming aroused. On January 22 he told the Washington press correspondents that he had directed the Department of Justice to observe the Public Lands Committee hearings in case evidence should be forthcoming that might require legal action. He also tried to reassure the country of the government's alertness. He told the reporters: "I don't suppose it needs to be stated that if any irregularities are disclosed, or any misdeeds on the part of any one, they will be subject to investigation by the Department of Justice, and such action taken as the laws of the country require. I want it to be understood in making that statement that I am not making any accusations against any one, or have any opinion about the outcome of the investigation."[2] In good faith Coolidge continued to press the Justice Department to observe the hearings and to take appropriate action to protect the government's financial interests and the integrity of federal agencies.

The most sensational revelation of the investigation came on January 24 when Edward Doheny, the owner of Pan-American Petroleum and Transport Company which had leased the Elk Hills naval oil reserves in California, appeared before the Public Lands Committee. The dapper millionaire admitted that he had lent $100,000 to Albert Fall in 1921. It was, Doheny insisted, just a business arrangement between two old friends and had no connection with the Elk Hills leasing of 1922. The next day one of Harry Sinclair's lawyers added more circumstantial evidence against Fall, when he testified that his boss had lent $25,000 or $30,000 to the former Interior Secretary in 1922.

Rumors now were circulating that the entire Cabinet, including Coolidge, had been in on the oil transactions. The question was put to the President on January 25 and he said he had no recollection that the leasing of oil lands had been discussed in the Cabinet meetings he had attended. He also restated his position on the relationship of the executive branch to the senatorial investigation, saying: "I don't want to be understood as jumping at any conclusion. I am very loath to believe that any one has been guilty of any criminal intent, but it is very evident that evidence has already been given up there that requires explanation. It requires investigation, and it points toward a criminal action." Yet, he emphasized: "You can't start a criminal action on mere rumor. It requires, of course, substantial evidence."[3] The President was warming up to the affair, but he was not going to indict his own party and Cabinet or conclude that loans were bribes without better evidence at hand.

One authority, Burl Noggle, has suggested that it was at this time that Coolidge invited in conservation publicist Harry Slattery to recount what he knew of the oil-leasing affair. After Slattery had presented his story he concluded that the President had been uninformed about the whole matter. Whether Coolidge began to take action now that he was informed or because pressures forced him to do so is a matter of conjecture, but he soon wound up in the middle of the oil mess.

As early as January 7, as a shot in the dark, Senator Thad Caraway of Arkansas had introduced Senate Joint Resolution 54 which would have directed the President to cancel Harry Sinclair's lease on the Teapot Dome oil reserve on the ground that it had been obtained corruptly. Caraway, after Walsh's return from Florida, had carried much of the burden of Democratic attacks on the Administration. On January 23 he went so far as to call Albert Fall a traitor on the floor of the Senate. Caraway's vituperation, based on the evidence that Fall had borrowed money from Doheny and Sinclair, made the leasing of naval oil reserves the prime issue before the Senate. Democrats were to have a grand time impugning the integrity of Republicans.

The Republican senators responded in a number of different ways, with some denying that there was any scandal, others charging that prominent Democrats were suspiciously involved with the Doheny and Sinclair interests, and still others contending that the whole affair was bipartisan in nature and in investigation. Coolidge himself remained cool, though he was increasingly under pressure both from without and within his party to do something.

Coolidge soon acted. Saturday afternoon, January 26, Senator

Walsh told the Public Lands Committee in closed session that the next Monday he intended to call up Caraway's resolution and substitute for it one empowering the President to sue to cancel the leases, to stop further tapping of the oil, and to prosecute where necessary with specially appointed counsel. At the time, the President was cruising on the Potomac in the *Mayflower* and discussing Teapot Dome with Senator George W. Pepper, Massachusetts Chief Justice Arthur P. Rugg, and National Committeeman William Butler. Whether or not Coolidge had been tipped off to Walsh's plans he decided to act in the oil lease matter. From the yacht, at 7 p.m., he telegraphed his secretary, C. Bascom Slemp, to be prepared to go to work. Two hours later Coolidge arrived back at the White House. After talks with Justice Department representatives, he drafted a statement, which was given to the press over the telephone. It read:

> It is not for the President to determine criminal guilt or render judgment in civil cases. That is the function of the courts. It is not for him to prejudge. I shall do neither; but when facts are revealed to me that require action for the purpose of insuring the enforcement of either civil or criminal liability, such action will be taken. . . .
>
> If there has been any crime, it must be prosecuted. If there has been any property of the United States illegally transferred or leased, it must be recovered.
>
> I feel the public is entitled to know that in the conduct of such actions no one is shielded for any party, political, or other reasons. As I understand, men are involved who belong to both political parties, and having been advised by the Department of Justice that it is in accord with former precedents, I propose to employ special counsel of high rank, drawn from both political parties, to bring such actions for the enforcement of the law. Counsel will be instructed to prosecute these cases in the courts, so that if there is any guilt it will be punished; if there is any civil liability, it will be enforced; if there is any fraud, it will be revealed; if there are any contracts which are illegal, they will be canceled. Every law will be enforced and every right of the people and the government will be protected.[4]

Coolidge had beaten the Senate investigators to the punch. He had lifted from Walsh the responsibility for investigation. He also had used the idea of employing special counsel. He had laid the possible guilt upon both the Democratic and Republican parties and was going to give both a share in acting. He had also relieved his party of having to carry the burden of the Department of Justice investigating and acting at a time when gossip of guilt was beginning to revolve around Attorney General Harry Daugherty. It was a masterful statement, magnificently timed, neither too late to seem late nor too early to seem harum-scarum.

Nevertheless, Coolidge was not out of danger. His opponents did not intend to let him get away that easily. They had not done all of the work on this matter in order to let him take the credit. After the White House statement had hit the press on Sunday, Senator Walsh implied that the President had been moved to act by what happened in Saturday afternoon's Public Lands Committee meeting. When the weekend had passed, members of the House and Senate began openly discussing the Coolidge Administration in connection with the scandal. Senator Caraway gibed, "The President was quoted on Saturday morning as having said he thought these contracts were good contracts for the government, but Saturday night at midnight he discovered that they were bad, after cruising down the river."[5]

The Republicans took their lead from the President. House Majority Leader Longworth shed crocodile tears about the partisanship that had been shown by some representatives in discussing Teapot Dome. It was a matter of national, not just partisan, concern. He then went on to reason that if Secretary of the Navy Edwin Denby was involved, as some had suggested, so had been his Democratic predecessor, Josephus Daniels, under whom the reserves had been taken out of the public domain. The Republicans had been shown the path by their leader, and it was a path they hewed to with some effect in the days to come.

Those days were made trying by the Democrats. They pushed adoption of Senate Joint Resolution 54 despite Coolidge's statement of January 26. The resolution was doctored to make Fall and Denby appear guilty of violating federal law in the granting of oil leases and to force the President to submit his appointment of special counsel to the Senate's approval. The resolution cleared the Senate unanimously as the Republicans agreed that they had no choice but to vote "agin' sin." It was later overwhelmingly approved in the House. Coolidge was reported by the New York *Times* to have given the resolution his blessing "in order that a prompt and thorough investigation may be made and appropriate action taken."[6] He took care, however, to give no opinion as to the facts stated in the resolution regarding Denby and Fall.

The President was delayed in his efforts to appoint the special attorneys. On January 29 he named former Attorney General Thomas W. Gregory, a New York Democrat, and Silas H. Strawn, a Chicago Republican, as counsel. Gregory soon withdrew because of business connections with Edward Doheny, and Strawn's name was withdrawn because the Public Lands Committee had objections to him. Former Democratic Senator Atlee Pomerene of Ohio was nominated to replace Gregory, and Owen J. Roberts of Philadelphia was named to take Strawn's place. Even the new nominees met with opposition, especially from Senator Walsh who had not been consulted by Coolidge. They were Easterners, the argument went, and would be at a disadvantage in considering Western land questions. Nevertheless they were soon accepted by the Senate, which was a bit worn out by the dallying of those senators who appeared to want to name the attorneys themselves. On February 19 Coolidge gave Pomerene and Roberts their commissions and they were on their way to do a successful and even distinguished job of handling the oil lease litigation in the courts. Largely as a result of his performance, Roberts was later appointed by President Hoover to the United States Supreme Court.

The maneuvers on the appointment of the special counsel constituted only a curtain raiser for a bigger show, the attack on Edwin Denby. The Secretary of the Navy had been mentioned from time to time in connection with the oil leases because of his assent to the transfer of the petroleum reserves to Interior Secretary Fall's jurisdiction. On January 28 the Democratic leader of the senate, Joseph T. Robinson of Arkansas, offered a resolution calling for Denby's resignation because of indicated misconduct in office. The debate went on for two weeks, during which time there was little defense of the Navy Secretary in the Senate and much unrest among his Cabinet colleagues. When asked about the Robinson resolution, Coolidge's response was, almost predictably, that he did not wish to discuss it.

Robinson's pressing of the resolution was meant partly to offset Coolidge's January 26 statement and partly to counterattack the whoopee that Republicans were making about the linking on February 1 of Edward Doheny with the leading candidate for the 1924 Democratic presidential nomination, former Secretary of the Treasury William Gibbs McAdoo. Robinson's resolution attracted progressive Republican as well as Democratic support. La Follette made a major speech in the Senate backing the resolution and indicting the entire Administration for doing nothing to stop Fall's oil lease policy. The Republican party had played, the Wisconsin senator said, "as sorry a part in this investigation as it did in the Ballinger investigation." Yet he took pains to point out that "Democratic administrations are not by any means free from like offenses. . . . There should be no politics on an issue like the present one."[7] Ten Republicans joined the Democrats to carry the Robinson resolution on February 11, 47 to 34.

Coolidge was up in the air on the Denby matter. He was convinced, with considerable justification, that the Robinson resolution was motivated by partisanship. The Secretary of the Navy was naive, but there was no evidence—and never has been—that he was guilty of misconduct. What could the President do? He gave moral support to Denby but seemed to believe that should the resolution pass he would have to ask for the Secretary's resignation. At least that appeared the case to Senators Borah and Brandegee one evening while at dinner at the White House.

As the two lawmakers were leaving, Brandegee asked Borah how he felt about it and the Idahoan replied, "Well, if he removes Denby on that resolution, I quit."

"Why don't you go back and tell the President that?" the Connecticut senator said.

They both returned and told Coolidge that the Senate could not force him that way. The President told Borah, "I wish you would dictate a message you would send to the Senate if you were President and such a resolution should be presented to you."[8]

Senator Borah accepted that request only as a compliment, but the next day Coolidge's secretary, C. Bascom Slemp, called to ask whether he had written the message. Borah then dashed off a draft in consultation with Brandegee. Coolidge drew on that heavily in preparing the public statement he made the day the Robinson resolution passed. "No official recognition," the President said, "can be given to the passage of the Senate resolution relative to their opinion concerning members of the Cabinet or other officers under executive control." In the oil lease case, action by the President must wait upon advice of the special counsel. Citing James Madison and Grover Cleveland on separation of powers, Coolidge added: "The President is responsible to the people for his conduct relative to the retention or dismissal of public officials. I assume that responsibility. . . . I do not propose to sacrifice any innocent man for my own welfare, nor do I propose to retain in office any unfit man for my own welfare."[9]

Denby held out for a week after the passage of the Robinson resolution but finally concluded, without pressure from the White House, to resign. Not only did he protest his innocence of any wrongdoing, but he defended his actions upon his resignation. He gave Congress time to dispute him through impeachment proceedings, by making March 10 the effective date of his resignation. He wrote Coolidge that he was leaving to keep "embarrassments" from mounting for the President. Coolidge expressed his regret at the Secretary's leaving, saying, "You will go with the knowledge that your honesty and integrity have not been impugned."[10] Yet Denby's resignation was not to end the Teapot Dome episode.

"Get rid of Daugherty," Senator Borah had told Calvin Coolidge soon after he assumed the Presidency.[11] That advice had been murmured by many others in the capital early in 1924 and as the Teapot Dome investigations grew in proportion it was to be shouted. Forces gathered quickly to condemn the Attorney General who had upheld the legality of the oil leases and who was a friend of Denby, Doheny, and Sinclair. On January 29 Senator Burton K. Wheeler had introduced a resolution calling for Harry Daugherty's resignation because of failure to prosecute corruption. After Denby's resignation the Montana Democrat pushed his resolution to the fore.

Coolidge was justifiably concerned with the developing attack on the Attorney General. Soon after Wheeler's resolution had been introduced, Senator Borah was summoned to the White House. When he entered the President's study he was asked to give his views on Daugherty, which he did, and they were against retaining the Attorney General in office. Within a few minutes Daugherty was ushered into the room. The President had brought the two men together to fight it out.

The Attorney General remarked sarcastically to Borah, "Well, don't let my presence embarrass you."

Borah, irritated with both Coolidge and Daugherty, retorted, "I think I should be the least embarrassed person here."

The senator and the Attorney General snapped at each other for an hour in the silent presence of the Chief Executive. The burden of Borah's comments was that Daugherty should resign because the people lacked confidence in him. Daugherty's position was that his political enemies were ganging up on him. When the Attorney General stormed out of the room, Coolidge finally opened his mouth to say to Borah, "Senator, I reckon you are right."[12]

The next day, Frank Willis and Simeon Fess, the two senators from the Attorney General's home state, Ohio, went to give the President their opinions. Daugherty's removal from office, they asserted, would give Ohio's electoral votes to the Democrats in the 1924 elections. They were right, too, Coolidge probably reckoned. The question would be allowed to simmer.

The Daugherty issue would get a lot of simmering before it was resolved. Fortunately for Coolidge, the time was available for it because the issue would not become crucial for several weeks. The President became caught up in a crossfire of urgings to remove and to retain Harding's friend and adviser. Several Cabinet members thought that Daugherty should resign. One day after a Cabinet meeting Secretary of State Hughes said to the President, "If it would be of any help to you, I think I could arrange to have all members of the Cabinet place their resignations in your hands; you could then reappoint those you wish to retain."

Coolidge, who was exiting from the room, called out: "No, don't do that. It might leave me alone with Daugherty!"[13]

At first Coolidge thought that the Teapot Dome investigation was merely an opposition plot to discredit the Administration and to divide the Republican party. Harding's judgment in men, he believed, could not have been so bad as the investigators made it out. Chief Justice Taft, among others, encouraged that kind of thinking. Taft viewed the matter as a repetition of the Ballinger-Pinchot affair that had occurred during his Administration and which he saw as an outrageous plot to dishonor men of good will and competence. Moreover, he was favorably disposed toward Daugherty, who had been a force in his appointment to the Supreme Court and had consulted him in the Harding Administration's judicial appointments. The conspiracy view led Coolidge not only to have contempt for the Teapot Dome investigators but also for the Republican regulars in the Senate who were tepid in their defense of the Administration. That was expressed when one day he blurted out to Taft that "the Republican senators are a lot of damned cowards."[14] For Coolidge, a man who was milder in words than in action, that was a violent curse.

Yet Coolidge had other reasons to retain his Attorney General. The Outlawry of War leader Raymond Robins, who was among those begging for Daugherty's dismissal, quoted the reasons Coolidge gave him for not doing so:

> First, it is a sound rule that when the President dies in office it is the duty of his successor for the remainder of that term to maintain the counsellors and policies of the deceased President. Second, I ask you if there is any man in the Cabinet for whom—were he still living—President Harding would more surely demand his day in court, would more surely not dismiss because of popular clamor than the man who was his closest personal and political friend? I am satisfied that you are right, the people would be pleased, the party would be helped, my campaign would be advanced, by the summary removal of Mr. Daugherty. We shall have to bear that burden. Regarding my being afraid to dismiss Mr. Daugherty, I can assure you, that if the attorney general does any act I regard as wrong while I am President, he will be removed.[15]

Perhaps Coolidge had told Robins all of his reasons for inaction. Yet that is doubtful because the President was under great pressure to keep, as well as to discharge, the Attorney General. In such a situation he had to placate both sides until it became clear that he should fire Daugherty or go all out to defend him. Coolidge may have been cautious, but he was neither a coward nor a fool. He had already demonstrated that he was not going to condemn a man on the basis of adverse public opinion or loose-knit circumstantial evidence, a virtue perhaps better understood after the McCarthyite scares of the 1950s than it was in the 1920s. Nor was he going to retain in office a man who had committed an unpardonable offense. It is true that the President occasionally appeared to favor both pro- and anti-Daugherty sentiments at the same time, but he did not act until there was clear reason to do so. If that ultimately redounded to his political advantage, so much the better for him. That is, however, retrospective thinking. At the time Coolidge's refusal to rush action, his insistence upon remaining silent while others roared, and the way he acted when he felt it necessary to act guaranteed him nothing politically. In short, he acted as much like a man who wanted to keep his self-respect as like a man who wanted to win the next election.

The pressures on the President were heavy. On February 20, the day after Wheeler revived his attack on Daugherty, Senators Pepper and Lodge told Coolidge that the Attorney General should resign for the sake of the party. Borah publicly called for Daugherty's retirement and Secretaries Hughes and Hoover stepped up their efforts to rid the Cabinet of their colleague. All that was not just politically inspired any more than was Coolidge's refusal to budge. Burton Wheeler later wrote of the conservative Republican senators who besought the President to discharge Daugherty that although they hoped to relieve their party of a campaign burden, they were "dignified, able, and honest senators. Daugherty was not their type but, more than that, they had a distaste for crooks in high office."[16]

Pressure on Coolidge also came from those who opposed dismissal of Daugherty. Republican National Committee Chairman John T. Adams of Iowa and many other influential members of the committee contended that it would smear the whole party and questioned whether the demands for resignations would stop if the Attorney General were discharged. One of the national committeemen, C. A. Reynolds of North Carolina, wrote the White House: "If I were the President, I would see that Democratic gang in Washington in Hell before I asked for Mr. Daugherty's resignation. . . . It would only be an inducement for them to be more destructive."[17] Yet men like Reynolds were unsuccessful in their representations. The President's only action, according to William Allen White, was to send Chief Justice Taft to suggest to Daugherty that he resign for the party's good. The Attorney General refused to do so under fire because it could be interpreted as a confession of some kind of guilt.

He told Coolidge: "If the time comes that you wish my resignation, just put it in writing and give me your reasons. It should be a matter of record."[18]

Yet the situation was deteriorating rapidly. The Republican National Committee attempted to tag Senator Walsh and former Secretary of the Navy Josephus Daniels with fathering the legislation which allowed leasing of naval oil reserves, but that maneuver failed. On February 29 the Senate Democrats mercilessly, and with little resistance from the Republicans, attacked Daugherty and the Administration for implication in the oil scandal. One of the Democrats, Thomas Heflin, Alabama's master of invective humor, put it:

> . . . the further this thing goes the worse it gets. It looks to me as if it is going to involve finally nearly every Republican official high in authority. Reaching, as it does, into nearly every nook and corner of the administration, it calls to mind two old familiar lines about a dog—

> > Whose name was Rover,
> > And when he died he died all over.[19]

That same day the Democrats also jammed through Senate Resolution 180 requesting the President to direct the Secretary of the Treasury to turn over to the Public Lands Committee the income tax returns of Albert Fall, Edward Doheny, Harry Sinclair, and the businesses they owned. Coolidge refused to comply with the resolution, holding it to be in violation of the Revenue Act of 1921. He did, however, promise alteration of the Treasury rules so that it would be possible for the committee's representatives to inspect the requested tax returns. The following day, March 1, the Senate resolved to investigate Attorney General Daugherty and the Justice Department for failure to prosecute corruption.

The Senate investigation of Daugherty began March 12 and soon a fantastic record of questionable transactions, deals, and actions by the Attorney General and his friends was revealed. The evidence was insufficient to jail Daugherty, but it was enough to disenchant all but his most ardent supporters. Yet the high law officer did not resign and the President did not move against him. Finally, toward the end of March, Daugherty took a step that brought the matter to an end. Senate investigators under Smith Brookhart of Iowa had

asked the Attorney General to open the Justice Department's files
to inspection. When Daugherty arbitrarily rejected the request,
Coolidge refused to back him. Daugherty had moved completely
beyond the line of propriety and would have to resign. The President wrote him on March 27, 1924:

> I do not see how you can be acting for yourself in your own
> defense in this matter, and at the same time and on the same
> question acting as my attorney general. . . . These two po-
> sitions are incompatible and cannot be reconciled. I am sure
> that you will see that it is necessary for me to have the ad-
> vice of a disinterested attorney general.[20]

Daugherty resigned the next day and a great weight was lifted from
the President's shoulders. Coolidge had kept his head and his self-
respect: he had not acted until he had unquestionable reason to do
so.

One should not be deceived that the Administration's critics
considered the President to stand above the charges of scandal. If
the names of Fall, Denby, and Daugherty were the ones most often
raised, the target was at the top, whether it was the dead President
Harding or his successor, Calvin Coolidge. If Coolidge did not bear
the brunt of the attack, it was mostly because of lack of evidence.
Once during the investigations, though, he almost became the Senate
investigators' number one public target. Presidential secretary C.
Bascom Slemp had been in Palm Beach early in January when Senator Walsh was seeking out Edward McLean and Albert Fall. The
Public Lands Committee concluded that it had to inquire whether
Slemp was in Florida, perhaps at Coolidge's bidding, to persuade
publisher McLean to say that he had lent $100,000 to Fall.

In what amounted to an attack on the White House, Senator
Walsh requested Slemp to appear before the committee on Monday,
February 25. The day before, Coolidge, his secretary, and Representative Walton Moore worshiped together in Alexandria's historic
Christ Church. Moore later in the day tutored Slemp as to the questions he might expect to be asked. Slemp believed that Coolidge
would forbid his testimony or at least give him some kind of encouragement, but his chief did neither. The President knew his man and
that it was possible that the veteran patronagemonger had been up to
something in Florida. Sunday night was sleepless for Slemp, who

feared, as he wrote William Allen White fifteen years later, that "any slip I might make would be given publicity and injure me personally as well as the administration."[21] He was so upset that by six Monday morning a physician had to be called to his side. He did not, however, make that public because it might be considered a sign of weakness.

Slemp arrived at the jampacked hearing room at ten-thirty that morning. His rambling testimony turned out to be of little value to the senators. He admitted that Fall and McLean had talked with him about the oil matter, but he mentioned little that was not already known to the Public Lands Committee. Walsh did ask him whether he had been in touch with the White House while in Florida, to which the President's secretary answered, "All communications that I would make to the White House I would have to reserve as confidential."[22] The overall impression given by Slemp was that he had been in Florida politicking with that state's Republicans and having a bit of vacation. If there was more, he succeeded in protecting himself and Coolidge.

Slemp's appearance before the committee did not end the questions about the White House. Senator Walsh introduced into the hearings a number of telegrams which had passed between McLean in Florida and various people in Washington. Two of the wires had been sent from Coolidge to the newspaper publisher. The first was dated January 12, the day after Walsh had questioned McLean in Palm Beach, and read: "Prescott is away. Advise Slemp with whom I shall confer. Acknowledge." The second one, sent February 12, went: "Thank you for your message. You have always been most considerate. . . ."[23] The latter raised no eyebrows, but the first was the cause of prolonged discussion in the Senate. Henry Cabot Lodge, however, gave a plausible explanation of it. At night after the White House aides had gone home, the senator said, the President had wanted information from Prescott, who was the chairman of the District of Columbia Republican Committee, but found him unavailable. Knowing that McLean knew of Slemp's whereabouts, Coolidge wired him to contact Slemp to tell him whom he should see in Prescott's absence.

It also turned out that Slemp had received telegrams, some in code, from McLean's employees. Suspicion was justifiable of a presidential aide who had been close to McLean and Fall at a crucial point in the investigation, who had been in touch with McLean's men, and who had told the Public Lands Committee that he would keep confidential any messages he had sent from Palm Beach to the White House. That suspicion was heightened when the contents of a telegram to McLean from one of his employees was revealed. It read, "Have arranged with Smithers at the White House, to have our end of the private wire opened at 6 o'clock tonight."[24] As it turned out McLean had leased a private telegraph wire between his Palm Beach cottage and his newspaper, the Washington *Post*. Smithers, the chief telegrapher in the White House, had taken the job of operating McLean's wire at night in order to supplement his salary. File copies of the messages dispatched over McLean's wire apparently had not been kept. When the publisher went before the committee in March to explain those and other things, he shed little light on them, but he succeeded in making a good impression on the committee. Interest in Slemp slackened immediately.

One other telegram came into question. That had been sent January 29 from Ira E. Bennett of the Washington *Post* to McLean and read: "Saw principal. Delivered message. He says greatly appreciates, and sends regards to you and Mrs. McLean. There will be no rocking of boat and no resignations. He expects reaction from unwarranted political attacks."[25] Bennett identified "principal" as Senator Charles Curtis, but the Republican whip in the Senate denied it. Even if, as many suggested, Coolidge had been "principal," the message was hardly startling because it represented his far from secret belief at the time that the investigation was a partisan plot to discredit his Administration. Moreover, McLean was never connected with the scandal other than as a friend of Albert Fall.

That did not save Coolidge from heavy attack in March. Newspapers raised questions and Democratic senators, both those seeking the truth, like Walsh and Wheeler, and those seeking partisan advantage, like Caraway and Heflin, bore down on the President from the Senate floor. Lodge rose to Coolidge's defense. He deplored public debate of matters that were still under investigation. He said that instead of leaving them to committees:

> . . . we have followed the plan here of discussing all the testimony and every newspaper rumor in addition, day after day, and with the character of that debate I am utterly out of

sympathy. I think it is lowering to the character of the Senate to have its time taken hour after hour in vilification of all sorts of men, whether guilty or innocent, and in exchanges of personal vituperation on the floor of the Senate among senators themselves.[26]

Lodge followed that statement with a strong testimonial to Calvin Coolidge's character. The senator was effective if only in making himself a target for those senators among the Democrats who were professional vilifiers. Like a shark scenting blood, one of them, Kenneth McKellar of Tennessee, asked Lodge whether Woodrow Wilson had been spared from attack in 1919. That was too good for any Democrat to miss: the man who had charged Wilson with every sin under the sun was now asking them to lay off Calvin Coolidge. Lodge deserved the ridicule he received, but the significance of it was that, intentionally or not, he had substituted himself as the prime target for the opposition thereby diluting criticism of President Coolidge. As public sentiment developed behind the idea that senators like McKellar were chiefly interested in besmirching reputations, even moderates like Walsh were listened to less often. Further attacks on Coolidge would build sympathy for him with the voters. It was not a case of the President's luck but of his critics hanging themselves on the rope they had made for his lynching. Coolidge's waiting game, whether aimed at that result or not, had paid off.

The President also aided himself by several actions he took in connection with the scandal. The appointments of Curtis D. Wilbur as secretary of the navy in March and of Amherst graduate Harlan Fiske Stone as attorney general in April helped. Although Wilbur, drawn from the chief justiceship of California, was a conservative and Stone, a former dean of the Columbia University Law School, was a Wall Street lawyer, both were considered several cuts above the men they replaced. Indeed, Stone proved to be an outstanding attorney general and Wilbur served effectively and honorably as navy secretary. Coolidge further helped himself, first by appointing a committee of experts to explore the problem of conserving the naval petroleum reserves and, later, by establishing the Cabinet-level Federal Oil Conservation Board to study the entire nation's problems of oil conservation.

Also helpful to the Administration over the years was the work of Special Counsel Roberts and Pomerene and of the government to clean up the messes created by the Teapot Dome and Elk Hills transactions. Those actions resulted in Albert Fall's conviction of bribery, with a sentence of a $100,000 fine and a year in prison being given. He was the first member of the Cabinet ever to be jailed for misconduct in office. Daugherty and Doheny escaped punishment because of the inconclusive evidence against them. Although Sinclair was not convicted of charges of bribery and conspiracy in connection with Teapot Dome, he was fined $1,000 and given three months in jail for refusing to appear before the Public Lands Committee. The oilman later received an additional six-month sentence for contempt of court. As for the controversial oil leases, they were finally canceled in 1927 after exhaustive judicial proceedings.

President Coolidge had handled himself satisfactorily in the oil lease scandal. He was cautious in acting, but caution when others are shouting their heads off is a virtue. In the Teapot Dome case he used prudence to keep the executive branch from becoming a tool of Congress, to clean up the scandal effectively, to preserve his political strength, and to keep that of his opponents, both Democrats and progressive Republicans, at a minimum. As for his relations with Congress that were to lead to the blocking of his 1924 legislative program, it is doubtful that anything he could have done then would have improved them. Stealing the investigation or denying that scandal existed would have further antagonized the lawmakers, and giving in to all their allegations would have destroyed whatever respect they had for him. In all, Coolidge had come through a great domestic crisis as well as could have been expected.

22

Frustrated in Congress

MUCH OF THE opposition that Coolidge faced on legislation in 1924 resulted from the tempers and suspicions raised by the Teapot Dome scandal. Not only did the affair disrupt Congress and gobble time and energy, but it created ill will that was bound to work against his program. He did his best to offset those consequences by not being intrusive in congressional affairs and by keeping his own anger under control. Senator Wheeler with the mellowness of his later years told of that:

> I was very much amused at the way he handled Walsh and me when we called on him to try to get the federal government behind a proposed road from Red Lodge, Montana, into Yellowstone National Park. O. H. P. Shelley, then Republican national committeeman in Montana, lived in Red Lodge and was going all out to line up support. Shelley got [Indiana Senator James] Watson interested in the project; soon Watson had a friend who wanted to get the contract to build the road. Coolidge got wind of this, and of course he was only too well aware that it was Walsh and I who had embarrassed the Republicans by our twin revelations of the Harding scandals.
>
> So when we went to the White House to discuss the matter, Coolidge didn't pay much attention to Walsh as he

talked earnestly about the merits of a new road. The President gazed thoughtfully out the window into the rose garden. When Walsh finished, all Coolidge said, in his extra-dry manner, was: "Well, I don't want to see any scandal about it."[1]

Yet Teapot Dome was not the only trying situation that upset Coolidge's relations with Congress. The revelations of the distribution of some $250 million in graft in the Veterans Bureau and of corruption in the Office of the Alien Property Custodian burdened his Administration. Another problem concerned the controversies and the charges of scandal that affected the legislative proposals closest to his heart, tax and debt reduction. The President fully supported his secretary of the treasury, Andrew Mellon, in seeking the reductions in 1924. Debt, from Coolidge's viewpoint, was almost sinful and should be retired as soon as possible. Federal taxes were high enough, he believed, to threaten the nation's prosperity. They must come down.

There were many observers, of course, who disagreed. A few held that the debt was not detrimental. More people were concerned with taxes. Some wanted a high level of taxation in order to pare the debt more rapidly; some wanted high taxes to finance additional public welfare programs; others opposed tax reduction so that the tariff could be reduced; still others objected that the government was trying to lower taxes too far; and yet others just disagreed with the proposed distribution of tax reduction benefits, contending that it would unreasonably benefit the wealthy at the expense of the poor. The clash of viewpoints was enough to insure great opposition to the Administration's tax and debt policies, and it was amplified by the reactions to the scandals.

Even worse for promotion of Coolidge's fiscal policies was the battle of the millionaires, Andrew Mellon against Republican Senator James Couzens of Michigan. Couzens, a member of the Senate Finance Committee, had written the Secretary of the Treasury questions about the Administration's tax reduction proposals. One thing led to another and the correspondence between the two officials became abusive. At one point the Secretary questioned the senator's huge investment in tax-exempt government securities and that led Couzens to inquire about Mellon's investments. Soon the decks were cleared for a showdown.

On February 21, 1924, Couzens introduced a resolution demanding investigation of the Bureau of Internal Revenue, which was in Mellon's jurisdiction. At the height of congressional furor about Teapot Dome, it was easy to get approval of the resolution. That hint of further scandal jeopardized the Coolidge-Mellon tax reduction program. In his spare time Coolidge had been imploring Congress to turn from its preoccupation with investigating everyone and instead consider cutting taxes, but the Couzens resolution undercut the President's pleas. Couzens' investigation revealed that a number of large corporations had received huge tax rebates and had been treated deferentially by the Internal Revenue Bureau. The Treasury Secretary described the investigation as "nonsense" and scoffed at the suggestion that the rebates were not routine. Coolidge attempted to stop the "nonsense," according to Couzens, by offering the senator appointment as ambassador to Great Britain.

Republican Governor Gifford Pinchot of Pennsylvania, who supported prohibition and opposed Mellon with equal fervor, got into the act. The old crusader suggested that there was scandal in the Internal Revenue Bureau in regard to enforcement of prohibition. He also told Couzens that the Senate Finance Committee should have an investigator familiar with tax affairs and nominated a veteran progressive, Francis J. Heney, for the job. Funds to compensate special counsel were lacking, so Couzens decided, "I will pay Heney out of my own pocket!"[2] Mellon was furious. He told the President that he would resign over the issue of making the investigation a fishing expedition and financing it from private funds.

Coolidge was on the spot. Mellon's resignation would cost him not only an adviser he was coming to regard as indispensable, but would remove some of the vigor from the Administration's tax proposals. The Republican leadership in the Senate, particularly James E. Watson of Indiana who was chairman of the Finance Committee, tried to block Heney's appointment, but was unsuccessful. Republican leaders in both the Senate and the Administration were alarmed. A general investigation of prohibition and tax administration backed by Pinchot and Couzens could, as Watson said, lead to "a saturnalia of vituperation and aspersion unequaled hitherto in the political annals of America."[3] The Administration did not need that as a topping for the scandals already facing it.

Mellon complained to Coolidge on April 10 that Couzens' sole

purpose was to "vent some personal grievance." In order to cooperate with the senator, Secretary Mellon had obtained waivers of
their right to privacy in tax records from the corporations under investigation. Yet when examination of those documents revealed no
irregularities, Couzens, instead of ending the matter, only pushed on
further without evidence to justify it. Referring to the senator's
payment of Heney, Mellon said, "If the interposition of private resources be permitted to interfere with the executive administration
of government, the machinery of government will cease to function."[4]

The President came to Mellon's support. He dispatched not only
his Treasury Secretary's letter to the Senate but sent a protest of his
own. To Coolidge it was "incredible" that the upper house would
authorize Heney, as the agent of one senator, generally to investigate a whole department of government without regard for that
agency's established procedures. The President added:

> Under a procedure of this kind, the Constitutional guar-
> antees against unwarranted search and seizure breaks down,
> the prohibition against what amounts to a government charge
> of criminal action with the formal presentment of a grand
> jury is evaded, the rules of evidence which have been adopted
> for the protection of the innocent are ignored, the Depart-
> ment becomes the victim of vague, unformulated and indefi-
> nite charges....
> Against the continuance of such a condition, I enter my
> solemn protests and give notice that in my opinion the de-
> partments ought not to be required to participate in it....
> It is time that we return to a government under and in ac-
> cord with the usual forms of law of the land.[5]

The Chief Executive was wide of the mark in his analogies, but
his point about procedures was well taken. Couzens had gone too
far by fishing in waters protected by federal law on the sanctity of
tax returns and by not fully taking advantage of the Treasury Department's willingness to cooperate. The Senate, however, was enraged by the President's and Mellon's letters. Senator Walsh said
that it was the executive that was telling another branch how to run
its business instead of the other way around. Senator James Reed
of Missouri offered a resolution to expunge the Coolidge and Mellon

letters from the record. Even the Republican leaders in the Senate were unhappy with the Administration. In the end a compromise was worked out. It favored Couzens by authorizing payment of a tax investigator from public funds, though Heney's place was required to be taken by an attorney satisfactory to all members of the Senate Finance Committee.

Over the years the investigations sponsored by Senator Couzens showed that, although the tax rebates were all legal, many companies, including those owned by Secretary Mellon, had benefited from liberal interpretations of the law by the Bureau of Internal Revenue. That evidence was not to lead to significant change in federal tax rebate policies even during the New Deal, which gladly used Couzens' data to condemn the Republican Administrations of the 1920s. The investigations did, however, end secrecy about the rebates and led to providing Congress with a permanent staff of tax experts. As for Coolidge, Couzens' crusade made it almost impossible to get favorable consideration of any of the Administration's tax proposals in 1924. Whatever the President achieved by way of tax reduction that year was crumbs from the congressional table. He would have to wait until 1926 to get enactment of the body of his tax reduction ideas.

Not only was Calvin Coolidge unable to secure approval of the major plank in his legislative program, but he was unsuccessful in persuading Congress to accept his solution to an issue of almost equal importance in his eyes. That was the disposition of Muscle Shoals. The Shoals was a strategic point on the Tennessee River where the Wilson Administration had begun an ambitious program of producing hydroelectric power and of manufacturing nitrates for national defense. The development of two nitrate plants, a quarry, and a steam plant had cost the nation $85 million, and some $16 million more of public funds had been invested in the construction, only one-third completed, of Wilson Dam. Of the batch, only the steam plant was in operation, leased to the Alabama Power Company.

Since the end of World War I much sentiment had developed in support of using Muscle Shoals to produce cheap fertilizers. Those who favored government operation of the project were in a minority. Most of the pressure was directed toward the sale of the project to private management that would get large-scale fertilizer production under way without burdening the taxpayers. Soon after taking office in 1921, Secretary of War John Weeks had asked for bids from private interests on the project. Henry Ford, the wonder man of the automotive industry, was urged by American Farm Bureau officials and those interested in development of the Tennessee River Valley to consider taking on the enterprise. During the summer Ford made a bid to use the project for producing fertilizers, while at the same time keeping the plants in readiness for war production. After much discussion Ford wound up offering to assume full control of the Muscle Shoals properties. For them he was willing to pay $5 million, maintenance costs, and semiannual payments that over the years, if invested properly, might yield the government at least $49 million.

The reaction to his offer came quickly. The Farm Bureau was joined in support of the industrialist by the Grange, the American Federation of Labor, most of the press, business, and politicians of the South, and the worshipers of Ford all over the land. The opposition, which was much smaller, was led by Governor Pinchot and George Norris, the chairman of the Senate Agriculture Committee. Norris compared Ford's offer to the thefts of public properties that had occurred during the Administration of Ulysses S. Grant. The opponents contended that in order to meet Ford's terms as to the condition of the property the government would have to spend at least another $40 million in Muscle Shoals. Ford's champions thought that the results would be worth it.

In June, 1922, the House Military Affairs Committee urged acceptance of the industrialist's offer in order to relieve taxpayers of the burden of carrying a white elephant any further. The matter dragged on, however, and was the subject of sporadic bursts of enthusiastic support or indignant opposition in Congress and the newspapers. Ford's motives, as usual, were muddled. That he was public-spirited is undoubted and that he wanted to use Muscle Shoals to develop a model industrial community is true. It was also clear that he was seeking glory and probable that he thought he would gain money and power from the undertaking. The manufacturer's motives justified both praise and criticism.

Soon after Coolidge took office as President, he talked with Ford about his bid. That was of interest for political reasons because a "We Want Henry" movement had developed behind Ford for the presidential race of 1924. It attracted further attention because Ford's interest in Muscle Shoals had cooled and it appeared that Coolidge was working to keep the automobile maker's bid open.[6] In December, 1923, another meeting took place between the President and Ford after which both men appeared pleased. Their conversations were never reported, but the manufacturer called off his political movement and the Administration backed his bid for Muscle Shoals. Talk of a "deal" began immediately. Nevertheless, in March, 1924, the House of Representatives voted, by a substantial margin, to accept Ford's proposition. In the Senate George Norris lashed out at the proposal, contending that if it were effected it would make "Teapot Dome look like a pinhead."[7] With scandal seeming to crop up on every side in 1924, Norris was able to make the most of his opposition. Carrying on almost alone, he fought the Ford bid to a standstill in the Senate and attracted the kind of publicity that made the industrialist happy to withdraw his proposal in October.

The President had been vanquished on Muscle Shoals as much by circumstance as by George Norris. Coolidge's astuteness in 1923 in getting Ford out of the presidential race and keeping him as a bidder to take Muscle Shoals off the government's hands turned into an embarrassment in 1924. Coolidge had thought that he had made a good arrangement for himself and for the country, but the apparent fact that a deal had been made left him vulnerable to attack after the Teapot Dome affair had been aired. Norris and the President had never gotten along well, but after the senator's battle on the Ford bid they were to be in a state of war that was not to end until Coolidge left the White House.

Although President Coolidge was battered, with the coming of spring he had more blows to take from Congress. In the next fight, that against the Japanese exclusion principle of the Immigration Act of 1924, he was enlisted in a good cause. Congress three years earlier had greatly restricted immigration and was now seeking to limit it further and discriminatorily against those not of northern European backgrounds. The acts of 1921 and 1924 were not partisan, for only a small band of Democrats and Republicans opposed them. Coolidge had accurately interpreted the mood of the country and Congress when in an article in *Good Housekeeping* in 1921 and in his 1923 State of the Union address he had called for tightening of immigration legislation.

The bill that was reported by the House Immigration Committee in February, 1924, however, was objected to by Secretary of State Charles Evans Hughes because it proposed to ban the immigration of Japanese. That question, the Secretary said, had been taken care of by Japan's agreement to regulate emigration of its nationals to America. The measure before the House would unilaterally revoke an effectively functioning agreement between the two nations. The bill was returned to the committee and revised. The new version was still unsatisfactory to Hughes but in early April was passed overwhelmingly, 326 to 71.

The Administration's chances looked better in the Senate. Not only was the composition of the upper house's Immigration Committee sympathetic to Hughes' position, but California's Hiram Johnson, the most ardent opponent of Japanese immigration, was absent early in the spring, campaigning against Coolidge for the Republican presidential nomination. The Department of State induced the Senate committee to write into its bill an annual quota of 250 for Japan. Had the department settled for that, it might have achieved its main goal, an immigration quota that would have kept the Japanese from being offended. Hughes and his aides went further, however, and asked for Senate recognition in the bill of the Gentlemen's Agreement on immigration. Since that had been an understanding between the executive branches of Japan and the United States, it was predictable that the Senate might be upset. When the bill was reported out of committee, many senators expressed fear that the State Department was trying to slip ratification of a treaty over on them and, at that, a treaty which would limit their power to regulate immigration as an internal affair. The agitation was contributed to by the return of Hiram Johnson to the Senate on April 9.

Alarmed by exclusionist sentiment in the Senate, Japanese Ambassador Masanao Hanihara sent a letter to Secretary Hughes on April 10 requesting that the quota be retained in the final bill. Hughes studied the letter and then, without referring it to the Cabinet, forwarded it to the Senate. Hanihara had written of "grave consequences" if the quota provision was not approved. Hughes let it pass because it was couched in a friendly context. That was one of the worst mistakes of the distinguished New Yorker's career. The senators, already exercised over Coolidge's and Mellon's protests against the Couzens' investigations, were prepared to be hypercritical in analyzing the ambassador's letter. Even the Republicans were excited enough to oppose the Administration on the Japanese quota.

On Monday morning, April 14, the Republican senators caucused to thrash out the matter. Stirred by Ambassador Hanihara's "grave consequences" phrase, which was taken as a threat, and by Hiram Johnson's vituperation, they came to oppose almost unanimously the provision for a Japanese quota. After the Republican caucus the majority and minority floor leaders arranged for an immediate closed session of the Senate on the question of Japanese exclusion. During that session Johnson summed up the feelings of most of his colleagues when he called Hanihara's letter "impertinent" and Hughes' failure to rebuke the ambassador "monstrous." The senators continued their mass tantrum during the open session that followed. Senator Shortridge, Johnson's colleague from California, asked, "Who is it that insolently and impertinently demands that we abdicate, that we surrender our sovereignty; that, indeed, we surrender our very independence of action as an independent nation?" Henry Cabot Lodge followed, describing the ambassador's letter as a "veiled threat" to the United States.[8] Then a vote was taken and the Senate noisily and deeply buried the Japanese quota and the Gentlemen's Agreement. Only the aging chairman of the Immigration Committee, Le Baron Colt of Rhode Island, and Thomas Sterling of South Dakota stood by the Administration on the question.

It was at that point that Coolidge entered the picture, trying to put the pieces together after Humpty-Dumpty had taken his great fall. The President talked with Senators Lodge and Willis about a veto, but was dissuaded by them on the ground that it would be a futile gesture in view of the overwhelming Congressional sentiment against a Japanese quota. After the House and Senate versions of the bill had gone to conference committee, Coolidge discussed amending the measure with members of the immigration committees of the two houses. He suggested that exclusion be de-

layed for two years to give the State Department time to negotiate
a treaty with Japan that would halt immigration. No, was the answer. Then he asked for a year in which to seek a treaty that would
allow the Administration and Japan to save face. Again the suggestion was rejected. Coolidge apparently then considered trying to
rush through a treaty with Japan before the new legislation became
effective but shelved the idea because it would have been viewed
unsympathetically by Congress and perhaps even by the Japanese
government.

The President persisted in his efforts to gain time for a treaty
and was able to persuade the conference committee to write an
amendment deferring implementation of exclusion until March 1,
1925. When the conference report reached the House and Senate,
however, Coolidge's amendment was ripped out. The immigration
measure that was finally passed by the two houses contained not one
concession to the Administration. Coolidge had been betrayed by
his friends and fellow partisans in Congress. He had been the victim
of errors of judgment by Secretary Hughes and Ambassador Hanihara. He had been overwhelmed by the nation's mean and shortsighted anti-Oriental sentiment and undercut by Congressional concern with the scandals bequeathed him by Harding. It was the country that really lost, for exclusion not only damaged Japanese-Ameri-
can relations in the mid-1920s, but contributed to Japan's feeling of
vexation that made easier the overthrow of her moderates by mili-
tarists and the coming of war in 1941.

Coolidge had one more decision to make on the issue of exclusion. What would he do with the Immigration Act? The decision
was an easy one to make. Vetoing the measure was out of the question. Not only was current immigration legislation to expire June 30,
but the new act was constitutional according to traditional standards. Moreover, the President, like a great preponderance of members of Congress and voters, favored most of its provisions. He did
make two gestures, however, that clearly recorded his disapproval
of Congress' handling of exclusion. In reply to a press conference
question about the Secretary of State leaving or being removed
from office, he expressed his confidence in Hughes: "We worked
together on [the exclusion issue] and will work together on whatever there may be to do further about it. There is no reason for any

suggestion that Mr. Hughes would resign."⁹ Although the President signed the Immigration Act, he also issued a statement that was aimed at mitigating Japanese reaction to exclusion. He said:

> We have had for many years an understanding with Japan by which the Japanese government has voluntarily undertaken to prevent the emigration of laborers to the United States; and in view of this historic relationship and of the feeling which inspired it, it would have been much better, in my judgment, and more effective in the actual control of immigration, if we had continued to invite the cooperation which Japan was ready to give, and had thus avoided creating any ground for misapprehension by an unnecessary statutory enactment. That course would not have derogated from the authority of the Congress to deal with the question in any exigency requiring its action. There is scarcely any ground for disagreement as to the result we want. But this method of securing it is unnecessary and deplorable at this time. If the exclusion provision stood alone, I should disapprove it without hesitation, if sought in this way, at this time.¹⁰

Coolidge's protest did little to calm Japanese sentiment, but he had had the will to write it with the knowledge that it could only worsen his relations with Congress.

In the midst of the furor over immigration legislation, the President plunged into controversy on the touchy question of veterans' affairs. The veterans' lobbies had pushed through the House and Senate the Adjusted Compensation Act to make up for the low pay World War soldiers had received while most citizens had gotten fat from increased profits and wages. The lobbies were also successful in securing legislation that increased pensions for veterans of earlier wars. Harding had been able to block the World War bonus, but sentiment had been building for the proposal at a time when the executive's influence over Congress was almost nonexistent. Coolidge had fought almost since his first day as President to prevent enactment of such measures, contending that veterans had in many instances been given bonuses by the states and that national fiscal policy could not countenance the drain on the Treasury that compensation would bring. He was successful in so far as he forced modification of the bill to offer veterans paid-up insurance instead of a bonus. Those policies would not be cashed in immediately, although the veterans were to be permitted to borrow up to one-quarter of the value of their insurance.

Coolidge was in the unenviable position of having Republican Floor Leader Lodge desert him and Senate Whip Charles Curtis actually introduce the veterans' pay bills. First, pension increases for veterans of earlier wars passed Congress, followed shortly by approval of the World War adjusted compensation bill. On May 3 the President vetoed the pension increase bill, justifying his actions on the grounds that the budget must be kept in line and that the advantage of one group could not be more important than the nation's welfare. That veto was sustained in Congress. Adjusted compensation was another matter, though, for there were more public sentiment and private interest behind it. The American Legion, then at peak strength, had used all the pressure at its disposal to push the measure through the House and Senate.

After the bill was passed, Coolidge extended himself to enlist support for a veto. He even used one of his congressional breakfasts to discuss the legislation. The President invited the Republican senators who had voted for the bill and bluntly asked whether they were going to stand by the Administration and the party. After a moment of embarrassing silence several said Yes, but others held out because they felt committed to supporting compensation for veterans. On May 15 Coolidge sent the bill back to Congress with his veto message. "The expenses proposed in this bill are against the interests of the whole people," he said. Their interests and that of economic prosperity demanded that the Treasury surplus be used to reduce taxes, not to pay men for services that could never be measured in cash. He argued:

> Patriotism which is bought and paid for is not patriotism.... Service to our country in time of war means sacrifice. It is for that reason alone that we honor and revere it. To attempt to make a money payment out of the earnings of the people to those who are physically well and financially able is to abandon one of our most cherished American ideals.[11]

The errand boys of the American Legion scurried back and forth on Capitol Hill to hold the line against the President. Both Republicans and Democrats were lined up by persuasion if possible and by intimidation if not. The result was a rebuff of Coolidge and a raid on the Treasury, which was only the smaller because of his resistance. Coolidge had stuck to his economic program even at the risk of losing the Presidency at the polls. If the veterans voted for him in 1924, it was because he stood for so many other things that they favored and because he acted promptly to implement the Adjusted Compensation Act.[12] Nevertheless, in May, 1924, it would have been politically easier to have let compensation pass unchallenged.

In June the President was fortunate enough to be given a victory over a special interest. This time the interest was farmers and they were a group that had serious grievances. Beyond urging more cooperative organization for marketing and encouraging expanded lending facilities, Coolidge had not thought much about agriculture. However, he was coming under increasing pressure to deal with farm problems. In addition he was caught between the crossfire of Secretary of Commerce Hoover and Secretary of Agriculture Wallace on farm policy. The President had been warned by Wallace and a number of senators that something had to be done to improve the purchasing power of America's farmers. After Senator Norbeck had told Coolidge that commodity surpluses could lead to grave political consequences and that action was imperative, the senator concluded, "I got nowhere; I went home disappointed."[13] When Burton Wheeler discussed farm problems with Coolidge, the President's attitude seemed summed up in a question: "When a man can't make any money in a business, what does he do?"[14] The senator answered that a farmer might seek higher tariffs. Coolidge probably had in mind the solution he had applied: quit the farm and seek another occupation.

The President could not dodge the problems of agriculture, but he was slow in acting on them. He let the two antagonists in the Cabinet fight it out, even though he probably favored Hoover's approach. He also let Congress thrash it out, wisely so since he had enough trouble on Capitol Hill without seeking more. The ambiguity of his position was seen in his answer to a press conference question in March, 1924, about the McNary-Haugen bill, which proposed government purchase of eight surplus commodities at an average of prewar prices and then their sale abroad for whatever they would fetch, with the hope that increases in farm prices at home would exceed the amount lost in the transaction. The President said that although he sympathized with the bill's objectives, "I have never been able to make up my mind entirely about the benefits that this bill would secure to the farmers, and for that reason I have had it under investigation by experts." Some agricultural specialists had said that the bill would benefit farmers, he continued. "If my investigation leads me to that conclusion, I shall favor it. If on the other hand my advice should lead to a different conclusion, and they seem to be conflicting at present, I should not want to favor it."[15]

Even though many of the highest officials in the Department of Agriculture, including Secretary Wallace, favored the McNary-Haugen principles, that did not mean that the President would. In fact, while the bill was being considered in Congress, Coolidge was backing other legislation, largely unsuccessful, to increase loans to farmers and to encourage crop diversification and marketing cooperatives. Fortunately for him, farm income began to rise, and, to boot, farmers and their champions disagreed sharply on how to solve agriculture's problems. Even Frank O. Lowden, later an ardent fighter for McNary-Haugenism, helped to defeat the bill in 1924. Coolidge was not yet on the spot on farm matters, as the McNary-Haugen measure was easily defeated in June without need for much involvement of the White House.

The defeat of the McNary-Haugen bill ended Coolidge's skirmishes with Congress before the 1924 elections. By June most of the capital's politicians had turned their attention toward the national party conventions and even beyond, toward the struggle among the parties for election to office. Coolidge had fought his first war with Congress and had come out of it about as badly as any President in the republic's history. Not one major part of his program and only a few minor ones had been enacted. His major legislative victories had been negative, the successful vetoing of the veterans' pension increases and of the proposed $68 million salary raise for Post Office Department employees. He also had seen McNary-Haugenism stopped, though little of the farm legislation he supported was approved.

The President's losses in Congress were huge. He had been defeated on Muscle Shoals, Japanese exclusion, and adjusted compensation. Not only had his tax proposals virtually been ignored, but publicity of income tax returns had been voted despite his unfulfilled threat of a veto. The only important legislation for which he could have claimed any credit, the Immigration Act, would have passed even had Andy Gump been President of the United States. Coolidge did fare well, of course, on the few major appointments he made, but that was, at best, in compensation for two members of his Cabinet being forced to resign. His greatest success was to uphold the integrity of the executive branch against congressional encroachment. He emerged from the train of investigations bruised but undaunted and, remarkably, not discredited among the voters. Largely by keeping cool during the Teapot Dome affair, he had stopped his opponents from pinning the donkey's tail on him.

In retrospect, the best that can be said of Coolidge's first round with Congress is that under the most difficult circumstances he had kept his head. He had kept little else and received little in recompense from Congress.

23

Nomination for President

MANY PEOPLE AT ONCE began to speak about nominating me to lead my party in the next campaign. I did not take any position in relation to their efforts. Unless the nomination came to me in a natural way, rather than as the result of an artificial campaign, I did not feel it would be of any value."[1] So Calvin Coolidge has written, but that was true only in terms of formalities. He was pleased by talk of his nomination for President and appeared determined to run in 1924. He certainly did nothing to discourage anyone from working for him. In fact, the Yankee President often chatted about the forthcoming Republican National Convention and, although he did not plan the strategy leading to his nomination, it was clear to his aides when he approved or disapproved of their efforts.

As soon as Coolidge had succeeded to the Presidency, talk began about who would be nominated the next year. Many observers thought there would be a race for the prize and that the new Chief Executive would not be the prime contender. They based their belief on the fact that, except for Theodore Roosevelt, an "Acting President" had never been continued in office and on the guess that the taciturn New Englander lacked the aggressiveness and astuteness needed to pull it off. Moreover, after two and a half years as Vice President, Coolidge was neither a party leader nor even well known in the party and gave little promise of overcoming those handicaps.

Yet he did. It began with statements like that of the Lion of Idaho, Senator William E. Borah, that Coolidge was the logical choice for the 1924 presidential nomination. And he had other factors working for him. As President he would have the publicity that no other candidate for the nomination could hope to attract and he had personally antagonized few people in the Republican party.

Coolidge may not have thought that he was actively seeking the 1924 nomination, but the appointment of his chief aide belies that. C. Bascom Slemp was a political professional, well experienced in dispensing patronage, raising funds from political hacks, and in maneuvering Republican convention delegates from the South, most of whom belonged to the highest bidder. The Virginian understood that his chief task was to secure Coolidge's nomination and election as President. Slemp's appointment as White House secretary drew immediate and widespread criticism because of his work in getting political funds, by levies and kickbacks, from Southern Republican officeholders.

The President was alarmed by the criticism and called Slemp to his office to discuss it. Coolidge told him that he "had better not have anything to do with politics."

The Virginian was astonished but replied: "I shall not take any part in politics except to do my best to see that you are nominated and elected. I feel that I have just got to do that. But I shall be discreet in what I do."

The President smiled, his blue eyes twinkling, and that was the end of the matter.[2] Politics on the state and regional levels was politics, but nationally it was statecraft, if conducted discreetly.

A number of people worked discreetly and effectively for Coolidge's nomination. The South was Slemp's special province, but he was also the President's contact with the Republican old guard, especially in Congress, where he had sat for so long, and on the national committee, of which he continued to be a member. Massachusetts National Committeeman William M. Butler was the White House's emissary to New England and the rest of the East, while National Committee Chairman John T. Adams of Iowa worked with Western Republicans. Joseph Martin stumped the country for the President. Even Chief Justice Taft talked or corresponded with a large variety of people in Coolidge's behalf. If the

President had not told them and others to work for him, he certainly did not discourage them from doing so.

Coolidge's nomination for President had to be worked for. In 1923 there were other Republicans mentioned almost as prominently in connection with the nomination as was he. There were the farmer's tribune, former Governor Frank O. Lowden of Illinois, and the California Caligula, Senator Hiram Johnson. Also spoken of were Senator La Follette of Wisconsin, Governor Pinchot of Pennsylvania, Henry Ford, and even Senate Whip Charles Curtis of Kansas. The goal was to discourage these men or, if necessary, to beat them. Curtis and La Follette caused little worry: the first, because he was at best a second choice of any delegate, even in his home state; the second, because he was too radical for almost everyone in the Republican party. The two senators would be catered to, in an attempt to enlist Curtis' support and to prevent La Follette from bolting the party. The other men were more potent contenders and had to be dealt with differently.

Pinchot, with his nationwide contacts and reputation as a dragon slayer, had first to secure his own state's large convention delegation. In that he had a chance, for he had Andrew Mellon, the man who could give him the delegation, in a corner. The Treasury Secretary might have been willing to have his home state vote for Governor Pinchot on the early convention ballots if he would stop his attacks on Mellon's lax enforcement of prohibition. The governor, however, was not the compromising kind and consequently not only failed to carry Pennsylvania's delegation but was even defeated for a place on it. Coolidge, for his part, permitted Pinchot to continue to seek dragons to slay and made him welcome at the White House. The old progressive dropped out of the race by January, 1924, and in fact supported the President throughout the election campaign.

Lowden was interested in claiming the Republican presidential nomination, which he felt he had been cheated out of in 1920. He seemed a threat to Coolidge because he was quite popular in the Middle West and had support elsewhere. Also, his views, except on agriculture, generally coincided with the President's and his ability was highly esteemed. Coolidge's offer of the ambassadorship to Great Britain probably was predicated in part on removing the former Illinois governor from the race for President. Yet Lowden's chances were less than they had been in 1920. His chief opponent was now already in the White House and, in contrast, Lowden no longer held public office. Equally discouraging, the Illinois Republican machine was controlled by his enemies, Governor Len Small and Senator Medill McCormick, who were working for Hiram Johnson. The fact that Coolidge was, as Lowden wrote in September, 1923, showing himself to be "an accomplished politician and able"[3] dulled the former governor's hunger for the nomination in 1924. That Lowden did not encourage his supporters led many observers to count him out, although Slemp and Butler never stopped worrying about him until Coolidge was nominated. Yet Lowden was no threat, for he had early persuaded himself that he could not win against Coolidge. Later, after the Harding Administration scandals were revealed, he became convinced that the nomination was not worth having anyway because the Republicans would lose in 1924.

Ford, of course, was dealt with by the President. The movement behind Ford, though enthusiastic, was amateurish. And Ford himself apparently was not greatly interested in it either for the purpose of seeking the Republican nomination or launching a third party. When Coolidge backed Ford's bid to take over Muscle Shoals, the automobile maker collapsed his boom and came out for the President for nomination and election. The industrialist seemed happy not to be involved in running for public office.

By January, 1924, Hiram Johnson was left as the only other substantial contender for the nomination. The Californian had retained his base of power as a senator and preserved the national organization that had made him a leading candidate in 1920. He could appeal to the West and to the 1912 Progressives because he had been Theodore Roosevelt's running mate on the Bull Moose ticket. He had a national reputation, was squarely opposed to internationalism, and was fully prepared to take advantage of the criticism of Coolidge that emerged from investigation of the Harding Administration scandals. Johnson eagerly sought the nomination in the hope that as the only man left in the field against the President he could pick up much of the support that would have gone to Pinchot, La Follette, and even Lowden.

The struggle between the White House and the senator began in December, 1923, when the South Dakota Republicans met to decide whom they would endorse for the March presidential primary. Slemp had entered Coolidge's name. Working with former Congressman Charles H. Burke, the White House secretary was able to swing the tide against Johnson and Peter Norbeck, his leader in South Dakota. Senator Norbeck failed to convince the regulars of his state that Coolidge "can no more run this big machine in Washington than could a paralytic. What we need is a regular Teddy Roosevelt house cleaning."[4] The South Dakota Republican convention did not view Hiram Johnson as a second Roosevelt. The Johnson forces, however, took the question to the voters in the March primary election. There they won, defeating Coolidge by 1,000 votes out of 80,000.

The President's men had magnified the importance of South Dakota in order to underscore their convention victory there and now they had to do something to erase the prominence given to Johnson's victory at the polls. That would be to defeat the senator in his own state of California. There the Coolidge men had to work hard because Johnson could and did take time off to campaign in familiar territory. Complicating the undertaking, Japanese exclusion came up during the primary campaign, and the senator pushed the issue in a state where anti-Oriental feeling was traditionally high. Coolidge was prudent enough not to go on record against exclusion until after the election had been held early in May. He also deputized Secretary of Commerce Herbert Hoover to take charge of his campaign in California. Hoover was able to split the Republican progressives and appeal successfully to conservatives and moderates on the issue of economic development of the state. Coolidge won the primary, with the result that Johnson was discredited as an opponent.

Of course, other things occurred. The Republican National Committee was forced by White House pressures to choose Cleveland as the site of the 1924 convention over Chicago, which was a Johnson stronghold and potentially a base for a Lowden revival. With help from the President, Slemp also persuaded the committee to set aside the rule that would drastically have reduced the number of delegates from Georgia, Mississippi, and South Carolina, delegates that were to be ardent supporters of Coolidge. Patronage was so discreetly distributed that the impression was given that it was not being used for political purposes. Moreover, the White House avoided taking sides publicly in primary elections for state and congressional offices. Except for the mistake of contesting Hiram Johnson in South Dakota, the campaign to nominate Coolidge for President was adroitly conducted.

The greatest worry that Coolidge's aides had was how the nomination would be affected by the Harding Administration scandals. Frank W. Stearns had been given the honor early in December, 1923, of announcing Coolidge's candidacy for the nomination, which the President confirmed a couple of weeks later at the Gridiron Club's annual dinner. Coolidge then appeared to be the front runner for the nomination. As the revelations of scandal came in January and February, 1924, he lost strength to Johnson and even La Follette, whose supporters contended that anyone who had sat in Harding's Cabinet could not win the presidential election. Yet Coolidge's handling of the scandals, in being cautious and acting well when he did act, accomplished two things for him. As the Democrats howled for his head, most Republicans felt that they had to support his nomination and election, for repudiation of an obviously prudent President would be repudiation of the whole party. The other result was that the Democrats made too much of the scandals. In the ferocity and scope of their attacks the Democrats appeared to be losing their heads while Coolidge was keeping his. Their exaggerations worked against them. Moreover, as it came out that some Democrats were involved with Sinclair and Doheny, the exaggerations hurt the Democratic party as well as the Republican.

Coolidge also may have helped himself, on the one hand, by refusing to admit any party responsibility for what individuals had done during the Harding Administration and, on the other hand, by contending that the Democrats were without reason self-righteous. On the latter point he was delighted when Charles Evans Hughes said to the New York Republican Convention in April, "Let not partisan pecksniffs affect a 'holier than thou' attitude; guilt is personal and corruption knows no party."[5] With the President's encouragement, the Secretary of State's view became standard ammunition for Coolidge men both before and after the national convention. As for Republican responsibility, Senator George W. Pepper told of Coolidge's reaction to a speech he made to the Maine Republican Convention in which he admitted that the party had some liability in connection with Teapot Dome. The President, who operated on the principle that enemies should be given no openings for attack, made it clear that he did not stand behind his friend's statement.

As the time of the national convention drew near, other steps were taken to protect the President. Coolidge would not go to the 1924 convention, as he had in 1920, with a divided delegation from his home state. Under William Butler's leadership the Massachusetts delegation was largely packed, and it was made clear to the few men of doubtful loyalty that they were to be considered probationers in Cleveland. The focal point of possible desertion, Henry Cabot Lodge, went as no more than a delegate. Indeed, the senator went as a delegate in disgrace because of the desire of many Massachusetts Republican leaders for revenge for what they regarded as Lodge's desertion of Coolidge in the 1920 convention and, later on, of so many Administration measures in the Senate.

They had their revenge, for Lodge, a leader in so many conventions, held no office and was not even given a committee assignment in the 1924 Republican National Convention. Coolidge had invited the old senator to the White House for dinner a short while before the convention. It was a dreary evening as no instructions were given the former giant and the President apparently did not want to tell him what was in store for him. Perhaps the invitation was Coolidge's way of trying to make up for the indignities he knew Lodge would suffer in Cleveland. When the senator arrived at the convention he was avoided like Typhoid Mary, and he found his room so inadequate that he had to seek refuge with his former assistant, Louis A. Coolidge. He was greeted at the convention with shouts from the gallery of "Down with Lodge!" and "Put Lodge Out!"

As the President's men controlled the Massachusetts delegation, so they controlled the convention. It was clear that a group quite different from 1920 dominated the party. In April Chief Justice Taft had written with feeling to Andrew Mellon "that the welfare of the country is critically dependent upon the success of President Coolidge. The Republican party has no chance without him. I don't remember a case in which a party is so dependent on a man."[6] In May almost all Republicans were saying the same, and by the time the convention met on June 10 the delegates felt, as Theodore Roosevelt, Jr., wrote in his diary, that Coolidge's "wishes should be taken as law." That such was not born of affection was indicated when the illustrious Teddy's son added: "With all this loyalty to Coolidge, there was a curious lack of enthusiasm for him. They accepted him as logical, inevitable; a good man, but one whom they did not particularly warm to."[7]

For the most part the 1924 Republican convention was dull. It was clear even before it opened that Coolidge would be nominated and that the platform would be largely a confirmation of his December, 1923, message to Congress. The Public Auditorium at Cleveland was usually just half full and the delegates shuffled about almost aimlessly on the floor. The gallery was bored and so were the press correspondents. The chief purpose of the convention seemed to be to teach the old guard to "Have Faith in Massachusetts." The old-guard Republicans were so taught and willingly played roles as supernumeraries in writing the platform and naming a candidate for President. The platform was driven through the convention, though the President's men had to give some concessions on agriculture and exert great pressure in order to secure endorsement of the World Court.

Soon afterward Coolidge was placed in nomination in a ridiculously long address by Marion L. Burton, the president of the University of Michigan, who had previously headed Smith College. Burton presented the candidate as "the virile man—the staunch American—the real human being—CALVIN COOLIDGE."[8] The demonstration following the speech was eighteen minutes in length. Then came an abundant number of seconding speeches and finally the roll-call vote for President, which was carried out with almost indecent haste. Coolidge was nominated and that was that.

William Butler, as Coolidge's regent at the convention, ran the proceedings from start almost to finish. The national committee chairman-elect named convention committee chairmen and freely altered assignments to the committees. He did not even bother to call the leaders of state delegations to confer on important questions. But others of power also were present. Imperial Wizard Hiram W. Evans of the Ku Klux Klan was in Cleveland to make sure that the Republicans were not so un-American as to condemn his brigades of nightshirt-wearers. Wayne B. Wheeler, the generalissimo of the Anti-Saloon League, was on hand to stop Republican wets from drinking up enough courage to try to push through an anti-prohibition plank. Both Evans and Wheeler were supported by plenty of publicity. The convention was not only the first to be broadcast by radio, but also to be recorded quickly in photographs, thanks to Telephoty, a new process of rapid transmission of pictures. Others were at the convention, though they might as well not have been. The delegation from La Follette's home state of Wisconsin sat through the proceedings as unconsulted and unheeded as if it had stayed at home. The convention was indeed, as William Allen White reported, "an outing of chambers of commerce and bankers and Rotarians" of which "Coolidge was the captain, of course, and a man of importance with the crew."[9]

Coolidge, chief engineer Butler, and the crew were having their way, but their way was not smooth toward the end. Their stormy weather, and the only exciting event of an otherwise monotonous meeting, was the nomination for Vice President. The problem was that insufficient attention had been given to the selection. The resulting farce was the first open contradiction of the idea that the President was a master politician. No top-notch political strategist would have gone into a convention which he dominated without knowing precisely who would emerge as his running mate, but Coolidge did.

There were those around the President who believed that the best vice presidential nominee would be Frank O. Lowden, who was Midwestern, conservative, well known, and yet a man respected by the nation's farmers. Stories of White House interest in Lowden hit the press, and friends of the former Illinois governor reported hearing of it over the party grapevine. Lowden himself talked of two direct approaches by men close to the President and took those approaches as coming from Coolidge. Not wanting second place on the ticket, he wrote the President to let him know that he would be better as "a voluntary supporter" than "as a spoke in his political wheel."[10] Yet no evidence has turned up to show that Coolidge was thinking of Lowden. It is likely that C. Bascom Slemp, who had been a Lowden manager in 1920, was the source of White House interest. Chief Usher Ike Hoover testifies that the names the President mentioned in connection with the vice presidential nomination were those of Secretary Herbert Hoover, Governor Arthur M. Hyde of Missouri, Representative Everett Sanders of Indiana, and especially Senator William Borah.

Borah offered many advantages as a running mate for Coolidge. He was a Westerner, a leading senator, a man widely respected or feared among politicians, a man the President knew and liked personally, and one who was as devoted to economy as was Coolidge. Moreover, the Idahoan could keep the Outlawry of War group under control. Coolidge in fact used the Outlawrists to feel out Borah about the nomination. Surprisingly, when Borah indicated to the intermediaries that he might accept it, Coolidge did not ask him. Since the boom for Lowden for Vice President had started at the same time, it is probable that the President did not intend to buck what appeared to be a Republican tide. The Lowden boom disappeared quickly, though, thanks to Lowden's unwillingness to be booked second class on a ticket that he believed was not going to take anyone anywhere.

In any event both Borah and Lowden were off the range for the time being. The Saturday, June 7, before the convention opened, a nominee for Vice President had still to be selected. An old-guard group tried to take the initiative away from Coolidge on the nomination for second place. Included in the group were Secretary Weeks, Nicholas Murray Butler, Secretary Mellon, Speaker Gillett, National Committeeman Charles D. Hilles of New York, House Majority Leader Longworth, Senator Watson, and Postmaster General New. After many hours of discussion they finally decided that Senate Whip Curtis should be the man. They took their decision to William Butler, who told them: "I have just been talking by telephone to the White House. We must nominate Borah for vice president."[11]

Claudius O. Johnson has told the story that on June 11 Coolidge asked to have Borah visit him immediately. The senator was tracked down riding his horse in Rock Creek Park. When he was ushered in to see the President, he was told that he was needed on the ticket. Borah snapped, "Which place, Mr. President?"[12] One may question that the senator said that. It is clear, however, that Coolidge wanted Borah, but Borah did not want Coolidge. In response to a number of urgings the senator flatly refused to consider the Vice Presidency. He also sent word to key people at the convention that he would not accept nomination to that post. He asked his old friend former Senator Albert Beveridge to make his position clear to the convention in case his name was presented to the delegates. He was not in the running and he wired Beveridge, "Do not accept any statement to the contrary."[13]

Somebody had erred. Perhaps Butler had misunderstood Coolidge on the telephone; perhaps Coolidge had misunderstood Borah; perhaps Coolidge or Butler had tried to force Borah to accept by putting pressure on him; and perhaps Borah had temporized with the President and then outside the White House decided firmly to refuse nomination. The important result was that Coolidge and Butler wound up in the middle of the convention without a vice presidential nominee.

If Butler had not been responsible for blundering on the Borah matter, he soon did so on others. Over Slemp's objections, he offered Judge William S. Kenyon as a sop to Middle Western liberals, but when pressed to know whether he had Coolidge's support, Butler found the President not interested in backing anyone if he could not have Borah. Unable to put the Iowa jurist across, Butler proposed Representative Theodore E. Burton of Ohio, the convention keynote speaker. That suggestion too was spurned by the leading delegates. The convention, much as it had in 1920, then took matters in its own hands and on the second ballot nominated Frank O. Lowden despite Butler's objections that the Illinois statesman would not accept. After Lowden had been nominated, his previously prepared letter of refusal was read to the delegates. He became the first man since Silas Wright in 1844 to reject a major party nomination. On the third ballot Butler tried unsuccessfully to put Herbert Hoover over as the vice presidential nominee. The congressional leaders and party rebels then took over and nominated General Charles Dawes, the former director of the Bureau of the Budget. It was to Dawes, as he wrote his friend Lowden, "about the most unexpected thing in my life."[14] And so it was for everyone, including Coolidge, who had already written Lowden a cordial letter of congratulations on his nomination.

24

★ ★ ★ ★ ★

The Campaign of 1924

T HE SURPRISE FLURRY of excitement in the Republican convention was nothing compared to what was coming. The Democrats were soon to assemble in convention, and the reform-minded Conference for Progressive Political Action was to act like a political party by endorsing candidates for national office. Both groups would provide plenty of lively copy for the press and would have a great impact on the 1924 campaign.

The Democrats met in New York City late in June and early in July. At first their chief objective was to lambaste the Republicans for wickedness and corruption in office and in general. That theme was picked up in every speech—and there were many—and was reiterated in the platform. Soon, though, the Democrats began raising issues that changed the delegates from a claque into a howling, raging mob. The minor issues that divided them were the League of Nations, which was endorsed, repeal of prohibition, which was not endorsed, and oil-tainted Democrats, who were condemned, even if there were not supposed to be any. The major issue was the racist Ku Klux Klan, which split the convention fifty-fifty. The result was a bitter battle over the platform and a compromise plank which indirectly deplored the Klan. The fights also carried over to the naming of a presidential standard-bearer. Oil drowned William Gibbs McAdoo, prohibition and Catholicism ruined the chances of

Governor Alfred Smith of New York, and Oscar Underwood of Alabama was destroyed by his criticism of the Klan.

Ballot after ballot passed as more than a million Americans listened over the radio to the sounds of a great party unable to reach a decision. June ran out and July came. Finally after 103 ballots, an all-time record, the exhausted Democrats turned to a Wall Street lawyer from West Virginia for their nominee. John W. Davis, the darling of the drys and a man seemingly harmless to the Klan, was the compromise choice of Western and Eastern conservatives. The Democrats, knowing their most prominent leaders only too well, had turned to a man who was unknown to the people to conduct its national campaign. Then, as if to repudiate what it had just done, the party quickly named for Vice President the brother of William Jennings Bryan, Governor Charles Bryan of Nebraska. The Democrats had ridiculously coupled a House of Morgan lawyer with a Bryan who represented all the reform vagaries of his famous brother. Yet the incongruity of the ticket was no match for an even greater burden—the unfavorable impression made upon the voters by the convention—that Davis and Bryan had to carry during the campaign. The nation had listened over the radio to the Democrats tearing themselves apart. That was more effective as criticism than any Republican oratory could be. If Davis had had the peak popularity of both Woodrow Wilson and Grover Cleveland, he would have been unable to overcome the impression created by his party's convention.

While the Democrats were trying to conclude their convention, an entirely different group of people was preparing to meet in Cleveland, in the same hall where the Republicans had met. That was the Conference for Progressive Political Action, which was made up of a variety of forces that rejected, not only the two major parties, but also the period in which they lived. Craftsmen, railway workers, preachers, priests, housewives, professors, Socialists, farmers, alienated Republicans and Democrats, and disgruntled small businessmen mixed in Cleveland in one of the few spontaneous mass movements in America's political history. They were searching for a way out of the conservatism and mockeries they saw in the United States in the 1920s.

As historian Kenneth MacKay has written, "These progressives were not convinced, as were many of the worshippers of Mammon in 1924, that telephones, washing machines, and six-cylinder automobiles were necessarily an index of political morality and economic well-being."[1] It was not that they did not want such things and more, but that they wanted them on their terms. They preached aid for farmers, recognition of labor's rights, housecleaning in government offices, protection of natural resources, popular sovereignty, and peace on earth. Robert La Follette summed up their goals when he said that they wanted "equal opportunity for all, special privileges to none" and believed that could be achieved by breaking "the combined power of the private monopoly system over the political and economic life of the American people."[2]

At Cleveland the Progressives endorsed the presidential candidacy of that magnificent loner, Senator Robert M. La Follette of Wisconsin. Only he would do, for as his inflexibility had irked most Americans, his articulateness, courage, and forthrightness were sure to rally a sizable number of voters around the Progressive standard. La Follette asked the maverick senator from Montana, Burton K. Wheeler, to be his running mate after the young Democrat had denounced both Coolidge and Davis as conservatives. Together La Follette and Wheeler would protest what they saw as control of the country by the priests of Mammon. They also had a hope, a scant one, that they could prevent any other presidential nominee from securing a majority in the Electoral College, thereby throwing the contest into the House of Representatives where La Follette might have a chance of election.

While the Democrats were yelling their final curses at each other and the Progressives were shouting hosannas to La Follette, Calvin Coolidge was on the verge of one of the great tragedies of his life. He had risen from humble origins to the Presidency and had just seen himself confirmed as his party's leader. He had married well and had been blessed with two sons. He was not a model husband and father. No successful politician can have the time necessary for the role, and in addition his domination of his family, his occasional tantrums, and his habitual teasing made him even less desirable as a family man. Yet he loved his wife and sons, however imperfectly that love was revealed.

Coolidge's favorite son was his namesake, Calvin, Jr., who had just turned sixteen. He was a bright, handsome boy, and particularly so in the eyes of his father, who wrote, "He looked like my mother's people, particularly my mother."[3] One summer day young Calvin played tennis on the South Grounds of the White House. He had worn sneakers without stockings. Afterward he noticed that he had a blister on one of his toes, but in the manner of most boys he kept quiet about it. Infection developed and soon he became listless and feverish. By the time a physician was called in, the lad's condition was serious and on July 3 he was moved to Walter Reed General Hospital. There was little to be done except to wait and hope for the best. The President went helplessly about official business, joining Grace Coolidge whenever possible at their son's bedside. As Coolidge poignantly wrote: "In his suffering he was asking me to make him well. I could not."[4] On the evening of July 7 the boy died.

Coolidge took his son's passing hard. The sympathy of the country, of friends and opponents alike, did little to help. He just went through the paces of the Presidency, and campaign planning was left to drag. He later said that when his son died, "the power and the glory of the Presidency went with him."[5] It certainly affected Coolidge's campaign and probably his remaining years in the White House. Some of his interest in politics was obviously missing. Just before the 1924 election Coolidge wrote to his father that he never again would be a candidate for public office. The President's feelings were best expressed in a story told by Colonel Starling, his Secret Service bodyguard:

Very early one morning when I came to the White House I saw a small boy standing at the fence, his face pressed against the iron railings. I asked him what he was doing up so early. He looked up at me, his eyes large and round and sad.

"I thought I might see the President," he said. "I heard that he gets up early and takes a walk. I wanted to tell how sorry I am that his little boy died."

"Come with me, I'll take you to the President," I said.

He took my hand and we walked into the grounds. In a few minutes the President came out and I presented the boy to him. The youngster was overwhelmed with awe and could not deliver his message, so I did it for him.

The President had a difficult time controlling his emotions. When the lad had gone and we were walking through Lafayette Park he said to me: "Colonel, whenever a boy wants to see me always bring him in. Never turn one away or make him wait."[6]

Despite the tragedy of young Calvin's death, the 1924 campaign ground on. Republican leaders would continue to plan and work, as would their opponents, even if the President could not for the time being. The new chairman of the Republican National Committee, William Butler, was given charge of his party's campaign. Blunder though he might on the vice presidential nomination, he had the President's confidence. Those who disagreed with him were forced to take a back seat. C. Bascom Slemp had fought Butler at Cleveland and lost. Afterward he offered his resignation as secretary to Coolidge, but it was rejected, probably to keep the appearance of harmony in the President's official family. To stop rumors of his leave-taking, Slemp told the press that he had not quit and that he would be active in the campaign, probably in a leading role. That led to a White House announcement that Butler was in full power as campaign manager. Coolidge stood behind that statement. Slemp was to operate during the campaign only as a minor functionary of the national committee chairman.

Butler operated the Republican National Committee headquarters and the campaign like the businessman he was. Funds were well budgeted, and expenditures did not exceed the money on hand. The chairman regularly scrutinized accounts and even brought in accountants to keep them in shape and to make public reports. The committee's money was used to achieve specific and justifiable goals, not just to be given to those politicians who could exert the most pressure on the national party headquarters. If there were to be less government in business and more business in government, there was also to be more business in Republican politics. Butler was also to try, with the President's encouragement, to set the goals and strategy of the campaign. In this he was almost as successful as he was in controlling Republican finances.

Coolidge and Butler were to stake the campaign on prosperity, economy, and respectability. If tax cuts and rising purchasing power were Republican bribes to the voters to forget other questions, they were compelling ones. To the President and the national committee chairman, economy and prosperity were fundamental issues. Both men believed that stability and harmony were vital to the nation's welfare and that they came from releasing as much money as possible for private development of the economy. Give hope that all men would share in an expanding prosperity, and many of the causes of strife and discontent in society would be removed. Moreover, the President and his party would be perpetuated in power by a grateful public. Of course, government would have to take care of the minor social and economic cankers that could not be remedied by private action, but nobody would object as long as it was done efficiently and on a small budget. Coolidge and Butler really believed that. To their opponents they might appear to be reactionaries and even hypocrites, but in their own minds they were acting courageously by restraining the impulse to chase hares over the countryside when the livestock in the barnyard needed tending. By doing the home chores the Republican leaders were convinced that they were building up prosperity and stability, not stirring up needless trouble. That they might do their chores badly did not occur to them any more than it occurred to their foes that they in turn might not know what to do with a hare once they had caught it.

In any event, prosperity, economy, and respectability, national stability and harmony would be stressed by the Republicans in 1924. They did not meet all the current issues, but they could transcend them. With a tax cut and prosperity at hand, who except small minorities could worry much about past scandals, religious or racial issues, or international questions? Prosperity, however distributed, was the leading issue among Democrats and Progressives as well as Republicans, and virtue was a close second. Coolidge had already made himself appear the procurator of prosperity and the symbol of virtue, and he had accomplished that almost by doing nothing at all. Most Americans found that they could identify with Coolidge but not with the Wall Street lawyer playing statesman or the Olympian senator playing holy prophet. After years of denunciation of evil by progressives and liberals, most citizens had become insensitive to cries of "Wolf." They were disillusioned by promises, largely unkept, of a bright new world through government action. They were ready to accept the idea that progress could come by letting people alone to seek it in their own private ways.

All that was well summarized by the veteran reformer Oswald

Garrison Villard in recounting what his business friends said of Coolidge: "He is just what the country needs, a quiet, simple, unobtrusive man, with no isms and no desire for any reform. The business world needs to be let alone to recover from the war strain and governmental interference in business and control along so many lines."[7] Coolidge was their man and that of most voters. He could achieve what Harding had promised, and the Yankee had given proof that he could achieve it without permitting the government to become a hothouse for another blossoming of Falls and Daughertys.

One other aspect of Coolidge's strategy was to get along with anyone who might support him for President. Of course, La Follette and the people who were pledged to him were black-listed, but those progressive Republicans who had not gone over to the Wisconsin senator were wooed by Coolidge's openness and courtesy with them. A man like Peter Norbeck could have worked vigorously against Coolidge's nomination and yet be welcome at the White House. Gifford Pinchot and James Couzens could have worked to demonstrate scandal in the Administration and yet as long as they supported Coolidge for President they could keep their standing in the party and even be flattered by the President. William Allen White could make scathing and mocking analyses of Coolidge and still command his confidence because he backed him in the election. Even those who did not support the national Republican ticket were not read out of the party as long as they did not come out for La Follette or Davis. George Norris could remain neutral without incurring the public wrath of the White House and William Borah could get by with merely saying that Coolidge was an honest man and a devoted advocate of economy.

Another Coolidge strategy was to speak as little as possible and without giving offense. In 1920 he had spoken less than either Harding, Cox, or Roosevelt. In 1924 he would again say less than any other leading figure. Although that was because of his official duties, his mourning for his son, and his low level of energy, it was also a matter of strategy. Coolidge was, of course, under great pressure to speak. He told the White House correspondents, "If I get cornered up by people wanting me to make speeches, and it is represented to me that on this occasion I am the only individual that can save the progress of civilization, and that unless I am to do it civilization is going to fail and I shall be responsible for it, when that proposal is made to anyone it is rather difficult for them to say they won't make a speech."[8]

Difficult though it was, Coolidge only occasionally agreed to make speeches. Except for his address accepting the presidential nomination, he confined his speaking to dedicatory occasions, historical commemorations, and talks before business and religious groups. Those speeches had political angles, but they were not partisan and they rarely dealt with issues. His talks were pitched to make him appear to be the acme of respectability and above the usual grubbing of politicians. He explained his strategy to the press by saying, "I don't recall any candidate for President that ever injured himself very much by not talking."[9] He did not say much during the 1924 campaign and he obviously did not injure himself.

Yet Coolidge was not the whole Republican effort nor could he control the entire campaign. There were those who were not content with silence and inaction. Chief Justice Taft was all for crushing La Follette on his proposals to have federal judges elected by the people and to authorize Congress to overrule invalidations of laws by the Supreme Court. That kind of radicalism called for "war to the knife" on the Progressives.[10] Many Republicans agreed with Taft. Senator James Wadsworth of New York wrote, "We know where [La Follette] is now officially, and we won't recognize him or any of his followers [as Republicans] hereafter."[11] Vice presidential nominee Charles G. Dawes argued that the changes proposed in the Constitution by La Follette posed the chief issue before the country. Despite discouragement from the White House, Dawes stressed the dangers of La Follette's constitutional propositions throughout his vigorous campaign across the land.

What there was of Coolidge's campaign began late and ran at a slow pace. His acceptance address was given in Washington in August. A rehash of the 1924 Republican platform, it exalted stability as the national goal, prosperity as the vehicle, and hard work and character as the means. After that the President took a vacation at Plymouth Notch in order to be near his son's grave, to visit with his father, and to think about the future. He did not, of course, discourage newspaper reporters and photographers and newsreel men from following him. He made droll remarks for the reporters and posed before the cameras as a statesman and as a Vermont farmer. As a President he looked passable, but as a farmer he made an odd picture chopping at a tree and pitching hay while he was dressed in a business suit and a homburg. Perhaps that is how he thought real farmers would dress to do their chores when prosperity got rolling.

Coolidge was also host to visiting delegations of politicians and business leaders. The most famous pilgrimage was that of Henry Ford, Thomas A. Edison, and Harvey Firestone, the aging symbols of the technological miracles of modern times. With the President they sat on the veranda discussing great affairs and being photographed and recorded in writing for the benefit of the public. Among their words were Edison's comment, "The United States is lucky to have Calvin Coolidge," and Ford's assertion, "Calvin Coolidge will be elected President and the United States is assured continued prosperity."[12]

Charles Dawes also visited for lunch one day. He and President Coolidge exchanged pleasantries and political observations, while Colonel John Coolidge sat eating silently. After John Coolidge had finished lunch, he left the other two men and Mrs. Coolidge and went outside. Some thirty newsmen, waiting for Dawes, surrounded the Colonel to question him. The President, who could see what was happening from a window, muttered, "I asked him to say nothing."

The First Lady answered, "I don't think you need worry."

When Dawes later saw the reporters outside, he asked what they and the Colonel had discussed.

"We asked him," they said, "what you and the President were talking about, of course."

"What did he say?" Dawes replied.

John Coolidge had foxily told the press, "My hearing ain't as good as it used to be."[13]

Dawes did more than pick up anecdotes at Plymouth. He discussed the farm problem with President Coolidge. To meet criticism that the government was doing nothing, Coolidge was preparing to name a commission to consider steps to alleviate agricultural distress. His running mate urged him to make it an impartial, nonpartisan, and competent group. He suggested as members his friend Frank O. Lowden, Democratic industrialist Owen D. Young, and Harvard economist Channing Bullock. Coolidge, however, was not appointing the commission to solve the problem but instead to ensure his election. When after considerable delay he appointed a commission, it was far from being impartial.

The Coolidge campaign consisted, of course, of more than newspaper publicity, presidential inactivity, and Dawes roaming the land living up to his nickname of "Hell 'n Maria." Great amounts of campaign literature, placards, and automobile stickers were distributed. Robert Washburn's friendly biography of Coolidge was edited to make it even more friendly and then handed out as a Republican campaign document. The President's relations with still and motion picture cameramen showed that he had a keen sense of the value of photography. He especially went out of his way to pose for newsreels. If his poses today seem artificial, they were natural at the time compared with those of Davis, who appeared either tired or pompous, and of La Follette, who too often seemed to affect a pose reminiscent of Napoleon Bonaparte. The Republican campaign managers also sought to have Republican speakers, many of whom were used as surrogates for Coolidge on the stump, laud the President. That was done to excess, for the Rock of Vermont was frequently portrayed, not only as the heir of Washington and Lincoln, but as the peer of Caesar and Charlemagne. Fortunately, Coolidge's photographs, which he delighted in handing out, and his speaking voice dispelled the notion that he was as highfalutin as his most enthusiastic supporters contended.

The Ku Klux Klan, which was at its peak postwar strength, was avoided assiduously as an issue by the President. In late August, though, Dawes decided to discuss the racist, anti-everything organization in a speech at Augusta, Maine. As Representative Fiorello LaGuardia commented, the vice presidential nominee "praised it with faint damn."[14] Coolidge, despite Dawes' speech and C. Bascom Slemp's urgings, refused to get involved, probably because he viewed the Klan as an organization that would shrivel and die if it were not fed publicity. Moreover, the Klan issue was not one that would win votes. Even Dawes came to agree that the Klan was not a rewarding issue and he backed off from further discussion of it. He later wrote that tranquillity "was the subconscious issue in the elections of 1924," a reaction "from the excesses of war."[15] That did not mean Republicans were united on how to handle tranquillity. Coolidge and Butler would do it by urging economy, prosperity, and re-

Of course the question comes up: What about the Davis-Bryan campaign? Governor Bryan turned out to have the family name but not the drive of his brother, William Jennings. John Davis offered an updated version of James Cox's 1920 campaign for President and with the same results. One view widely held about Davis was expressed by Henry L. Mencken, the bitter wit of Baltimore, who wrote: "Dr. Coolidge is for the Haves and Dr. La Follette is for the Have Nots. But whom is Dr. Davis for? I'm sure I don't know, and neither does anyone else. I have read all of his state papers with dreadful diligence, and yet all I can gather from them is that he is for himself."[23]

What happened was that large numbers of Americans concluded that Davis offered no alternative to Coolidge. The Democratic nominee was a bore as a speaker and, like most of his fellow partisans, he drove the Teapot Dome issue into the ground. He was hampered by his conviction that he could not win. He later commented: "I went around the country telling the people I was going to be elected, and I knew I hadn't any more chance than a snowball in hell. . . . Not only was the Democratic party ripped apart, but it was impossible to hang the responsibility for the Harding era ills on Coolidge."[24] Davis also spoke about the League of Nations and of reviving Wilson's economic liberalism, which could not compete with Republican talk of expanding the prosperity that was already on the scene or with Progressive promises to farmers and workers. Only in denouncing the Progressives did Davis rival the President and only in condemning the Republicans did he compete with La Follette, and that was insufficient to win the election.

The Republicans spent a great deal of time and money on their campaign. The national receipts of the Republicans totaled $4,360,-478; of the Democrats, $821,037; and of the Progressives, a puny $221,977. Large numbers of orators went out on the stump for Coolidge, even reluctant ones like Albert Beveridge, Frank O. Lowden, and Raymond Robins. Cabinet members and other high officials were asked to speak, including Secretary of Commerce Hoover, Attorney General Stone, and Secretary of State Hughes. Moreover, pains were taken to offend none of the touchier members of the Republican Administration. When the vice chairman of the Tariff Commission, William F. Culbertson, was the target of high-tariff advocates for occasionally supporting Democratic tariff views,

Coolidge refused to force him to resign. After Assistant Attorney General Mabel Willebrandt wrote a letter highly critical of federal district attorneys in enforcing prohibition and it mysteriously found its way into Democratic hands, she was not reprimanded, but instead told to keep "plugging away at 'em."[25] Other things were conveniently left fallow. When on October 17 the Federal Trade Commission made a report indicating the need to investigate Andrew Mellon's Aluminum Company of America, nothing was done except for the White House to announce that the commission "was letting itself be used for political purposes."[26]

Action was taken, however, to meet partisan charges. One story concerns the use of the lofty State Department for political purposes. The week before election the Democratic National Committee made public the names of twenty-seven American diplomats who were absent from their posts in order to campaign for the Coolidge-Dawes ticket. The President called Under Secretary of State Joseph Grew to ask whether he had remembered correctly that John Davis, when serving as ambassador to London, had campaigned in the United States for Cox in 1920. Grew almost eagerly rummaged through the department's records. The search confirmed the President's recollection and also turned up evidence that twenty-one diplomats were home traveling the Democratic campaign trail in 1920.

Coolidge also had help from other sources. He was accused of taking $250 for addressing a veterans organization while he was Vice President. Rising to his defense was Woodrow Wilson's Vice President, Thomas R. Marshall, who told the press: "I went on the Chautauqua lecture platform and received compensation for addresses while vice president. I either had to do it, steal, or resign."[27] It bore out Coolidge's contention that "a great many times if you let a situation alone it takes care of itself."[28]

Also bearing out that idea was the farm situation. Coolidge was the beneficiary of rising agricultural purchasing power. Farm costs had started declining earlier in 1924, and as the election campaign progressed, farm income jumped. In October hogs were up over 50 percent from July and grain prices were all increasing. Farmers were finding it difficult to remain discontented with more money in their pockets. Coolidge also was fortunate that no crises either at home or abroad occurred during the campaign. Everything seemed to be well handled and he did nothing to contradict that impression.

The campaign came to an end for Calvin Coolidge with a speech on election eve over the largest radio hookup until then assembled. His voice was carried to almost every voter who owned a radio set and cared to listen. The President stressed the importance and the patriotism of voting but did not refer to his own candidacy. He ended folksily telling his audience good night, "including my father, up on the Vermont farm, listening in."[29] The result of the campaign was a convincing victory for Coolidge. He polled 15,718,211 votes to 8,385,283 for Davis and 4,831,289 for La Follette. The President ran away with the vote in the Electoral College, receiving 382 ballots to 136 and 13 respectively for his two opponents. He could indeed afford to look as Joseph Grew described him after election: "He was all smiles and looked just as happy as might be expected."[30]

Why had Coolidge won? For one thing it was a case of Davis putting the voters to sleep, La Follette not being able to arouse many of them, and Coolidge not even trying. The President had bent his efforts to appear a man of dignity who was attentive to duty, and the more he was attacked by Progressives and Democrats, the more he appeared to be that. Moreover, while his opponents were promising better things to the country, he seemed to be delivering them. There were no crises facing the nation, farm prices were rising, business was getting better, and labor conditions seemed to be improving. The campaign slogan of "Keep Cool with Coolidge" summed up the President's view that one should not tamper with a good situation. Although the campaign had its share of *Sturm und Drang*, Coolidge's way won out. Davis and Bryan bored the public, La Follette and Wheeler attracted only a small part of it, and the more active Republicans did not disturb its serenity. Solicitor General James M. Beck in his campaigning found "everywhere . . . a profound indifference" on the part of the voters.[31] Coolidge had guessed correctly: the old shouts and cries, whatever their source, would make no impact. What the majority wanted was to be left alone and Coolidge did that masterfully.

Americans by 1924 wanted prosperity and peace in which to enjoy it. Progressivism and internationalism had, in the minds of most men, either gone far enough or had failed. The conclusion in either case was the same: tranquillity was needed. That was summed up by, of all people, Supreme Court Justice Oliver Wendell Holmes when he said, "While I don't expect anything very astonishing from

[Coolidge] I don't want anything very astonishing."[32] Of course, there were those who were unhappy with what they saw about them. The Hoosier knight, Albert Beveridge, wrote of "a swirl of crosscurrents beneath the surface which I . . . cannot make heads or tails of. So I am not altogether at ease about the future."[33] Gifford Pinchot observed it "is perfectly clear that this country is at the moment falling back under a more complete domination of the plutocracy than for many years past, and eventually something has got to be done about it."[34]

All that those worthies could think to do, however, was to vote for Coolidge. And why not? Davis, both in 1924 and in his career as a defender of conservatism in the courts, gave no signs of doing better, especially with the howling, divided mob of the Democratic party behind him. La Follette, while presenting a clear alternative, did not offer a program or an organization that could command the confidence of a majority of voters. Even worse, his platform of nationalistic reform promised to do even less for a troubled world than the programs of Coolidge or Davis. There was really no choice for most voters in 1924 except Coolidge. He did not understand the postwar age, but neither did his opponents, and he was so much more reasonable in his misunderstanding of it than they were. Sooner or later, though, the result would be calamitous for the American people, who out of the depths of their misunderstanding had developed leaders who had confused all sense of direction.

25

Overture to a Second Term

I<small>N</small> W<small>ASHINGTON</small> <small>ON</small> March 4, 1925, the skies were clear and the temperature demanded no more than a topcoat to keep warm. Calvin Coolidge was to be inaugurated as President in his own right, the first elected from New England since Franklin Pierce seventy-two years before. Coolidge's inauguration was to be the first ever broadcast by radio, and large crowds were promised in attendance because of the mild weather. It should have been a great day for the President, but it did not go too well for him.

The first order of business was the induction of the Vice President in the Senate chamber. In his address, Charles Dawes gave the senators a piece of his mind, telling them that their rules were "inimical . . . to the principles of our constitutional government" and calling for restriction of the right of unlimited debate.[1] The new Vice President's comments came as a surprise, for he had not given the press corps advance copies of his message. It did not put the senators in the mood to be receptive to the President's inaugural remarks. Moreover, on the way outside to the presidential inauguration, Senator Ashurst reported, "The feet of the President were trodden upon, the justices of the Supreme Court were jostled, ambassadors straggled out, and the senators white from rage at the V.P. trooped to the east front of the Capitol."[2]

Coolidge's address could not compete with that of Dawes. After taking the oath of office on his grandfather's Bible, the President faced the radio microphones and the audience to tell how good things were in America and to urge the defense and realization of the nation's unique ideals.

> Here stands our country, an example of tranquillity at home, a patron of tranquillity abroad. . . . Here it will continue to stand, seeking peace and prosperity, solicitous for the welfare of the wage earner, promoting enterprise, developing waterways and natural resources, attentive to the intuitive counsel of womanhood, encouraging education, desiring the advancement of religion, supporting the cause of justice and honor among the nations.[3]

The applause the President received was deservedly polite.

After the ceremonies at the Capitol the parties of the Chief Executive and the Vice President returned to the White House to prepare to review the Inauguration Day parade. The whole occasion was to be lacking in color and festivity as compared with past inaugurations. It was conducted with a view toward saving time and money. The customary luncheon for high executive officers and members of the inaugural committee was omitted. Coolidge had the Daweses join him and the First Lady in their quarters for sandwiches and coffee. The others were expected to cool their heels downstairs or go to the reviewing stand. A buffet lunch had been set up for military aides in the State, War, and Navy Building next door, and Colonel Clarence Sherrill gallantly invited the hungry members of the Cabinet and other officials to share it. The result was that when the Coolidges and the Daweses came down to go to the reviewing stand, their parties had vanished. For the next hour, much to the President's annoyance, officials straggled to the stand from Colonel Sherrill's lunch. To make the situation worse White House aides had notified Coolidge and the Vice President to go to the stand too early. There they fidgeted for a half hour in their splendor and glory without any paraders to review. When the marchers came Coolidge looked on in silence. After the parade had run its course he returned to the White House for a short rest and later a reception for delegations from various states. Then he relaxed before going to a dinner at which only the members of the family, the Frank Stearnses, and Mrs. Reuben Hills and Miss Laura Skinner, friends of

Grace Coolidge, were present. Later Coolidge attended a party given by his old Massachusetts associates. He soon returned to the White House and was in bed before ten, exhausted by the day's activities and frustrations.

Senator George W. Pepper of Pennsylvania has written, "Everybody was 'out of tune' and harmony was 'mute' in the Senate following the inauguration of Coolidge and Dawes."[4] He ascribed that to bitterness over the use of the Teapot Dome issue in the 1924 election campaign. Pepper was right about the mood of the Senate, but the reasons were more numerous than he indicated. There was a residue of unrest and resentment from the battles between Coolidge and Congress in 1924 and in addition bitterness between progressive and regular Republicans as a result of the election campaigns. This discord was clearly evident before Coolidge's inauguration and in fact was aggravated during the lame duck session of the Sixty-eighth Congress that met from December, 1924, to March, 1925. The President had been an astute politician in winning election, but he was to prove himself a poor one in dealing with Congress.

His program was, as expected, largely a restatement of his earlier legislative goals. In his message to Congress of December 3, 1924, he emphasized tax reduction and economy in appropriations. He favored sale or long-term leasing of the Muscle Shoals properties. On defense matters he warned against arms races and urged consideration of further international agreements to limit armaments. The President endorsed adherence to the World Court, but almost contradictorily called for sympathetic examination of the idea of outlawing war. In short, there was nothing astonishing or really new in his message except more stress on arms limitation and the throwing of a bone to the Outlawrists. Yet his program irritated his opponents, both Republican mavericks and Democrats, who were pleased with little in it.

Coolidge's legislative program was one he felt obliged to support regardless of sentiment in the House and Senate. After the election he had written former Secretary of State Elihu Root:

I feel that the Republican party have made definite promises to the people as to what they would do if the people gave them authority by their votes to do it. I do not see how, under the circumstances, it would be honest to disregard these public pledges and put the conduct of the affairs of the people and the government of the people in the hands of those who have opposed the policies which the Republican party advocated.[5]

Not only did the President make no concessions to the malcontents in Congress, but he took few steps to enlist their support or acquiescence. He remained aloof to the election of officers and composition of committees in Congress. He told the press on November 21, "I think that is a matter that the House and Senate particularly ought to decide for themselves." Their choices, he was confident, "would be persons entirely acceptable to me."[6]

Not only did he refuse to influence the organization of Congress in order to smooth the way for his legislative proposals, but he also did nothing to moderate the majority leadership's plans for vengeance against Robert La Follette and his supporters. All Coolidge did to mollify Congress was to agree not to oppose a raise in their pay from $7,500 to $10,000 if no fuss was made. Although a fuss *was* made throughout the country, he did not veto the appropriation, which was passed toward the end of February, 1925. Congress did not appreciate his gesture any more than it did his hands-off policy on organization. He was to find both the lame duck session of the Sixty-eighth Congress and the special session of the Sixty-ninth Congress equally balky.

War to the knife on La Follette and his followers in the Senate began soon after the 1924 election. On November 28 La Follette, Edwin F. Ladd of North Dakota, Smith W. Brookhart of Iowa, and Lynn J. Frazier of North Dakota were read out of the Republican party caucus. When Congress convened in December the Republican leadership also moved to strip the four senators of their seniority on committees. Indeed, a resolution was overwhelmingly adopted by the Senate to remove La Follette from the chairmanship of the Committee on Manufactures, which he had held since 1921. Coolidge had not called for the action against La Follette and his supporters, but he was blamed and with good effect by progressive Republicans. The four disgraced senators, along with Farmer-Laborite Henrik Shipstead of Minnesota and five or six other sympathetic Republicans, would embarrass the President time after time. The Republican leadership had the power to discipline progressives but not to dictate their votes.

Coolidge resorted to his earlier tactics in dealing with Congress after his election. He relied on the leadership chosen by the House and Senate Republicans. That leadership had changed and, at least in the House, for the better. Frederick Gillett had been elected to the Senate and was succeeded as speaker of the House by Nicholas Longworth. The son-in-law of the late President Roosevelt was a slicker and more forceful article than his predecessor. He emphasized party regularity and usually received it. Thanks to that, to his integrity, and to a slightly larger Republican majority in the new Congress, Speaker Longworth was able to secure more favorable consideration of Administration measures than had Gillett.

The Senate presented a greater problem for Coolidge. There the nominal Republican majority was small and less responsive to its leadership. The old floor leader, Henry Cabot Lodge, had died of a cerebral hemorrhage on November 9, and his successor, though learned in the ways of the Senate, had neither Lodge's prestige, oratorical ability, nor sagacity. Charles Curtis was a fairly dependable hack, who was regarded as one of the boys and a square shooter. He would, unlike Lodge, take orders from Coolidge, but he would not be as successful in having his way with his Senate colleagues. The situation was complicated by the fact that the new Senate leadership was split. William E. Borah had also risen a notch because of Lodge's death. He had become the chairman of the Foreign Relations Committee and was to use that position to set up a second Department of State as well as to expand his influence on all party and Senate matters. Although Curtis would take orders from the White House, Borah had to be treated like a foreign potentate.

Another complication was the new Vice President, who if not really a leader, acted like one. Charles Dawes too would not accept direction from the President, and almost as bad, when his views coincided with Coolidge's there was the possibility that his work on behalf of Administration measures would hurt them. In short, he was eagerly used by Coolidge's opponents and resented by many of the President's allies. He had incurred the hatred of many senators and he kept that hatred alive by his forthrightness and frequent tactlessness. He even stumped the nation in the summer of 1925 seeking support for changing the Senate rules on debate. For his bull-like integrity Dawes was to become recognized as one of the few outstanding Vice Presidents, but for the same reason he was as often to hamstring the Administration as he was to help it.

In addition to relying on the Republican legislative leadership for assistance, Coolidge did his undynamic best to cultivate individual members of Congress. The strange breakfasts with lawmakers continued as did invitations for often silent and dull weekends on the U.S.S. *Mayflower*. Although the President kept the highest levels of patronage to himself, he usually considered the wishes of Republican senators on federal appointments in their own states. Thanks to his determination to avoid scandal, the competence of his appointees was above Harding's and certainly as good as Wilson's. Coolidge also courted dissident elements. The progressive Republicans who had not backed La Follette and the moderate mavericks, like Farm Bloc leader Arthur Capper, were treated cordially by the President. In fact, some conservative Republican senators were to complain that Norbeck, McNary, and Capper had better access to the White House than they did.

Coolidge's moderation was reflected in kinder treatment by congressional leaders of the progressive Republicans who had remained loyal to the party during the 1924 campaign. After the election Peter Norbeck noticed the absence of the "go to h——" attitude he had previously encountered in the Senate and he was even placed on the Republican steering committee.[7] Some Democrats too were courted by Coolidge, perhaps because he liked them and perhaps because they occasionally backed him on legislation. In 1928, over Speaker Longworth's objection, Coolidge sent Representative Sol Bloom to Rome as a delegate to the convention of the International Copyright Union. The President explained to Longworth that he was giving the Democrat that choice appointment because "Sol is the best informed man we could send, and he won't play politics."[8]

Yet Coolidge's use of the personal touch sometimes backfired. George Norris told of the time when the President was pressed by California Republicans to appoint a man of questionable qualifications to the federal bench. Coolidge called Norris, who was then chairman of the Senate Judiciary Committee, to the White House for his opinion. The senator told him: "Your problem is simple, Mr. President. You are convinced this man lacks the qualifications for a federal judge. Simply refuse to nominate him."[9]

After leaving the President, Norris went to his automobile and found Senator Borah sitting in it, waiting for a ride back to Capitol Hill. The two men discovered that they had been to the White House on the same mission. Coolidge had been advised by both of the senators that the man under consideration lacked the qualifications to sit on the bench. They knew the President would now make the nomination in the belief that they would block the appointment. That way he could satisfy the Californians and yet keep a mediocrity out of office. The strategy failed, however, as the nomination was favorably reported by the Judiciary Committee and confirmed by the Senate, perhaps out of spite.

Coolidge was also willing to make deals. He never did favors for members of Congress without hoping for something in return, and sometimes he was explicit about what he thought would be adequate as *quid pro quo*. Peter Norbeck has told of asking the President to appoint the bibulous campaign manager of Senator-elect W. H. McMaster as United States marshal for South Dakota. Coolidge made it clear to Senator Norbeck that he wanted him to hold the line against pay increases for Post Office Department employees. Norbeck went along with the President because, he said, he intended to anyway. Soon afterward McMaster's man was appointed a federal marshal.

Calvin Coolidge tried to master Congress, but despite his efforts in that direction he lacked the shrewdness to succeed. Even had he been more astute his goal would have been difficult to achieve because Republican party solidarity was weakening. Economic issues, not party loyalty, increasingly moved members of Congress, and those interests had plenty of articulate, able, and independent spokesmen. Coolidge felt forced to play the game of picking up support where he could, either in favor of his program or in order to prevent Congress from passing its own proposals. Although he did rather well at obstructing Congress, he usually failed to find enough support to gain approval of the Administration's program. His failure was heightened by his ineptitude in using force and lures to stiffen party regularity. He was also unsuccessful in finding proposals that could be offered as a compromise between his interests, which were usually those of the Cabinet officers, and the ideas of members of Congress. In that respect he was inferior to Harding and almost as bad as Wilson at his worst. Under Coolidge the White

House legislative program was made by the executive branch with little concern for what Congress suggested. The concern came later when the program was under formal consideration in Congress, and then it was too late. Coolidge's approach was based on both principle and habit. He believed that the executive should formulate proposals for consideration by the legislators, who would then decide what should be done. Executive pressure on them was usually something that should be limited to stopping enactment of measures that ran contrary to the Administration's wishes. In a Congress where the President's party was often only nominally in the majority, that approach would usually lead to stalemate.

Moreover, Coolidge's method of picking up support where he found it was to help weaken Republican party regularity. In courting the Cappers, Borahs, and Norbecks, he made it all the more difficult for the Curtises and Watsons to keep them in line. His method lessened the influence of the old guard, for which he did not grieve because he disliked its assumption of political superiority. But in weakening the old guard he dissolved the band of discipline that had held most of the party together from 1916 to 1923. He was to discover that flattery, friendliness, and occasional deals would not keep his party together the way that the cement of compromise or the force of discipline could. Under President Hoover, who was even less astute at Congressional politics than Coolidge, the result was disastrous. It was not to be until 1937, when Republicans feared for their very existence as a party, that regularity again became a significant aspect of Republicanism.

As a consequence of increasing independence among Republicans and his inability to cope with it, President Coolidge more frequently used the veto to block Congress. By the time of the Seventieth Congress, 1927–29, he felt it necessary to impose twelve vetoes compared with a total of five in the Sixty-eighth and Sixty-ninth Congresses. As Vice President Dawes prolixly wrote:

> The steadily increasing unreliability of nominal party majorities in Congress in upholding in legislation the platform policies which have won a party victory has tended to emphasize in the public mind that it is the President, possessing among other powers the right of veto, who must be relied upon after election to guard in the government the policies the public has approved.[10]

Coming from a man who considered himself independent of party leadership, that statement carries authority.

If Coolidge usually found it impossible to ride the wild horses of his own party in Congress, those of the opposition would gladly trample on him. Only occasionally could he count on Democrats for support. Moreover, some of his habits and manners made him vulnerable to the darts of the pygmies among the Democrats who believed that discourtesy was an acceptable form of revenge for the way Woodrow Wilson had been treated on the League of Nations issue. An example was the insistence of Representative Fred Vinson of Kentucky on commenting on the newspaper story that the President, thrice daily, rode a mechanical horse. Coolidge used the wire-and-wood steed to save time from other forms of exercise and because riding flesh-and-blood horses irritated his delicate nose and throat. Of course, it appeared slightly ridiculous, particularly as the President came to enjoy his artificial horse rides, even to the point of whoopeeing like a cowboy while astride the electrically operated mount. Nevertheless, the caprices of Chief Executives are normally not commented upon in Congress aside from introducing press articles on them into the *Congressional Record*. Vinson pushed beyond an objection by Representative Robert Luce, though, saying, "The gentleman from Massachusetts forgets that the *Record* of yesterdays brimmed full to overflowing with the snaps and snarls toward a world figure, declining in health, who occupied the executive chair." Then Vinson read to the House doggerel of his own composition, "Cal's 'Hobbyhorse' ":

> The Prince of Wales, astride a steed,
> Is a picture of world renown.
> When the horse bestirs, as is its need
> The Crown Prince hits the ground.
>
> Silent Cal is a more cautious chap
> Than the young Prince, brave and good.
> He profited by the princely mishap,
> And bought a horse of wood.[11]

And so on for twelve stanzas did the Democrat, who was later to sit as chief justice, mock the President as Presidents had not often been mocked in Congress.

26

★ ★ ★ ★ ★

Congress and Administration

THE FACT THAT the 1924 election had had little effect on relations between Coolidge and Congress was made clear as soon as the House and Senate reconvened in December. Senator George Norris, following up on his victory over the Administration on Henry Ford's bid to take over Muscle Shoals, introduced a bill for public development of the property. His proposal was scheduled for debate on December 3, but on the previous day Senator Oscar Underwood of Alabama, with Coolidge's support, offered a substitute bill to empower the Secretary of War to lease Muscle Shoals as a unit. Party and economic lines were scrambled for and against the measure offered for the Republican President by a leading Democrat. Many senators would vote for Underwood's proposal because the issue seemed to be a question of that or nothing. Others voted against it, not because they opposed private leasing, but because the bill did not provide for congressional regulation of whatever lease might be negotiated. Norris fought assiduously for his own bill and against Underwood's, but his cause appeared to be lost.

In January, 1925, the Underwood bill was passed by Republican-Democratic coalitions in both houses of Congress. Inconsistencies in the House and Senate versions had to be reconciled by a conference committee and that committee reported on February 7, but Coolidge and his allies made the mistake of not having the report considered by Congress until February 19. Norris found new material in the conference bill and therefore was able to invoke a seldom used Senate rule to send the measure back to committee. The Nebraska senator's maneuvers and the recommittal took up valuable time toward the end of the session so that he could threaten to stop all business with a filibuster unless Congress blocked final consideration of the Underwood bill.

Norris had won by a thread and the President had been dealt an embarrassing setback. More important, Norris' victory turned the tide on the disposition of Muscle Shoals. When the Administration recommended leasing measures to later Congresses, the senator more easily blocked them. By 1928 he had even worked up enough sentiment in Congress to secure approval of a bill for government development of Muscle Shoals. That measure was blocked by Coolidge in a pocket veto. Yet Norris had persuaded a majority in Congress that the progressives could and would prevent private operation of Muscle Shoals and that therefore if the property were to be developed it would have to be through public operation. Throughout Coolidge's second term battle raged between progressives and conservatives in Congress and between farm organizations and electric power interests over the country. The result was an inglorious stalemate for the President that undoubtedly had an adverse effect on his other legislative proposals. The question of what to do with Muscle Shoals was finally resolved during the Franklin Roosevelt Administration, when the property was used as the basis for the development of the Tennessee Valley Authority.

Coolidge had been certain that his program for Muscle Shoals would, with Democratic support, be approved, and it would have if consideration of it had been properly expedited. That was, however, the only favorable sign he saw for his program in the final session of the Sixty-eighth Congress. He would wait to push the rest of his proposals until the opening in March, 1925, of the Sixty-ninth Congress, in which Republicans had larger majorities. In the Sixty-eighth Congress the President's party had only fifteen- and six-seat majorities, respectively, in the House and Senate compared with sixty- and sixteen-seat majorities in the forthcoming Sixty-ninth Congress. Given the unreliability of many Republicans but of few Democrats to their parties, the larger majorities seemed worth waiting for. There were, however, some actions that could not be postponed until the new Congress met. Requiring prompt attention were confirmations of appointees to take the places of Secretary of Agriculture Henry C. Wallace, who had died October 25, 1924, and of Justice Joseph McKenna, who had resigned from the Supreme Court.

Wallace's death put the President on the spot. It was not his loss from the Cabinet so much as when it came. One can surmise that the dissenting Iowan's days in the Administration had been numbered anyway. But to have the Agriculture post left vacant just before election and Wallace's successor confirmed by a difficult Congress was discouraging. Coolidge soon felt pressure to name this or that man to the job. To gain time and relieve himself of the pressure, he temporarily appointed Wallace's assistant secretary, Howard M. Gore, to the post. That could not solve the problem, however, because Gore had been elected governor of West Virginia and would have to leave the secretaryship in January. Coolidge offered the post to Herbert Hoover, since his ideas on agriculture had now to a large extent become those of the Chief Executive. Hoover turned down the position, probably reasoning that he could remain secretary of commerce and still have a man of his way of thought appointed to head the Department of Agriculture. Vice President Dawes pressed Coolidge to appoint Frank O. Lowden, but the President decided against it because of the probability that Lowden would not agree with him on farm policies and might use disagreement to further his own political ambitions.

Politically Coolidge did the wisest thing by turning to Senator Arthur Capper of Kansas for advice. Not only would that flatter the Farm Bloc leader, but would undoubtedly lead to Senate approval of a man who, like Capper, was critical of the McNary-Haugen plan. The President was under great pressure, for, as he told Capper, he had seventy-nine applicants or nominees for the secretaryship of agriculture. Probably both as a matter of courtesy and flattery, he asked Capper whether he wanted the job. When Capper indicated that he did not want it, the President said: "Well, there are two men that, as far as I can see now, would make pretty good agricultural secretaries, and they come from out in your country. I have called you down here to find out what you think of them. One is John Fields, now the president of the Farm Loan Bank at Wichita, and the other is Dr. Jardine, president of the Agricultural College at Manhattan."

The Kansas senator replied that both men were good, "but if I was naming a man myself, I would probably name Jardine."[1]

The following day Coolidge sent William Jardine's name up to the Senate, where it was confirmed. The President had made a good choice both politically and technically. The nomination benefited from Capper's support and from the good name Jardine had made for himself with the American Farm Bureau and the land-grant colleges. As secretary of agriculture, he was to do his administrative job competently, with little fuss, and he was to be an effective bulwark against McNary-Haugenism. Jardine was helped by his long experience as an agricultural scientist and as an educator, as well as by the fact that he was genial and reasonable with both his supporters and opponents. Under him the McNary-Haugen advocates in the department left and the forces of those favoring the cooperative movement were strengthened. Coolidge could well afford to be pleased by Jardine's appointment.

The nomination to the Supreme Court that Coolidge sent to the final session of the Sixty-eighth Congress should have caused little controversy. As it turned out, not only did the appointee, Harlan F. Stone, draw considerable fire, but the nomination in March of Charles Beecher Warren to take Stone's place as attorney general led the President to his most embarrassing moments with Congress. Stone, a graduate of Amherst, had served with distinction during the months he had headed the Justice Department. It is unclear why he was selected for the Supreme Court. Perhaps it was a reward for his ability as attorney general and for political speechmaking during the 1924 campaign. Perhaps it was a matter of the President appointing the most distinguished lawyer he knew personally or perhaps it was the influence of Chief Justice Taft, who favored Stone. Or perhaps it was to remove Stone, who was showing signs of becoming an overactive trust buster, from the attorney general's post. With Coolidge, whose habit was to weigh all advantages and disadvantages of a course of action, it is probable that all of these factors were considered.

Stone's nomination to the Supreme Court early in January, 1925, was generally well received by the bar and bench and by lay commentators. Yet soon after it was made the Attorney General began a legal action that would raise opposition to him in the Senate. Harry Daugherty, when still the Administration's chief legal officer, had instituted proceedings in Montana against Senator Burton K. Wheeler for practicing law before a government agency while a public official and for conspiracy to defraud the government. Although Stone was convinced that Daugherty had acted only to discredit one of his antagonists on Capitol Hill, he also believed that a legitimate legal question existed about Wheeler's activities. Stone assigned investigation of the question to Assistant Attorney General William J. Donovan, and on the basis of Donovan's report suggesting prosecution, the Attorney General brought the case before a District of Columbia grand jury early in 1925. Stone could have ducked the issue by deferring it until he had been confirmed as a Supreme Court justice or by leaving it to his successor, but the fact that he did not gives credence to belief that he acted in good faith against Senator Wheeler.

On January 19, 1925, after Stone had brought the Wheeler case before a grand jury, the Senate Judiciary Committee recommended his confirmation as a member of the Supreme Court. However, Thomas Walsh, the other senator from Montana, successfully demanded that the recommendation be recommitted. Coolidge refused to withdraw the nomination but did not object to recommittal, and Stone was called before the Judiciary Committee for testimony. He made a good impression there. As his chief inquisitor, Senator Walsh said, "The very excellent impression I formed of him . . . before this time, was confirmed by his demeanor before the Committee on the Judiciary."[2]

Again the nomination was reported favorably to the whole Senate. Walsh, despite the "excellent impression" he had of the Attorney General, joined Thomas Heflin and George Norris in attacking Stone on the Senate floor. Walsh charged the Attorney General with retaining Daugherty's men as Justice Department employees, and Heflin and Norris condemned his former connections with Wall Street. The attack failed as Stone was, on February 5, confirmed by the Senate, 71 to 6, with Wheeler and Walsh abstaining. An interesting sidelight was that Senator Wheeler was later acquitted of the charges against him.

The upshot of the Stone appointment was that an outstanding

justice had been added to the Supreme Court, one who under President Franklin D. Roosevelt would be elevated to the chief justiceship. The short-range result of the Stone incident was that Calvin Coolidge was plunged into the greatest controversy of his presidential career. Failing to block Stone, progressive Democrats and Republicans in the Senate had been primed to take advantage of any opening that the President might give them. Their chance was to come soon with the nomination of Charles Beecher Warren to take Stone's place as attorney general.

In naming Warren, Coolidge made one of the worst political blunders in the nation's history. He had abundant forewarning that the progressives were aiming to embarrass him. By not intervening against the exclusion of La Follette and his three supporters from the Senate Republican caucus and the stripping of their committee assignments, he had encouraged them to think of revenge against him. The battle with George Norris on the Muscle Shoals issue had only made a bad situation worse. The progressive opposition to Stone, a man of stature, should have warned the President to move carefully in his next appointment. He either failed to read the signs properly or chose to ignore them. Moreover, Warren was about the worst choice Coolidge could have made to present to the Senate. The Michigan Republican politician was known, as Chief Justice Taft said, as a man who resorted to "evasion and concealed methods."[3] Warren's arrogance had irritated many other Republican leaders and, even worse, he had been a prominent figure in the Sugar Trust that was still under indictment. Adding further to the blunder was the President's failure to consult party leaders on the matter.

On Inauguration Day Coolidge sent the nomination up to Capitol Hill. He thought that Warren's service as ambassador to Japan and Mexico, his prominence as a lawyer and a businessman, and his service to the party as a contributor and national committeeman and to Coolidge as a 1924 convention floor leader would assure confirmation. Moreover, there was a Republican majority in the Senate as well as the tradition that a President's Cabinet nominations would not be rejected. The nomination was favorably reported by the Judiciary Committee on March 6.

The following day the progressive Republicans with plenty of Democratic support forced the Senate to take the unusual step of considering the report in open session. Walsh led the attack on Warren for his work as counsel and confidential agent for the sugar industry and as long-time president of the Michigan Sugar Company, one of the organizations cited by the Federal Trade Commission for controlling the marketing of sugar pulp. Confirmation of the nomination, the Montana senator charged, would put a man under indictment in a position to judge his own case. Walsh also questioned whether Warren's legal background was of the nature to qualify him for service as attorney general. James Reed went further, denouncing Warren as a scoundrel and a criminal. "What will people say," the fiery Missouri senator asked, "as they behold the spectacle of the trusts naming the attorney general of the United States, of the Sugar Trust presiding over the Department of Justice, and from that high place protecting the combinations of the past and the present?"[4]

Few attempts were made to answer the charges against Warren. The Republican Senate leaders felt they had enough votes to pull him through. On March 9, though, Senator Curtis knew his majority was slipping away under the blows of Walsh, Reed, and progressive Republican James Couzens, and he unexpectedly called for a vote. As the senators were being polled it became apparent that he had waited too long. Vice President Dawes, who had gone to the New Willard to take a nap in the belief that there would be no problem, was summoned to return immediately. While he was riding up to Capitol Hill in a taxicab, the Senate tied 40 to 40 on the Warren appointment. Before Dawes could get into the chair to cast the tie-breaking vote, Senator Overman went over to Warren's opponents and the nomination was blocked. For the first time since Henry Stanbery was rejected as attorney general in 1868 a presidential Cabinet appointment had been refused by the Senate.

Coolidge was furious. Republicans had betrayed him, Democrats had gone against tradition, and there was the suspicion that Dawes had intentionally absented himself during the vote. Curtis and other Senate leaders advised the President to nominate someone else, telling him that they could secure approval of anyone but Warren. Coolidge was adamant, however. He was going to send Warren's name up to the Senate again. Pressure built up on him not to do so and the signs became clearer that the renomination would not succeed.

Yet the more the President was pressed to drop Warren, the more determined he became to stand by him. He considered the Senate's rejection an insult to his judgment and unfair to Warren. Coolidge renominated the Michigan Republican for attorney general and announced his hope "that the unbroken practice of three generations of permitting the President to choose his own Cabinet will not now be changed, and that the opposition to Mr. Warren, upon further consideration, will be withdrawn in order that the country may have the benefit of his excellent qualities and the President may be unhampered in choosing his own method of executing the laws."[5]

The President called upon the Republican leaders in the Senate for support and pressed the rank-and-file to go along. He held a lengthy and, for him, somewhat sarcastic press conference on March 13, commenting that he could not find men who lived up to the standards some senators had in mind. "I have to appoint human beings to office," he told the reporters.[6] He also hinted at a recess appointment for Warren should the Senate again fail to confirm him.

The defense of Warren in the Senate was taken up by the junior Republican senators, led by George W. Pepper. The old pros kept out of harm's way. Senator Pepper valiantly served Coolidge, calmly outlining reasons for Warren's confirmation. But he and his supporters were no match for veteran lawmakers like Norris, Reed, and Walsh, especially now that the issue encompassed the right of the Senate to reject presidential nominees for office. Pepper's work was further complicated because of adverse reaction to the President's hint of a recess appointment for Warren. During the debates progressive Republicans were visibly happy about the prospect of a monumental defeat for their foe in the White House and with the knowledge that that defeat would dramatize his inability to control Congress. On March 18 Warren's nomination was again rejected, this time by a vote of 46 to 39. Warren wisely refused to consider a recess appointment as attorney general.[7]

Coolidge had apparently anticipated defeat, for on March 17 he telegraphed to an old friend, John Garibaldi Sargent, "Hope you can come at once."[8] The former Vermont attorney general, who in size, dress, and bearing reminded one of a St. Bernard dog just back from a romp in the Alps, traveled to Washington to discover that he was to be the new attorney general of the United States.

Sargent was nominated at once and confirmed unanimously by the Senate. His administration of the Justice Department would be honest and conservative. He would heed his master's command to heel on all actions that might lead to controversy. As for Coolidge, he got a measure of revenge on his antagonists. If he had ever thought of appointing a progressive to high office to placate the Republican insurgents, that thought was banished. The President also sought to avoid discussing federal patronage in the states with those Republican senators who had voted against Warren's confirmation. Coolidge pointed this up when during spring, 1925, he refused to include Senators Norris and Howell in a meeting with the members of Congress from Nebraska regarding patronage there. Both senators had opposed Warren.

The Chief Executive had one other major appointment to make in 1925. On January 5 Charles Evans Hughes had submitted his resignation as secretary of state effective two months later. Hughes, who possessed some vanity, felt "a little as if I had been fired."[9] He had apparently expected Coolidge to ask him to stay on, but Coolidge took his resignation at face value, perhaps because he wanted a secretary who would be less his own boss. Yet the President wrote a letter of reply that was for him fulsome with praise. "I cannot refrain," he told Hughes, "from expressing my feeling of personal loss at the prospect of your retirement, and also the loss that must inevitably ensue when one of your ability and experience goes out of an office which he is so well qualified to fill."[10]

Later Coolidge asked Hughes whether he desired the chief justiceship. Hughes did not take the question seriously and replied that he did not. It is difficult to know what the retiring Secretary of State expected from the tight-lipped Yankee. He must have misjudged his chief, for Coolidge bestowed upon him twice the amount of flattery and courtesy he had on any other member of the Cabinet. Furthermore, as a private citizen, Hughes was often invited to the White House for long and candid discussions of public affairs, which was certainly a token of the President's high esteem for him. Equally important, Hughes named his successor, Frank B. Kellogg, in the State Department.

Kellogg, who was a former trust buster, later conservative Minnesota senator, and at the time of his appointment ambassador to Great Britain, had indicated his wish to leave government service by spring, 1925. In December, 1924, however, Hughes told him that the President wanted him to be the next secretary of state. Mrs. Kellogg, who would have been much happier returning to Minnesota, advised her husband that if he thought he could do the job he had a duty to accept it. He felt up to heading the Department of State and so informed Hughes. Coolidge nominated Kellogg and he was quickly confirmed by the Senate. Here the President had acted wisely because the senators would find eminently suitable for the Cabinet a former colleague who was personally well liked and not suspect of being an advocate of the League of Nations.

The Senate and the President were to be satisfied with Kellogg. He was an industrious, if less than brilliant, secretary of state. He occasionally caused crises in his department by his explosive temper and by not keeping his subordinates fully informed of the state of affairs, but that was offset by his usual geniality and his willingness to do more than his share of the work. More important, although Kellogg, like Hughes, was given great freedom in carrying out his duties, he was, unlike his predecessor, almost always willing to acquiesce whenever the President disagreed with him. This was early demonstrated when Kellogg proposed that Dwight Morrow be appointed under secretary of state. Coolidge vetoed it, saying, "No, I don't think that would do."[11] Kellogg did not object and was to wait two years before he got a second-in-command of his own choosing and liking.

After Coolidge's election victory in 1924 there was speculation about whether he would act differently now that he was President in his own right. He soon met that speculation. At his November 11 press conference he said: "I don't anticipate to change very much. I have tried in the conduct of my office to be natural and I don't want to change that attitude. There are two or three other people that have served with me in the conduct of the affairs of the United States that I should be pleased if they changed a little—that I have to change from saying 'no' to saying 'yes.' "[12] That statement gave a key to what Coolidge expected in his Administration. He wanted men who saw things the way he did and he got them. Secretary of the Navy Wilbur proved to be such a man, as did Secretary of Agriculture Jardine, Secretary of State Kellogg, and Attorney General Sargent. Most of the Cabinet holdovers either bent themselves to Coolidge's will or saw eye to eye with him. Only Herbert Hoover followed a fairly independent course.

A compliant Cabinet was essential to Coolidge. If he could not persuade Congress to follow him, he was determined to have as few adversaries as possible in his own house. Because the President had to shape government policy mainly through administration, he needed administrators who would take his orders and carry them out effectively. He could abide Hoover because of the support the Commerce Secretary had outside the government and because he and the President agreed often enough on policy to make their relations tolerable. With a subdued Cabinet and by juggling and jiggling the economy, Calvin Coolidge could eclipse Congress or at least move in his own orbit. He was helped in that by the budget control system established in 1921. Its shakedown cruise had about ended when he succeeded Harding, and now that the Bureau of the Budget was operating effectively he had both complete information on the fiscal condition of the executive agencies and the power to approve or deny their appropriations requests and expenditures. For the first time a President had the power to control the finances of federal agencies and Coolidge used that control, against considerable bureaucratic opposition, to gain compliance with his demands.

A second thing the President sought from his subordinates was that they do their work. The veteran chief clerk of the White House, Rudolph Forster, commented of Coolidge: "He knows what he is doing and what he wants to do. He doesn't do anyone else's work either." That was illustrated when Edward T. Clark asked Coolidge, on behalf of Secretary James J. Davis, whether he agreed with one of the decisions made in the Department of Labor. On offering the President the necessary papers, Clark was told: "I am not going to read them. You tell ol' man Davis I hired him as secretary of labor and if he can't do the job I'll get a new secretary of labor."[13]

As Coolidge did not expect to be burdened with other men's work, he also did not want to take the risk of being embarrassed by being innocently involved in making departmental decisions that might go wrong. As he told the Cabinet one day: "There are many things you gentlemen must not tell me. If you blunder, you can leave or I can invite you to leave. But if you draw me into all your departmental decisions and something goes wrong, I must stay here. And by involving me you have lowered the faith of the people in their government."[14]

Coolidge wanted men as subordinates, not seekers of thanks. Senator Pepper told of a time when the Coolidges and the Peppers had attended church together. The sermon was on gratitude and had as its text: "Were there not ten cleansed? but where are the nine? There are not found that returned to give glory to God, save this stranger." At lunch following the church services, the President asked the senator what he thought of the sermon. Pepper said he liked it, but Coolidge responded: "I'm not at all sure that the man who came back and prostrated himself was a bit more grateful than the nine who went about their business. When I appoint a man to office I don't want him to thank me. I want him to go and make good."[15] Overlooking Coolidge's inadvertent blasphemy, it can be said that he did expect his men to work and not to fawn. Conversely, he rarely thanked a man for doing his job. Thanks was, in his eyes, to be offered for a gift, not for discharging a duty.

Coolidge did his best to secure able, though usually conservative, men for jobs in his Administration. Although he heeded requests of congressmen for patronage, he would dicker with them to get subordinates who were competent. The influence of members of Congress was more revealed in the conservatism of the appointees than in their lack of ability, and that conservatism was not something that had to be pushed upon the President. It is also true that when he was considering a man for a job, it was not just for any job or for one that the candidate wanted. After the 1924 elections Coolidge offered defeated Senator Thomas Sterling of South Dakota a position on the International Joint Commission. Sterling refused it, asking instead for appointment as secretary of state or attorney general, to which the President would not consider nominating him. When Sterling became convinced that he could not have a Cabinet post, he consented to take a place on the commission. Coolidge, however, had already given it to another man, and consequently the former senator wound up with the humble position of field secretary of the Commission for the Celebration of the 200th Anniversary of the Birth of George Washington.

The President refused to gratify job-seekers unless it served his purpose. That was illustrated by his handling of C. Bascom Slemp. The presidential secretary had apparently taken a position in the

White House in the hope of later being appointed to the Cabinet. When it became clear that his hope was not Coolidge's wish, he resigned. Not only did Coolidge refuse to elevate Slemp, but he froze him out of the White House staff in order to replace him with a more diplomatic chief secretary, former Representative Everett Sanders of Indiana. A tribute to Coolidge in such things was that despite Slemp's frustration he and the President remained on cordial terms.

Despite the President's cracking of the whip over agency finances and his expectation that his executive officers would "do the day's work," he was not regarded as a poor boss. Most of his chief subordinates went out of their way to report that he was candid with them and far from being an icicle or humorless in conversation. The officials with whom he worked closely found that he could even be sentimental. Yet his success in keeping the loyalty of his aides was attributable to more than discipline and personality. The extra quality was succinctly stated by Henry L. Stimson, the governor general of the Philippines, when he wrote: "Mr. Coolidge was a wholly satisfactory chief; he gave his chosen subordinates unreserved confidence, and he never let them down."[16] That confidence amounted to giving a tremendous latitude for arriving at decisions, for Coolidge did not intend to do his assistants' work for them. Yet when their decisions were made, unless way off base, he fully supported them. Fortunately for him, indefensible decisions were rarely made by his subordinates.

As efficient as Coolidge was as Chief Executive, there was one aspect of administration he found difficult to handle. That was the no man's land of the regulatory commissions. Budgets are not usually of prime concern to such agencies, so presidential control could seldom be developed by manipulating their finances. Moreover, Congress had given the President little or no formal control over the regulatory agencies. Yet they had such influence over the nation and its economy that all the Presidents have tried to bring them to heel. The Chief Executive's only powers, though, have been to nominate the members of the commissions and to scrutinize their budgets.

Coolidge set out to bring the regulatory commissions in line. He was fairly successful in that through his nomination of conservatives to commission posts. Under his and Harding's Administrations the character of the commissions' work changed from regulation of business abuses to encouragement of business freedom. "More business in government and less government in business" was the slogan that still governed. Coolidge's remaking of the commissions often led him to abandon standards of administrative conduct that he prized. He shuffled the Tariff Commission by appointing a protectionist Democrat and letting a low-tariff Republican swap his place on the commission for appointment first as minister to Romania and later as ambassador to Chile. Coolidge also tried to get members of various commissions to give him predated letters of resignation to be used if he wanted them out of office. He got more bad publicity from that approach than letters of resignation. Coolidge was so often frustrated in getting Senate agreement to his nominees that several times he made recess appointments to the regulatory agencies of men who would serve him but could not be confirmed in office.

The President's tactics led him to serious embarrassment in dealing with the oldest regulatory agency, the Interstate Commerce Commission. In 1925 he nominated a Democrat, Thomas F. Woodlock of New York, who was sympathetic to the arguments of the railways that they needed less regulation. Southerners blocked confirmation of the New Yorker by protesting that there had been only two commissioners appointed from their region during the ICC's history. The President gave Woodlock a recess appointment. When the next vacancy came up Coolidge named an Alabaman and that removed Southern objections to Woodlock, but Pennsylvania then objected until the President promised it the next opening on the commission. That finally led to Woodlock's confirmation. Coolidge was, however, left in a position where he not only had to get men whose views he approved but who would also satisfy the demands of the various regions. Pulling the commissions in line was one of his toughest chores, but it can be said that he generally succeeded. His success was, of course, just to be a pain in the neck for his successors, who were to spend years in getting commissions responsive to their wishes.

27

★ ★ ★ ★ ★
═══════════
═══════════

A Restless Man

B EING PRESIDENT, Thomas Jefferson said, is a splendid misery. Calvin Coolidge certainly found it so. He enjoyed living in the executive mansion, having aides at his beck and call, being greeted in public by the playing of "Hail to the Chief," driving in limousines, yachting on the *Mayflower*, and being the center of attention wherever he went. He also enjoyed many of the famous and great people he met on the job. Yet it was all so confining. Along with the power came great responsibility. Along with the gold and the trumpets came the tinsel and the tinhorns. And along with the famous and the great came the bores and the self-seekers.

Coolidge's routine as President was heavy in emotional toll if not in hours spent. A great deal of it was ceremonial. At 12:30 every working day he shook hands with an average of four hundred tourists visiting the White House. When business pressed he abandoned the handshaking and instead let the tourists file through his office to be treated to a glimpse of the President at work or even in conference. Often at midday Coolidge would also go to the South Grounds to be photographed with groups of citizens who wanted proof of their visit to the White House. Lunchtime meant an hour with guests who were too important to be satisfied with a handshake or a group photograph. The rest of the afternoon, following naptime, was usually taken up by the signing of masses of military commissions, civil service appointments, Treasury orders, and the like. Coolidge spent a good deal of time helping people who had complaints regarding claims, pensions, and government jobs. He did that whether or not they had political influence and often to the point where the work of his staff resembled that of a social service office. The greater part of the ten thousand or so letters that arrived every week was handled by his aides, but several hundred were left to be read and answered by the President in the morning or after dinner. Coolidge also gave time to inscribing personal photographs and books for well-wishers and autograph hunters.

His regular business was normally conducted in the morning. Twice weekly short Cabinet meetings and not-so-short press conferences were held. New ambassadors or ministers from foreign nations had to be formally presented to the President, and American diplomats given send-offs by their chief. Of course, there were other visitors, some from Congress, some from the executive departments, some from the regulatory agencies, as well as a number of ordinary citizens. Coolidge devised what he thought was an effective way to handle talkative visitors. He told his successor, Herbert Hoover: "You have to stand every day three or four hours of visitors.... If you keep dead-still they will run down in three or four minutes. If you even cough or smile they will start up all over again."[1]

There was also the capital social life, which was headed by the President. The White House functions consisted annually of the formal Cabinet dinner, the reception and dinner for diplomats, the judicial reception, the dinner for the Supreme Court justices, the reception for members of Congress, the dinner for the speaker of the House of Representatives, and the Army-Navy reception. A couple of thousand people might turn out for the receptions and from fifty to ninety guests were invited to the dinners. Additional guests would troop into the East Room after the dinners for a musicale. The President became expert at handling receptions quickly. At one Army-Navy affair Coolidge whisked the line of 2,096 people through in one hour and five minutes, probably an all-time record. Although Coolidge liked shaking hands with ordinary citizens at the midday sessions, he disliked the formal receptions. There were too many people at them and too many of those people were self-important. Snobs he found difficult to tolerate. Colonel Starling said: "Whenever he spotted a particularly bejewelled dowager down the line, or a social leader of rank and distinction, he would nudge me and say, 'Colonel, stop the line at that lady there. I've got to rest' Then, while the lady waited, he would go and sit down for five or ten minutes."[2]

One other presidential chore was the entertaining of persons of great rank or eminence at the White House. The visits of the Prince of Wales, the Crown Prince of Japan, the Crown Prince and Princess of Sweden, the Premier of France, and the Presidents of Cuba, Eire, and Mexico went off well. The visit of Queen Marie of Romania in October, 1926, was a fiasco. All the White House plans went awry thanks largely to the fickleness of the visiting royal personage. Marie made a circus of the White House reception and at her return reception she had photographs taken when it had been expressly forbidden by the Coolidges. At the state dinner she acted less a queen than like a girl at her first dance. Coolidge was a confirmed republican after Marie's visit. The great humorist Will Rogers was a well-behaved and surprisingly solemn guest, although he made fun of the President afterward and was never invited back. Charles Lindbergh was a house guest after his famous flight to Paris in the *Spirit of St. Louis*. The Lone Eagle and his mother were splendid guests, though Coolidge was perturbed at being overshadowed by the young aviator during his stay. Usually there were other overnight guests in the White House and they were left largely to their own devices by the Coolidges. Never did the President and the First Lady breakfast with their guests, for the first meal of the day was reserved to the family and their most intimate friends, and members of Congress. A house guest had to be content with lunch or dinner and a short chat with the Coolidges.

Short chats with visitors were what Coolidge became famous for. This, many have said, was part of his development of a legend. George Mayer has commented in his history of the Republican party that, "with an unexpected flair, Coolidge carefully nurtured the public image of 'Silent Cal.' "[3] Of course there was an advantage in it, for as Gamaliel Bradford wrote, "Silence always suggests mystery and vast uncomprehended intellectual depths, which may be there or may not."[4] Coolidge was aware of the political value of silence, but he did not have to cultivate it because he was naturally shy and frugal in speech with people he had not come to know well.

Moreover, he was not a man who felt altogether well. His extraordinary amount of sleeping and napping, up to ten and eleven hours a day, suggests that. He felt plagued by irritation of his nasal and throat passages and suffered from chronic indigestion, probably induced by his constant nibbling on nuts, candies, and sandwiches. His medicine cabinet was filled with nostrums and occasionally he was forced to a diet of more easily digested foods.[5]

Coolidge was a man who kept most of his worries and woes to himself, though when he did let off steam it was in the form of a great explosion within the family or White House circles. His love of daydreaming probably contributed to that because the daydreamer not only dwells on pretty thoughts but builds up grievances in his mind. Coolidge was caught in a vicious circle. He could not release his emotions well. Except for a few years toward the end of the Presidency he engaged in no sports, and he felt compelled to be quiet around most people, seeking release only occasionally in wisecracks and major explosions. The code of emotional restraint that had been drummed into him as a child and his feelings of duty made him determined to appear to the world the model of composure. His self-imposed quiet probably contributed to his feelings of illness and they in turn contributed to the need he felt to shun people.

The result of Coolidge's shyness and concern for health was, as Henry Mencken wrote, that "his ideal day is one on which nothing whatever happens."[6] That considerably explains both Coolidge's silence and his lassitude as President. His laissez-faire philosophy of government contributed, but they were almost dictated by his emotional need to take things easy. Certainly he avoided irritation where he could. Editorials in *Wallace's Farmer* against Herbert Hoover once caused the Commerce Secretary to complain to Coolidge.

The President asked, "Do you mean to say that a man who has been in public life as long as you have bothers about attacks in the papers?"

"Don't you?" replied Hoover, mentioning a stinging attack on the President in *American Mercury* by Frank Kent.

"You mean that one in the magazine with the green cover?" Coolidge said. "I started to read it, but it was against me, so I didn't finish it."[7]

Coolidge worked out of habit and felt safe in well-established routines. Order and system were essential to him. Surprises, risks, and irritations were to be avoided so that the loads on his emotions and energy could be kept manageable. Order was infused in everything: his daily schedule, official relations, and household matters. Everything was to be under control—his control. He had to watch himself. He was even careful not to say grace before people outside the family. Sometimes his principles, habits, and fears collided. His thrift led him as President in 1924 to travel to Chicago in a regular Pullman car drawing room, but he became such an object of curiosity that he could not stand it. Money or no money, thereafter he would travel in a special train.

With friends or trusted advisers he could let presidential decorum slip, put his feet up on the desk, and talk on and on. But when people were around whom he did not know well, he sat apart from them and spoke rarely. Yet the silent, severe-looking, and even inscrutable President could be caught off guard. If he could not show emotion in public, he was at a loss to defend himself against those who did. Queen Marie flustered him by her emotional ups and downs. Senator Pepper told of how emotion got the President to approve his bill for a national arboretum in the Anacostia River valley. After the bill passed Congress, one of its most earnest advocates, Mrs. Frank Noyes of Washington, rushed to the White House after hearing that Coolidge planned to veto it for economy's sake. In the middle of her presentation, Mrs. Noyes suddenly broke into tears. The President was aghast. He stammered, "Why, Mrs. Noyes, I had no idea that you felt so deeply about this matter." Still crying, she assured him that its veto would break her heart. Coolidge signed the measure into law.[8] He had little defense against persistent emotion, a fact that fortunately for him few discovered.

Control was necessary for him. He was the active, not just the titular, head of his family. He reviewed and altered Mrs. Coolidge's guest lists for White House parties. Using his prerogative as captain of the ship, he selected the guests for the runs of the *Mayflower*. He made it clear to White House employees that he was the master of the house and to test his control he often made difficult demands on his servants. With feeling, White House Usher Ike Hoover wrote, "Coolidge took notice of everything, butted in."[9]

He also felt his control of the government to be personal. All the heads of departments were his. They were "my" secretary of state, "my" secretary of war, "my" secretary of agriculture, and so on. His friends were also subject to his need to run things his own way. Frank Stearns, as has been noted, was kept in his place. He would be drawn into Coolidge's life and expelled from it as the President saw fit. Dwight Morrow found that the same was true for him and indeed his role for some time was one of being excluded. Although Coolidge later assigned missions to his Amherst classmate, he never called upon him for advice on general affairs of state. Morrow was pestered by people who thought he was in constant touch with the White House, but, as he wrote a friend: "I seldom write to the President and he hardly ever writes to me. But everybody is convinced that we maintain a constant correspondence and this gives me, I am glad to say, a quite unwarranted reputation and much influence with people unconnected with the White House."[10]

Although Coolidge tried to control all those around him, he saw a large number of people and sought advice from them. Bernard Baruch lived up to his reputation as adviser to Presidents, even Republicans, with Coolidge. Occasionally the President asked the financier for his views and Baruch responded with memoranda on a variety of subjects. William Randolph Hearst often visited the White House and became an admirer of Coolidge's. The Rockefellers had an attraction for the President. Indeed, Coolidge liked the advice of men of wealth, probably because he believed that those who had made money knew what economics and management were all about.

When Coolidge was in control, he was happy. With the press he was affable and even charming if the reporters followed his rules. If they did not, they could count on being chided. Yet he respected the need for a good press and would not think of asking to have a legitimate news story suppressed. He was particularly aware of the value of photography.

William Allen White told of an afternoon in December, 1924, when a newsreel man yelled to the President's party, "Look pleasant and for Heaven's sake say something—anything; good morning or howdy do!"

Coolidge remarked with a poker face, "That man gets more conversation out of me than all Congress."[11]

The presidential comment was all the more amusing because in the days when motion pictures were still silent the conversation would be lost to all the world. His love of publicity was not just a matter of political shrewdness. Coolidge enjoyed the attention and even the fun of it. Posing as a cowboy for the cameras or becoming an honorary Sioux Indian or Boy Scout were things he did without protest. It was somewhat true, as he once shouted to Grace Coolidge, "Oh, Mammy, they're making a perfect fool of me."[12] But he enjoyed it. Perhaps it was true, as Colonel Starling said, that Coolidge was enjoying a delayed boyhood.

Coolidge's intellect and erudition have often been discussed. Nicholas Murray Butler, the Republican party's intellectual-in-chief, said that the President "was wholly lacking in imagination."[13] Gamaliel Bradford, the self-appointed psychoanalyst to the nation, said that Coolidge's frequent references to the classics sounded "more like the respect of one who reveres afar off than with any intimate daily acquaintance."[14] To some extent both men were correct. Coolidge did not live with the classics because he had little time for them. He did not use much imagination on public issues because he saw his intellectual task as that of applying a philosophy which he had acquired by the time he had left Amherst.

That is not to say that Coolidge was not bright or had no scholarly interests while in the White House but, instead, that his intellectual capacity was cramped by a variety of things. His philosophy of service, stressing politics as it did, excluded concern for most other things. Moreover, the press of his work and his health reduced all of his activities. The time and energy he had left for other things he spent on the study of history and oratory. Although Coolidge ranked low among the Presidents in artistic appreciation, he certainly was not alone among them in possessing a tin ear, in having a lukewarm attitude toward the theater, or in disliking any but the most pictorial types of art. Thanks to Amherst and his own reading over the years, however, he had as good a fund of cultural knowledge as Franklin Roosevelt and Taft, and better than Truman and Eisenhower. In thought he was more logical than any twentieth-century President except Hoover and Kennedy. As Coolidge's prime critic, Gamaliel Bradford, conceded, "When any situation is brought before him, he works it out to the very bottom, as far as his comprehension goes, and with a minuteness of small detail sometimes astonishing to those who know both him and the subject best."[15] This was the benefit of his upbringing and his Garmanesque education. And it was amply supplemented by his ability to master quickly the necessary facts to support his logic. The weakness was that he did not use his intelligence to see ahead, confining it instead to "the day's work."

The promise and failure of Coolidge's mind was well illustrated in his speeches. Like all Presidents he turned out pages and pages of printed dullness, punctuated occasionally by an epigram or an energetic phrase that newsmen and his admirers could quote. His speeches and other state papers also sought to reflect his knowledge, studded as they were with statistics, historical references, or quotations from the classics. The number of ideas in his public pronouncements was limited, but not lacking in idealism. In an age that hooted at absolutes and jeered at fundamentals, Coolidge was a great idealist. In furnishings, his intellectual mansion might have been almost bare, but in faith in man's perfectibility, it reached as high as a cathedral.

To Coolidge the development of character was the highest ideal, for on it depended the achievement of other ideals: service, justice, spirituality, and the stability of society. Character meant not only the development of the individual's talents, and thereby of society's, but also the self-restraint of evil impulses. The President told a meeting of the National Education Association: "Envy, malice, uncharitableness, class jealousies, race prejudices, and international enmities are not realities. They do not abide. They are only the fictions of unenlightened comprehension. Those who preach them are not safe advisers and not sound leaders. Nothing but discord and disaster at home and abroad can result from following these policies."[16]

It was clear in that and other speeches that if character had to be developed it was for the sake of stability. Coolidge's ideal day—the one on which nothing disturbing happened—was a good alternative to the ripping apart of the soul and the flesh which so many people in so many places were urging. Yet that stability had to be constructed by individuals. It could not be imposed, and particularly not by government. That belief stamped his remarks at Philadelphia's Sesquicentennial International Exposition, where he commented on what the Founding Fathers of the Republic had in mind.

It was to establish a free government, which must not be permitted to degenerate into the unrestrained authority of a mere majority or the unbridled weight of a mere influential few. They undertook to balance these interests against each other and provide the three separate independent branches, the executive, the legislative, and the judicial departments of the government, with checks against each other in order that neither one might encroach upon the other. These are our guarantees of liberty. As a result of these methods enterprise has been duly protected, the people have been free from oppression, and there has been an ever-broadening and deepening of the humanities of life.[17]

Those results were the things that could lead to solution of the problems of the twentieth century. Change for good came from the people, Coolidge believed, not from the government. High personal character was both the end and the means, and government's role was to encourage its development and to serve its needs.

Coolidge's brightness was not expressed in his public statements or his policies, but in his humor. He had not long been in the White House when stories attributed to him were being told all over the nation. Justice Holmes wrote that Coolidge was becoming recognized as a witty man. Under Secretary of State Joseph Grew said of the President: "He is not chatty at the table, but now and then makes a dry remark which is very amusing. He has a distinct sense of humor."[18] Coolidge's humor was pointed, even mischievous. It was often in the form of a squelch, which fitted in well with his nature, for that kind of humor was likely to stop conversation instead of encourage it. Certainly no one would try to top the President of the United States in a wisecrack. His humor was all the more penetrating because he seldom smiled when unburdening himself of a retort.

One story was of a lady who came up to Coolidge to say, "Mr. President, I was *so* anxious to hear your speech at the opening of Congress yesterday, that I had to stand the *whole* forty-five minutes."

He quacked in reply, "So did I."[19]

His friends in Congress frequently asked him for copies of photographs in order to stock their own private collections or to give to constituents, and Coolidge complied gladly. Once, though, when a new picture was available, and Representative Allan T. Treadway requested it, the President could not resist saying: "I don't know what you want another for. I'm using the same face."[20]

His humor could also be silent. At one of his breakfasts for members of Congress, Coolidge poured cream and coffee in his saucer. His guests looked dismayed, but a few followed his example and then waited for him to swallow his *petit café au lait*. He bent down, however, and put the saucer on the floor for his dog, leaving the copycats with their saucers awash.

Coolidge's victims did not have to be on hand in order to be ribbed. Claude Bowers told of the time when the Jefferson Centennial Commission was meeting in the East Room of the White House. President Coolidge came in

> —a slight, slender man, looking down his nose, not even glancing to his right or left or making any sign of recognition to the Congressional leaders who were his friends. He sat down at the table and, without once looking up, began reading a telegram from [Felix] Warburg. Thus far it was clearly the silent Coolidge of the gossips. Then having read the telegram, in which Warburg offered to contribute $100,000 to the Monticello fund if a like amount would be subscribed by a Catholic and a Protestant, Coolidge soberly said, "I will authorize Senator Robinson to notify Vice President Dawes that it is the sense of this meeting that he donate a like amount." Then he smiled.[21]

Sometimes Coolidge victimized himself as well as the person to whom he was talking. In preparing to write about the President, William Allen White interviewed him at the White House. "Well, just what is it you want?" asked Coolidge. The Sage of Emporia replied that he wanted a peek at the man behind the mask. The President gazed quizzically for a moment and then said, "I don't know as I can help you." He paused, finally adding, "Maybe there isn't any."[22]

There was a man behind the mask, a tired, not-always-well man. He was not lacking in good intentions and ideals or in warmth and character. Behind the mask he had a private life. He revered his mother. Her picture was ever on his desk and he always carried a silver locket with him encasing a smaller picture of her. He talked often of her with his few intimates. Edmund Starling, who adored his dead mother much as Coolidge did his own, said that in the President's many talks about Victoria Coolidge:

> He seemed to remember every day he had spent with her.

She died when he was young, and he nourished his memories so that now they were living things, as real to him as the days he was now living. He communed with her, talked with her, and took every problem to her. "I wish I could really speak to her," he said one night. "I wish that often."[23]

The President's affection for his father was almost as strong, if less often expressed. He worried about the aging John Coolidge, now alone in Vermont, and wrote him as often as possible. By early 1926 it was clear that the colonel was failing rapidly. His son urged him to come to the White House, but the old gentleman was determined to stay in Plymouth Notch. The President kept in constant touch with the colonel's physician and had a direct telephone wire installed between the White House and the home. When word came in March that his father could not live long, arrangements were made to speed the President by train and automobile to the Notch. The presidential train got the green light all the way and all roads were cleared as Calvin and Grace Coolidge raced to Vermont. Coolidge later, though, had to write: "When I reached home he was gone. It costs a great deal to be President."[24]

Coolidge also gave a great amount of thought to the raising of his surviving son. Now that Calvin, Jr., was gone, the President became overprotective of young John. He tried to shield him from the publicity that a Chief Executive's son naturally attracts, both for the lad's sake and for fear that an adolescent's activities might reflect adversely on the Presidency. He paid close attention to John's schooling. Once when he thought that his son was studying too little at Amherst, he detailed Colonel Starling to watch over him and to protect him from diversions, a task appreciated by neither the young man nor the Secret Service operative. John Coolidge was also put on a strict protocol basis at home. One day he returned from a tea dance in Annapolis to the White House just a few minutes before the dinner hour. John asked, since he was so late, whether he might dine without changing into more formal clothing. He was told by his father, "You will remember that you are dining at the table of the President of the United States, and you will present yourself promptly and in proper attire."[25] John Coolidge would be brought up right. He was the son, now the only son, of the Chief Executive, and he would not be allowed to forget it.

The President's prime love on this earth was his wife. Grace Coolidge was also his greatest support. Gamaliel Bradford put it well when he wrote, "The man would not have been what he was without the woman, and most of all precisely because of her infinite, exquisite tact in effacing herself."[26] Coolidge guarded her as his most precious possession. When she was at home he was with her as often as possible; when she was away he mooned over her like a lovesick boy. Almost every minute of her life was regulated by him, and heaven help her if she departed from schedule or did something unapproved by the master of the White House. She occasionally left Washington, seeking relief for her sinus trouble and attacks of the grippe or to visit her mother who now lived in the Coolidge house in Northampton. When Grace was absent, she wrote her husband almost every day and he would seem to count the minutes until the mail arrived. When the presidential mail came he would go so far as to sort through it. Upon finding her letter, he would go off by himself to read it, taking up to a half an hour to mull over it.

Coolidge also seemed jealous of his wife. Relations between the President and whichever Secret Service operative was assigned to protect the First Lady were never cordial. There was a day in 1927 when Grace Coolidge and her guard, James Haley, hiked over the South Dakota hills while the White House office was established there for summer vacation. They misjudged time and distance, returning more than two hours late. Coolidge had a fit and transferred Haley from the White House detail. The press interpreted it as jealousy, perhaps correctly, though Coolidge undoubtedly saw the whole matter as gross inefficiency by both Grace Coolidge and her Secret Service escort. In any case, the President did not speak to his wife for days.

Coolidge had other loves. It has been said that his love of nature, of which he so often spoke, was superficial. Yet for all his summer vacations he chose places where the flora and fauna were interesting and varied. He definitely was a lover of pet animals. Grace Coolidge's white collie, Rob Roy, was often by the President's side, and there were other dogs in the White House menagerie for whom Coolidge showed affection. Some guests said that he showed more attention to the dogs than he did to them. Coolidge was also fond of cats. One of the White House felines was named Tige and when it was a kitten the President would frequently walk from the executive offices into Grace Coolidge's sitting room with the cat draped around his neck. That performance also was carried out on occasion with a pet raccoon, Rebecca, who enjoyed favor only with the President and at his insistence was permitted to run loose about the White House.

Many men would have been content with the life led by Calvin Coolidge, but he was not. On New Year's Day, 1926, the President wrote his father: "I suppose I am the most powerful man in the world, but great power does not mean much except great limitations. I cannot have any freedom even to go and come. I am only in the clutch of forces greater than I am."[27] Coolidge tried to escape the misery, though not the splendor of the Presidency. His walks were more for the sake of gaining privacy than exercise. He probably spent more time in his family quarters than any other President of modern times. He certainly was on vacation more often. Every summer he took several months of vacation, uprooting his family, much of the White House staff, the press corps, the Secret Service detail, and a force of over one hundred soldiers and marines.

He spent the summer of 1924 at Plymouth and Northampton. The next summer he was at Swampscott, Massachusetts, where Richard Jervis, the head of the White House Secret Service detail, reported, "He is restless and wants to do something every minute and we will have a very busy summer."[28] The following summers the President vacationed at White Pine Camp close to Saranac Lake in New York, South Dakota's Black Hills, and Cedar Island in Wisconsin. After the election of 1928 he sought relaxation in Virginia and Sapelo Island, Georgia. In 1927 he had an unavoidable escape from the White House. It had become clear that the building badly needed renovation. The necessary funds were appropriated and in late winter the Coolidges moved out of the White House and into Eleanor Patterson's mansion at 15 Dupont Circle, where they stayed for much of the year.

It was at White Pines in 1926 that the restless President, at Colonel Starling's urging, took up fishing. He began the sport almost grudgingly but soon developed zest for it, and by the end of his term he had become a passable fisherman. In South Dakota in 1927 Coolidge abandoned his mechanical horse for the real thing. He was always given a responsive animal to ride, which led him to believe after a while that he was quite an equestrian. In fact his confidence in his horsemanship became so strong that Grace Coolidge and Starling had to use all their influence to stop him from riding a wild horse. The vacations benefited the President, for he returned from them feeling both mentally reinvigorated and physically fitter. Their effects, however, did not last. Coolidge's restlessness and feeling of fatigue always came back soon.

28

Taxes, Airplanes, Farmers, and Elections

THE PRESIDENT'S BATTLE with Congress resumed in December, 1925. Coolidge had prepared well for it simply because he had decided to ask little of the lawmakers. Indeed his previous two messages to the House and the Senate would look dynamic and full of requests for action compared with the one he sent up to Capitol Hill December 8, 1925. President Coolidge opened his 1925 message by stating:

> Members of the Congress . . . it is exceedingly gratifying to report that the general condition is one of progress and prosperity. Here and there are comparatively small and apparently temporary difficulties needing adjustment and improved administrative methods, such as are always to be expected, but in the fundamentals of government and business the results demonstrate that we are going in the right direction. The country does not appear to require radical departures from the policies already adopted so much as it needs a further extension of these policies and the improvement of details.[1]

What were especially needed, he went on to say, were "economy and efficiency" so that the public debt could be further reduced and taxes cut in order to give additional stimulae to prosperity. The most important contribution to economy could be made by Congress in holding the line on appropriations. Other things could help, too. Congress should encourage government efficiency, extend the civil service merit system, authorize reorganization of the executive departments, and encourage state and local governments to assume more responsibility for projects like reclamation and prohibition enforcement. This was not a program to keep the nation's problems from being met. It was one designed to encourage the states, localities, and private interests to solve their problems when they could and to make the federal government most efficient in solving its own. Moreover, it was aimed at creating a national wealth that could do wonders in the future. As Coolidge told Congress, "When the country is prosperous and free from debt, when the rate of taxation is low, opportunity exists for assuming new burdens and undertaking new enterprises."[2]

The President's budget message was sent on to Congress the following day, December 9. It contained no surprises, except for his request for an increase in appropriations for the aeronautical activities of the government. Again it was clear that he wanted the House and the Senate to keep appropriations low enough to provide for a tax cut and to reduce the national debt.

Coolidge could not be accused of bringing down too much hay. Only one legislative measure, tax relief, was emphasized. For that he would fight, and he had great support. Much public sentiment had been marshaled behind the tax cut and with congressional elections coming soon it was clear that that sentiment could make itself felt. If Coolidge had earlier been lacking in astuteness in handling Congress, he was masterly in preparing the ground for a tax cut in 1926. There would be few diverting issues. Scandal could not be raised because the Harding scandals had lost their force and there was no Coolidge scandal. No major appointments to office were coming up and the President proved to be circumspect in dealing with minor appointments. He was not asking for any controversial powers and appropriations, and any that might be asked for in Congress would only focus additional attention on the tax reduction issue.

The few diversions from the tax questions were taken care of satisfactorily by Coolidge. Prohibition was the sorest one, but by luck and by design the President slipped neatly between the wets and the drys. Wayne Wheeler, Bishop James Cannon, Jr., Gifford Pinchot, and other dry leaders kept constant pressure on Coolidge to perfect enforcement of the prohibition laws. The President did sponsor the negotiation of treaties with other nations to stop illegal imports of alcoholic beverages, but otherwise he tried to keep from being personally involved in the prohibition question. He referred inquiries to either the Secretary of the Treasury or the Attorney General, who were respectively in charge of prohibition enforcement and prosecution. Letters that could not be referred elsewhere, Coolidge had one of his secretaries answer. The President also sought to send the devotees of dryness chasing over the countryside by his tactic of urging the need for more state and local action on prohibition enforcement.

Coolidge did not drink while he was President, but that did not make him a crusading dry. The steps he took to deal with the problems of prohibition enforcement were well publicized, but largely ineffective. For example, when he was pressed for action by the National Citizens Union of a Thousand on Law Enforcement, he invited their most prestigious representatives, John D. Rockefeller, Jr., Elbert Gary, and S. S. Kresge, to breakfast at the White House. Coolidge's idea was that those who wanted action would, over breakfast, pledge themselves to act in place of pressing him to do so. It was clear that the President was directing the Attorney General and the Secretary of the Treasury to make of prohibition laws what their own consciences required. Attorney General Sargent needed to think about the problem, in fact for the four years of his term of office, and Secretary Mellon showed little interest in what his enforcement agents were doing. It also became suspected that Coolidge himself had no sympathy for dry legislation, although he went through the motions of enforcing it. Colonel Starling later wrote that the President thought that "any law which inspires disrespect for the other laws—the good laws—is a bad law."[3] But Mellon and Sargent were criticized for weaknesses in enforcement. The drys did not have the courage to attack Coolidge for fear that he would do less than he was doing and the wets largely left him alone for fear that he might just get his back up and try to do more. The result was that prohibition did not become a major stumbling block for Coolidge, although it was a constant irritation for the whole country.

Another issue that threatened to divert attention from tax reduction was air development. On the one hand, advocates of expansion of the airways had been besieging Congress and the executive agencies for subsidies and support for years. Every city of size was contending to become the center of both air transportation and airplane manufacturing. On the other hand, railroad interests and the rapidly growing trucking and bus businesses were fighting them. Even fundamentalist theologians got into the act, shouting that if God had wanted man to fly, he would have given him wings and a beak.

Coolidge had already shown interest in orderly development of aeronautics and the nation's airways. In December, 1923, he had urged Congress to establish a Bureau of Civil Aeronautics in the Commerce Department to engage in research that would enable the United States to keep up with other nations in the development of military and naval aviation. His request was passed over, but the government through a number of agencies subsidized airmail service and experiments in the design and construction of aircraft. Those programs and Coolidge were criticized on the ground that taxpayers' money was being wasted. The President defended his Administration in a February, 1925, press conference, when he said:

> We have to make experiments with planes of different makes, patterns, engines, and everything of that kind, and oftentimes the experiment only demonstrates that if you want to secure a result you have to proceed in another direction. That costs money. So I don't think it is a real criticism that although we have spent a great deal of money we have not accomplished altogether results on the practical side.[4]

Coolidge was embarrassed by fierce competition and law suits among the couple of dozen aircraft manufacturers. To meet that he had tried to encourage them to cooperate with one another, saying that stability was needed in the industry so that it could produce large numbers of planes in times of crisis.

Yet those problems took a back seat to the affair created by the charges of the crusading advocate of air power, Colonel William Mitchell, that the Army and Navy were incompetent and negligent in the development of aviation for national defense. Mitchell became so brash in his attacks on the armed services that he was brought up on court-martial charges. Coolidge acted to allay public criticism of the Administration by appointing a board to investigate Mitchell's contentions and to consider the best ways to develop aircraft for the national good. Dwight Morrow finally entered the President's service when he was appointed chairman of the board in September, 1925. That was not a sudden thing, for Coolidge had told his friend the previous March, "I have in mind that I may have you look into the subject of airplanes for me."[5]

The Morrow Board did the job of getting the Administration off the hook by making a good case for the position that the United States was not menaced by foreign air power nor would be in the foreseeable future. Its position, contrary to Mitchell's, was that radical changes in America's air defense system were then without justification. The Wall Street lawyer permitted Mitchell to talk without harassment before the board and the colonel talked until he meandered far afield and wore himself out.

The Morrow Board gave support to the President's views by recommending patient study of all phases of aviation, the designation of assistant secretaries of War, Navy, and Commerce for air with coordination of their activities, and the establishment of a Bureau of Civil Aviation. Although Colonel Mitchell later became celebrated as the patron saint of air power, he was convicted by a court-martial in December, 1925. He had been farsighted, too much so for his time, but he had also been guilty of insubordination so gross that he would have been disciplined severely by any military organization at any time.

Using the Morrow Board Report and the Mitchell affair, a President who never went aloft in an airplane achieved an orderly advance in American aviation. Coolidge asked Congress for, and received, a substantial appropriation for aviation in his December 9, 1925, budget message. In requesting $76 million he asked for one of the few large increases in his budget. His goals were pursuit by the government of "an orderly policy toward building up its air services" and subsidization of "a normal and proper growth in [the aircraft] industry." He pointedly told Congress, "If we continue this policy, there need be no fear of our national defense situation in so far as air strength is concerned."[6]

Coolidge was also able to get congressional approval of most of the Morrow Board's recommendations for coordination of the government's air activities. If future advocates of air power were to say Coolidge lacked vision, it was because he did not go along with them completely. His program of urging and even buying tranquillity in the aircraft business and of subsidizing the industry's development was a significant step in the direction of enabling the United States, when the demand came during World War II, to surpass any other nation in air power.

Yet most important to Coolidge at the time was that he had handled the aviation question in a way that did not distract from accomplishment of his prime goal, tax reduction. Public pressure was developing behind the President's demands that taxes be cut substantially. Tax reduction clubs from all over the nation gave ample testimony before the House Ways and Means Committee in fall, 1925, that taxes had to be lowered in order to continue the country's prosperity. An abundant number of economists, bankers, industrialists, and other businessmen pressed Congress to act. Coolidge himself was instrumental in gathering federal and state representatives together to discuss inheritance and estate taxes. When the first conference, in February, 1925, failed to give adequate support, a second meeting was called for November, which did go along substantially with the President's proposal that there should be no federal estate taxes.

With constant pressure from Coolidge and Secretary Mellon, and with no distractions allowed, an easy victory was achieved in Congress. The Revenue Act of 1926 passed the House, 390 to 25, in December and the Senate, 58 to 19, in February. The gift tax was repealed, estate taxes snipped in half, surtaxes on great wealth slashed up to 50 percent, and income tax rates lowered for all. The only reverse suffered by the Administration was that the corporation tax was slightly increased instead of being lowered as requested. About one-third of the citizens who had paid taxes the preceding year would now be exempt from taxes.

The new law cut federal revenue by almost 10 percent and would release for productive investment some $350 million annually. Of course, the tax measure made the government more reliant on the high tariff for revenue, but that was an added dividend for an Administration that sought to protect American producers from the dumping of competitive foreign products. Coolidge was delighted with the Revenue Act and went so far as to bestow upon the body of lawmakers the title of "the most efficient Congress that we have had for a great many years." Buoyed by his success, he also promised future tax reduction, not in 1927, but "as the debt is reduced, as the business of the country expands and revenue increases and expenses decrease."[7]

Now that the prime Administration measure was out of the way, Coolidge could look to the task of turning back threats to increase the federal budget. The chief threat was to come from the developing McNary-Haugen movement. America's most obvious economic problem in the 1920s was found on the farms. The farmers knew that they had a problem, but they did not know why or what to do about it. They demanded relief, almost any kind as long as the symptoms of their problem were alleviated. The causes of the farm crisis of the 1920s were legion. Farmers had borrowed too much during World War I in order to meet the nation's needs and to make profit for themselves in an expanding market. When demand and prices fell after the war, the agriculturalists were left holding a bagful of debts. The problem was how to pay off the debts and make a decent return on their labor and investment. The answer seemed to lie in using new methods, particularly mechanical ones, to increase production in the hope of increasing income. Agricultural production did increase, but faster than demand, with the result that income remained low.

Farmers also had other burdens thrown upon them. The expansion of state services, especially highway improvement, increased the tax load. Farmers found that in mechanization they could reduce the number of farm animals, but in doing so they released more feed and livestock for the market. Foreign competition became sharper as agriculturalists in other countries encountered troubles. Quotas and tariffs rose abroad, and subsidies were given by many foreign governments to farmers raising products that competed with those grown on American farms. The American farmer answered as usual by increasing his production, but that merely contributed to depressing prices. Production was further boosted by better control of crop- and animal-killing diseases and the development of superior strains of seed and animals. The margin between production and consumption was lengthened by a decreasing birthrate at home and reduction of immigration. The coming of the fashionable slim figure of the 1920s also cut demand for agricultural commodities.

Caught up in constant economic peril, farmers refused to heed the advice of patience which came from so many sources. They used the recommended cures for their problems—mechanization, crop diversification, soil conservation, businesslike farm management, cooperative marketing, and better rural credit—not to limit production to demand or to cut the costs of production, but instead to grow more produce for an already saturated market. The result was, of course, to keep prices low. The howling mob that had been called the backbone of the nation was thrashing around in its own misery. It lashed out in every direction to find relief, but found little. Then along came the McNary-Haugen idea of subsidized dumping of American agricultural surpluses abroad, and gradually great segments of the agricultural community embraced it as fervently as they might a religious faith. They had tried federal credit, tariff increases, and cooperation, but found them wanting. The farmers demanded help right away and most of them expected that the government would provide it.

If the farmers were not patient, Calvin Coolidge was. He had come to favor a several-pronged attack on the farm problem. He would not go over to a program of crop restriction that some of the men around Herbert Hoover favored or to price-fixing that was advocated by some agrarian radicals. He knew well, as he said in his December, 1925, annual message, that despite piteous pleas for help "the farmers as a whole are determined to maintain the independence of their business. They do not wish to have meddling on the part of government."[8] Cooperative marketing, more information on crop and market conditions, cooperation between agriculture and business on economic matters, improved transportation, better agricultural education, and additional credit were what he proposed. Those might turn the trick, and without government dictation or great cost to the taxpayers. What Coolidge had in mind was that farmers should act like astute businessmen who thought "in terms of safe and sound economics."[9] They would have to cooperate

among themselves and with others to know when to adjust their production to market needs and to learn how to cultivate new markets
and to secure efficient farm operation. Coolidge was not sanguine
that even his proposals would work, but he was convinced that
other things would fail and that something had to be tried.[10]

Although farm costs had declined and farm prices increased
somewhat in 1924 and 1925, few farmers were sharing in America's
postwar prosperity. Farm sentiment increasingly swung over in support of the McNary-Haugen nostrum. In October, 1925, no less a
leader than Frank O. Lowden came to back subsidized dumping of
farm surpluses abroad in the hope of bolstering market prices at
home. It was said that even Vice President Dawes favored the idea.
With sentiment building behind McNary-Haugenism, Coolidge
moved to counterattack. On December 7, 1925, he spoke in Dawes'
and Lowden's backyard, Chicago, before the American Farm Bureau Federation convention in a nationally broadcast address. Price-
fixing and tariff revision were out of the question, the President said.
He would stand behind the agricultural proposals that he had out-
lined in his annual messages to Congress. Action beyond those, and
particularly price-fixing, would lead to the destruction of the independence that farmers so valued. Without mentioning McNary-
Haugenism by name, he labeled it as an insidious proposal for price-
fixing, saying that "the moment the government engages in buying
and selling, by that act it is fixing prices." He urged farmers to support the cooperative movement for "a more orderly marketing calculated to secure a better range of prices."[11]

The battle was carried to Congress. The McNary-Haugen bill
was introduced as were the various measures suggested by Coolidge
in his annual message. Stalemate, however, was the result. The
President's proposals made little progress and when Charles Mc-
Nary pressed for action on his own bill in the Senate, James Watson,
the chairman of the Republican steering committee, replied that the
majority leadership saw no reason to act on it. Secretary of the
Treasury Mellon entered the debate on the issue by writing Representative Haugen that "if the bill were to become law it would present
the unusual spectacle of the American consuming public paying a
bonus to the producers of the five major agricultural products."[12]

In an effort to break the log jam in Congress, Agriculture Secretary Jardine and Commerce Secretary Hoover worked out an Ad-

ministration bill, one that Coolidge unenthusiastically approved, to tie in low-interest loans to farm cooperatives with controls on production. The carrot with the stick attached was introduced as the Curtis-Crisp bill and provided specifically for establishment of a Federal Farm Board with $250 million to lend to cooperatives in order to keep nonperishable crops off the market when surplus production threatened to depress prices.

The counterattack of the McNary-Haugenites was made of lace and satin. They tried to appease the Administration by writing a section in their bill that would support expansion of agricultural cooperatives. McNary became convinced that if his bill passed it would escape a presidential veto because of that cooperative clause. The Oregon senator was encouraged because President Coolidge in conference with him said nothing to indicate that he was considering using his veto power. Additional impetus came for the McNary-Haugen bill when Bernard Baruch spoke out for it and when in June one of the bill's chief supporters defeated a leading Republican regular for Senate nomination in Iowa. But the Administration also had forces working for it. When a great cotton crop threatened to flood the market, Coolidge appointed a commission to distribute some $30 million to assist cotton growers in keeping their surplus off the market. The final result in 1926 was stalemate. The McNary-Haugenites without the support of cotton and relatively prosperous tobacco interests could not attract sufficient congressional support for their bill. They were, however, strong enough to prevent the Curtis-Crisp bill from passing. The only significant piece of farm legislation in 1926 was an act that established a Division of Cooperative Marketing in the Department of Agriculture.

On the whole Coolidge could be pleased with the action of Congress on domestic matters in 1926. His tax and aviation recommendations had generally been enacted and Congress had restrained itself in its appropriations. McNary-Haugenism had been thwarted, but cooperativism had advanced. On lesser requests, like funds for development of inland waterways and for improvement of government buildings in Washington, the President had been successful. He had gotten most of what he had wanted and had stopped most of what he had not wanted. Never again was he to have such a successful legislative record on domestic issues.

Coolidge and the members of Congress also were very much aware that 1926 was an election year. The President pointed to the Republican record with pride in the hope that the voters would uphold his majority in Congress. At White Pine Camp on August 3 he reviewed the record in one of his press conferences. "This is the [third] anniversary of my being President. The country has made a great deal of progress in the past three years. It hasn't been so noisy as it has at some other times, but judging from the general condition of the country it has been fairly successful." He listed the accomplishments of the government. The German reparations problem had been solved. The public debt had been reduced steadily, taxes had been cut twice, and federal expenditures kept "as low as possible." Business had been better than during any three years in the nation's history, yet there had been a decline in commodity prices and wages were up a bit. He did not hesitate to give his tax reduction policy credit for that. He did recognize that some sectors of the economy—farming and textiles—were lagging but contended that the fact that others were advancing would go "a long way toward making all the business of the country productive and prosperous." Relations had been resumed with Mexico, the new immigration law put on the books, railroad labor-management relations improved, and further efforts were being made to limit armaments.[13]

That record was in effect Coolidge's platform for his party during the 1926 elections. The country was flourishing and prosperous and, under Republican leadership, would flourish and prosper further. No one disagreed that the United States should flourish and prosper. The disagreement was with whether that state had really been achieved and how prosperity for everyone could be achieved. It was largely on those bases that the congressional elections would be fought, particularly by farmers who demanded immediate relief and workers who asked for more than a bit of increase in their wages. Despite signs that there would be serious opposition at the polls, Coolidge followed the same policy with regard to politics as he had with respect to government. He did little. Indeed, the national party organization did little. The President gave almost no help to regular Republican candidates who were faced by insurgents in the primaries or to the Republican nominees who were chosen in those elections. National Chairman William Butler was involved in his own tight race in Massachusetts for election to the United Stares Senate and could not, even had he wished, organize an effective national campaign for his party.

One issue cropped up unexpectedly during the campaign and had widespread repercussions. The national origins aspect of the Immigration Act of 1924 had not yet been settled and Americans of foreign birth had become greatly concerned about the size of the quotas that would be assigned to various countries. The pressure from foreign-born voters became so great that even Representative Albert Johnson, the law's author, telegraphed Coolidge in August asking him to come out against the national origins scheme of determining who should enter the United States as immigrants. He told the President, "My opinion is that a pronouncement by you in plenty of time before the general elections will save to our party not less than twenty districts in states where German, Irish, and Scandinavian people are disturbed over possible further restrictions under national origins section."[14] If the groups most likely to be favored in immigration quotas were disturbed, it could be easily inferred that less favored groups like the Italian-Americans would be almost rebellious.

Coolidge passed Johnson's telegram on to the secretaries of State, Commerce, and Labor, who were responsible for recommending definition of the national origins clause. It appeared the President hoped that the secretaries would find a face-saving device, but his hope was not realized. Whatever disappointment they felt with the national origins provision was as successfully concealed from the public as was Coolidge's. What the President had done, and was to do until after the 1928 elections, was to ignore the national origins scheme in the hope that he would offend neither its champions nor foreign-born Americans. That policy perhaps helped his party secure victory in 1928, but it contributed to a number of Republican losses in 1926. As Senator Irvine L. Lenroot of Wisconsin, after his own defeat, ruefully wrote Coolidge, "I doubt if many members of either house knew just what the effect of the section would be."[15]

Aside from talking about prosperity, Coolidge did not help any Republican candidate until late in the 1926 election. Then he returned to Massachusetts to support Governor Alvan T. Fuller for re-election and William Butler in his fight to save his Senate seat. Republican National Chairman Butler, who had been appointed to fill Henry Cabot Lodge's place in the Senate, was a poor candidate for elective office. He was a mediocre campaigner and had over the years accumulated a large number of enemies both within and without his party. Moreover, Butler was a textile manufacturer in a state where that industry was depressed and he was opposed in the election by former Senator David Walsh, who had been the most successful Democratic politician in Massachusetts. Governor Fuller was in political trouble because of widespread resentment over his failure to intervene to insure justice in the sensational Sacco-Vanzetti murder case.

Coolidge wanted to stay out of the Massachusetts contests, but he was drawn into the campaign by the efforts to use his prestige to bolster the state's Republican ticket and obscure the real issues. The Boston *Transcript* wrote, "There can be no doubt now that a vote for Butler is a vote for Coolidge, and conversely that a vote against Butler is a vote against the . . . head of the Republican party." The Republican state chairman said, "The issue in Massachusetts this year is Calvin Coolidge," and a newspaper advertisement asked, "Do You Believe in Calvin Coolidge Your President? If You Do You Have No Alternative But to Vote the Republican Ticket."[16] Having been made the chief issue in the Massachusetts elections, Coolidge concluded that it was his responsibility to help Butler and Fuller. On October 25 the President sent a widely publicized letter praising the two nominees and he later decided to travel to Northampton to cast his vote on Election Day. The results of the election were not gratifying, for although Fuller won, Butler was rejected by the voters. Coolidge's critics were quick to crow that the defeat of the Republican National Committee Chairman represented a repudiation of the President's policies in his home state.

What had happened in Massachusetts had also frequently happened elsewhere over the country. The Republican majority in the House of Representatives was cut from sixty to thirty-nine and in the Senate from sixteen to two. Even worse, the insurgent Republicans in the Senate were joined by John J. Blaine of Wisconsin and Smith W. Brookhart of Iowa. The Republicans had retained a majority, but it was only nominal. Democratic and insurgent Republican senators would be in a position in the new Seventieth Congress to block the President's legislative requests at will and occasionally to enact their own proposals.

29

Coolidge and Business

I F CALVIN COOLIDGE was dismayed by the 1926 election returns, he remained happy with his own record. He particularly rejoiced in the economic good times that were being given the name of the Coolidge Prosperity. That prosperity he intended not to forsake. Nor did he intend to forsake business, which he was convinced was its chief support.

It would be unfair to say that Coolidge was antilabor or antifarmer. He was, to be sure, a business President, but not because he opposed other groups in American society. His reasons for favoring business were political, constitutional, economic, and personal. He believed that it was the President's duty to represent the wishes of the people. As he saw it, and not too incorrectly, a majority of Republicans and Democrats approved of giving business a good deal of freedom and encouragement. A majority in Congress might develop for something like the McNary-Haugen bill, but that was a majority that Coolidge decided was clearly out of line.[1] He represented majority sentiment on that question as far as he was concerned.

His position on business was that most Americans wanted a minimum of government interference—even the American Federation of Labor opposed a strong antitrust policy—and that representations for privilege from farm, labor, and other interests pointed toward strictly class legislation that lacked a majority. In short, as he saw it, favor for business derived, not only from business' strength, but from the support of a majority of interests. There was also a constitutional prop for Coolidge's position. The national government was restricted by the Constitution in how far it could intervene in the lives of its citizens and in the works of state and local officials. For the federal government to fix farm prices, regulate workers' hours and wages, and tell businessmen how to run their businesses was clearly unconstitutional to Coolidge and most jurists of the time. For the government through its inactivity to encourage citizens to meet their own problems was, however, definitely constitutional.

Coolidge was sincere about his political and constitutional views. He believed that he represented the will of the people. In view of Harding's election victory in 1920 and his own in 1924 and in view of the strong support among Republicans and Democrats for free enterprise, it must be concluded that Coolidge was more right than wrong. His interpretation of the Constitution was narrow, but it was in line with the thinking of most Americans in the 1920s. Because of that, business would have been privileged even if Coolidge had been impartial. The retreat of government from regulation, which was demanded at the polls, would have accomplished that. Moreover, for farmers, workers, and sectional interests to gain amounts of privilege equivalent to what business had gained from government inactivity alone would have required positive legislation. Such legislation, however, would have run counter to the wishes of most Americans and equally important would have collided with the traditionalist outlook of the nation's courts. Agriculture, labor, and the sections were willing to strive for government favor and to test the nation's organic law, but they were seldom willing and never eager to support one another in their efforts. The result of that paucity of cooperation was, as Coolidge recognized, that a majority would only occasionally be available for positive government action on behalf of farm, labor, or sectional interests. Majorities both among the people and in Congress were reserved almost entirely for government action and inaction that would encourage business expansion.

The President's political and constitutional views were bolstered by his conviction, widely shared, that by minimizing regulation of business the whole country would prosper. "We are not able to make much progress in other directions," he told the press in 1926, "unless we have sound business conditions."[2] Prosperity came because expanding business meant expanding labor. Furthermore, expanding business meant that people must buy goods and services, and business, out of enlightened self-interest, would make the necessary adjustments in wages and salaries to permit that. Even critic Gilbert Seldes in his classic tract on the Great Depression and its causes said: "Coolidge was quite hard-headed and realistic in his approach. . . . He seemed to be aware of the new economics of capitalism which created demand and in which a steady and steadily growing demand, even to the point of extravagance, was essential to prosperity."[3] Coolidge was a true believer in the new economics. He believed in frugal government and in his own personal thrift, but mass spending to buy the products of business was highly acceptable, as his proud citations of booming sales figures in his speeches and statements made clear. He also believed that businessmen knew what they were doing. The nation's economy, he thought, was safe in the hands of the men who had developed America into the world's greatest industrial and financial power.

Coolidge's attitudes toward business were conditioned by another factor. He had been imbued with the idea that the unfettered right to acquire and keep property constituted true personal liberty. That view came with him from the Vermont hills all the way to the White House and he had never seen any reason to discard it. He once said of the people of Vermont: "My folks are happy and contented. They belong to themselves, live within their incomes, and fear no man."[4] The key to their contentment, he believed, was that they owned their property and ran their own businesses and thereby had secured liberty. The man who was prevented from owning and retaining goods and lands could not have true freedom. The corollary, to Coolidge's way of thinking, was that a man was hampered in his freedom to the extent that he was subject to taxation and regulation by other men. Such things must be kept at a minimum. Apparently it did not occur to him that the amount of property one held could grow so large that it would deprive others of the right to acquire property. Similarly the fact that freedom could be obtained in other ways was an idea Coolidge had not thought about seriously, although paradoxically whatever freedom he had enjoyed had come more from his political career than from his business ventures.

It has been said that Coolidge's White House guest list looked like an interlocking directorate of great industry and finance. And there is some truth to that. Certainly he liked to have around him men like William Butler, Andrew Mellon, and Frank Stearns. He seemed to enjoy John D. Rockefeller, Jr., William Randolph Hearst, Bernard Baruch, and even that antagonist of the Administration, James Couzens. And if he had the Babbitts' awe of the Dodsworths, he also had the Babbitts' great respect for his fellow Babbitts. Yet Coolidge's esteem for those who had made or were making money was not a dominant strain in his thought. Far more important was his concern, which he derived from his childhood training, education, and political experiences, to keep things harmonious.

That harmony was of central concern to Coolidge was evidenced in a number of ways. Throughout his career he had shown great dislike for strife. Conflict unsettled men's minds and hampered their progress. Moreover, it was too often used as an excuse for unnecessary government interference. His approach was a gentle, reasonable one. Conciliation had settled the Lawrence textile strike back in 1912 and the coal strike in 1923. Conciliation could solve most disputes. Even better was for forces that tended to conflict to come to understandings before strife developed. Conciliation and understanding were Coolidge's keys to harmony. There were occasions, however, when emergency required more dynamic intervention. At such times government under Coolidge did intervene, for example, in trying to bring stability to the radio industry by establishment of the Federal Radio Commission to stop the ugly scramble for broadcasting rights. His interventions, except for his reluctant action in the Boston Police Strike, were mild, for they were aimed at getting people to work together to regulate themselves and to solve their own problems.

In his concern for harmony, understanding, and self-regulation the President was an idealist because he believed that men had the character and intelligence to solve their own problems if encouraged to do so by higher authority. Although he carried it to extremes, Coolidge was not alone in his belief, for Herbert Hoover and many leading economists and businessmen saw intelligent self-regulation as the way to reach national prosperity and harmony. Even Democrats, no less a one than Franklin D. Roosevelt, were advocates of the idea of voluntary regulation. The 1920s was the testing ground for the concept and it failed miserably. It was not that the ideal was faulty, but instead that people lacked the necessary understanding and will to adjust themselves to the needs of society. Coolidge's failure was his inability or refusal to recognize that harmony through conciliation and self-regulation was too high an ideal to be achieved at that time.

Of course, the ideal was supported by Coolidge's constitutional views and his lack of energy. When in 1926 Professor William Z. Ripley of Harvard University drew his attention to the fact that pyramiding holding companies and rigging of stock markets threatened the United States with serious economic consequences, Coolidge was concerned. Yet in searching Ripley's arguments, he could not find any legal justification for federal intervention. Coolidge seemed relieved when he told a press conference that the states had jurisdiction over corporate matters and that any federal action would have to be decided in the courts. The President was worried about the activities of holding companies and stock market rigging, but he was not going to draw upon his short supply of energy to act on those problems as long as other remedies were available. He made it obvious by speech and inaction that the White House was the last place to take domestic economic problems.

That was made even clearer in his statements regarding the federal regulatory commissions. Although he wanted those agencies to be responsive to his wishes whenever he had any wishes, his prime interest was that they do their day-by-day work without involving him. In response to a reporter's question in 1927 about the Federal Reserve Board he said that the board "does function and ought to function entirely apart from the executive." He conceded, "I have sometimes made some comment on what they have done and the beneficial effect that I thought had accrued from it, but I do not recall that I have ever made any suggestion to the Board as to any action that it ought to take." In fact, the less he knew about the detailed activities of the regulatory agencies the better. That was evinced in his answers to questions about government regulation of the economy. Studding his press conference transcripts are replies such as, "I am not familiar enough with the exact workings and practice," "a matter that I wouldn't happen to know anything about," "I have no information," and "I have very little information."[5] Of course, that was in part his way of deflecting embarrassing questions, but it was also a reflection of ignorance. To concern himself much with economic regulation would run contrary to his constitutional, political, and economic convictions as well as drain his energy.

Secretary of Commerce Hoover repeatedly asked him to seek additional control over private banking and financial practices and Senator Watson expressed his fear that speculation in stocks had gone too far. The President, however, was happy just to ride on the whitecaps of the Coolidge Prosperity. His job was to act only in case of emergency and no emergency threatened, as far as he could see. Coolidge contented himself with urging business expansion. This encouragement is seen in many of his presidential speeches, from the statement in his 1925 inaugural address that "we appear to be entering an era of prosperity which is gradually reaching into every part of the nation," to his proud recitation of economic figures in the 1928 campaign that "illustrate the life and development of our country."[6] His many words and statements had had, according to the New York *Times*, "the effect of converting an aimless, colorless stock market into a lively buoyant affair."[7]

Indeed, Coolidge did use words to keep the stock market buoyant. On January 6, 1928, a reporter asked him whether brokers' loans, which had jumped to almost $4 billion in value, had expanded too rapidly. He could not answer the question, saying only he had no evidence that the amount of the loans was too large. He was, however, bothered by the question and by recent breaks in the stock market and therefore had a formal statement prepared. His statement declared that brokers' loans were not excessive because they reflected steadily increasing bank deposits and the larger number of securities on the market. To give emphasis to his reassuring view, he allowed it to be quoted directly in the press. The result was to bolster a defective market instead of permitting it to seek healthier lower levels of value.

A few days later H. Parker Willis, who was editor-in-chief of the New York *Journal of Commerce*, discussed the statement with Coolidge at the White House. The President indicated that his official view and his personal opinions were divergent. He said, "If I were to give my own personal opinion about it, I should say that any loan made for gambling in stocks was an 'excessive loan.' "

Willis replied, "I wish very much, Mr. President, that you had been willing to say that instead of making the public statement you did."

"Why did you say that?" Coolidge asked.

"Simply," Willis said, "because I think it would have had a tremendous effect in repressing an unwholesome speculation, with which, I now see, you have no sympathy."

The President argued: "Well, I regard myself as the representative of the government and not as an individual. When technical matters come up I feel called on to refer them to the proper department of the government which has some information about them and then, unless there is some good reason, I use this information as a basis for whatever I have to say; but that does not prevent me from thinking what I please as an individual."[8]

There it was. More than following his own conclusions, Coolidge was fulfilling his conception of the officeholder as a representative, in this case as a representative of those who ought to know. As usual he was not going to overrule his subordinates. Nevertheless he did feel uneasy and he kept in touch with the Federal Reserve Board on the situation. He placed himself in an anomalous position, on the one hand making statements that led people to believe that everything was fine, and on the other hand not discouraging Federal Reserve officials from trying, however ineffectively, to slow down expansion of credit and the rise of stock market prices. Coolidge was unable to act for he was stalled on dead center. The influence of his business friends, his distaste for federal intervention, his pride in the Coolidge Prosperity, his hope that things would work themselves out naturally, his lassitude, and perhaps his mounting dividends, outweighed his suspicions that serious economic trouble was in the offing.

The Coolidge Prosperity has not been misnamed. By tax and debt reductions, statement and inaction, the President had greatly encouraged business to expand and it responded to his encouragement. The results were temporarily magnificent. Never before had so many Americans prospered so much. It was, however, a prosperity built largely on airy expectations. It defied the economic laws of gravity and when it came down it landed calamitously. It would be unfair to say that Coolidge's policies lacked public approval or that he could have prevented the consequences of the world's shoddy economic and political reconstruction after World War I. Yet it will forever be held against him that he did not see further and more clearly than his fellow Americans, and with some justice, for he had qualms and failed to act on them. His representative Presidency and his ideal of achieving harmony and prosperity through a minimum of federal regulation in the long run contributed to discord and economic collapse.

30

Congress and Domestic

Issues, 1927-1928

THE MESSAGE Coolidge sent up to Congress after the 1926 elections was much like his preceding annual messages. He did not ask for much. It was largely an expression of pride and of promise. He wrote: ". . . in reporting to the Congress the state of the Union, I find it impossible to characterize it other than one of general peace and prosperity. . . . What the country requires is not so much new policies as a steady continuation of those which are already being crowned with such abundant success." The keys to success, past and future, were "economy" in government, "elimination of many kinds of waste," and "a general raising of the standards of efficiency." He left it up to Congress to decide whether the anticipated surplus of revenue should be used in 1927 for tax reduction or for debt reduction. Either would help boost the national economy through release of large sums of money for investment and consumption.

There were, however, other things that the President asked Congress to authorize: railroad consolidation that should reduce rates, development of roads and inland waterways, land reclamation, regulation of radio wave lengths, extension of emergency government powers to compose disputes in the bituminous coal industry, authorization of branch banking by national banks, and continued beautification of the nation's capital. Such measures could greatly benefit the people. They also, if not allowed to become too costly, would fit into Coolidge's conception of what America's goals should be:

> . . . its face ought always to be turned upward, its vision ought always to be fixed on high. . . . To relieve the land of the burdens that came from the war, to release to the individual more of the fruits of his own industry, to increase his earning capacity and decrease his hours of labor, to enlarge the circle of his vision through good roads and better transportation, to place before him the opportunity for education both in science and in art, to leave him free to receive the inspiration of religion, all these are ideals which deliver him from the servitude of the body and exalt him to the service of the soul. Through this emancipation from the things that are material, we broaden our domination over the things that are spiritual.[1]

Coolidge may have wanted little from Congress, but he received a lot in terms of disturbing his equanimity, and much of the disturbance revolved around the stormy issue of McNary-Haugenism. He tried in his annual message to deflate the movement. At great length he recited what the federal government had done for farmers since 1921 by way of easing credit, encouraging cooperative marketing, conducting research on agricultural products and their uses, improving transportation, increasing tariffs, decreasing taxes, and regulating packers, stockyards, and warehousing. He reasoned that by further product research, encouragement of cooperatives, railroad consolidation, additional farm education, and general stimulation of the economy, the problems of farmers could safely be brought under control. His effort was of little avail because too many farmers wanted those things in addition to implementation of the McNary-Haugen plan.

The McNary-Haugenites had gained strength since their last joust with Coolidge. Vice President Dawes was now squarely in their camp. Indeed, he was so firmly linked to them that when an Illinois attorney told the President, "Mr. Dawes seems to have a good many friends among the farmers," Coolidge replied, "Yes, I have noticed that the McNary-Haugen people have their headquarters in his chambers."[2]

Not only had the Vice President gone over, but also such financial and industrial leaders as Bernard Baruch and Owen D. Young. Coolidge's position was further weakened because he could no longer rely on the regular Republican leadership for help. Dawes had converted James Watson of Indiana to support of the scheme to dump farm surpluses abroad, and Charles Curtis of Kansas was not carrying out the White House's orders on the issue. The President was left with the active support of only one of the Senate giants, Borah of Idaho, who could hardly be counted on to lead as much as to antagonize. Almost as bad was that the Administration was not united behind Coolidge. None of the Cabinet members supported the McNary-Haugen bill, but Secretaries Hoover and Jardine took advantage of the situation to push their proposal for a Federal Farm Board that would use cooperatives to control production through the extension of credit at low interest rates. Coolidge did not oppose that, but he did view it askance. He was almost alone in his position, being able to look only to Secretary Mellon and Frank Stearns for solace.

The new McNary-Haugen bill was introduced in December, 1926, and its advocates campaigned all over the country to gather support. The measure's appeal was great. Farmers were offered immediate relief without the government controls on production that were included in the Hoover-Jardine proposals. Businessmen serving agriculture were promised a share of whatever prosperity the farmers would receive and the bill even guaranteed middlemen reimbursement of any losses they might suffer under the plan's operation. The objections of much of the South had been eliminated by including cotton and tobacco among the commodities protected, and cultivators of those two crops could now appreciate the bill, for their production was running far ahead of demand. Midwestern Republicans thought that McNary-Haugenism offered them a way to retain their seats in Congress and perhaps to gain control of their party in 1928. Even if Coolidge vetoed the bill, its Republican supporters in Congress could say that they had been on the side of the angels. Many Democrats viewed the bill another way. To them it appeared to be an avenue to election of one of their own as President in 1928. As one of the Democratic leaders in the House, Henry T. Rainey of Illinois, wrote: "There are some farm leaders who think the President will veto the bill. If he does, God help the Republican party in 1928."[3]

Thanks to its increased attractiveness, the McNary-Haugen bill was passed by a substantial majority in the House. In February, 1927, the measure barely passed the Senate and only because of intervention by Vice President Dawes. Coming up for action at the same time as the McNary-Haugen bill was the Pepper-McFadden bill, which authorized branch banking by national banks. Those who favored the first bill largely opposed the other, but both groups were eager for success and their leaders were not particular about how it was achieved. Dawes, who favored both measures, arranged a marriage of the contending forces for the purpose of exchanging support, with the result that the two bills were approved by the Senate. Now it remained to be seen what the President would do.

Coolidge gladly signed the branch banking bill, for it was an Administration measure, but he concluded that the interests of a majority of Americans required him to reject McNary-Haugenism. His veto message of February 27 was lengthy and forceful. His general objection was that the bill "is not framed to aid farmers as a whole, and it is, furthermore, calculated to injure rather than promote the general public welfare." Then he listed, sometimes repetitiously, specific objections. The bill put "a premium on one-crop farming" and upheld "as ideals of American farming the men who grow cotton, corn, rice, swine, tobacco, or wheat, and nothing else." Why did it, the President asked, leave out a dozen or more other lines of important agricultural endeavor? Why would it penalize the farmer who diversified his crops and, he added by implication, the farmer who tried to restrict his production to demand? The measure would guarantee a profit, to be taken out of the pockets of farmers, only to exporters, packers, millers, cotton spinners, and other middlemen. The equalization fee to be charged to finance the program would unconstitutionally fix a tax, not for revenue, but for the benefit of a few. Another effect of the fee would be "employment of the coercive powers of government to the end that certain special groups of farmers and processors may profit temporarily" from the artificially higher prices charged for their products in the home market. That additional income for a minority of Americans would encourage them to produce more although inflationary prices would soon decrease domestic demand. The eventual result would be to expand, not control, the farm surpluses which gave rise to the problem the bill sought to remedy. McNary-Haugenism would also dump agricultural surpluses on the international market which would depress the world price of those commodities and lead either to retaliatory dumping in the United States or to the erection of tariff walls so high that American farmers could sell few of their products abroad.

The bill, Coolidge continued, would establish an administrative monstrosity. The program was to be carried out by a board which would be legally unrestricted in its power and from which no appeal would be possible. That fantastic delegation of power alone made the measure unconstitutional. Moreover, the board would have set before it an almost impossible task of dealing with and coordinating the efforts of thousands of businesses and millions of farmers. Not only would the McNary-Haugen program subject farmers to "the tyranny of bureaucratic regulation and control," but because of its scope and methods would seriously dislocate distributive and marketing practices and channels. The bill was further unconstitutional in that it proposed that farm organizations instruct the President whom he should nominate for membership on the board.

McNary-Haugenism also violated fundamental rules of order and conservation, according to Coolidge. "Instead of undertaking to secure a method of orderly marketing which will dispose of products at a profit, it proposes to dispose of them at a loss. It runs counter to the principle of conservation, which would require us to produce only what can be done at a profit, not to waste our soil and resources producing what is to be sold at a loss to us for the benefit of the foreign consumer." In short, the President told Congress, the bill could not be approved because of its "unconstitutionalities, invasions of executive authority," and its provisions for "overproduction with its inflation and inevitable crash . . . indirect price fixing . . . [and] creation of huge bureaucracies."[4]

Coolidge had vetoed the bill and Congress was unable to override it, but McNary-Haugenism was not a dead issue. Its supporters rewrote the bill to try to meet the President's constitutional objections on the next go-round. Indeed, Charles McNary went so far in meeting the White House's objections that he thought Coolidge might sign the new bill should it pass Congress, although the senator wrote that what the President "doesn't know about 'sech' things would fill a great big library."[5]

Coolidge may not have known much about farm matters, but he seemed to be aware that the fervor of McNary-Haugenism's supporters was weakening. As McNary's biographer has written, "It appeared [in the summer of 1927] that the political rumblings against Coolidge were mostly thunder without the torrents."[6] Vice President Dawes had to be pressed to support the bill again and others were tiring of the battle.

Chester Davis told George Peek, one of the fathers of the original plan: "George, this is the last heat I trot. We can't dump surpluses over the sort of tariff walls they're rearing over the water now."

"The hell we can't," Peek replied.[7]

Yet Peek's enthusiasm was not representative. In vetoing the measure, Coolidge had rallied the opponents of McNary-Haugenism. The Southern-Western coalition backing agricultural dumping started coming apart, going off in divergent directions to seek ways to counter the President, and then disagreeing on what they returned with. The Administration added to their disagreement by tossing in what a young farm editor, Henry A. Wallace, called "red herrings."[8]

Yet the danger that a new McNary-Haugen bill would become law had not disappeared. The enthusiasm of the bill's supporters may have lessened, but their majorities in Congress had increased thanks to the larger agrarian element in the new Seventieth Congress. In 1928 the measure was approved by large majorities in both the House and Senate. Coolidge again vetoed it, in May, this time with unrestrained ridicule. In his message he described the bill and its provisions as "bureaucracy gone mad," "autocracy," "ponderously futile," "vicious devices," "delusive experiments," "fantastic promises," "preposterous economic and commercial fallacy," "naive," "futile sophistries," and "a system of wholesale commercial doles." The McNary-Haugen bill was no longer constitutionally objectionable, but it was "nonsense" to the President and therefore deserving of rejection.[9]

Again Coolidge's view prevailed, for Congress upheld his veto. The McNary-Haugenites determined to appeal his decision to the 1928 Republican National Convention in the hope that their plan would be adopted as official party policy. A number of farm and political leaders called for a march of 100,000 farmers on the convention, which was to be held in Kansas City, but few showed up. The McNary-Haugen plank prepared by Peek, Senator Watson, and others had even less success. Coolidge was upheld by the convention and that was in effect the end of McNary-Haugenism.

The movement had been done in by the inability of its own supporters to stay hitched together, the President's staunch opposition, and slightly improving farm conditions. The McNary-Haugen plan had been conspicuously foolhardy. It would have encouraged further overproduction of the farm commodities it sought to protect and therefore probably would have brought only temporary relief to those farmers and businessmen covered by its provisions. By dumping surpluses abroad it certainly would have aggravated an already bad international economic situation. The only constructive contribution of McNary-Haugenism was to press, with a bit of success, a languorous Administration to do something for the farmer. It can be conjectured, however, that the movement siphoned off pressure for more orderly and scientific approaches to agricultural problems. Coolidge did well to stand firmly against the McNary-Haugen movement, although he failed to develop an effective plan to deal with the problems of his country's farmers.

There were other domestic troubles with which Coolidge had to contend during his years as President. One concerned civil rights. Northern Negroes were part of the Republican voting coalition in the 1920s and they were increasingly pressing Coolidge for help and recognition as they became greater in numbers and better off financially. They particularly asked him for action against the Ku Klux Klan, which was terrorizing Negroes in much of the country. Other leading matters of interest to them were restoration of voting rights in the South, relaxation of racial tensions in the cities, courteous treatment by federal officials, a desegregated civil service, and more political appointments. Coolidge's response, though no worse than Harding's and better than Wilson's, was not vigorous. On several occasions he requested Congress to use its power to punish lynching. He referred complaints of violations of voting rights to the Department of Justice for routine investigation and he secured some increases in appropriations for the education of Negroes. The President allowed the Ku Klux Klan to burn itself out, but by remaining aloof he vexed many of his party's colored supporters. Indeed, they would note well that it was during his Administration, in 1925, that the Klan, despite a great wave of public protest, paraded through the streets of the national capital.

Coolidge was often in touch with a number of Negro leaders, especially Dr. Robert R. Moton, the principal of Tuskegee Institute; James Weldon Johnson, the secretary of the National Association for the Advancement of Colored People; and the dynamic William Monroe Trotter, the corresponding secretary of the National Equal Rights League. All of them frequently made suggestions and representations to him but only with occasional results, such as enlisting his support for better educational appropriations, improved opportunities for employment in the civil service, and the Dyer federal antilynching bill. Perhaps those leaders were responsible for a few high-level appointments to federal office, such as that of W. T. Francis as Minister to Liberia. Yet Coolidge's actions on behalf of Negroes were viewed by most civil rights leaders as only gestures, and rightly so. He failed to make the most of the power he had to secure desegregation of the civil service or polite treatment of Negroes by public officials. In 1925 he obviously sidetracked his interest in antilynching legislation in order to enlist maximum support in Congress for tax reduction. He also did virtually nothing to build on Harding's restoration of Negroes to high office after Wilson had purged them. No one expected Calvin Coolidge to institute the Kingdom of God on earth, but he did have opportunities to improve the conditions of Negroes in the United States. His policy of making gestures where substantial improvements could have been made was to contribute to the wholesale abandonment of the Republican party by Negroes during the New Deal years.[10]

Another problem facing Coolidge was flood control. Floods had for years ravaged parts of the country with great loss of life and property. The Army Corps of Engineers and the Department of Commerce had become increasingly interested in stopping the waste caused by floods but had been able to do little because of the public's general lack of concern. In spring, 1927, however, the nation's attention was dramatically called to the matter when a series of floods on the Ohio, Missouri, and Mississippi rivers brought the worst natural catastrophe that the midlands had ever suffered. Over two hundred people died, a million and a half persons were driven from their homes, and hundreds of millions of dollars in damage was inflicted on property with even more being lost because of the discontinuance of industrial productivity in much of the area. The federal government moved quickly to cope with the great flood.

Coolidge placed Secretary of Commerce Hoover in charge of a gigantic coordinated effort by local, state, federal, and private agencies to calm the rampaging waters, rescue the stranded, control disease, give shelter and food to the homeless, and provide loans for reconstruction. As if to show that severe flooding was not the problem of one region, New England in November, 1927, was hit by the worst flood in its history, which led to the loss of 112 lives and untold property. Once again the Coolidge Administration acted promptly to give assistance.

As a result of these two disasters great pressure was placed on the Administration to take steps to prevent serious floods in the future. The President was not pleased, because a large federal flood control program would throw his budget out of line, but the amount of support within the government and over the country for action was too great to resist. Therefore in his December, 1927, annual message to Congress he asked for federal flood control projects along the Mississippi River, though emphasizing the need for the property owners who would benefit to carry a substantial part of the cost. Coolidge was intent upon restricting appropriations for flood control. He had, however, made a tactical error in not specifying in his annual message the kind of program he wanted. Congress, it appeared, wanted an expensive one that would be financed completely by the government.

In February, 1928, Coolidge clarified his position, saying that what he had in mind was the $180 million program proposed by General Edgar Jadwin, the chief of the Army Engineer Corps. The President had in his December annual message vaguely referred to a one-third contribution by the benefited property owners, but he was forced to retreat by February to one-fifth. He also was willing for the Treasury to lend money to landowners so that they could handle their share of the cost. In any event he did not consider a 20 percent levy to be a great burden to the property owners since it would average about three cents on each acre of land to be protected by flood control projects.

At the end of February Coolidge had thought there was general agreement among all those concerned with flood control work, but by April it was clear that the situation had gotten out of hand. Congress had increased the anticipated cost from $180 million to $1.4 billion and was resisting the principle of charging those persons and corporations to be benefited a share of the cost. What was almost as bad was that the bill before the House of Representatives, the Jones bill, left a loophole whereby the United States government could be considered financially responsible for all flood damage along the lower Mississippi River in case federally constructed levees broke. On April 10, 1928, the President took his fight before the people. He told newspaper reporters that the situation in Congress represented "a scramble to take care of the railroads and the banks and the individuals that may have invested in levee bonds, and the great lumber concerns that own many thousands of acres in that locality, with wonderful prospects for the contractors." He also opposed the legislative provision that would take the administration of the program away from the Corps of Engineers and put "it into the hands of a new body that are to hold office forever . . . unresponsive to anybody or anything."[11]

The $1.4 billion flood control program was approved by the Senate in April, so Coolidge accelerated his campaign to swing the House behind the Jadwin plan. As for the Senate bill, he told the press that it was "extortionate" and added that the upper house had not "understood it, what its implications were, or what is behind it."[12] He named the lumber interests as the chief villains in this plot to drain money from the federal Treasury. The House gave him some concessions in its bill, but not enough. The President was willing that the United States assume some liability for damages that occurred as a result of government levee construction, but he resisted the idea of a $1.4 billion program and the principle that property owners should contribute nothing. He made a veiled threat to send a special message to Congress on the subject in order to focus public attention on what was happening. When the Jones bill passed the House toward the end of April, he commented that it was no better than the Senate measure and in fact if anything was more expensive.

Coolidge turned his attention to the conference committee, urging it to come up with a bill he could sign. He condemned the bill before Congress as one that would benefit absentee property owners far more than the people who lived in the areas threatened by floods. The House and Senate conferees ignored the President in drawing up their report, but after he complained bitterly they decided to consult him. Consequently he was able to impress upon them that the voters would not stand for a raid on the Treasury. The bill finally agreed upon in Congress the middle of May was not what Coolidge had wanted, but the price had been marked down to about $500 million and essential responsibility for flood control projects remained with the Army Corps of Engineers. Moreover, the measure provided for some local contributions to the cost of flood control. Coolidge decided to sign the bill because public opinion seemed strongly to favor it. In an election year the representative President had no feasible alternative.

One other money-gobbling program that Coolidge worried about concerned the development of water resources. That was a program in which Secretary of Commerce Hoover and Secretary of the Interior Work were greatly interested. The pressures for it from the West were tremendous and the progressive Republicans supported the concept of water development, if not the Hoover-Work interpretation of it. As early as 1925 Hoover was vigorously pushing for the establishment of land reclamation and hydroelectric power projects in California's San Joaquin and Sacramento valleys and along the Columbia River basin. Push and pull as he might, though, the Commerce Secretary could not get the President's backing. In fact in 1926 while Hoover was barnstorming the country speaking out for water development projects, he received a telegram from the White House objecting to such talk because of the amount of appropriations that would be required for them. Coolidge would go along with Hoover on the improvement of rivers as arteries of transportation because that was a traditional government activity and enjoyed great public support, but he believed that hydroelectric power projects were an entirely different matter.

Hoover and Work were more successful in carrying out plans for the development of the Colorado River basin. There had been much discussion of damming the river for the purposes of irrigation, power development, flood control, and water supply. Although acrimony often characterized the discussions, the fact was inescapable that there was a great deal of public and congressional support for a federal water project on the Colorado. Here, unlike the California and Columbia River projects, a large number of states were involved, including Arizona, California, Colorado, Nevada, New Mexico, Utah, and Wyoming. As early as 1922, under Hoover's leadership, those states had agreed to ask Congress to approve an Interstate Compact on distribution of the Colorado River's waters and construction of a huge dam. The agreement did not last long, for Arizona's governor reneged on his state's promises, and Senator Hiram Johnson, seeking an election issue, induced California to demand that the compact not be effective until the big dam, Boulder Dam, was authorized by Congress. It took four years to gain ratification of the compact and several years to get the President's support

Coolidge backed development of the Colorado River project in December, 1925, and confirmed his interest in his 1926 and 1927 messages to Congress. It should be noted, however, that his interest slackened after the 1926 elections were held, which suggests a political motivation. The project, which he had described as imperative in 1925, was only favored by the President in late 1926 and 1927. Legislation authorizing a big dam on the Colorado became a major issue in Congress and in the West. Coolidge, Hoover, and Dr. Work, who was elected Republican National Committee Chairman in 1928, became caught between those, like Senator Johnson, who advocated public operation of the dam's electric power facilities and those who opposed it. In an attempt to appease everyone and to permit Hoover to carry California in the 1928 elections, the question of public operation was left open. Once Hoover became President the use of the power produced by the dam was given over to private interests, though California was thrown a sop in being authorized to regulate the rates charged consumers. Hiram Johnson contended during the debates on the Boulder Dam bill, which he sponsored, that the Administration was only "pretending to be for it."[13] The California senator complained that his bill had been delayed so long in the House by Coolidge's men and private power interests that the Senate was unable to consider it before the 1928 elections. The measure was finally passed by Congress, however, and signed by the President in December, 1928.

Although one should never take anything Hiram Johnson said at face value, circumstantial evidence bears him out. Politics was an important factor in determining how Coolidge would support the Colorado River project. By backing the Johnson bill but delaying its passage, the President would antagonize the least number of voters, senators, and representatives. More important, he had his own prime interests to consider and those were further tax and debt reductions in 1928, which would be jeopardized by the appropriation of some $125 million called for in the Boulder Dam bill. From Coolidge's standpoint it was better that the sum be spent in 1929, after the fiscal reductions had been carried out.

That Coolidge was determined to cut the federal debt and taxes in 1928 was made clear in his December 6, 1927, annual message. He told Congress that retirement of the debt "should be continued for the purpose of relieving the nation of the burden of interest . . . and releasing revenue for internal improvements and national development." Of greater importance was the paring of taxes:

> The immediate fruit of economy and the retirement of the public debt is tax reduction. The annual saving in interest between 1925 and 1929 is $212,000,000. Without this no bill to relieve the taxpayers would be worth proposing. The three [tax] measures already enacted leave our government revenues where they are not oppressive. Exemptions have been increased until 115,000,000 people make but 2,500,000 individual taxable returns, so that further reduction should be mainly for the purpose of removing inequities.[14]

The President got down to specifics in his budget message. He recommended that taxes be lowered by $225 million, which, when added to earlier reductions, would mean that the annual tax yield had been sliced by $1,604,000,000 during the Harding and Coolidge Administrations.

The President's fiscal program was threatened from the beginning of the Seventieth Congress in December, 1927, and it continued to be in peril until the legislators adjourned a half year later. During the closing days of Congress Coolidge enumerated, to a press conference, the threats to his budget:

> The number and the amount is appalling. . . . Of course, there is this flood bill. It is impossible to estimate what that will cost. If it is carried out as suggested, I think $500 million would probably be the minimum. Nobody knows what the maximum might be. There is the farm bill calling for $400 million. The Boulder dam bill. I think the lowest estimates on that are $125 million. Other estimates run to $250 million. There is a pension bill, running $15 million or $20 million. The salary bill, the so-called Welch bill, of about $18 million. The Muscle Shoals bill, which I think was reported to me would cost perhaps $75 million. . . . In addition to that

there is the Post Office pay bill of I think $20 million, and the reduction of postage payments which has been reported in the Senate I think calls for—it seems as though it is $38 million.

When asked about the effect of these measures on tax reduction, the President replied: "Well, there is a tax reduction bill of $203 million reported to the Senate and $289 million as it passed the House. If all these bills went through and became law I should think it would not only endanger tax reduction at the present time, but would make necessary the laying of additional taxes."[15]

Coolidge fought these threats rather successfully. It was probable that his actions led to deferring passage of the Boulder Dam bill until the following fiscal year. He vetoed the McNary-Haugen bill and gave a pocket veto to the Muscle Shoals bill. He was able to get several other appropriations, like the flood control bill, substantially reduced in cost. In the long run the President was able to keep expenditures in line so that the tax bill could be approved. To his great pleasure he also found that his January, 1928, estimate of a revenue surplus of $252 million was $146 million less than the actual surplus for the fiscal year. That not only aided tax reduction but also permitted a much larger paring of the public debt than he had anticipated.

The tax law enacted by Congress in May gave Coolidge and Secretary Mellon most of what they had requested. The corporation tax was reduced by one-ninth and the credit given taxable corporations was increased from $2,000 to $3,000. By reductions in certain categories, the graduations in income tax rates were made less sharp. A large number of exemptions were granted on entertainment and other special taxes. What the Administration failed to get was repeal of the federal estate tax, and what it got but did not want was repeal of the lucrative 3 percent tax on manufacturers' prices on automobiles. Nevertheless Coolidge considered himself highly successful. Debt and tax reduction had been furthered, and that, he was convinced, would on the one hand promote prosperity and on the other hand dispose of revenue surpluses which would tempt Congress to yield to the sin of fiscal extravagance. The Administration's tax program was also a good lure for the voters to keep the Republican party in power in the 1928 elections. All was well that ended well as far as the President was concerned.

31

Over There

Dᴵꜱᴄᴜꜱꜱɪᴏɴ ᴏꜰ ᴏɴᴇ highly important aspect of Coolidge's elected term as President has been saved until now. That is foreign affairs, and it has been saved because these matters run like a thread throughout the period from late 1924 to his leave-taking from office in March, 1929. It is true that Coolidge left most questions of foreign relations in the hands of the Department of State. Yet there were times when he was unavoidably drawn into them, other times when he wanted to be involved, and when, because of domestic policies, he thought it necessary to take a hand. His significance therefore lies in the fact that not only was he constitutionally responsible for the State Department's actions, but also that he occasionally called the tune or gave it strong accompaniment.

One policy he encouraged was European prosperity. By 1925 most European nations had reached their prewar levels of production and by then the Coolidge Administration's objective was to push them beyond that point, on the assumption that Europe's and America's prosperities were intermeshed. The problem was to find acceptable ways to promote the development of Europe's economy.

Two methods that the United States refused to consider were reductions in tariffs and in debts owed it by foreign governments. That America would not entertain tariff revision had been made clear by Harding, and Coolidge reiterated it in every one of his annual messages to Congress. The high tariff was, they believed, essential to protection of ailing and not-so-ailing domestic businesses. As for reduction of foreign debts, few Americans favored it. The majority of both Republicans and Democrats were in agreement with the comment, "They hired the money, didn't they?" which was attributed to Coolidge. America's intransigence on reducing intergovernmental debts had first been expressed by Woodrow Wilson at Versailles. He, no less than Harding and Coolidge, correctly interpreted the people's wishes that America's loans to its erstwhile allies be returned since the nation already had too many losses to show for its participation in the World War. Moreover, cancellation or even significant reduction of the debts, which with interest ran some $13 billion by 1923, could cause a financial panic in the United States and would certainly throw a great burden on a government that collected little more than $4 billion in annual revenue. With a government administered by Republicans who were committed to reducing domestic taxes and debts, assumption of the financial obligations of other nations was out of the question.

There were, however, other ways that the United States could and did try to stimulate European prosperity. One was to renegotiate the interest rates and the number of years over which foreign debts were to be paid. The Coolidge Administration did that, and liberally so, against a certain amount of opposition at home. The President wrote George Harvey in March, 1926:

> Some opposition has developed to the Italian debt, but in the last few days a very marked shift has taken place in favor of the settlement [of a 0.4 percent interest rate]. It now looks to be certain of adoption. I hope that those who have been telling us that it was none of our business what was done in Europe will not now suggest that we are going to be influenced by the actions of Mussolini, and that others who have said we ought to do more for Europe are not now going to say we have done too much.[1]

Coolidge had a right to feel irked, for the amount of pressure on him was considerable. Too often it is forgotten that he operated in a sea of "hands-off" sentiment that threw up huge waves against whatever the government did that might be considered as internationalist. The reduction of interest rates and American leniency in often permitting deferral of payments of both principal and interest allowed much foreign money to remain in Europe for internal development or to be used in international trade.

Even more significant was the government's encouragement of private American loans to foreign nations and businesses. Herbert Feis has written:

> The soldiers and sailors had done their part [in the war], the dollar was counted on to carry on their work. It was regarded as a kind of universal balm, good for all peoples and all ailments. The American executive shared this attitude, though wistfully aware that the mien and response of some foreign nations was not all that could be wished.[2]

The result was that American dollars poured abroad, rising from a total investment of $7 billion in 1919 to $17.2 billion by 1930. The loans were spurred because they were thought to be good business as well as good neighborliness. The great danger came from the fact that the government had retreated from regulating the flow of dollars beyond America's borders. President Wilson had maintained, through a Cabinet committee, some restriction on the investment of dollars abroad, but that was weakened under Harding and virtually abandoned under Coolidge. Both listened to the pleas of Andrew Mellon and other industrial and financial giants to keep hands off.

Yet there were other pressures to which Coolidge felt it necessary to respond. Almost any action taken by the government to discourage unwise financial transactions—those that were bad risks, those that supported tyranny, and those that contributed to economic and political disorder—were greeted by cries at home of dictatorship. In some cases the protests came from investors and in others from liberals who believed that the United States had no right to tell other peoples what they should borrow, buy, or sell. Occasionally complaints came from both groups. When, for example, in 1927 the State Department asked to clear loans going abroad, it was assailed by Democratic Senator Carter Glass of Virginia, the bankers' friend, and by Republican Senator Borah, no banker's friend, who maintained that if loans had to be restricted Congress was the agency to do it. Coolidge took an intermediate position, holding that the government had the right to give advice on the investing of American money abroad. Yet as it turned out the government's advice was seldom sought. The result was that during the 1920s American dollars, without regulation, marched abroad to help build a flimsy façade of prosperity for the world. The many bad investments that were made weakened the international economy and a large number of the loans, good and bad alike, were lost when the Great Depression came.

Yet it would be absurd to assume that government advice could have helped the situation much. After all the Coolidge Administration's policy was to encourage private loans to foreign businesses and states. Moreover, the Administration was largely responsible, under the Dawes Plan, for the greatest investment fiasco of the time, the lending of American dollars to prop up German's currency and economy. The $2.5 billion that was lent to aid Germany corresponded to the amounts that that country paid in reparations, which in turn corresponded to the war debt payments that the United States government received from its wartime allies. In effect America was almost singlehandedly supporting the whole structure of reparations and debt payments, while congratulating itself on the progress that was being made in reducing those burdens. The triangle of payments was, as Winston Churchill said, "insane." In fact the whole American policy of promiscuously encouraging loans to Europe was insane, for it was the Yankee dollar that financed the artificial world prosperity of the 1920s. It not only enabled European nations to avoid coming to grips with the problems of war debts and reparations, but, as historian Hajo Holborn has pointed out, "made it possible to postpone the adjustment to the structural changes of the world economy produced by the war."[3] That postponement could only last so long and when it came to an end it plunged the world into a terrible new era of depression and political upheaval.

America's failure was not so much one of intentions, which were good, but of lack of knowledge and caution. Despite the force of anti-internationalist sentiment the Coolidge Administration tried to contribute to world economic stability. The whole problem was greatly aggravated by the policies of other countries. Their citizens and officials were seldom more cautious about borrowing and spending than America was about lending. They were wildly nationalistic about developing their economies and erecting trade barriers. There is also much to the contention that some foreign nations were not playing fair. No European state was in such bad condition financially that it could not have improved its efforts to pay both interest and principal on intergovernmental debts. Well-considered tariff reductions by the United States could have helped the world's economy, but the high American tariff was only one strand in the composition of the crazy-quilt international economy of the postwar era. The World War had created new economic yarns for the world and no nation knew or seemed willing to learn how to weave them into a durable fabric.

Although the Coolidge Administration was unsuccessful in its foreign economic policy, it made a stride forward in raising the caliber of American representation abroad. Pressure had been exerted for years to remove politics from the Foreign Service. Some progress had been made during the Roosevelt and Taft Administrations in the development of professionalism among State Department employees, but it suffered during the early years of the Wilson Administration when the department was regarded as a source of high-prestige patronage. Although Wilson tried to correct that during his second term, much damage had been done. President Harding's appointments represented no improvement over those of his predecessor. Coolidge was more amenable to pressures to protect the Foreign Service from politics because of his conviction that efficiency went hand in hand with the merit system for public servants. In his first message to Congress he asked for legislation to regularize the consular service along civil service lines. That led to the passage of the Rogers Act of 1924 to classify consular officials and to provide for merit procedures in their selection, promotion, and retention. Coolidge also showed interest in professionalization of the diplomatic corps by drawing upon career men to fill supervisory positions in the Department of State and occasionally to head American legations. In fact, once when fourteen ministerial and ambassadorial posts were vacant abroad, Coolidge nominated career men to fill six of them. His Administration fostered the real beginning of a professional American foreign service, and the nation would consequently in the future be better prepared to live in a world that was growing ever more tense.

If Calvin Coolidge was a lucky man, his luck was best observed in the few foreign crises that confronted his Administration. It was particularly seen in America's relations with China. That nation was undergoing upheavals of international significance during the 1920s. Civil war gripped the country, with the forces of the North, the South, and miscellaneous war lords vying for whatever booty they could pick up, including mastery of the entire land. The situation was complicated by the involvement of foreign powers and interests, ranging from Russian Communists to American missionaries, each rooting for its favorite generals. The war-torn Oriental nation was also being swept by wave after wave of protest against foreigners. The antiforeign sentiment forced all of the fighting factions to demand revision of treaties that maintained the extraterritorial rights in China of various countries and the virtual alien control of China's tariff system. The Chinese insisted that the powers keep the promises made during the World War and the postwar Washington Conference that tariff and extraterritorial treaties would be revised.

The position of the United States had been to avoid the appearance of backing any of the contending forces for power in China. In December, 1924, a new Chinese government indicated that it expected treaty revision and a half year later that government formally requested the Washington Conference participants to revise their treaties with China. The reaction of Secretary of State Frank B. Kellogg was favorable. The American chargé d'affaires in Peking was told to advise other diplomats there that the United States wanted preparations expedited for meetings of the Chinese Customs Tariff Conference and the Commission on Extraterritoriality. Kellogg believed that gradual progress toward revision of the treaties was the cure for China's internal instability. As he reported to President Coolidge:

> I feel that the critical conditions in China require some action to allay the public agitation. I am quite aware that this antiforeign sentiment is due partly to Bolshevik activities and propaganda, but there is no use disguising the fact that there has been growing for some time in China a nationalistic movement resentful of foreign control.[4]

Coolidge's reaction was one of cautious support. From his 1925 summer vacation site at Swampscott, Massachusetts, he expressed confidence in Kellogg's judgment, but he repeated what he had already told the Secretary, "keep in harmony with the other interested powers."[5] That was not an idle suggestion because the other powers concerned with treaty revision were not all standing shoulder to shoulder with the United States. Great Britain was willing to agree to the early convening of the tariff conference but thought that discussion of altering extraterritoriality then would be taken by the Chinese as an indication of weakness. The British also wanted proof of China's ability to restore order and repress the antiforeign elements. As for Japan, its government was under great pressure at home not to give in to Chinese demands, but the ministry was edging its way toward the United States in the situation. The other major power, France, had not yet ratified the Washington Conference agreements and therefore its views were not crucial to the situation. The minor powers indicated that they would endorse whatever America, Britain, and Japan decided. That led Acting Secretary of State Joseph Grew to conclude, "I feel very strongly that it is up to us to take the lead in insisting on carrying out the obligations of the Washington Conference."

Both Grew and Kellogg worked to convince Coolidge to accept this view. Indeed, on July 11 Kellogg cut his own vacation short to go with Grew to visit the President. During a long afternoon conference they talked to persuade him. There he sat by the sea listening to the Secretary and Under Secretary and using his marine glasses, as Grew wrote, "continually to watch every ship that passed."[6] Despite his seeming indifference, Coolidge did authorize the State Department to work actively to bring Britain and Japan in harmony with America's views on China.

In a note to the British dated July 13, 1925, the United States agreed that China should give effective assurance that foreign lives and property would be safeguarded. It was stressed, however, that one of the best ways to secure that was for foreign governments to adhere to the Washington Conference agreements. "This government cannot believe that a policy which consists in carrying out agreements undertaken in good faith and already overdue can be interpreted as a sign of weakness."[7] Although Great Britain and Japan were reluctant to go as far as the Americans wanted, they were very much interested in making an identical response to the Chinese request for treaty revision. Exchanges of views and of proposed drafts of an answer went out among the British, Japanese, and Americans over a period of a month before agreement was reached. The United States government insisted that both tariff and extraterritoriality revision be started. The government even went so far at one point to notify its minister to China, J. V. A. MacMurray, that the American view be given formally to the Chinese government even if the other powers failed to agree. Finally the British and the Japanese gave in and preparations were made for meetings of the tariff conference and the Extraterritoriality Commission. The work of the conference and the commission ultimately led to tariff autonomy for China and substantial reduction of the extraterritoriality rights claimed by foreigners.

Yet treaty revision did not end the troubles in China. In December, 1926, rebel military operations threatened to close the road from Peking to the sea, in violation of the Boxer Protocol of 1901. Acting Secretary of State Grew, with Coolidge's approval, warned the opposing forces to keep the road open and further ordered that American naval forces were to permit no blockade of the Taku Channel below Tientsin. Grew got into trouble with Coolidge, who had not completely comprehended the position he had endorsed. The President called Grew in and, waving a newspaper, quacked, "What does all this mean?" Grew reviewed their conversation on the matter and Coolidge in a characteristic motion wheeled around in his swivel chair and gazed out the window at the White House lawn for a few minutes. Then he wheeled back to face Grew, remarking merely, "All right, Mr. Secretary."

Grew's position had been advised by Minister MacMurray, but it was in opposition to the views of Secretary Kellogg, who was under heavy pressure from missionary groups backing the rebel Feng Yu-hsiang, the so-called Christian General. When Kellogg had returned from his Christmas vacation, he summoned Grew to his office and told him sarcastically, "I understand, Mr. Secretary, that during my absence you have declared war on China."[8] Grew's days as under secretary of state were probably dated from that point.

In any event, America's warning did not stop the crisis in China. Foreign interests were under heavy propaganda attack, and in fact both lives and property were threatened, especially in Shanghai. American agitation for sending in armed forces, which had been stimulated by British troop movements, was calmed by Coolidge himself. On January 26, 1927, he announced that it was unnecessary to dispatch American forces, for the United States, unlike Great

Britain, had no official concessions to protect in China. When Senator Borah suggested that endangered Americans be evacuated, the President replied that they had a right to be there and would be protected by the United States if China could not do so. However, when Britain asked that the United States send forces to join her troops in Shanghai, Coolidge rejected the idea as one that would inflame all China and jeopardize Americans residing in areas outside the Chinese metropolis. He further contended that, if necessary, the American Navy in the Far East could protect those Americans who were in Shanghai.

The President, who had already sent several thousand marines into Nicaragua, was probably leary of another military expedition. Toward the end of January Kellogg prepared a note proposing neutralization of Shanghai during the revolution, although, because of Minister MacMurray's objections, he changed it to neutralization of only the city's International Settlement and additionally offered American participation in negotiations concerning the settlement's future. Coolidge supported that on February 5 by emphasizing America's willingness to negotiate all issues with both the contending northern and southern governments of China. With Administration encouragement, the House of Representatives resolved by an overwhelming vote on February 21 in favor of scrapping all treaties with China and negotiating treaties that "will in no way offend the sovereign dignity of either of the parties."[9]

Neither position of the United States—neutralization of the International Settlement or wholesale treaty renegotiation—was fruitful. Shanghai was probably saved from a serious incident by the intervention of British armed forces, not by American promises. When a similar situation in Nanking led to loss of life and great destruction of property in March, 1927, the United States remained patient and pacific. Threats of economic sanctions by other foreign powers and splits in Nationalist Chinese ranks were responsible for preventing the Nanking riots from getting worse than they were. It was clear that America's conciliatory policy was not working, and after the Nanking incidents the President held 1,500 marines and an aviation unit in readiness for police work. Fortunately, the situation in China stabilized itself and Coolidge did not have to make a decision about using the marines.

The counsel of patience had not been entirely a failure, for

America's reluctance to use force helped to prevent wholesale foreign intervention in China, which, because of her new-found spirit of independence, could have led to a great international war. Despite the unsettling news from China in 1927, Coolidge and Kellogg had held firmly against the actual use of force and the imposition of economic sanctions. Aloofness, fear of an inconclusive war in a huge, far-off land, anti-imperialism, and sympathy with the emerging China largely motivated Americans to support the Administration's views. As the Washington *Post* wrote on April 12:

> The United States in dealing with China has nothing in common with other powers. Its interests are not their interests and its purposes are not their purposes. They may resort to force if they wish. The United States cannot resort to force without arousing a furor of protest from the American people.[10]

That was an able summary of the views of both the Administration and the President.

Coolidge had another occasion on which to repress conflict between the United States and China in March, 1927. The Japanese-controlled South Manchurian Railway had been seeking a loan from American financiers and the question was brought up in a Cabinet meeting. Coolidge was willing to permit the Japanese government to borrow money directly, but he had serious doubts about loans to the railway because they might be construed as American recognition of Japan's claim to a special interest in Manchuria. The American bankers were impressed by the President's position and were able indefinitely to delay lending money that might embarrass their country in its relations with China.

In 1928 the Coolidge Administration extended diplomatic recognition to the Chinese Nationalists, who had captured control of their nation's government. To the end the Administration had consistently supported revision of tariff and extraterritoriality treaties and had followed a policy of reason and persuasion in Far Eastern affairs. Coolidge's role had been mainly to support the convictions of his Secretary of State on those matters, although it cannot be overlooked that Kellogg's ideas squared with the President's policies of avoiding military involvement and extraordinary appropriations.

Kellogg may have been an idealist in formulating his country's policies with China, but Calvin Coolidge was not, except that he believed in following the public mind. Certainly, the President's policies were not, as one scholar has written, "bold and imaginative."[11] They were dictated by the ordinary concerns of a Chief Executive: maintaining the budget, catering to public opinion, and keeping out of a situation where the nation's interests did not justify the risk of involvement. If Secretary of State Kellogg had idealistic motivations, so much the better, so long as his policies fitted in with what Coolidge wanted.

There was one other continual trouble spot in the Far East during Calvin Coolidge's Presidency, and it was one that involved Coolidge more directly than did China. That spot was the Philippine Islands. One can be forgiven for considering this in relation to foreign affairs, for to most Americans and to Coolidge the Philippines were foreign. Moreover, America's position there had to be considered in the context of international relations. The situation in the Islands was none too good when Coolidge took office. The governor general, Leonard Wood, had antagonized broad strata of Filipino life, and a move for independence was under full steam. Wood's predecessor, Francis B. Harrison, had encouraged autonomy among the Filipinos. He had also sat by while the economy of the Islands deteriorated. Wood had succeeded in bolstering Filipino business and finance and in improving some government services, but in doing so he had acted like a military martinet and as something of a racist. By the time Coolidge became President, Governor General Wood was ruling the Islands without a cabinet and without formal consultation with the Philippine legislature.

Coolidge upheld the governor general from the beginning in his tiffs with the Filipino politicians. The President left no doubt of his position when he was asked to review Wood's veto of the legislature's action in remitting a land-tax penalty. There was a question as to whether the governor general had the power to veto purely domestic Philippine legislation. Coolidge upheld Wood saying that his veto power was complete, not only by law, but also because the governor general's chief task was to guide the development of self-government in the Islands. When a memorial of grievances against Wood's restrictive government was presented to Coolidge in January, 1924, it was rejected. The President's justification, given in February, indicated that the Philippines were unable to support autonomy. Economically they could not afford it and politically their lack of cooperation with Wood gave abundant evidence that they were unready for additional self-government. Coolidge pointed out, too, that the strongest support in America for Philippine independence came from those who wanted to relieve the United States of a drain on its energy and treasury, not from those who wished the Islands well. The Chief Executive emphasized that the United States government would not abdicate its responsibilities toward the Philippines. He also made it clear that the Filipinos would have to cooperate effectively and completely with the government before additional autonomy would be recommended.

At the time Coolidge replied to the Filipino memorial, enough sentiment appeared to have developed in Congress to pass a bill granting independence to the Islands by 1930 or 1935. The President's insistence that at least twenty more years of guidance were needed broke up that voting bloc. Moreover, there is some evidence to indicate that the Filipino leaders were using the idea of independence only as a pawn to gain increased autonomy and that they worked to calm down the sentiment for Philippine independence in the United States Congress. Coolidge's election victory in 1924 crushed whatever hopes there were in the United States and the Philippines for independence or even the granting of additional autonomy.

Friction continued between Governor General Wood and the Filipino legislature in 1925 and 1926, and Coolidge, now less sure of himself, dispatched Colonel Carmi Thompson to the Philippines to investigate conditions there. The Ohio politician reported in 1926 that independence for the Islands was then impossible because of their financial instability, lack of homogeneity, and the probable damage to America's trade and political position in the Far East. As for the deadlock between Wood and the legislature, Thompson recommended that the governor general be given civil advisers to help him carry out his tasks, which the legislature had refused to authorize, and that the legislature be given increasing autonomy in Filipino domestic matters. Coolidge commended Thompson's report to Congress, though indicating that he did not agree with all of it, presumably the increase in legislative autonomy. No immediate action was taken on the report.

Whether despite, or because of, Colonel Thompson's report, the deadlock between Leonard Wood and the Philippine legislature continued. It was to be broken only with the coming of a new governor general, and that was soon to occur. Wood, who was suffering from old and new injuries, returned to the United States early in summer, 1927, for medical care. He died August 7 in Boston during a brain operation. In December Coolidge appointed Henry L. Stimson, Taft's secretary of war and a man who had done yeoman service for Coolidge in Central America, to succeed Wood as governor general of the Philippine Islands. It was a good choice because Stimson combined the virtues of both a soldier and a diplomat, with few of their drawbacks, and he was a national figure who had been a friend of Wood and also met with the favor of the leading Filipino politicians. Coolidge was to support Stimson as he did Wood, but with different results. His only order to the new governor general was "to do a good job."[12] Stimson took the time necessary to become acquainted with the Islands, and he treated the Filipinos as intelligent human beings, not as inferiors as had Wood. The results were happy ones, for the Filipino situation was one problem that was under control when Coolidge left the White House in 1929.

32

Neighbors to the South

THE MOST DANGEROUS problems of foreign relations that confronted Coolidge concerned Mexico and Nicaragua. The United States had extended diplomatic recognition to Mexico in 1923 after years of disagreement. The placid relations of Coolidge's early days in the White House were soon to change as it became clear that Álvaro Obregón's successor as President of Mexico, Plutarco Calles, did not feel bound by all of the agreements made between Obregón and the United States. In late 1925 the Mexican Congress, at Calles' urging, passed two laws that perturbed Americans. One allowed foreigners to own land only if they renounced any right of protection by their homelands. The other limited to fifteen years any oil rights acquired in Mexico before 1927 and required applications for renewal of rights by 1927 or loss of those rights to the nation. Resistance and protest against the oil law came from such large petroleum interests as Doheny, Gulf, Sinclair, and Standard. The ambassador of the United States to Mexico, James R. Sheffield, encouraged the companies' recalcitrant attitudes by questioning his own government's "neglect of American rights under international law" and characterizing Mexican practices as "bolshevist."[1]

Coolidge tried to allay hostile American reactions by his statements that the two nations were getting along well. In January, 1926, he urged upon the press the view that Mexico had its difficulties and that its government "expects to abide by the terms of its treaties" and wished to cooperate in the "adequate protection" of the interests of American citizens.[2] Even Secretary of State Kellogg, who was not as patient as the President, was determined that there should be no break in relations between the United States and Mexico or any question of the use of force.

The situation worsened, however, when in April, 1926, the bishops of Mexico revived another issue. They declared that the Catholic Church would combat nationalization of Church property and other restrictive measures of the state. Consequently the Mexican government cracked down on the Church, closing convents and religious schools and requiring all priests to register with the state. At the end of July the hierarchy retaliated with an interdict on the performance of public religious services, which was complicated by a campaign of terrorism against the government by armed bands called Cristeros. American Catholics howled and demanded that the United States do something about Mexican persecution of their church. Coolidge, however, continued trying to calm the American people by emphasizing that negotiations were being carried on to adjust disputes and that they had led to some significant concessions and adjustments.

Illustrative of his tranquil approach was his remarkable statement to the September 8, 1926, press conference:

Mexico has been in a condition of uncertainty and there have been quite a number of years of burglary and revolution, but for the past three or four years that has been getting less and less, so that I don't think there is much complaint now about a condition of disorder that has characterized Mexico in some years past. The present government keeps a very fair condition of order. Of course we are not able in this country to prevent considerable lawlessness. We have constant outbreaks of burglary, highway robbery, and things of that kind. I don't suppose anyone would say it is because the government is lacking in authority. We make every effort to apprehend anything of that kind and punish it. But I think generally speaking over practically the whole of Mexico there is a very good condition of order. . . . The complaint is rather about prospective, rather than present, interference, with the rights of our citizens. There has been a good deal of recession on the part of the Mexican government in the claims that it has made of the privilege of interfering with the rights of our citizens. We still have some unsolved questions touching the rights of our citizens to hold property and conduct business there, but the general statement that I would make in relation to that is that the Mexican government has receded very materially in the claims that it had put out as to its right to interfere with the business of our citizens in Mexico. On the domestic difficulty that they are having there, over the religious question . . . we deal with that as we would deal with any other question that might affect the rights of property of our citizens. When those are affected beyond the practice of the government relating to religion or the carrying on of business or anything else, we try to protect the rights of our people.[3]

One might ask, "What did he say?" But that is the point: by being vague he tried to reduce anti-Mexican pressures and point up the reasonableness of negotiating and of staying calm.

Calmness was not, however, to continue for long. A new crisis was to arise, in Nicaragua, which not only in itself reached feverish proportions but also intensified American disagreements with Mexico. Nicaragua had been one of the less stable of the Central American nations and under the terms of the Roosevelt Corollary had been occupied by United States marines in 1912. By 1925 the country's finances and state of order appeared satisfactory enough to withdraw the last of American forces. Within a short period of time, though, chaos ruled Nicaragua. The Liberal Vice President, Juan Sacasa, was forced to leave the country and then the Conservative President, Carlos Solórzano, was ousted, making way for establishment of a dictatorship by General Emiliano Chamorro. The United States tried to make peace between the contending political factions, but succeeded only in persuading Chamorro to relinquish the Presidency in favor of a chief of state, former Conservative President Adolfo Díaz, chosen by the Nicaraguan Congress. Coolidge attempted to support Díaz by declaring that his election was legal. It was in vain, for Dr. Sacasa, who claimed the Presidency by virtue of his right of succession to Solórzano, returned to the country and established a rebel government in December, 1926. By then

Nicaragua was in a state of civil war, a tragedy complicated by the fact that Mexico supported Sacasa with arms' supplies, while the United States backed Díaz.

In late December, 1926, Coolidge and Kellogg decided to send in marines. Of Nicaragua, the President told the press:

There is a revolution going on there and whenever a condition of that kind exists in Central American countries it means trouble for our citizens that are there and it is almost always necessary for this country to take action for their protection. . . . That is what is being done at the present time. This government is not taking any sides, one way or the other, in relation to the revolution.[4]

Coolidge failed, however, to secure full American backing for the intervention in Nicaragua. He was attacked in a number of influential newspapers and in Congress. Senator William Borah, the chairman of the Foreign Relations Committee, changed from grudging support of the Administration to criticism of the landing of marines, and many other senators and representatives showed skepticism of the President's policy. Coolidge, feeling great pressure, decided to send a special message to Congress. On January 10, 1927, he reviewed the background of the situation for Congress and then attempted to justify the intervention. The Administration, he said, was permitting the Díaz government to purchase weapons in the United States because Mexico had refused to join in an embargo on supply of arms to Nicaragua. Moreover, the lives and property of Americans and other aliens were in danger and needed protection, and America's canal rights in Nicaragua had to be protected.

Secretary of State Kellogg tried ineptly to back up the President by explaining to the Senate Foreign Relations Committee that intervention in Nicaragua was prompted by the need to offset Communist influences there. That comment riled the congressional forces opposing the Administration's policy. Representative Fiorello La Guardia of New York called it "aldermanic stuff" and wrote Kellogg that America's actions would "play into the hands of people slimy with oil, greedy, and having only their own selfish interests in mind, who are seeking to embroil this country into armed conflict with our sister republics of the south."[5] After Kellogg's implication that Communists controlled Mexico and were seeking a beachhead in Nicaragua, Senator George Norris twitted the Administration with a parody of James Whitcomb Riley's poem, "The Goblins."

Onc't they was a Bolshevik, who wouldn't say his prayers,
So Kellogg sent him off to bed, away up stairs,
An' Kellogg heerd him holler, an' Coolidge heerd him bawl,
But when they turn't the kivvers down, he wasn't there at all.

They seeked him down in Mexico, they cussed him in the press;
They seeked him 'round the Capitol, an' ever'wheres, I guess,
But all they ever found of him was whiskers, hair and clout;
An' the Bolsheviks'll git you ef you don't watch out.[6]

Norris, Borah, Burton K. Wheeler, and the other progressive Republicans and Democrats in the Senate pounced all over the Administration, calling for detailed information on American interests to the south and on their correspondence with the State Department. Repeatedly they introduced legislation to prevent American armed forces from going abroad. Borah tried unsuccessfully to get Senate authorization for the Foreign Relations Committee to travel to Mexico and Nicaragua to investigate the situation in an attempt to tie the Administration's hands until the committee made a report.

Congressional resistance, increasing antagonism between Mexico and the United States, fear of simultaneous military involvement in China, and the fact that the disorders in Nicaragua had not been lessened by the presence of marines all had their impact. Coolidge and Kellogg began to seek some other solution to the situation. By March the President decided to make an extraordinary attempt to stop the carnage in Nicaragua, which threatened to draw the marines into the civil war. The odds for peace were good because both the Liberal rebels and the Conservative government had been disappointed by the bloody stalemate that had been achieved. Moreover, President Calles of Mexico had communicated to Coolidge on March 21 his desire for amicable talks on the issues between their two nations. All parties seemed to be coming to their senses.

Coolidge, at the State Department's suggestion, summoned

Henry L. Stimson to the White House on March 31 to undertake a mission of an "important and emergent nature." He asked the former Secretary of War to investigate the entire situation in Nicaragua and added, "If you find a chance to straighten the matter out, I want you to do so." After studying the situation for a week in Washington, Stimson sailed for Central America. Before leaving, he asked Coolidge whether it would not be seen as a sign of weakness "to reopen question of recognition of Díaz." The President agreed that it would. Then Stimson asked whether he was willing to risk election of a Liberal as President in 1928. Coolidge allowed that he could not see how it could be avoided. They both agreed that force should be used to resolve the situation only with "very great reluctance."[7]

Stimson arrived in Nicaragua on April 15 and immediately began gathering information and arranging talks with both Conservatives and Liberals. By May 11 he had secured the assent of almost all military and political leaders on both sides to immediate peace and amnesty, press freedom, support of Díaz in office with Liberal participation in the government, and elections in 1928 to be held under American supervision. That agreement was put into effect with the result that most American forces were withdrawn by 1931 and completely withdrawn by 1933.

While Stimson was working toward a peaceful settlement of the Nicaraguan situation, others were concerned with the deteriorating relations between the United States and Mexico. Oil and gas magnate Henry L. Doherty, officials of the Southern Pacific Railroad, and others with business interests in Mexico had been trying to reduce tensions between the two countries. Indeed, Paul Shoup, the Southern Pacific's executive vice president, and former President Álvaro Obregón of Mexico were constantly working together to bring pressure on the White House and the Calles government for a mutually satisfactory settlement of oil and land questions.[8] In his March communication the Mexican President had asked Coolidge to send a "personal representative" for a confidential talk that would permit Calles to express his "absolute sincerity and friendliness in all of his dealings with the American government." That plan did not materialize, but it is noteworthy that the crusty American ambassador in Mexico, James R. Sheffield, did not gain Coolidge's support for a harsher policy toward that country. In April President

Coolidge, probably at the prompting of Under Secretary of State Robert E. Olds, stated that "we do not want any controversy with Mexico. We feel every sympathy with her people in their distress and have every desire to assist them."⁹

The Administration then went about finding a replacement for Ambassador Sheffield, who had decided to resign. Frank Stearns, Olds, and Kellogg recommended Dwight Morrow for the job. Coolidge told Kellogg that he did not think that Morrow would accept but that there was no objection to talking with him, which the Secretary did in late May or early June. Certainly if Coolidge had earlier been reluctant to appoint his Amherst classmate and a House of Morgan partner to an important post, that had been overcome as a result of Morrow's highly satisfactory service as chairman of the Aircraft Commission in 1925. In June, 1927, Coolidge invited Mr. and Mrs. Morrow to spend some time with him at the temporary White House on Dupont Circle. Then, as Mrs. Morrow noted in her diary, the President "talked to him about Mexico and practically offered that place to him."¹⁰

On July 14 Coolidge actually offered the ambassadorship to his classmate. Time passed as Morrow thought it over and weighed the pressures on him from Coolidge and the State Department to take the job and those from Mrs. Morrow and Wall Street to decline. Coolidge was the most persuasive, as Morrow indicated in a letter of August 19. Then he wrote J. P. Morgan that the President "said to me that you were probably right that I could do more good where I was than in Mexico. He said, however, that that was not the whole story; that it was not the business of the government to do good but to prevent harm, that when governments tried to do good they generally got themselves and other people into trouble, that he felt that I should probably prevent a good deal of harm if I went to Mexico now." Go to Mexico Morrow did. In September Coolidge announced his appointment and in October the new ambassador left. Coolidge told Morrow before he went, "My only instructions are to keep us out of war with Mexico."¹¹

Morrow was a splendid choice. Not only did he help reverse what Coolidge feared was a drift toward war with Mexico, but he showed that cooperation and real friendship could obtain between the two countries. Before arriving in Mexico, Morrow had said, "I know what I can do for the Mexicans. I can *like* them."¹² He did more than that. He plunged himself into a love affair with the Mexican people and their customs and found that his love was reciprocated. He elicited recognition of America's foremost personalities for them, showing Charles Lindbergh and Will Rogers around the country. He negotiated armistices between church and state and between capitalists and officials. He was patient, he was ever willing to discuss things, he was happy to give advice and assistance to help Mexico and her people. Morrow did not settle the differences of opinion between Americans and Mexicans, and what he did accomplish derived partly from the willingness of others who were involved to lessen tensions. Yet he was successful in taking full advantage of the situation and gaining results that reduced tensions, removed any threat of war, and set a good example for the development of a policy based on reason and good will instead of on force and bluster. Coolidge was impressed with his choice as ambassador to Mexico, so much so that he recommended Morrow to Herbert Hoover as the next secretary of state.

Coolidge involved himself directly in one other aspect of Latin American affairs. In summer, 1927, President Gerardo Machado of Cuba invited him to address the opening session of the Sixth Conference of American States at Havana the following January. Coolidge was reluctant to attend, partly because of his natural reluctance to do anything that was not essential and partly because no United States President had ever attended such a conference. Secretary of State Kellogg prevailed on him to visit Havana as a good will gesture that might offset the widespread Latin American criticism of United States intervention in Nicaragua and of the retention of marines in Haiti. The President's decision to go was later reinforced by information that a number of American nations were considering switching their prime concern with international organization from the Pan American Union to the League of Nations. Care was taken to make the United States delegation prestigious to meet the move of some Latin American countries to force adoption of a resolution forbidding intervention in any Western Hemispheric nation by another. With that in mind the United States was also represented by Charles Evans Hughes, as chairman; Ambassador Morrow; and Stanford University President Ray Lyman Wilbur.

President and Mrs. Coolidge boarded a special train for Key West on Friday, January 13, which turned out to be no ill omen.

At Key West they boarded the light cruiser *Memphis* and six miles out were transferred to the battleship *Texas*. The twenty-one-gun salute from the *Texas* upon entering Havana harbor was answered from the ancient forts of Cabanas, Morro Castle, and Punta. President Machado personally welcomed President Coolidge at the dock. When the presidential party entered the city, it found the streets packed with cheering people, with thousands more perched on the roofs and flag-draped balconies. Roses were thrown down toward the presidential automobiles. Coolidge was caught up in the enthusiasm, smiling broader than ever before and even making gestures with his arms to the crowd.

Coolidge went before the conference to address it on January 16. His speech was replete with praise for the republics of the Western Hemisphere and their institutions. Independence, self-government, peace, and the striving for progress were the things that had made the American nations unique and great. Furtherance of those things in a cooperative fashion and of understanding and friendship would make for fulfillment of Christopher Columbus' hope that in the New World God would be able to write a new story of mankind. Coolidge sweetened his address by adding that the United States would work to assist its sister republics in building highways and establishing air transportation routes.

The President's speech was greeted with almost cordial response, which was gratifying in view of the widespread hostility toward the United States among the delegates. He left for home on the U.S.S. *Memphis* January 17 happy with his reception in Havana. Even if he was criticized for not dealing with Nicaragua and Haiti and the general question of intervention, his visit and address had made a favorable impression. The President's appearance helped the American delegates at the conference to prevent adoption of an anti-intervention resolution and to make progress toward a hemispheric agreement to submit inter-American disputes to conciliation or arbitration. If the United States would not be forced by other American countries to abandon the practice of intervention, it should be noted that it was making progress toward voluntarily relinquishing its claim to that right. The practice of intervention had declined under Coolidge's Administration, and in late 1928 Under Secretary of State J. Reuben Clark drafted a memorandum in support of repudiation of the right of intervention in Latin American nations. The Clark Memorandum, though it was never official American policy, symbolized the nation's general policy of nonintervention for a generation after the document's publication in 1930.[13]

Calvin Coolidge made substantial contributions to the betterment of relations between the United States and the republics to the south. Since the Administration of Theodore Roosevelt, relations had badly deteriorated, thanks to the policy of intervention and the lack of sympathy with the nationalistic movements under way in so many Latin American nations. Coolidge's recognition of the Mexican government in 1923 and the removal of the marines from Nicaragua in 1925 constituted the first fumbling steps toward better relations between the Yankee state and the Latin Americans. The growth of new tensions between the United States and Mexico and the Nicaraguan episode in 1926 and 1927 represented a serious setback. Yet most of the time Coolidge strove to minimize those tensions in order to keep passions under control in his own country. Despite the momentarily belligerent attitude in early 1927 of Coolidge and especially Secretary Kellogg, efforts for peace and friendship were renewed that spring. The Stimson mission to Nicaragua, Morrow's appointment as ambassador to Mexico, Coolidge's visit to the Pan American Conference at Havana, and his support of President-elect Hoover's tour of Latin America were the beginnings of an era of harmony among the American republics, an era brought to fruition by Presidents Hoover and Franklin D. Roosevelt. Calvin Coolidge had few fine hours as President, but his role in the conduct of inter-American relations was well played. Indeed, it represented him at his best. Although he did rely considerably on others to fashion his Latin American policy and to carry it out, his support and contribution went well beyond what he normally thought to be the call of duty.

33

World Court and Arms
Limitation

THE FAR EAST was important, Latin America was touchy, but most vexing to Calvin Coolidge was the question of international organization for peace. It was vexatious because of the passion Americans invested in considering the issue. Those who opposed affiliation with a world organization thought they were fighting to save the republic from destruction; those who urged United States membership in the League of Nations and on the International Court of Justice worked with the fury of men who saw doom for mankind should they not succeed; and those like the Outlawry of War advocates struggled just as diligently and vehemently for their cause as the only one that could cure the world's ills.

Coolidge knew that he would be damned regardless of what he did. He felt a moral commitment to work for international cooperation in maintaining peace and he also felt bound by Harding's commitment to work for American membership on the World Court. Even more he felt committed to represent the wishes of the people. That was what he fell back upon. He took his election as President in 1924 as a sign that the people approved the World Court and that was what he worked for. It is probable that he felt less restrained immediately after the election because of the death of Senator Lodge, the chief opponent to America's adherence to the Court. There had been other favorable signs. In August, 1923, Assistant Secretary of the Navy Theodore Roosevelt, Jr., believed that Coolidge would do little about the Court, but as time passed the President made it clear that he favored membership on that body. Confronted with that fact, many of the Eastern anti-Court Republicans agreed to support Coolidge on the Court if, as Roosevelt said, it were "absolutely separated from the League of Nations."[1] Moreover, both the major party platforms in 1924 had asked for American adherence to the World Court protocol.

In his December, 1924, message to Congress Coolidge indicated his favor of American membership on the Court of International Justice, provided "that our country shall not be bound by advisory opinions which may be rendered by the Court upon questions which we have not voluntarily submitted for its judgment."[2] That cautious statement was as far as he would go. His reasoning was simple. Each power on the League of Nations Council had the right to set aside advisory opinions by the Court and the United States should likewise as a major power have the right of veto. In his March, 1925, inaugural message he repeated his endorsement of the Court, as he did throughout the rest of the year while Congress was in adjournment.

When Congress met again in December, 1925, he emphasized the Court issue because of the public support that had developed for it during the year. For example, a survey of over a thousand daily newspapers showed that 83 percent of them approved Court membership. Yet Coolidge indicated his willingness to accept four conditions that many senators insisted on attaching to American approval of the Court protocol. Those were that the United States would, by adherence to the protocol, not be considered to have assumed any obligations to the League of Nations, that America have equal voice in the election of Court justices, that Congress determine the nation's financial obligations to the Court, and that the World Court statute not be amended without consent of the United States. He also reiterated the condition, "that we are not to be bound by advisory opinions rendered without our consent."[3]

By accepting the five conditions, Coolidge had signaled that he was unwilling to go far in fighting for the Court. He had also handed the Court's opponents a weapon they would use to make the terms of adherence repugnant to the forty-eight nations that were already members. There were reasons for the President's action. The intense campaign of propaganda against the Court had weakened his will to support it. Former Senator Albert Beveridge, whom Coolidge respected, tried to convince him that the "League Court" was "merely a method for getting us into the League."[4] Senator Borah, who declared that the Court issue meant "that a crisis was at hand,"[5] spent a great deal of time working on the President against the Court. The Outlawrists constantly pushed their claim on Coolidge that he would ask Congress for serious consideration of Outlawry of War as an alternative to the Court. Raymond Robins particularly was active in trying to cool Coolidge's interest in the World Court.

Former Secretaries of State Elihu Root and Charles Evans Hughes, both New Yorkers, labored to keep Coolidge behind the Court. The voices coming from New York State, however, could not be as powerful as those the President heard from Capitol Hill and in his White House office. There was also a practical consideration. Coolidge had to think of support for his entire program in Congress and especially of his reliance on Borah for backing of tax and budgetary measures. Coolidge obviously concluded to give no more than endorsement to the Court, reasoning that if its advocates were as strong as they seemed they would carry it through the Senate, and if they were not that strong there was doubt that the people really wanted adherence to the Court. In either case no one could seriously criticize Coolidge. He had recommended adherence, as he had promised, and he had left it to the Senate to act, as the Court's opponents wanted.

The senators fighting for approval of the World Court protocol were given no encouragement from the White House, even when they went to consult the President. Coolidge gave the impression of constitutional impartiality while the struggle went on in the Senate. It was quite a fight. Senators Borah, James A. Reed of Missouri, Cole Blease of South Carolina, and others launched a filibuster in the middle of January, 1926, "to keep," as Blease declared, "this iniquitous, infernal machine from being put on the people of America."[6] It took imposition of cloture on January 25 to keep the protocol from being talked to death. The next day the Senate agreed to adherence, by a vote of 76 to 17. The instrument of adherence contained the five reservations which Coolidge had said he would accept, although a cumbersome addition had been made to his proposal on advisory opinions: no advisory opinion could be rendered without giving interested nations advance notice and allowing them to require a public hearing on the question. Another complicating factor was the stipulation that the Senate's reservations had to be accepted through individual exchanges of notes with each of the forty-eight signatories of the Court protocol. Secretary of State Kellogg was too timid and Coolidge by now too indifferent to uphold the right of the executive to determine the means of assent. The result of the Senate action was well stated by Senator Norbeck of South Dakota when he wrote, "I believe with the reservations that it carries that it is entirely harmless (if not helpless)."[7]

The fuss over the World Court protocol did not die with the Senate's approval of adherence. Senators Borah and Reed, among others, spoke all over the country against the Court and against senators up for re-election who had voted for American membership on it. The question also was debated in almost every community, newspaper, and magazine in the nation. The continued high interest in the Court influenced Coolidge to seek, though cautiously, to enlist public support for adherence. In February, 1926, he told the press that the Senate's action on the Court was "an expression of the sentiment of desiring to cooperate, and a desire to put America on the side of having differences settled by orderly procedure and as near as they can be in accordance with international law, friendly conferences and settled rules, rather than to resort to force and have the question settled because one country or the other has a larger army or navy." As for those who charged that adherence to the protocol was a step toward taking the United States into the League of Nations, he added that the Senate's reservations were "a rather definite expression of the fact that we don't want to become identified with the League."[8]

Coolidge was, however, passive in securing agreement of the member Court nations to the American adherence and the five reservations. Although Congress was in adjournment from March to December, 1926, he just sat and waited for the approval of the signatory nations. When questions were raised by the nations, he appeared offended by them instead of being irritated with the handful of senators who had caused the difficulty. That spring he rejected an invitation from the League of Nations for a conference to discuss the reservations. He said: "We are dealing . . . directly with the nations concerned. We are adhering to the Protocol, which is the technical name of the Statute that created the Court and which is the action of forty-eight different nations. The League has nothing to do with it and can't do anything with it if it wanted to."[9]

The assent of the forty-eight nations to the first four American reservations was promptly given, but only a few of the Court members could accept the one on advisory opinions. In September twenty-one member nations of the Court offered to negotiate on that reservation. After six weeks of smoldering at the nations' audacity and after the congressional elections, which the Court's opponents contended favored their position, Coolidge rejected the offer. The Court members could take the reservation on advisory opinions or leave it. There was nothing to negotiate. The President was determined not to get involved in prolonged warfare with the Senate that would jeopardize his legislative program and probably not lead to any revision of the instrument of adherence. The Court was a dead issue as far as he was concerned. Borah and the other opponents of the Court had won.

Nevertheless, sentiment for American participation in international action for peace remained strong and Coolidge's own thoughts in that direction were still favorable even if vague. He was looking for a resolution of the problem that would not split the country and the Senate wide open. He was still cool to Outlawry, adherence to the World Court seemed lost, and membership in the League of Nations was politically out of the question. Only one avenue, further disarmament, appeared open, and that greatly interested Coolidge. There was considerable public support for arms limitation, and the President personally believed in it as a cure for war. It also appealed to him as a way of economizing on public expenditures both here and abroad and of stimulating business, which he thought to be another way to insure peace, for nations that prosper are unlikely to go to war. Again he was thinking as an idealist. He believed that ideals and economics could protect the boundaries established by the postwar treaties and stand in the way of possible aggression by Soviet Russia, Italy, and Germany. Coolidge was not a fool in the matter. He knew that trust would take time, as would the development of economic prosperity to divert aggressive forces in Europe and Asia. His immediate goals therefore concerned restriction of naval vessels, with limitations on land armaments to come later as conditions became more stable.

For his own country he worked to keep down appropriations for military supplies and naval vessels and to delay construction of ships already appropriated for. He worked on that with the civilian heads of the War and Navy departments, the press, and senators and representatives. He chided military officers and the newspapers for spreading "stories about the destitute condition of the navy and the deplorable plight of the army."[10] Repeatedly he called for elimination of needless activities in the armed services in order to save money and he condemned pressures for an arms race between the United States and other countries. His objective was to maintain only minimal forces for national defense. To accomplish that he was willing to buck the military, veterans groups, and defense-minded members of Congress, in the belief that he would be supported by peace groups and by taxpayers interested in seeing fewer of their dollars going to the government.

Yet limitations of weapons and armed forces in one country would not keep the world at peace. Coolidge took a number of actions to get agreement from other nations on international arms restrictions. He called for and received funds from Congress to finance United States participation in the League of Nations Preparatory Commission for the Disarmament Conference, although that conference did not meet until 1932. In his annual messages Coolidge often deplored sentiment for an arms race. In December, 1924, he told Congress:

> We have been constantly besought to engage in competitive armaments. Frequent reports will reach us of the magnitude of the military equipment of other nations. We shall do well to be little impressed by such reports. . . . I believe thoroughly in the army and navy, in adequate defense and preparation. But I am opposed to any policy of competition in building and maintaining land or sea armaments.[11]

From the beginning of his Presidency in 1923 he continually sent out feelers to other nations and spoke out publicly for further arms limitations. Sometimes he was thwarted by other nations and other times he found that League of Nations actions or conferences made it inauspicious for him to push too hard or too far. But his interest in the limitation of naval and military strength did not weaken until toward the end of his Presidency.

By fall, 1926, Coolidge decided that the time was right for a major international effort at arms reduction. The League of Nations was proceeding too slowly, yet reports indicated that other major powers might be interested in such a conference with the United States. Toward the end of the year America expressed its willingness to consider with other nations extension of the ratios of the Washington Conference to all types of naval vessels. The response of the powers was taken by Coolidge as favorable. Therefore on February 10, 1927, he formally proposed to France, Great Britain, Italy, and Japan that they join with the United States "to negotiate and conclude at an early date an agreement further limiting naval armament, supplementing the Washington Treaty on that subject, and covering the classes of vessels not covered by that treaty." He justified his action to Congress, saying:

> The support of all measures looking to the preservation of the peace of the world has long been established as a fundamental policy of this government. The American government and people are convinced that competitive armaments constitute one of the most dangerous contributing causes of international suspicion and discord and are calculated eventually to lead to war. A recognition of this fact and a desire as far as possible to remove this danger led the American government in 1921 to call the Washington Conference.... We felt then . . . and feel now, that the policy we then advocated—that of deliberate self-denial and limitation of naval armament by the great naval powers—promised the attainment of at least one guarantee of peace, an end worthy of mutual adjustment and concession.[12]

Coolidge picked Geneva, Switzerland, for the site of the conference and recommended that the delegates should be the delegates that the five powers had appointed to the League's Preparatory Commission for the Disarmament Conference. He hoped that that way the objective of further restriction of naval armaments would gain from the work of the League of Nations. Geneva was accepted as the place of the naval conference, but Great Britain and Japan each insisted on sending a delegation headed by a man of Cabinet caliber. That disturbed Coolidge and he asked Charles Evans Hughes to represent the United States, but the former Secretary of State indicated that it was impossible for him to attend. The President then, in his eagerness for success, suggested an all-star delegation including Secretary of State Kellogg, Secretary of the Treasury Mellon, and Senator Claude Swanson. Kellogg opposed it, however, writing Coolidge that "it would look like overloading the delegation and make it appear to the other countries that we were overanxious to have an agreement."[13] Kellogg, who believed that the United States should rely on competence instead of prestige, finally persuaded the President to approve a delegation headed by a career diplomat, Ambassador to Belgium Hugh Gibson, and Rear Admiral Hilary Jones.

The Geneva Naval Conference opened June 20, but it seemed ill-fated from the beginning. France and Italy refused to participate, and it was clear that the United States, Britain, and Japan did not see eye to eye on what restrictions should be imposed. Yet Coolidge, with a father's pride, was optimistic that the conference would lead to agreement among the three participants and that France and Italy would later adhere. He was to be disappointed. There was dissension between the diplomats and naval officers of each of the three powers at the conference, and it appeared that there were pressures from armaments interests on the delegates to scuttle the whole program. Yet most significant was the inability of the United States and Great Britain to agree on cruiser tonnages. The United States regarded the British demand for a minimum 600,000 tons as an extension instead of a limitation of cruisers. As Coolidge's secretary, Edward T. Clark, wrote Frank Stearns, the British were aiming at "an agreement for the largest naval armament ever known."[14] Britain, however, viewed America's proposal to reduce cruiser tonnage to 250,000 tons and even its later willingness to accept a maximum of 400,000 tons as inadequate to maintenance of the Royal Navy's world obligations. The Japanese let the two English-speaking nations fight it out, and fight it out they did until the Geneva Conference went down in August with flags flying.

Coolidge was chagrined. His pet hope for peace had been scuttled. He had been embarrassed at home and abroad, and, as bad, he now had little heart to continue resisting those who demanded substantial expansion of the American Navy. His unhappiness was increased in 1927 and 1928 as other powers entered into discussions of naval limitations that aimed at allowing them to build what they wanted while sharply restricting classes of ships in which the United States was interested. His grand step toward peace had turned out to be a stumble that could help other powers build their war strength at America's expense. As Coolidge put it in an Armistice Day speech in 1928:

> . . . the movements have been discouraging. During last summer France and England made a tentative offer which would limit the kind of cruisers and submarines adapted to the use of the United States, but left without limit the kind adapted to their use. The United States of course refused to accept this offer. Had we not done so, the French army and the English navy would be so near unlimited that the principle of limitations would be virtually abandoned.[15]

His reaction, and that of most Americans, was reflected in the budget he presented to Congress in December, 1927, in which the largest recommended increase in appropriations was to finance the beginning of a nine-year, billion-dollar naval development program. Coolidge never completely surrendered hope that the powers could agree to restrict their sea strength, but as a naval arms race was obviously under way he felt he could take no chances with his country's defenses.

34

The Outlawing of War

THE COOLIDGE ADMINISTRATION would try to take another great step toward world peace, but it was an attempt that the President had to be shoved into. That was the outlawing of war under the terms of the Pact of Paris of 1928. Coolidge had been flirting with the advocates of Outlawry since 1923. By promising consideration of their panacea, he had skillfully strung them along and gained their political support. That situation would probably have continued to the end of his elected term as President had it not been for France. That nation had been a source of distress to the Coolidge Administration in many ways. France had been the country hardest to sell on the Dawes reparations plan; it had given the United States the most difficulty in arranging payments and interest on wartime loans; it had adopted retaliatory and highly restrictive measures on world trade; it had been reluctant to agree on arms limitations; it had pressed the hardest for some form of American guarantee of the postwar territorial boundaries; and it had been most active in making military alliances. In short, France, in the American government's view, had revealed the least trust of any nation in international understanding and prosperity as viable means of peace.

In 1927 one of the leading advocates of international cooperation, Professor James T. Shotwell of Columbia University, planted the Outlawry idea in the mind of French Foreign Minister Aristide

Briand. The statesman was not naive or taken in by the earnest scholar. He came to see the Outlawry of War concept as a way at least to reduce the ill will that had grown between the French and American governments and perhaps to secure an American guarantee of Europe's national boundaries. Should the two countries agree to outlaw war, would that not give France the moral right to call upon the United States to help defend *la patrie* in case of attack by another power? Moreover, it might facilitate better treatment of France in future negotiations over debt terms and give France a higher reason for not participating in Coolidge's naval conference at Geneva. France could not lose by making a gesture, Briand thought, especially as the idea originated with an American and had strongly organized support in the United States. As for Shotwell, he looked to the French to put the American government on the spot, to force the consideration of Outlawry that Coolidge had so long promised. Furthermore, as was true of Briand, the Columbia University professor believed that should a Franco-American Outlawry treaty be ratified, a demand might follow to implement it with some expression of force against aggressors. Unlike Briand, Shotwell also hoped that the treaty would be followed by Outlawry pacts with other powers and eventual American entry into the League of Nations.

Briand acted on April 6, 1927, the tenth anniversary of America's entry into the World War. In an address directed to the American people he pledged France's readiness "to subscribe, with the United States, to any mutual engagement tending, as between those two countries, to 'outlaw war.'"[1] If the French foreign minister's prime goal had been to force consideration of the idea by the American government, he had succeeded by addressing himself to the people instead of taking up the matter through diplomatic channels. Both Coolidge and Secretary of State Kellogg were displeased, even irritated, with Briand and the amateur diplomat Shotwell, but they could not ignore a proposal made publicly.

The Administration bid for time, indicating that it would consider Briand's proposal when it was formally submitted. Coolidge could not and did not close the door on the subject, even though he recognized that the French were motivated less by the ideal of Outlawry than by the goal of bolstering their position on the continent of Europe. He could not ignore the issue, because of the surge of good feeling in France and America following Charles A. Lindbergh's record-breaking flight from New York to Paris and because of the publicity for Outlawry that had been spurred by Briand's address and pumped up by the Outlawrists. That the President did not shut the door was seen in his press statement of May 31, when he said that the idea "is one which I have been very glad to observe is being studied and which I should be very much pleased to find had been put into a practicable form."[2] Public interest in a Franco-American Outlawry treaty had mounted to such a point that on June 11 Kellogg instructed the American ambassador in Paris, Myron T. Herrick, to notify Briand that the United States was willing to discuss his proposal.

The French foreign minister's proposed pact of perpetual friendship was given to the United States embassy in Paris on June 21, the day after the Geneva Naval Arms Limitation Conference opened. The draft pact provided:

Article 1 The high contracting powers solemnly declare in the name of the French people and the people of the United States of America that they condemn recourse to war and renounce it, respectively, as an instrument of their national policy towards each other.

Article 2 The settlement or the solution of all disputes or conflicts of whatever nature or of whatever origin they may be which may arise between France and the United States of America shall never be sought by either side except by pacific means.[3]

It is worth noting that though the proposal was similar to what Professor Shotwell had suggested to Briand, it bore an even greater resemblance to France's most recent defensive treaties with other European nations. It served to confirm the Coolidge Administration's fear that Briand was interested mainly in seeking American favoritism that could be flaunted in Germany's face.

Neither Coolidge nor Kellogg was impressed with the draft pact. Their tactic was to stall for time, hoping that the proposal would abort or that something else would come along that they could use to kill it. Their hopes that a successful conclusion of the Geneva Conference would accomplish that were to be frustrated, as were their hopes that public interest in the Briand proposal would subside. The Outlawrists kept up their campaign of pressure on Coolidge and other government officials. As Raymond Robins said to the President at a summer luncheon, "Mr. President, you have immortality lying all around you in this proposal to outlaw war and you are doing nothing about it."

Coolidge answered, with more hope than assurance, "Well, the people are not interested in that proposition: they probably think it is impractical."[4]

The Outlawrists went all out to interest the people and to convince them that the draft pact was practical. Senator William E. Borah was openly interested in the idea, and no one could ignore the dynamic Idahoan, especially when he was speaking as chairman of the Senate Foreign Relations Committee. Indeed, he not only helped to keep up the fires of public interest, to Coolidge's disgust, but also advocated making the pact multilateral instead of unilateral, to Briand's disgust.

Delay, Coolidge and Secretary Kellogg believed, was the key to the situation. They decided that the United States would make no response to Briand's proposal during the Geneva Naval Conference in the hope that the conference would succeed and that they could then press France to adhere to its results. Even if public interest in Outlawry continued to be high and the Geneva Conference failed, Coolidge and Kellogg agreed that the Administration could not rush into a pact with France. There were too many angles to it and particularly ones that might involve the United States in the dangerous political maneuverings of France on the continent.

In putting off the French, Kellogg used the excuse that he had no opportunity that summer to go to the President's South Dakota vacation place to discuss the draft pact. He added that not much could be done anyway because Congress was in adjournment until December. The Secretary of State noted that "neither the President nor I thought it was advisable to enter into a treaty unless we had some assurance that it would receive the ratification of the Senate."[5] The collapse of the Geneva Conference fortified Coolidge's and Kellogg's resolve to move cautiously on an Outlawry pact with France, who could share much of the blame for the conference's failure. Their latent suspicion that European diplomats could not be trusted had been brought to the fore.

After Coolidge's return to Washington in September, Secretary

Kellogg used Ambassador Herrick's illness and his own pressing business further to delay discussing Outlawry with French Ambassador Paul Claudel. It was not an adroit move, but it gained time, for weeks, then months passed before anything happened. Coolidge meanwhile was making clear his opposition to the Briand proposal. During the fall the President complained of the premature amount of attention given the draft pact and of the irregular way in which it had been first proposed. He also told Wickham Steed, the editor of the London *Review of Reviews*, of his belief that the Senate, "a very curious body," would not ratify an Outlawry treaty with France.[6] Coolidge suggested to his November 25 press conference that the Briand proposal might be considered unconstitutional on the basis that it would conflict with a congressional prerogative. He alluded to the possibility that, by binding the United States to perpetual peace with France, Congress would lose its power to declare war on that nation, a tricky bit of logic to say the least. He also told the reporters: "There isn't any short cut to peace. There is no short cut to any other salvation. I think we are advised it has to be worked out with fear and trembling."[7] That statement was more sensible and closer to his heart than the question of constitutionality.

Yet public interest in Briand's draft pact would not recede. In fact, as the convening of Congress came closer and as Coolidge ventured his opinion about Outlawry's constitutionality, the interest increased. Dr. Charles Clayton Morrison sent the President a public inquiry in order to try to pin him down as to whether he really thought Outlawry was unconstitutional. Coolidge evaded Morrison's question by having his secretary reply that the President could take no responsibility for how the press interpreted his statements.

Senate interest in Outlawry also seemed to be rising. In November Senator Arthur Capper of Kansas announced that he would offer a resolution in Congress to seek agreements with other nations to renounce war. Coolidge could find that interesting because Capper was known as a senator who was exceedingly sensitive to the tides of public opinion. One could also say that if Kansas was ready for such a resolution so was the rest of the nation. From that point on the President fairly well decided to let events take their own course. If the people wanted to try a short cut to peace, he, as their chief representative, would not obstruct them. His only condition was that a better formula than that proposed by Briand had to be found. Accordingly, on December 10, he told a delegation from the Women's International League for Peace and Freedom that official conversations on Foreign Minister Briand's draft pact would begin upon Ambassador Herrick's return to France.

The formula that Coolidge wanted had been under his nose all the time. That was the suggestion championed by Senator Borah that Outlawry of War be made multilateral. Borah had the opportunity to press this upon the Administration when Secretary Kellogg came before the Foreign Relations Committee in closed session December 22, 1927. The Secretary was advocating a treaty for arbitration of disputes between France and America, which he apparently hoped would mollify the peace forces. The committee was unimpressed and Borah told him that an arbitration treaty would not dispose of Briand's proposal. The Idaho senator stressed that "the American counterproposal should be a pact to outlaw war between all nations of the world. We should point out that this is too important to confine only to this country and France."[8] The fact that no opposition to Borah's suggestion was expressed in the committee probably impressed Kellogg. He discussed the idea with Coolidge who, seeing a formula that might safely be offered to France, replied, "We can do that, can we not?"[9]

December 28, 1927, was a momentous day in the history of the negotiation of the Pact of Paris. Briand was either becoming nervous over the rise of sentiment for a multilateral agreement or losing hope that the United States would seriously consider his proposed treaty. On the 28th the French foreign minister drafted a note that edged him in the direction of calling off the whole affair. Before it was dispatched, though, Kellogg sent a note of his own. The American secretary wrote that "it has occurred to me that the two governments, instead of contenting themselves with a bilateral declaration of the nature suggested by M. Briand, might make a more signal contribution to world peace by joining in an effort to obtain the adherence of all the principal powers of the world to a declaration renouncing war as an instrument of national policy."[10]

Kellogg, probably more than he knew, had outmaneuvered Briand. A multilateral pact would put a crimp in the instrument of policy, military force and alliance, that France was building to contain Germany or any other potentially hostile power. An Outlawry treaty with the United States would have bolstered that policy, at least by keeping America out of the camp of France's enemies in case of war and perhaps by drawing her in on France's side. The Kellogg proposal, if implemented, would pose a legal barrier to any preventive war undertaken by France and make any hostile gesture on her part embarrassing. The beauty of Kellogg's suggestion was, however, that Briand could not reject it if other nations were willing to approve it. The foreign minister had advocated Outlawry too well and too long to withdraw now. Moreover, he was, as a Nobel Prize winner, too well identified with peace to reject the American Secretary of State's ingenuous proposal to achieve it. There is also the possibility that, despite his wiliness, Briand was tempted to pull off the stroke of modern times by being the co-author of a world peace plan that might actually work.

While Briand waited to see what international reaction would be, Kellogg grew enamored of multilateral Outlawry. The Secretary circulated his proposal among the leading world nations and found that it was readily accepted by Germany, Italy, and Japan. After negotiations that continued through spring, 1928, the governments of fifteen countries, including France and Great Britain, agreed to sign the proposal, which was now popularly called the Kellogg-Briand Pact. The document itself bound its ratifiers to "condemn recourse to war for the solution of international controversies, and renounce it as an instrument of national policy in their relations with one another." They also pledged themselves to settle all disputes among themselves "by pacific means."[11] As it had become Kellogg's hope that all nations would adhere to the pact and that thereby war would be universally and legally abolished, the treaty was left open for additional states to sign.

Coolidge did not become enthused about the pact as had his Secretary of State. He took the treaty as it developed and hoped that it would not cause trouble and that it might perhaps even do some good, though he appeared doubtful of the latter. As a concession to the French, and possibly because it would be cheaper to send a few Americans to Europe instead of playing host to a great number of foreign dignitaries, the President assented to the signing of the pact in Paris in August. America's share in bringing about the treaty was recognized in the provision that ratifications were to be deposited in Washington.

Coolidge agreed in July, 1928, to send Kellogg to Paris to sign the pact. The President's spirit was, however, almost that of a man who felt the farther away the Kellogg-Briand matter was carried off the better. Yet Kellogg almost did not go. Coolidge was irked by the Anglo-French naval limitation agreement of July 31 that cut a pattern that was as unfavorable to the United States as it was favorable to Britain and France. From Superior, Wisconsin, where the summer executive offices were, the President advised Secretary Kellogg on August 3 to do nothing about the naval agreement. He added:

I do not especially like the meeting that is to be held in Paris. While it is ostensibly to sign the treaty, I can not help wonder whether it may not be for some other purpose not yet disclosed. Of course, so far as this government is concerned, it will neither discuss nor decide any other question of any kind or nature at the Paris meeting.[12]

Yet the Department of State had already officially reacted to the Anglo-French naval agreement by asking the British to explain unclear statements in their note on the agreement. That inquiry further irritated Coolidge, who ordered the department to do nothing further. On August 7 Assistant Secretary of State William Castle confided to his diary: "All I am afraid is that he will get so angry that he will tell the secretary he cannot go to Paris after all. This would be an utterly impossible situation and the secretary says that if it should by any chance arise he would have to tell the President that he must either go or resign."[13]

Whether Kellogg actually stated those alternatives to Coolidge or not, the President calmed down. He got some of the irritation out of his system by making the statement that he did not foresee a reduction in the strength of America's armed forces, because they were defensive in character. He did, however, take petty revenge on the British by forbidding Kellogg from making a scheduled stop in London on his return from Paris. That the Secretary was permitted to visit Dublin in the Irish Free State made clear to the world that Coolidge was angry with the British.

Since the beginning of 1928 President Coolidge had been largely noncommittal and certainly unenthusiastic in his public statements on the Kellogg-Briand proposal. Yet he warmed up to it somewhat as the presidential election campaigns got under way that summer. It became obvious to him that his political party had found an accomplishment that compensated for some of the frustrations of the World Court and Geneva Conference episodes. The Republicans were working themselves up to going before the voters with an internationalist nominee, Herbert Hoover, and as the party of peace and accomplishment. As Robert Ferrell has written:

> For the Republican party, embarrassed for years with its negative record on foreign policy, the antiwar pact was heaven-sent. Leaders of the Grand Old Party realized with fond anticipation that the Coolidge administration—a Republican administration—had "out-covenanted" Woodrow Wilson himself.[14]

In Wausau, Wisconsin, Coolidge did his bit to keep up his party's ballyhoo about the Kellogg-Briand Pact. There on August 15, before some fifteen thousand people, he lauded the treaty as the kind of instrument that might have saved the world from the Great War. He also took the occasion to put in a word to urge obedience to it by the nations and indirectly to encourage its ratification. "It holds a greater hope for peaceful relations than was ever before given to the world," said the President. "If those who are involved in it, having started it will finish it, its provisions will prove one of the greatest blessings ever bestowed upon humanity. It is a fitting consummation of the first decade of peace."[15] To Coolidge's surprise the Wausau speech was widely and highly praised. He took more interest, and pride, in the reaction than he had in responses to his public statements for several years.

Coolidge's campaign pose did not mean, however, that he had changed his basic attitude toward the peace accord. His position was still that of letting public opinion take the lead and of hoping for the best results. If he became more interested as time went by, it was because of his wish that the pact would be ratified by the Senate, and without too much trouble. To that end he did his share. One indication of it was his call, in an Armistice Day address, for building up the navy for defensive purposes. The address reflected his willingness to cooperate with the advocates of a big navy since the Geneva Conference had failed and the League's efforts toward a disarmament conference had flagged. The Armistice Day speech also reflected the President's attempt to assuage the big navy senators in order to win their assent to the Pact of Paris. Of course, peace movement leaders sharply criticized him for urging armament on the verge of the Outlawry of War. Let them criticize, he must have thought. After all they were committed to support of the pact and would, for the most part, oppose enlargement of the navy. He probably knew that some of the peace people would defend him, as indeed they did. Salmon Levinson, the father of Outlawry, told Coolidge's critics that "they had better direct their fight against the British Tories that had irritated and insulted the President and thwarted all his moves for limitation of naval armaments, rather than fight the man who was our greatest power in securing the consummation of the peace treaty."[16]

Beginning in November Coolidge moved further in support of the treaty. Britain and France had indicated that their ratifications of the pact would include reservations. Coolidge cautioned Americans not to let that alarm them; the important thing was the inclusion of the two powers as ratifiers, regardless of their reservations. He also worked against members of the Senate who sought to seize upon foreign reservations to justify home-grown reservations. As he told the press: "I do not think any reservations ought to be attached. . . . I can hardly comprehend the nature of any reservations that any one might think would be desirable. I think the treaty itself carries all the reservations that are necessary to protect our rights and protect our interests."[17] From almost any other President that would sound weak, but from Coolidge, who was devoted to simplicity, that direct statement carried conviction. The reservationists had been warned that he would fight.

Soon after Congress convened in December, 1928, Coolidge took the occasion of his State of the Union message to recommend ratification of the Pact of Paris.

One of the most important treaties ever laid before the Senate of the United States will be that which the fifteen nations recently signed in Paris, and to which forty-four other nations have declared their intention to adhere, renouncing war as a national policy and agreeing to resort only to peaceful means for the adjustment of international differences. It is the most solemn declaration against war, the most positive adherence to peace, that it is possible for sovereign nations to make. It does not supersede our inalienable sovereign right and duty of national defense or undertake to commit us before the event to any mode of action which the Congress might decide to be wise if ever the treaty should be broken. But it is a new standard in the world around which can rally the informed and enlightened opinion of nations to prevent their governments from being forced into hostile action by the temporary outbreak of international animosities. The observance of this covenant, so simple and so straightforward, promises more for the peace of the world than any other agreement ever negotiated among the nations.[18]

This recommendation was simple and straightforward. Coolidge spoke under no delusions as to what had been accomplished at Paris during the summer. Perpetual peace had not replaced war because of the signing of a sheet of parchment. Peace would come only if the people of the nations enforced the pact, both by acting against aggressors and by preventing their own governments from undertaking aggression. The treaty offered the world an opportunity, slim though it was, to seize peace. Without reservation Coolidge was willing to accept that chance and by his praise of the pact he indicated that he expected the senators to do likewise.

The move to ratify the Kellogg-Briand Pact began well. Senator Borah guided it, without any alterations, through the Foreign Relations Committee. Yet it was clear that the reservationists, even if they were diminished in influence by Borah's and Coolidge's clearcut advocacy of the treaty, would strike. On December 17, 1928, Republican Senator George H. Moses of New Hampshire and Democratic Senator James Reed of Missouri tried to attach three reservations. These were:

(1) That the treaty does not impair or abridge the right of the United States to defend its territory or other vital interests in accordance with traditional American policies, (2) That the treaty imposes no obligation on the United States to resort to coercive or punitive measures against any offending nation, (3) That the treaty does not obligate the United States to the conditions of any treaty to which the United States is not a party.[19]

Of course, taken at face value in comparison with the text of the pact, those reservations were unnecessary, and with strained interpretation by future Chief Executives and lawmakers the first exception could completely contradict the treaty's meaning.

Borah and Kellogg, with occasional assistance from Coolidge, worked hard to stymie the Reed-Moses resolution. The Idahoan looked in every corner of the Senate to secure approval of the treaty without reservations and Kellogg talked with whomever he could to line up support. The Secretary of State pointed out that the reservations of the other nations were inconsequential. He also indicated that because the United States in June had asked the signatory powers to accept the pact without conditions, American reservations would prove embarrassing to the government and set a bad example for the other nations that were in the process of ratifying the treaty. Kellogg invoked the President's name to condemn the Reed-Moses reservations as unnecessary.

While the Secretary argued, coaxed, and pleaded for approval of the treaty, others joined in to hamper or to help. In January, 1929, some of the Farm Bloc senators declared that they would stop ratification of the pact until relief for farmers had been passed. Senator Borah came back, saying that that would work both ways, for he and his followers would block agricultural measures until the treaty had been ratified. President-elect Hoover broke that stalemate by promising to call a special session of Congress to consider farm relief.

As 1929 arrived Coolidge personally took steps to encourage ratification of the pact. He invited recalcitrant senators to the White House in order to persuade them to uphold the Administration, but his attempt had no apparent effect. Although the Reed-Moses resolution was no longer a threat, interest was rapidly growing among the senators to make an interpretative statement on the treaty before bringing it to a vote, and even Borah's efforts to stop that had thus far failed. On Sunday, January 13, Coolidge called upon Vice President Dawes for help. Dawes who believed that failure to ratify without qualification would humiliate the United States and who also wanted to encourage support for a big navy promised that he would "steam up" for action.

On January 14 Dawes got word out that the Kellogg-Briand Pact and the naval appropriations bill had to be seen as meshing.

Together they represented, he said, "the declared and unified policy of the United States."[20] That view appeased a number of senators, but not enough. The following day Borah proposed a compromise for those who wanted the treaty encumbered with an interpretive report, which could be seen as a listing of reservations. His compromise was to offer the Foreign Relations Committee's explanatory report, which specifically denied being a statement of reservations, as a summary of the Senate's feelings. It explained little and altered nothing, but the document satisfied the great majority of senators. Dawes telephoned the President to tell him what had been done and Coolidge approved, saying "I think you have done all you can."[21] The President himself, at a White House press conference, had given ratification a final shove on January 15, and that afternoon the Senate approved the pact by a vote of 85 to 1. Coolidge's last ordeal with Congress, and especially with that "very curious body," the Senate, had come to a happy conclusion.

On January 17 the final scene in the ratification of the Kellogg-Briand Pact occurred. Then members of the Cabinet and leading senators gathered in the East Room of the White House to witness Coolidge's signing of America's instrument of ratification. The great moment turned out to be a great irritation to the President. He was bothered by the unusually large and noisy number of photographers and newsreel men. Then he was irked by the hovering of a minor State Department official who had been assigned to assist at the ceremony. While the employee was trying to blot the President's signature, Coolidge snapped at him: "Who are you? I don't know you. Go away." Assistant Secretary of State Castle noted that "the President's face looked like murder."[22]

It was soon to look like genocide, as the ceremonial pen ran dry before he had completed his signature. Impatient, he maneuvered a heavy inkwell on to the table in order to fill the pen. All that, of course, was being recorded for posterity by some twoscore still and movie cameras. The President's peevishness was contagious and the official photograph of Coolidge signing the document, with Dawes and Kellogg flanking him and Senators Robinson, Borah, Swanson, and Thomas Walsh standing behind him, showed all of them looking tight-lipped and grim-faced. There had been no peace during the peace pact ceremony, as Vice President Dawes later commented.

The pact itself turned out to be more ceremonial than real in effect. As Coolidge had cautioned, there was no short cut to peace. And as he had observed, the treaty's effectiveness depended upon public opinion. Public opinion turned out to be a weak reed upon which to lean, as it ran wild during the following decade, with the revival of militarism. Most peace crusaders were either crushed by the new spirit or fought it with lilies and more utopian formulas. The Kellogg-Briand Pact proved to be a swordless sheath; the peace efforts of the Coolidge Administration proved to be only a respite between world conflagrations. The best that can be said for the pact was that it was a magnificent gesture and as such provided a standard toward which men of good will would continue to strive. The best that can be said for Coolidge was that he tried, despite considerable nationalistic opposition at home and abroad, to lay some foundations for an extension of the peace won on the battlefield in 1918. That he failed was not surprising. His levels of conviction and drive were too low to overcome the tensions, ambitions, and cynicism of other statesmen and other nations.

35

I Do Not Choose To Run

B Y SPRING, 1927, the quadrennial silly season of American politics had arrived once again. Speculation on the stock market was small compared with private and public speculation on who would be nominated by the Democrats and Republicans for President the following year. The number of Democratic possibilities seemed infinite, but among Republicans the question was, is Coolidge going to seek renomination and re-election? Those who asked that question had received no hint of an answer from the President.

Much support had developed for Coolidge's re-election. As early as July, 1925, Chief Justice Taft wrote one of his Court colleagues that another term for the President "would be very satisfactory."[1] During 1925 and 1926 similar comments were frequently expressed among Republican politicians and in the press. Of course, others— Borah, Hoover, Hughes, and Lowden—were mentioned as possibilities, but that represented mostly wishful thinking by their admirers. Charles Evans Hughes himself probably reflected the attitude of most Republicans when in May, 1927, he stated, "I am for President Coolidge, first, last, and all the time, and I believe that he will be renominated and re-elected."[2]

Coolidge was buoyed by such expressions of confidence and support, but he had serious doubts about running again. The President's chief Secret Service aide, Colonel Starling, interpreted a conversation they had in spring, 1927, as an indication that Coolidge planned to step down. The colonel expressed it well:

> The novelty of being President had worn off; the glory of it had gone with Calvin's death; there was no great national crisis which demanded a continuation of his leadership. From now on the office was more a burden than anything else. The steady grind of work was wearing him down, and the duties of the First Lady, plus Washington's weather, were weakening Mrs. Coolidge's health.[3]

Of course, there were other factors that Starling had not mentioned. The President was at loggerheads with the McNary-Haugenites, facing the possibility of a rebellion in his party. He had been made to look foolish on the World Court fiasco. If the forthcoming Geneva Naval Conference failed, he would look worse, and if it succeeded, he would have reached the pinnacle of his career. Moreover, that spring of 1927 the Mexican and Nicaraguan situations appeared to be coming apart at the seams. There were also doubts in the President's mind that the Coolidge Prosperity could continue indefinitely.

During the summer Coolidge went to the Black Hills of South Dakota for his annual vacation, perhaps to arrive at a decision about seeking renomination, perhaps just to enjoy himself for the first time as President, because he could see an end coming to the splendid misery. He did set out to enjoy himself. He got out more among the people, and he plunged himself into fishing and into horseback riding, even wearing high-heeled cowboy boots. His moods and tempers were also more exposed than ever before. Coolidge stayed at a South Dakota state game lodge a few miles away from Rapid City, with Senator Peter Norbeck serving as host. There Coolidge was warmed by Western hospitality and openness, and by, to Norbeck's chagrin, the prominent conservatives of the Northwest who flocked in to tell the President how wise his McNary-Haugen veto had been. In the Black Hills Coolidge also seemed to enjoy playing cat-and-mouse with Norbeck on support for the sculpture of presidential visages on the side of Mount Rushmore. Coolidge was a benevolent cat, and Norbeck a proud mouse, when the President in a speech August 10 said that the project deserved the "support of private beneficence and the national government."[4]

Yet the big news of the summer came on the fourth anniversary of Coolidge's succession to the Presidency. The drizzly morning of August 2 the Chief Executive, accompanied by Senator Arthur Capper, was driven from the game lodge to Rapid City High School, where his summer offices had been established. The chief purpose was to hold a routine press conference, or so Capper thought. At the high school, Coolidge went to his office where he summoned his secretary, Everett Sanders. He gave Sanders a short statement which he in turn took to stenographer Edwin Geisser to type out copies for the press. When that was done, Sanders returned with the releases.

Shortly before noon the President, several of his aides, and Senator Capper went to the mathematics classroom. The thirty or so newspapermen soon filed in, full of much speculation and a bit of irritation because the press conference had been delayed a couple of hours. On the desk were two-by-nine-inch slips of paper. Coolidge told the reporters "that the line forms on the left" and then as they passed by he handed each man one of the slips. On them was typed a sentence that relieved both the speculation and irritation of the newsmen. "I do not choose to run for President in nineteen twenty-eight," read the announcement. There was no comment by Coolidge, no explanation. The room exploded into activity as the reporters scrambled to get to telephones and telegraph. Only Sanders had known about the statement before that day and he had only been told about it, not consulted. Grace Coolidge had not been informed of her husband's intention. It was Senator Capper who gave her the news.[5]

Reaction was instantaneous over the land. Some people took the statement at face value; others thought it to be a crafty bid for a draft nomination; many did not know how to take such an unusually worded announcement. Reaction was also to be long-lasting, for most of the Republican leaders of the time were to try during the next generation to decipher Coolidge's statement. Most Democrats, out of hopefulness, accepted the President's words as reflecting his determination to bow out of office. Claude Bowers told the joke that pancake eaters would have to do without maple syrup the following year. When asked why, he replied, "Because the Vermont sap chooses not to run in 1928."[6] Frank O. Lowden, who for the third time was considering running for the Presidency, spent much time trying to figure out Coolidge's meaning. One of the President's friends, Matthew C. Brush, assured Lowden's supporters that Coolidge meant what he had said, but Charles Dawes believed that the President "ardently desired" renomination.[7] There was and still is no absolute proof of what Coolidge had in mind. The significance of his announcement was, however, well sized up by Carl Smith, one of Senator Charles McNary's political allies: "Whether Calvin meant it or not I believe he is fairly out of it. The country has in a large measure accepted the statement at face value, and the active candidates will occupy the field without much elbow room remaining."[8]

That is precisely what happened. Commerce Secretary Hoover appeared to hold the lead, but he had a plethora of contenders, including, as he saw it, almost every Republican senator. Chief among the other contestants were former Illinois Governor Lowden, Senator Frank Willis of Ohio, Senator James Watson of Indiana, Senator Charles Curtis of Kansas, and Senator Guy D. Goff of West Virginia. Some support also was mustered for former Secretary of State Hughes, Senator Norris, Vice President Dawes, and two of his fellow Illinoisans, Senator Charles S. Deneen and Chicago Mayor "Big Bill" Thompson. Yet the stampede for the nomination led to the contention that the President had removed himself from the race in order to win it. By withdrawing, the speculation went, he would be able to demonstrate that he stood head, shoulders, and waist above his possible successors.

As it became clear that Coolidge was not going to amplify his statement, Hoover's supporters worked to create the impression that the Secretary of Commerce was the President's choice for the Republican nomination. They got some mileage out of the logic that if Coolidge really wanted another term he would not allow one of his Cabinet members to build up strength and another, Interior Secretary Hubert Work, to serve as his campaign manager. Hoover himself tried to get clarification and support from Coolidge. In September, 1927, he went to the White House and told the President that he wanted to see him renominated. Then the Commerce Secretary asked whether Coolidge's "do not choose" statement was conclusive. As Hoover recounted the story: "He made no direct reply. I stated to the press that Mr. Coolidge should be renominated. The

President certainly enjoyed the amazing volume of curiosity and the discussion that his statement had evoked and apparently did not want to end it. Nor did he ever do so."9

Hoover made two other attempts to draw Coolidge out. He received what might be considered as encouragement, but no public support from the man in the White House. In February, 1928, the Secretary was anxious to enter the Ohio presidential preference primary against Senator Willis, who, he knew, was not well thought of by Coolidge.

Hoover asked whether the President was allowing his name to be entered in Ohio.

"No," answered Coolidge.

When Hoover then asked whether he should enter, the President said simply, "Why not?"

By May Hoover thought he had the loyalty of some four hundred of the one thousand Republican National Convention delegates. Again he went to Coolidge. He told of his four hundred delegates, but indicated that he would gladly influence them to vote for the President for renomination.

Coolidge replied, "If you have four hundred delegates, you better keep them."10

Although he was never sure, Hoover convinced himself that Coolidge did not, either directly or indirectly, seek the 1928 presidential nomination.

What was behind Coolidge's attitudes? He was just pixyish enough to enjoy the guessing game that was going on about his intentions and the squirming of contenders for the nomination. He was unlikely to spoil his own fun by supporting one of the candidates for the nomination. Yet there were more serious possible reasons. One was personal. He had made his statement about running and he was not the kind of man to waste words or attract embarrassment by amplifying it. As White House Secretary Edward T. Clark wrote to Frank Stearns in September, 1927, in opposing further statement by the President, "I should hate to have him admit in this way that after thinking about the matter for months, as he must have done, the best he could compose was cloudy and indecisive."11 If there were those who would not believe his words, it was not Coolidge's fault.

As to underscoring his statement by supporting one of the candidates for the Republican nomination, several reasons militated against that. In case of a serious national crisis it might become his duty to step forward again for service. He also professed belief in the concept that the people should make their own decision on such matters, through their convention delegates. For him to try to choose his party's 1928 nominee would be a serious violation of that belief. Then too he must have been aware that his endorsement of a successor would antagonize large numbers of Republicans, and especially those in Congress with whom he was already having enough troubles. Perhaps he felt that as long as so many senators were itching for the nomination they would be more amenable to suggestions from him if it was obvious that he was not opposing any of them. Moreover, as a man who detested failure, he would feel greatly embarrassed if his chosen candidate failed of nomination. The defeat of a protégé would make Coolidge appear repudiated by his own party, which neither the fortunes of the party nor his ego could afford. There is always some possibility too that the conjecture of the New York *Evening Post* on April 21, 1928, was true. That was that Coolidge would come forth as a candidate for renomination if Lowden or Dawes appeared to be edging toward success.

Many of Coolidge's admirers were working for his nomination. Taft, Slemp, Butler, and Stearns were all of the opinion that the President would accept a draft, chiefly because he did not crack down on their activities in his behalf. Others felt that way too. Senator Robert M. La Follette, Jr., introduced a resolution in the Senate on January 31, 1928, that stated that the idea of serving as President for only two terms "has become, by universal concurrence, a part of our republican system of government."[12] The young Wisconsin senator made it clear that he was trying to head off any draft-Coolidge movement. Others must have agreed with La Follette because his anti-third term resolution was adopted as the sense of the Senate by a vote of 56 to 26.

Yet the belief of many, both admirers and opponents, that Coolidge was open to nomination is supported almost completely by negative evidence. If he indicated to anyone that he would accept renomination, there is no testimony to it. Those who thought that the President was aiming at re-election had their own reasons for doing so. Men like William Butler, Andrew Mellon, and Everett Sanders were so convinced that Coolidge had to be renominated—

for the sake of the country and to retain their own political positions—that they could easily believe, without any sign from him, that he wanted to be renominated. A man like Irwin Hoover, the chief White House usher, thought that the President was tricky and happily put the worst connotation on whatever his boss did or did not do. Then there was always the possibility that some politicians spread the word, as Edward Clark accused New York Republican Committeeman Charles Hilles of doing, that Coolidge was available for renomination in order to serve their own purposes.[13]

Actually the evidence is strong that Coolidge intended to retire from the White House in 1929. He never encouraged those who were booming him and even occasionally discouraged their efforts. That was probably first seen in September, 1927, when Edward Clark, who never did anything from the White House without Coolidge's knowledge, wrote Frank Stearns disapprovingly of activities in Massachusetts in favor of the President's renomination. "If our state," Clark wrote, "refuses to take the [Rapid City statement] seriously, what of other localities."[14] In December Coolidge himself told the Republican National Committee that he was out of the race. That and other signs were not lost on one astute politician among the Coolidge men, C. Bascom Slemp, who in February, 1928, switched to support of Hoover. In March, 1928, the President went further. Then he answered a query from the Wyoming State Republican Committee about a draft-Coolidge nomination by saying that he was not available. More significant to perceptive politicians should have been the fact that an experienced vote-getter like Coolidge did nothing to hang on to the delegate votes that were offered to him. Any man receptive to a draft nomination would have kept those in reserve.

Further evidence of Coolidge's wish to retire was the extent to which he shared with others his disinclination to remain in Washington. On the way back from making his "do not choose" statement, he told Senator Capper: "It's four years ago today since I became President. If I take another term, I will be in the White House till 1933. . . . Ten years in Washington is longer than any other man has had it—too long!" He also appeared to be worried about whether the stock market would continue to hold up. Colonel Starling and presidential secretary Edward T. Clark both thought that Coolidge saw financial disaster ahead for the nation. Grace Coolidge was another witness to that. Responding to a guest's question about the President's Rapid City statement, she said, "Poppa says there's a depression coming."[15] The First Lady was the source of additional information about her husband's intentions. She told of the time the President said to a member of the Cabinet: "I know how to save money. All my training has been in that direction. The country is in a sound financial condition. Perhaps the time has come when we ought to spend money. I do not feel that I am qualified to do that."[16]

Perhaps Mrs. Coolidge was merely recalling an account told by Senator Watson or perhaps Watson adds a similar story. The Indiana senator, whose presidential ambitions had been extinguished by spring, 1928, wrote in his memoirs that he and New York National Committeeman Charles Hilles were working strenuously for Coolidge in order to keep Hoover from nomination. About three weeks before the Republican National Convention, Watson took the matter up with Coolidge. The President told him: "You and Charley Hilles are bad boys, and I want you to behave yourselves. I have studied it all over and have finally concluded that I do not want that nomination." Coolidge added that someone else was needed as Chief Executive. He had been all right until then because his policies fitted in with the requirements of postwar reconstruction. "From this time on," he said, "there must be something constructive applied to the affairs of government, and it will not be sufficient to say, 'Let business take care of itself.'" Positive and probably expensive government steps had to be taken to allay discontent in order to save the value of business to the country and to stop the loss of political party discipline. The President declared: "I do not feel that I am the man to fill that sort of position or to undertake to meet the demand occasioned by that situation. Somebody can do it, but I do not want to undertake it."[17] Grace Coolidge, Starling, Clark, Capper, and Watson may have exaggerated the President's attitudes, especially since they told of these things after the fact of depression, but it is unlikely that they made up their reports.

Health cannot be overlooked as a factor in the President's decision to leave office. Mrs. Coolidge's sinusitus was aggravated by Washington's humid climate and she found the task of White House hostess increasingly wearing. The President felt worse. He was painfully sensitive to his nose and throat difficulties and his chronic indigestion. Grace Coolidge wrote Frank Stearns that her husband was exhausted when he arrived at Cedar Island for vacation in June, 1928, and is "having quite a lot of trouble with his asthma—or whatever it is. This is not known outside." The First Lady described one of the steps taken to keep that secret. When the Coolidges went to church in Brule, Wisconsin, "The President took his 'spray' along in the car and we told Mr. Jervis if we had to come out before the service was over to say that I was not very well and had to leave."[18]

Coolidge was further bothered by the worries of his office and, as a taciturn man, could only seldom find release for his feelings. Certainly it did not seem that life would become easier for the President during another term in office. The deadlocks, defeats, and pressures caused by the farm question, foreign affairs, arms limitation, and other issues promised to continue. It is understandable that Coolidge would no longer wish to be involved in a series of national arguments that gave little hope of being settled.

The Republican National Convention came in June. Some of Coolidge's supporters were still hopeful that he would give a sign of interest in the nomination. However, the only interest the President showed in the convention was that he wanted the McNary-Haugenites defeated, both on the platform's farm plank and on nominations for office. Coolidge's unwillingness to be nominated was finally taken as being official when Secretary Mellon and National Chairman Butler advised their home state delegations to join in the nomination of Hoover for President. Charles Curtis, Coolidge's usually faithful Senate majority leader, was given the vice presidential nomination. The Republican ticket had been harmonized and during the 1928 campaign would sing hosannas to Coolidge's record as loudly as had the delegates during the convention.

Much has been made of the fact that Coolidge expressed dislike for the new Republican presidential nominee. Indeed, Irwin Hoover and William Allen White indicated that the President detested Herbert Hoover. In support of that has been quoted Agriculture Secretary Jardine's story that when he sought backing for Hoover's nomination, Coolidge snorted, "That man has offered me unsolicited advice for six years, all of it bad!"[19] The Chief Executive could say such things about anyone in a fit of pique. It may have been, and probably was, that he was constitutionally in rebellion against the idea of a man with some positive views on government succeeding him. Chief White House Usher Irwin Hoover was exaggerating when he said that Coolidge would not have been unhappy had Herbert Hoover been defeated at the polls, yet relations between the President and his Commerce Secretary were strained. When the new presidential nominee visited Coolidge in Wisconsin in summer, 1928, to pick up some campaign publicity, the two men posed together for photographs and newsreels. They sat almost silently, for Hoover could not get a conversation going and Coolidge apparently would not try. The cameramen asked the President to say something to Hoover, to which Coolidge replied surlily: "Let him talk. He's going to be President."[20]

The problem was that Coolidge, like Hoover, Roosevelt, Truman, and even Eisenhower after him, suffered from the rarest form of Potomac fever—that which afflicts only Presidents. That form decreed that he could view no prospective successor with equanimity. Yet what is significant is that Coolidge had kept Hoover on as a Cabinet member despite their many disagreements and that he had done nothing to oppose his nomination. In fact, if Coolidge encouraged any one it was Herbert Hoover. Moreover, during the 1928 campaign, Coolidge was cordial in his letters to Hoover and backed the nominee adequately if not enthusiastically. The fact is that during the nomination and election campaigns Coolidge did not treat his would-be successor as badly as Wilson had treated Cox in 1920, nor did he turn on Hoover after the election as Teddy Roosevelt had turned on Taft. If Coolidge disliked Herbert Hoover, it must be remembered that he disliked many men. He did not have to be pleased with Hoover to find him acceptable either as a colleague or a successor.

After Hoover was nominated Coolidge usually seemed content and even at times happy with the prospect of leaving office. His occasional happiness was observed by the press when he told reporters in September that although he had been constantly running for office and being elected, "This time the only thing I was a candidate for was retirement and apparently I am going to be successful in that."[21] He may even have been happy with Hoover's nomination after the Democratic candidate, Governor Alfred Smith of New York, kidded the President for being so pinchpenny as to remove colored stripes from mail sacks, wear pencils down to their stubs, and use the back sides of obsolete government forms for note paper.

After Hoover's election in November there remained little for Coolidge to do. There was the lame duck session of Congress, but that demanded little from him except for his urging ratification of the Pact of Paris. When he sent his annual message to Congress on December 4, the President gave the impression of being in a highly self-satisfied frame of mind. His message sounded like a eulogy to himself instead of a legislative program. The tone was set in the first paragraph:

> No Congress of the United States ever assembled, on surveying the state of the Union, has met with a more pleasing prospect than that which appears at the present time. In the domestic field there is tranquillity and contentment, harmonious relations between management and wage earner, freedom from industrial strife, and the highest record of years of prosperity. In the foreign field there is peace, the good will which comes from mutual understanding, and the knowledge that the problems which a short time ago appeared so ominous are yielding to the touch of manifest friendship. The great wealth created by our enterprise and industry, and saved by our economy, has had the widest distribution among our own people, and has gone out in a steady stream to serve the charity and the business of the world. The requirements of existence have passed beyond the standard of necessity into the region of luxury. Enlarging production is consumed by an increasing demand at home and an expanding commerce abroad. The country can regard the present with satisfaction and anticipate the future with optimism.[22]

Dr. Pangloss could not have painted a better picture of "this best of all possible worlds." Indeed, not many Americans would have disagreed with the President's delusions. The plain fact was that Coolidge was happy with the times, which he felt he had had such a large part in creating. He would become equally unhappy with the future as it unfolded, for it clearly revealed the extent of his delusions in 1928.

36

Back to Northampton

"T HE PRESIDENT AND Mrs. Coolidge evidently are looking forward
to the time when they lay down their official cares," wrote
Vice President Dawes after the Cabinet dinner of November 8,
1928.[1] Coolidge did seem to be more relaxed than usual in the
months between the election and his leave-taking in March, 1929.
He accepted private dinner invitations a few times, something he had
not done in the capital since he had become Chief Executive. At one
of the dinners, at Vice President Dawes', he even stayed well
beyond his bedtime to see a showing of the film *Abie's Irish Rose*.
He also sought rest and recreation, traveling to Virginia's Blue Ridge
Mountains for a few days in late November and spending the Christmas holidays on Georgia's Sapelo Island.

Coolidge showed less restraint than usual in his conversations
with other people. He complained about the burdens of the Presidency, telling William Butler that it was a job of terrific responsibility
and loneliness. His distaste for dedicating buildings, memorials, and
the like was made clear in the response to a reporter's question in
December about his traveling to dedicate Edward Bok's Singing
Tower in Florida. Coolidge was asked what Bok's Tower was and he
wryly answered, "He is dedicating it as a bird sanctuary and putting up these bells to interest the birds in music."[2] He would
also have his little joke with his successor. After Coolidge had en-

dorsed the President-elect's decision to make a good will tour of Latin America, Hoover asked him for the use of a battleship in making the journey. Coolidge recommended a cruiser—"it would not cost so much."[3]

If President Coolidge had little work to do in regard to Congress, he had a great deal to do to wind up routine matters in the White House. Packing was a problem. Perhaps out of sentiment, perhaps out of New England frugality, he wanted to keep the many gifts he had received. By February 12, 150 boxes had been packed. He cackled during one of his press conferences, "I am having rather more trouble in getting out of the White House than I had getting in."[4] It also seemed like the last-minute details of administration would not be wound up. Moreover, he was not pleased with the flood of stories that Hoover would accomplish miracles as President. Coolidge combined his irritation over those two minor vexations by telling his office staff to forget about this or that problem— "We'll leave that to the wonder boy."[5]

As Inauguration Day approached, the President had fewer and fewer visitors. Attention was concentrated on the incoming, not the departing Chief Executive. Those few who did pay their respects to Coolidge thought him to have mellowed and came away believing that he was pleased to be retiring. Supreme Court Justice Harlan F. Stone was one of his visitors. The justice said that he hoped the President would return to the capital as a senator. Coolidge talked about it thoughtfully but concluded that it would not be a good idea. He seemed to indicate that it could be embarrassing to too many people, including himself. A former President could never sit in the Senate like other men, especially in the eyes of the new leadership of his party and of the incumbent President. Stone told Coolidge that he was wise to leave the White House, because the worst economic convulsion since 1873 appeared to be coming and the people would not be in a happy mood. The President replied, "It is a pretty good idea to get out when they still want you."[6]

Coolidge met with his Cabinet for the last time the morning of March 1. He thanked its members for their service to him and the nation, and the pleasant relations he had had with all of them. That afternoon he held his last press conference, thanking the reporters for their "constant kindness and consideration" and wishing them many happy years ahead. He also gave the correspondents the last news story of his Presidency when he said, "Perhaps one of the most important accomplishments of my administration had been minding my own business."[7]

On Inauguration Day, March 4, the President arose early. He dressed and then wandered all over the White House looking to see whether anything had been left unpacked. After breakfasting and finishing up some work in his office, he looked about the family rooms as though to bid them good-by. Then he changed into formal dress for the inauguration ceremonies. Upon coming downstairs to depart for the Capitol, he found that Mrs. Coolidge had lined up the White House staff for a farewell. The President looked surprised, nodded to the employees, and barked something that might have been a greeting or a good-by. He was more demonstrative when told it might rain. "Well, I hope not," he said, "but it always rained on my moving days."[8] The Coolidges then left the White House, the President with President-elect Hoover and Mrs. Coolidge with Mrs. Hoover. At the Capitol they sat in chill weather while Hoover was inducted as the new Chief Executive. After the ceremonies the Coolidges, accompanied by a small army of press and radio reporters, went to Washington's Union Terminal to catch their train for home.

Home was Northampton and the town's citizens greeted the former President and First Lady with a great reception. Home was also 21 Massasoit Street. There the Coolidges tried to take up residence again in the duplex as though nothing had happened during the preceding eight years. The local people left the couple alone, but the house became an attraction for out-of-town motorists. With automobiles passing as often as ten a minute, Coolidge could not feel relaxed rocking on the porch or strolling up and down the street. It was also becoming clear that the public did not think much of a duplex as the residence of a former Chief of State. When he heard one tourist comment uncomplimentarily, "I don't think much of this place," Coolidge muttered to a companion, "Democrats!"[9]

The smallness of the home at 21 Massasoit Street and its lack of privacy finally led the Coolidges to seek a better dwelling. They bought The Beeches, an estate at the end of Munroe Street, and moved into its shingled house during spring, 1930. With the nine acres, eight hundred trees, tennis court, swimming pool, and the twelve-room house of The Beeches, Coolidge not only had a home befitting his station, but some of the seclusion from the public that he craved. To make it more private he had the entire property fenced in. At his new home he could sit on the porch and smoke, read, or just gaze at the meadows that swept down to the Connecticut River. The Beeches was also the kind of place where he could put up visitors without embarrassment. And that he did from time to time as loneliness led him to invite old friends and associates, like Stearns, Sanders, Slemp, Starling, and Clark, to visit.

There were joys and sorrows in retirement for the former President and his wife. John Coolidge had been graduated from Amherst College in 1928 and had taken a position, out of the public eye, with the New York, New Haven, and Hartford Railroad. Calvin and Grace Coolidge were overjoyed when in September, 1929, their son married Florence Trumbull, the daughter of Governor Robert Trumbull of Connecticut. The Coolidges' sorrow came with the death in October, after a long illness, of Grace's mother, Mrs. Goodhue.

Life for Coolidge in Northampton quickly became routine. He rose early in the morning to read. After breakfast he was driven in his car to the Masonic Building where he worked in the five-room office which he shared with Ralph Hemenway, his old law partner. There, often with one of his feet propped in an open drawer of his desk, Coolidge dictated replies to the many letters he received from well-wishers, friends, and former associates. He used his influence to help acquaintances—almost always people of modest means—settle their problems with the government, relying heavily on one of his former secretaries, Edward T. Clark, to serve as go-between for him in Washington. On his way to and from his office the former President could not avoid noticing the marquee of the vaudeville and movie theater that had been named The Calvin in his honor. It was probably a dubious honor to his way of thinking.

Coolidge was not a recluse during his retirement. He attended meetings of the Northampton Literary Club, a men's club composed only of those who could afford to smoke expensive cigars regularly. The Coolidges attended Edwards Congregational Church almost every Sunday. It was said that the former President spent as much time when in church figuring out who was absent as in listening to the sermons. He made his only return visit to Washington in July, 1929, when he attended a White House luncheon in celebration of the Kellogg-Briand Pact. He arrived and left unescorted, but during his brief stay he was surrounded by former colleagues and newspaper reporters. Coolidge spent time that summer at Plymouth Notch, exchanging the boredom he felt creeping up on him at Northampton for the reveries he thought he would enjoy at the scene of his childhood. And he did enjoy the Notch somewhat, partly because of the memories he connected with it and partly because of his and Grace's activity in planning to enlarge and, with Sears, Roebuck fixtures, to refurbish his father's house.

The only long trip of Coolidge's retirement years came in January, 1930, when Grace and he traveled to find warmth and diversion in the South and West. They journeyed to Florida, New Orleans, and California where they found the crowds of curiosity seekers irritating. When the Coolidges arrived in Hollywood, former Republican National Committee Chairman Will Hays, who was then czar of the movie industry, arranged for them to be dragged all over the film capital. Coolidge found more to his liking his visit to William Randolph Hearst's imperial estate, San Simeon. It had the touch of grandeur and polish that the former President missed. Part of it was put on, for, in honor of the Coolidges, everyone at the usually informal castle wore dress clothes. If the New Englander was shocked by staying at a place where the lord of the palace was living with a woman, actress Marion Davies, who was not his wife, he gave no sign of it. Indeed Coolidge appeared to enjoy immensely his stay at the grand but isolated estate. He even took a drink, perhaps for the first time since prohibition went into effect. Hearst asked him whether he would prefer a cocktail or an *apéritif.*

Coolidge said, "I don't drink."

"Neither do I," the publisher replied. "But I find that a sip of this wine is an excellent appetizer."

The former President asked, "Is it alcoholic?"

"Not perceptibly," Hearst said. "The alcoholic content is slight."

Coolidge tried a glass of Tokay, found it to his liking, and had another. Then he said brightly, "I must remember this."[10]

Yet the main result of Coolidge's tour was to avoid others like it. Traveling and being the center of attention was now too much for him. He would content himself with a fishing trip to Swampscott in summer, 1931, and occasional business trips to New York City. Northampton in winter and Plymouth Notch in summer were good enough for him. In fact when Grace Coolidge traveled to Newport News, Virginia, in February, 1931, to christen the Dollar Lines' new passenger ship, the *President Coolidge*, the former Chief Executive stayed in Northampton, pleading that the burdens of his work demanded it.

Coolidge did have work to do, but not much of it was remunerative. He wanted work to do. He fought off inactivity and loathed the idea of becoming an elder statesman. Yet finding suitable employment was difficult. He could not take up the practice of law again. Not only was he rusty, but it would not do for a former President to dabble in collections, drawing up wills, and settling squabbles among small-town merchants. He could not move to a big city to take up a more dignified and lucrative practice, partly because he disliked big cities and partly because he drew the line at receiving fees more for his name than for his legal ability. Related to that was his refusal to allow the Coolidge name to be used for advertising purposes. Albert D. Lasker, one of the giants of the advertising business, offered the former President $75,000 to use Mrs. Coolidge's name in a contest to promote a product of one of his clients. Coolidge turned it down, saying only, "She wouldn't like it."[11]

Coolidge's job-hunting did not mean that he was in financial distress. He had entered the White House with money at hire and left it with a small fortune. His returns from interest and dividends in 1928 indicated that he had investments amounting to at least $200,000 face value. In addition he held considerable land and buildings in Vermont. Not only had he benefited from the Coolidge Prosperity and inherited his father's holdings, but he had saved a good deal of his presidential salary. He had invested wisely and therefore did not lose too much during the economic decline beginning in 1929. He had also been one of the prominent Democrats and Republicans, including among others Charles Francis Adams, Newton D. Baker, Charles D. Hilles, and William Gibbs McAdoo, on the House of Morgan's preferred lists of buyers. Such favored persons had been permitted to purchase stocks at reduced prices before they were put on public sale. Indeed Coolidge was well fixed financially, but he continued to look for employment in order to keep active.

In fall, 1929, he was intrigued by the possibility of becoming czar of the petroleum industry, to referee its many problems of over-production, waste, and allocation of resources. Although he wanted a job that would keep him out of controversy, he concluded he could not avoid it. Of the oil industry position he wrote Everett Sanders: "I have come to think I would find it agreeable work. . . . I cannot find any place, even writing, where there are not problems and criticism of what I am doing."[12] The oil job did not materialize, but the former President had in 1929 found agreeable and essentially noncontroversial work as a director of the New York Life Insurance Company. For the remainder of his life, for fifty dollars a month and traveling expenses, he faithfully studied insurance statistics and attended the company's monthly meetings in New York City.

Coolidge's main source of income after he left Washington was from writing. Even before retiring from the White House he had put together notes for an autobiography. That basically dull and unrevealing work was published serially in *Cosmopolitan* beginning in spring, 1929. Later it appeared in book form under the title *The Autobiography of Calvin Coolidge*. He was paid a premium rate for his literary effort and must have netted a fortune as large as that which he had already accumulated. Despite his autobiography's absence of literary merit, he found no lack of offers to write for money. He did three articles for *Ladies' Home Journal*, one for *Collier's*, and a number for the *Saturday Evening Post*. In 1930 the McClure Syndicate engaged him to write a couple of paragraphs daily of newspaper commentary. Almost one hundred newspapers carried his column, and for the year it ran it earned $203,045, a substantial part of which went to Coolidge.[13]

He tried to make the daily "Thinking Things Over with Calvin Coolidge" paragraphs easy on himself, relying for help on his secretaries, Herman C. Beaty, who had formerly been an Associated Press writer, and Harry Ross, who succeeded Beaty in spring, 1931. Coolidge read the public prints assiduously for information and occasionally requested economic data from the Department of Commerce for his writings. His routine was to write a draft of the column at night and to dictate the finished version to a stenographer at his office the following morning.

The former President's syndicated column on the whole avoided partisan political controversy. He wrote like a humorless David

Harum, usually offering platitudinous prescriptions for the nation's problems. Typical of his comments were:

> Success comes to people who are not considering the narrow question of what they are paid for but the broad question of what they can do to be helpful. . . .

> Whatever insures peace and really promotes commerce anywhere in the world will be in harmony with the policy of our best thought. . . .

> The right to vote is the very essence of the right to self government. . . .

> The campaign of 1930 has closed. . . . Some people will be disappointed and some will be elated. . . .[14]

Of recurring interest to Coolidge the columnist was the nation's economic decline, which had started in fall, 1929. One of his first pieces of advice on how to deal with the depression was:

> We need more faith in ourselves. Largely because of some decline in trade we have set about finding fault with nearly everybody and everything. . . . Yet our government, our physical properties and our industries have changed very little from a year or two ago, when people were fairly content. . . . It will help somewhat to increase public and private construction. But the principal consuming power is in the people who have work. Unless they buy of the other fellow, he cannot buy of them. If those who have the means would pay all their retail merchandise bills and in addition purchase what they need and can afford, a healthy commerce would quickly be created.[15]

Coolidge's thought on the subject of coping with the deepening depression was simple, as set forth during the year his column ran. The American people by intelligent individual action could reverse the situation. Personal spending, along with some governmental expenditures, and a willingness to bear losses without complaint could do the job. Indeed, they had to, he wrote, for fanciful remedies like price-fixing and government subsidies would only make the depression worse by prolonging the necessary natural adjustment of market conditions. Yet that advice on how to retrieve prosperity clashed with his explanation of the causes of depression. Coolidge contended that overborrowing and overextension of credit in Europe as well as the dumping of cheap Russian farm commodities on the world market had been basically to blame. (He admitted that too much speculation in the United States had contributed, but he defended his Administration by saying that the government had warned against the practice.)

The argument of foreign causation, which was also enthusiastically expounded by President Hoover, constituted a plausible defense of Coolidge and Hoover against charges that they were responsible for the coming of depression. The disadvantage lay in casting doubt on Coolidge's assertions that prosperity could soon be restored in one nation—America—by the private action of its citizens. Coolidge was caught in a dilemma that he never grasped. If on the one hand, as he contended, individuals in America could work themselves out of depression by spending as much money as possible, then a necessary corollary was that they had worked themselves into depression by tightening up their expenditures at some point. If on the other hand, as he also held, depression had fundamentally come to the United States from abroad and especially because of the policies of foreign governments, then it was logical to conclude that the efforts of individual Americans could not deal with the problem. Because the large-scale effort required could be handled only by government and because the alternative argument demanded that he admit considerable American responsibility for the depression (and especially during his Administration), Coolidge could never bridge the great divide between his view of what had caused the depression and what could solve it. Consequently he was left in a position of prescribing a cure which only in small part could attack the disease he had diagnosed.

Coolidge also wrote in his column on other issues, ranging from support for the Jewish Joint Distribution Committee fund raising to deploring the dropping of Greek and Latin as required college courses. On a more important question he stood foursquare for peace but was pessimistic about its maintenance. As he wrote in July, 1930, while the London Naval Arms Reduction Treaty was being debated in the Senate:

> The world does not make real progress as fast as some expected. Like backward people with free constitutions revert-

ing to revolution, the nations have made numerous agreements with each other for peace and then turned their attention to preparation for war. In spite of all the high resolutions, all the solemn treaties, all the carefully prepared organizations set up for the peaceable adjustment of international disputes, the world is arming more heavily than before the war, and we hear too many utterances of hostility. This is a disconcerting change from the spirit of the Paris Peace Conference. Then there was disagreement about reparations and allocation of territory, but absolute accord by friend and foe alike on the principle of reduction and limitation of armaments and the maintenance of peace.

It was so nominated in the Treaty of Versailles. Germany consented to disarm on the agreement of the other parties to the treaty to disarm. Yet only the United States has proposed and secured any practical agreements for limitation of armaments. It has not been possible to secure much real reduction. The war curbed for a time but has not greatly changed the spirit of the nations.[16]

Coolidge had no ready solution to the problem except to continue urging reduction of armaments upon the nations and to hope for the best. The new Treaty of London, however, did not offer much hope. There were too many signs that it was only a gesture toward arms limitation and perhaps even a screen for secret armament. It was obvious from his column that he was drifting toward the isolation of America from world affairs, the direction in which most of his countrymen would travel during the coming years of broken agreements and world rearmament.

The labor of writing the columns wore on Coolidge. Increasingly he felt physically drained and he disliked the press of daily deadlines. Perhaps he also became aware that fewer and fewer people could agree with his views on domestic affairs. In any event after writing the column for a year, he gave it up.

That did not mark the end of his writing career, because in 1932 he wrote three *Saturday Evening Post* articles, for which he was well paid. In one, "Debts and Taxes," he reasserted the view that debts of any kind were honorable obligations that had to be paid for the economic welfare of the nation. He also supported an increase in taxes to avoid impairment of the federal government's fiscal integrity. In a second article, "Party Loyalty and the Presidency," he dealt with the theme that a strong party was one that backed its chief to the full. That was a view undoubtedly appreciated by President Hoover, who was facing rebellion on all sides in his party. The third piece, "The Republican Case," was a contribution by Coolidge to the 1932 election campaign. He characterized the Republicans as the party of peace and good will, the party that would use the protective tariff to maintain "America's Markets for Americans." The Democrats he saw as intending "to give away the money which someone else has earned."

Coolidge also emphasized that, in all justice, people should "stop blaming President Hoover for the conditions of depression, the devastating effects of which arose almost entirely outside of his jurisdiction and beyond his control, and judge him in accordance with the patience, courage and success with which he has been able to propose and supply remedies." World events, the former Chief Executive reiterated, had brought the depression, and only wise private action, coordinated where necessary by the government, would lead to economic salvation.[17] Coolidge was too comfortable and too far removed from those who felt the sharpest pains of depression to entertain other views. Moreover, his concept of party loyalty dictated that he go along with the party chief, Herbert Hoover, even if he did things as President that smacked too much of government interference for Coolidge's taste.

During the years of his retirement Calvin Coolidge resisted, usually with success, being engaged in activities that required him to go before the public. He did, however, try to render public service. He served as honorary president of the Harding Memorial Association, and although while serving as Chief Executive he had refused several invitations to dedicate the Harding Memorial at Marion, Ohio, he joined President Hoover for that purpose in June, 1931. Most of Coolidge's service, though, had no political connotations. In 1930 he became president of the American Antiquarian Society, which appealed to his considerable interest in the New England heritage. Until his death he never missed a meeting of the society's council.

Coolidge also served as an Amherst College trustee, as he had since 1921. Although he was not a very active trustee, he stood, as could be expected, for fiscal soundness in the affairs of the college. Once, another trustee came to discuss appointing Charles Andrews, who had been one of Coolidge's classmates, as college treasurer. Coolidge went to his study with the trustee, sat in his swivel chair, pulled out a desk slide, and draped his leg over it. Then he asked his colleague, Stanley King, "Have we enough money in the budget to pay his salary?" When King assured him that there was, Coolidge delivered a sermonette: "I don't believe in deciding to do something we haven't got the money for.... If our institutions and our cities and states and nation only spent the money they had in hand, we wouldn't be in the mess we are today."[18]

One other aspect of the former President's service to Amherst concerned the Folger Library, which was to become the center of Shakespearean studies in the United States. Henry Clay Folger had been an Amherst alumnus and his will provided a sizable endowment for the establishment in Washington of a library bearing his name. The library was to be administered by the college's board of trustees. Coolidge procured a distinguished Amherst graduate, who was resident in the capital, to chair the Special Committee on Plan and Scope for the new library. That man was Supreme Court Justice Harlan F. Stone, who was largely responsible for overseeing the successful early development of the Folger Library.

Only one part of Coolidge's public service after he left the Presidency concerned government. In 1932 he consented to serve on the National Transportation Committee. This group, the members of which, among others, included Alfred E. Smith and Bernard Baruch, undertook the task of making recommendations to the nation on how best to meet the burgeoning problems of the transportation industry. Coolidge was active in working on the committee, though he died before it made its report, which recommended a much expanded Interstate Commerce Commission. Coolidge's suggestions for dealing with the industry's problems went well beyond those of the committee. He called for a high-powered bureau in the Department of Commerce or even a full-fledged federal department of transportation that would have regulatory jurisdiction over all forms of interstate transportation. A proper balance, he believed, among air, water, rail, and highway carriers could be achieved only by an agency that had the scope and power to deal with all of them. Coolidge's recommendations could be read with profit decades after he had made them.

37

★ ★ ★ ★ ★

I Know My Work Is Done

THE TENOR OF Coolidge's life after leaving the White House was well illustrated by his public service. Avoid controversy and publicity, and when you serve, do little. That was partly because he had been overexposed while President, but more because he was wearing down at a rapid rate. If he did little it was not entirely because he wanted it that way. His officemate, Ralph Hemenway, said that Coolidge was obviously bored in Northampton. The simple fact was that he could do little to escape the yawning chasm of ennui, because he had been drained of most of his energy during his years in the White House. He was shy, but he was not by nature a recluse. He did not, as William Allen White has suggested, sit on the side lines because he hated his successor and because he had lost interest in politics. Coolidge just did not feel physically able to do much. That was clearly revealed in his political activities after leaving office.

Even before his departure from Washington, there had been mention of nominating Coolidge for senator from Massachusetts in 1930. Although he had discouraged such talk, the movement grew in 1929 and finally he had to be blunt in putting an end to it. Even after that, various people from time to time suggested him for one office or another. He gently discouraged them. In summer, 1931, a Hearst syndicate reporter asked for a comment on a statement by his boss. Mrs. Coolidge reported the conversation:

> I heard the Hearst man ask him something about the statement Mr. Hearst put out about [Coolidge's] running for the Presidency. He replied that he didn't care to discuss politics. The man said he wasn't asking for publication only from personal interest. In his best drawl, Calvin said, "Well, as long as I live I suppose I'll be mentioned whenever there is a vacancy in any office."[1]

Coolidge's refusal to consider running for office did not come from a lack of interest in politics. He encouraged Dwight Morrow to run for the Senate from New Jersey in 1930. He advised his Amherst classmate: "Talk as little as you can, but if you have to talk, talk about patriotism. They seem to like it."[2] Coolidge enjoyed the newsy letters about the Washington scene that he got from his former secretaries, Everett Sanders and Ted Clark, though his responses to them were usually brief. He also kept up with affairs in his newspaper reading and showed interest in Massachusetts politics.

Yet despite his continued concern with political matters Coolidge was reluctant to become actively involved. Many writers visited him looking for good copy, but they went away disappointed. Many politicians asked him for help, but they were no more successful than the writers. He succumbed to requests for help only once in 1930. Then he went on the radio in support of his old political associate, William Butler, for senator and Frank Allen for re-election as governor in Massachusetts. Coolidge told his listeners, "This is no time for rash experiments in men or measures."[3] His advice went unheeded as both the Republican nominees were rejected by the voters.

The defeat of Butler and Allen and his reaction to what he took as a radical tone in the country fortified his aloofness from political activity. He had little hope for the future the way the nation was going. He did not trust even Republicans to stay hitched to Hoover's wagon. As he wrote soon after the lame duck Congress of 1930–31 had convened, "I suppose this session of the Congress will load the country up with no end of expense, and, probably, they would also like to reduce the taxes."[4] After his 1930 political speech Coolidge refused to make personal appearances and radio talks. During summer and early fall, 1931, he retreated to the isolation and quiet of

Plymouth Notch, where he spent most of his time, as he wrote Ted Clark, "in repairing my buildings and working on my land."⁵

During 1932 it was more difficult for Coolidge to avoid political involvement. It was a presidential election year and he was badgered by the press and politicians for action, statements, and speeches. He complained: "I have kept away from Washington because I get so much newspaper reaction if I go anywhere that the only place I am safe is at home. All the newspapers expect me to function just the same as if I were in public office."⁶ He continued to resist pleas for help. He refused to send a letter to Senator Reed Smoot to aid him in his campaign for re-election. Coolidge told Ted Clark, "If I should give out one letter everybody else would claim one or blame me for hurting them."⁷ Time and energy, which were running out for the former President, were not to be wasted in writing letters or giving speeches for every Republican in the nation. That was made clear in late May when Coolidge refused the requests, apparently emanating from the White House, to attack Democratic opposition to bills providing for increased taxes and government economy. "My throat is not in good shape to make a speech, you know it always bothered me some, and besides that I should not know what to say," he wrote Clark. For what it was worth, he did observe: "Of course, almost every Democrat thinks the sovereign remedy for any of our ills is an appropriation of public money. A good many Republicans always think so too."⁸

Lack of interest in politics was not Coolidge's problem. It was obvious from the letters he wrote in 1932 that his concern for his party and country was high. His letters were longer and covered more subjects than ever before, even though they rambled. The former President was pleased with passage of the tax increase bill in June. It might stop the increase in the federal debt, which he believed could be disastrous in terms of cutting down on necessary private spending in the future. His conviction of the need to avoid an unbalanced budget carried some hurt pride with it. He did not happily witness his years of effort in paring the public debt being thrown away by deficit spending. He was sarcastic in his letters about the failure of Congress to economize on appropriations for salaries. He wrote Ted Clark: "I was a little disturbed when I thought the four or five hundred men on the government payroll attending the national convention might get a ten per cent cut. I judged that all danger is passed." Melancholy could also crop out in Coolidge's letters. He had often tried to get jobs for people of his acquaintance who were "little fellows." "Probably I am no different," he wrote, "than everybody else but it does seem as though anyone that I tried to help get employment is dropped at the first opportunity."[9]

In addition to the pressure on him to participate in politics in 1932, Coolidge was confronted with a situation that perturbed him. That was the development of maneuvers to put him in candidacy for President or Vice President. The presidential movement was not serious because one could be sure that the party would not embarrass itself by repudiating Hoover and that Hoover would not let it do so in a convention packed with his supporters. Moreover, no one of importance in the party was behind the Coolidge-for-President movement. The vice presidential movement was serious, though. There was substantial sentiment among Republicans to retire Vice President Charles Curtis, for he was considered a liability to the party because of his social-climbing antics and his reputation as a political hack. Apparently influential New York Republicans, led by National Committeeman Charles Hilles, had devised the strategy of offering Coolidge for the purpose of preventing Curtis' renomination. Coolidge instructed Everett Sanders "to stop any movement of this kind."[10] Sanders and others were successful in keeping Coolidge's name from being offered for nomination. The former President could relax. As he wrote Clark, "I am glad that conventions do not come oftener than once in four years."[11] Coolidge also took pride in the fact that his protégé, Everett Sanders, had been elected Republican National Committee chairman at the convention.

Soon after the convention's end Coolidge left Northampton to spend an indefinite period of time in Plymouth in hope of escaping political pressure and of improving his health. He felt only slightly better at the Notch and he did not escape the pressure to participate in the campaign. He wrote his *Saturday Evening Post* article in support of Hoover and the party, but that just seemed to encourage Republicans to seek more from him. He had little to give. Even Sanders, who visited him in late July, thought Coolidge had lost color and weight. The former President had been bedridden from what he called pollen poisoning, and when called upon to substitute for Hoover in opening the Olympic games in Los Angeles, he refused for fear that "to go across the plains and through the fields of blossoming vegetation would . . . probably land me on the coast totally unable to function."[12]

The pressure on Coolidge to speak increased during the summer. In September he wrote almost pathetically from Plymouth of his situation:

> I am besought to make speeches in the campaign. I have every disposition to help in any way I can but I do not know what I could say other than what I put into the *Saturday Evening Post* and my throat is not in good condition. . . . If I were to speak the public would expect something of as much importance as I was able to give when I was in Washington. I have no one to look after my throat and no sources of information. I know little about what the government has been doing or what the results of what it has done have been. . . . After being out of things for three years it is about the same as though you had never been in it so far as any knowledge of what is going on and the issues at stake."[13]

Again he felt hampered by his health and the fear of being embarrassed by what he might say. Lack of knowledge had stopped few politicians from speaking out, but it was an obstacle to the former President, who feared he might sully his reputation by speaking with less than complete information and authority for his statements.

Although he resisted speaking, he was willing, through Sanders and Clark, to give advice and encouragement to Herbert Hoover. The Republican party needed organization much more than oratory, Coolidge said. What President Hoover should do was make clear to the people what he had been trying to accomplish and what the results of his efforts were. As for encouragement, Coolidge wrote, "I think it would be a great calamity if Mr. Hoover were not reelected and I cannot believe that he will be defeated."[14]

Coolidge was unable to hold out much longer against the appeals for him to speak in support of the national Republican ticket. The implication that he owed it to the party, especially in a campaign to defend his and Hoover's records, and the intimation that his speaking out could mean the difference between victory and defeat led him to succumb. He agreed to speak in New York City and Chicago in October. Coolidge drew on Ted Clark for ideas and material for the New York speech, but he could not reconcile himself to the idea that he had made the right decision. "I find it terribly hard to know what to say," he told his former secretary. "You know that I would not relish making any attack on the opposition candidate. My entire training has been in speaking when I had some authority back of my word."[15]

The former President came down from Plymouth to New York to make his speech on October 11. In the cavernous Madison Square Garden he told his audience that he had come to "reiterate my support of the President, and reassert my faith in the Republican party, the most efficient instrument for sound popular government ever entrusted with the guidance of a great nation." He went on to praise President Hoover, the tariff, sound money, and the indirect relief efforts of the Administration. Then Coolidge criticized the Democrats for obstructionism and gave the news that "things are much worse in other parts of the world."[16] Some thought he sounded cranky in delivering the address, and almost all listeners agreed that his voice sounded thin. It was his ailing throat. What many of his former colleagues had taken for an excuse to stay out of politics turned out to be an explanation of his real condition. He was a sick man. Because of the strain and restraint in his delivery, his speech was, as he himself said, "almost ineffective."[17] He consequently had the Chicago speech canceled.

Yet Coolidge's interest in politics remained high. He was almost outraged when he heard that Democratic nominee Franklin D. Roosevelt, if elected President, intended to appoint a coalition Cabinet. The idea was "preposterous" to the former Chief Executive who believed so much in party loyalty and responsibility. "If [Roosevelt] does not feel able to handle the situation with his own associates he ought to tell the country so in order that they might get a man who can."[18]

That kind of reaction and the continued pressure on him to help his party led Coolidge once more to participate in the campaign, this time in a way more suitable to him. The night before election he joined President Hoover and Senator Capper in a national political broadcast. Speaking over microphones set up in his study at The Beeches, Coolidge advised his listeners: "When the American people make a major decision like the election of a President they do not offer themselves to the highest bidder.... Promises and good intentions are not enough. We cannot afford rash experiments.... All the teachings of common sense require us to reelect President Hoover."[19]

Coolidge could not stem the tide running against Hoover and the Republican party. Indeed, he probably did not understand it. As he wrote Ted Clark after the election, "I do not know enough about politics these days to express any intelligent opinion about the election so I take the easy method of charging it to the depression."[20] Yet he did not give up trying to understand what had happened and might happen. In late November he took satisfaction in an analysis and prediction he had formulated: The Republican party had won in 1920 with the help of dissident elements and had almost been wrecked as a result; the Democratic party had been elected in 1932 by malcontents and it too would suffer from the party-wrecking talents of its new-found allies.[21] As economic conditions got steadily worse and the hurt of his party's defeat became less intense, Coolidge became mellower. He grasped the seriousness if not the nature of the crisis confronting the nation and was inclined to be generous toward the Democratic President-elect. Coolidge wrote on New Year's Eve: "Of course a new man is new. Ordinarily he can wait a little. The difficulty now is that everything is in an emergency requiring immediate action. I would be glad to tell anybody anything I know and I think it is a time when partisanship ought to be laid aside."[22]

The former President's grasp of the situation could not develop further. He had almost reached the end of his life. Never a man of great energy, he had given most of what he had to the Presidency. What remained he had carefully conserved after leaving the White House, but even that amount seemed to run off quickly. During 1932 he repeatedly complained of asthma, indigestion, and bronchitis. He was always bothered by his throat and his bad breathing, and he tired rapidly. His worries for his nation and party and the pressure on him to help his party only burdened his frail constitution further. His four-month stay at Plymouth Notch and his dropping of commodity after commodity from his diet were desperate and unsuccessful attempts to secure physical comfort.

His last letters and comments to friends reflect his low state of mind. Public service was impossible for him in the future. To Everett Sanders he spoke of the "terrible burden" and the "sacrifices" his running for office had imposed on his friends.[23] To C. Bascom Slemp he wrote with a tone of relief: "I am glad that you and I are not in politics during these terrible times. I retired at the right time and am more and more thankful every day."[24] When Coolidge had written Ted Clark of the need for nonpartisanship in the dark days of late 1932 and of his willingness to give information, he had added that it could not go beyond that. "I should not want to serve on any bodies or commissions. The fact is that I feel worn out. No one can tell these days what a short time or three or four years may bring forth but of course I know my work is done. I could not pick it up again."[25]

"I feel worn out." That was the theme of Calvin Coolidge's last week. Indeed, when Charles Andrews and other friends visited after New Year's, he told them, "I'm afraid I'm all burned out."[26] And to Colonel Starling, in a belated season's greetings note, Coolidge wrote, "I find I am more and more worn out."[27] And he was. The morning of January 5 he arose at seven and went to the office at half past eight. He finished his correspondence a little after ten and told his secretary, Harry Ross, that he wanted to go home. After he arrived back at The Beeches he went into the library and fitted a few pieces into a jigsaw puzzle picture of George Washington. Then he spoke to Ross of the past summer and fall in Plymouth. Coolidge went to the kitchen for a glass of water and to the cellar to watch the furnace being stoked. Then he went upstairs to his room. When Grace Coolidge went to fetch him to lunch, she found her husband lying on his back in his shirt sleeves in his dressing room. He had died quietly and quickly, a victim of coronary thrombosis.

The funeral services were held in Northampton, with President and Mrs. Hoover, Chief Justice Charles Evans Hughes, Cabinet members, governors, members of Congress, and diplomats in attendance. President-elect Roosevelt was represented by his wife and his son James. After the great ceremony at Northampton a smaller party accompanied Coolidge's body to Plymouth Notch, where burial took place in the Coolidge family's plot. The Vermont Yankee had come home to stay.

38

A President Restrained

At the beginning of the 1924 election campaign, George Harvey said that Calvin Coolidge would be elected or rejected by the people "not for what he has said nor what he has done, but for what he is."[1] Harvey was largely right, for the new President had done and said little, but as a public figure he contrasted sharply with his competitors and, equally important, with his two immediate predecessors, Woodrow Wilson and Warren G. Harding. Coolidge's character was not as well known as it would become, but it was remarkably like the general portrayal of it in 1924. It was already clear that he was a man of honesty and integrity and a believer in representative and constitutional government. He was thrifty, cautious, and shy. He believed in fattening the golden goose of big business, so that it might produce bountifully for all society.

Coolidge's ordinariness inspired confidence. Physically, he was of average height and of facial features that, however delicately chiseled, were not commanding of attention. He exuded an appealing balance of modesty and self-confidence and left no doubt that he had good reason to be both modest and confident. If he was no Harding, neither was he a Wilson. He exalted stability, unity, and harmony, and after the ups and downs of the Wilson and Harding Administrations, most Americans were ready to settle for the genius of the average. Reliability, not brilliance or good fellowship, was what Calvin Coolidge held up as the prime virtue before the nation, and he personified it. If he was slow to judge, he was also unlikely to prejudge. Certainly, he appeared to have enough strength, intelligence, knowledge, and tough-mindedness to run the government. He was also intent upon discussing the promise of the future instead of the troubles of the past. For a nation that was tired of having the ship of state rocked, he was a reassuring skipper.

Of course, Coolidge was other things, about which the public either did not care or was not informed. Although his ideas of God and religion were mystically vague, it was clear he believed that man had a duty under God's laws to give service. Yet there was no reason why service could not be both pleasant and profitable. Because of that Coolidge could be a happy Christian since he prospered from politics and usually enjoyed the attention which public life brought him. Not that anyone at the time much cared, but the President narrowly focused his intellect on the work that came before him day by day. In dealing with large, long-range issues he substituted his broad idealism for intellect. And make no mistake, Coolidge was an idealist. He wanted to do right by all men and see others do likewise. He believed in man's perfectibility, in terms of honesty, dependability, industry, service, fairness, kindliness, tolerance, and harmoniousness. The problem was that he did not know how wide the gap was between belief and achievement.

Yet Coolidge cannot be considered just on the basis of his character and beliefs. What he did, or did not do, obviously is more important in its effects on people. Although he is seldom remembered for his accomplishments, a number of them must be credited to his Presidency. Most outstanding, after the Harding days, was his retrieval of public confidence in the office he held. As the Democratic senator from Arizona, Henry F. Ashurst, wrote in his diary when Coolidge left office, "Time's perspective will appraise Calvin Coolidge, but with certainty it may *today* be said that he restored the White House to a symbol of dignified and moderate living." Ashurst also praised the departing Chief Executive because he had "defied politicians who advocated nostrums."[2] Such praise, one can suggest, Coolidge most deserved for his resistance to the McNary-Haugen bill, which, by adding to inflation at home and by dumping surplus farm products abroad, would have created problems at least as bad as those it might have solved.

Another accomplishment of note was administration, an aspect of the Presidency often underappreciated by the public and even scholars. Coolige made his mark as an administrator by demanding able and economical performance from public servants, by making maximum use of the Bureau of the Budget, and by extending the civil service merit system. In related functions he deserves credit for the release of the remaining political prisoners and for helping to raise the level of competence among career Foreign Service officers and federal judges. Government under Calvin Coolidge did not undertake all that it might have, but what it did it accomplished with considerable efficiency.

Relations with Congress were another matter, for Coolidge, however able as an administrator, was clumsy in dealing with the House and Senate. The President and the lawmakers got out of step during the Teapot Dome conflict of early 1924 and only occasionally got together again. Nevertheless he got Congress to give him the program closest to his heart and the one he most esteemed among his accomplishments. That was his fiscal policy of holding down appropriations, with the surplus to be applied to reducing taxes and paring the national debt. The rising levels of income and of stock prices, which were labeled the Coolidge Prosperity, proved to him that his fiscal policy was a success. Yet his pride was mocked as the prosperity was shattered in the Great Crash of 1929 and as government expenditures and debt mounted quickly to meet the exigencies of the consequent depression.

The Administration's other accomplishments were achievements that the President either encouraged or allowed. His interest in them ran all the way from his determination to improve relations with Latin American nations to his unhappy support of naval development after his international arms limitation program had failed. The result of the former was the dawning of the Good Neighbor policy of the 1930s and in the latter lay the germ of America's preparation for World War II. Other accomplishments of the Coolidge Administration include harmonizing the relations between the United States and the Philippine Islands, development of waterways, orderly growth of civil and even military aviation, regulation of radio broadcasting, expansion of the technical and information services of the Departments of Agriculture and Commerce, straightening out of some of the fierce disputes over use of Colorado River waters, encouragement of cooperative solutions to farmers' problems, and negotiation of the Kellogg-Briand Pact, which still stands as a statement in international law of the goal that men of good will hope to achieve. All together the record of his Administration was substantial in terms of the number and variety of works, even if the President was less tied up in its making than most American Chief Executives have been in making the records of their administrations. The flaws in the Coolidge Administration's accomplishments were that, in most cases, they were too puny and too tardy to be effective in dealing with the problems that were to lead to economic calamity and eventually to another world war.

Equally important were the Administration's failures. On some things the deck was stacked against Coolidge. The League of Nations had not a wisp of a chance in the United States and genuine arms limitation enjoyed only little more favor abroad. It is true that he fumbled America's adherence to the World Court, although it is farfetched to believe that the nation's membership on the Court would have stopped the rise of aggressor powers during the 1930s. Other failures represented the Administration's lack of vision. Its inflexibility toward Communist Russia and unquestioning acceptance of Fascist Italy dissipated whatever moderating influence the United States might have had over those totalitarian powers. Regarding international economics, the American government's policies were imaginative, but to the point of foolishness. To try to insure repayment of war debts by financing the effort with Yankee dollars only worked the United States deeper into the mire of European politics and economics from which the nation hoped to extricate itself. And that went on while America was engaged in the absurdity of trying to boost sales abroad while fortifying barriers to international trade.

If the idea of a world economic conference ever entered President Coolidge's head, he probably expelled it. He certainly turned aside ideas of federal control of American investments abroad or of speculation at home and of reorganization and regulation of banking and public power. In other areas, he failed to make more than gestures in support of a federal antilynching law, he ignored pressure for desegregation in the civil service, and decided to let the Ku Klux Klan burn itself out instead of providing the moral leadership which his code of service sanctioned. He even refused to push for adoption of one of his favorite ideas, the reorganization of railway transportation.

Coolidge's share of responsibility for the inadequacies of his administration derived largely from his restraint in both thought and action. He was like the naval officer who runs his ship according to the letter of the book, on the premise that nothing can go wrong that way. Coolidge's book was the Constitution and he interpreted it almost literally as far as the Chief Executive's powers were concerned. He addressed himself only to those problems *clearly* provided for in the Constitution and by judicial interpretation of it. As Coolidge saw it, the Constitution did not authorize the President to fuss over problems that belonged to other jurisdictions or to posterity.

He stated his view well in his comments, "Do the day's work" and "If you see ten troubles coming down the road, you can be sure that nine will run into the ditch before they reach you." Although there is much to be said for letting evil forces spend themselves, there is great danger that those that do not run into the ditch will gather so much momentum that they will become overwhelming. Coolidge had neither the conception of duty nor energy to enable him to deal effectively with all of the many problems that kept coming down the road.

In short, Calvin Coolidge was a statesman of the later nineteenth-century kind. He had modeled his career on what he had found there. By training and by feeling he was unable either to look forward or to comprehend satisfactorily the tendencies of his time. He thought he was presiding over the renovation of society, when, in fact, he was floating on top of a nation that was drifting into a new era. A man of his time, Coolidge was not a man for his time. As such he did not seek problems. That was, however, what most people wanted. In the 1920s the prime concern was to make money, and the rising tide of prosperity seemed to confirm that that was the thing to do. The result was that most Americans felt secure with Coolidge in Washington. As Henry Stoddard happily wrote in 1927, "They have faith in him beyond any they have shown in any other President of my time.... He inspires a deep, nation-wide confidence that all will go well with the country while he is in the White House."[3]

Yet the consequences of Coolidge's popularity in the 1920s went further in terms of his reputation. During the middle of the Great Depression of the 1930s, mining magnate John Hays Hammond said that "part of the resentment which even today is directed towards him is due to the fact that thousands of his former constituents believe that, had he chosen to run again, he would somehow miraculously have saved their personal fortunes and the country from depression."[4] Coolidge was doubly blamed for his failures. He was reproached for pursuing the domestic policies he did and for not pursuing them for four more years. That was also true in foreign affairs where he was to receive blame, on the one hand, for not bringing enduring world peace and, on the other hand, for not sufficiently preparing the nation for the collapse of peace.

Coolidge's signal fault was his pursuit of the policies approved by most Americans. When such policies fail, the people blame the President. They do not expect him to be representative unless his policies succeed. They do expect him to have special insight. That Coolidge lacked, as did the people. As Hammond remarked, with a hint of confession: "While many people attribute the financial collapse of 1929 in part to some of his policies, I consider the justice of this debatable. I would ask them if these same policies had not been their own."[5]

Even if Calvin Coolidge were representative of the majority when a leader was needed, he was also responsible for looking only to the day's work when vision was required. It is probable, of course, that had he been a leader and man of some vision, he would have failed to prevent depression and another great war because of the monumental disorder created by World War I and of the popular craving for political simplicity. But there was a good chance that had he been a less restrained Chief Executive the civil rights movement would not have been so long impeded, a chance that depression and aggression might not have reached such devastating proportions, and even a miniscule chance that they might have been averted.

As Walter Lippmann wrote in 1927, Coolidge had stopped the "nationalizing tendency" of the Republican party. "He has just stopped it, mind you. He has not replaced it with anything."[6] Like his time, Coolidge had the opportunity for greatness, a greatness born of his actual accomplishments and of his possible accomplishments. But he refused to seek the power to achieve more. He might not have achieved more for the seeking, but even noble failure would have saved him from Peter Levin's apt assessment that "Coolidge, the success of his times, is a failure in history."[7] A struggle to accomplish more might have saved his party, for which he cared, from disintegration and have reduced the loss of confidence during the early 1930s in the nation's leaders.

The lesson of Calvin Coolidge is that of a man bred and trained to avoid the daring. From that background he never freed himself. Consequently the story of Coolidge's life is more of what he became than of what he did. As a representative of the people, he rose to eminence; as the same, he failed to use his position to any great end. Yet in fairness it must be recalled that in Coolidge's days of national prominence, Harding was also President, Friedrich Ebert and Paul von Hindenburg were presidents of Germany, Stanley Baldwin and Ramsey MacDonald were prime ministers of Great Britain, and failure after failure trooped in and out of office as premiers of France. Italy's Benito Mussolini and Soviet Russia's Nicolai Lenin towered over all other chiefs of state, but it must be said of Coolidge that if he did not have their flair for leadership, neither did he possess their megalomania or their instinct for terror.

What Coolidge was and did are not too difficult to comprehend. Why at bedrock he was what he was, however, is a question that can at best be only plausibly answered. Yet the question should be asked for no other reason than that Coolidge was a most untypical man. His attributes of honesty, reliability, unpretentiousness, thriftiness, and caution, his ideals, his interest in public service, and his sketchy political and economic philosophies clearly derive from his family training and his school and college experiences.

His was a heavily idealistic upbringing, one that was fortified by what he learned at school, academy, and college. His religious vagueness came from his mother and the unstructured nature of church in Plymouth Notch. His mother also contributed to the development of his sentimentality and apparently transferred to him her desire for life beyond the Notch. Both contributions were complemented by his father, who increasingly during Calvin's adolescence relied on the boy for sentimental comfort as John Coolidge's father, wife, and only other child were taken from him by death. His mother, Calvin's grandmother, was too flinty a person to be an emotional anchor. Yet, because the boy and the father were taciturn, their affection was more understood than expressed, which must have been a frustrating business for them both. As for leaving the Notch, that might have been young Coolidge's way of proving himself to both his father and mother and of intentionally seeking to beat his father at his own game of public leader. One can guess that Calvin's mild hypochondria also derived from his mother, whose illnesses were an integral part of his first dozen years. His lack of expressiveness came in part from the model set by his father and from his grandmother's disapproval of much expression by the boy. This may permanently have fettered his imagination or at least have internalized it in the form of elaborate daydreams.

Calvin Coolidge also was influenced by the community of Plymouth Notch. It was a democratic society, one not much bothered by intrigue or chicanery and one without serious social distinctions. Coolidge carried that spirit of easygoing democracy with him the rest of his life, not only politically, but also in terms of being personally rather free from bigotry, snobbishness, and prejudice. As a lawyer he had to serve a widespread clientele which fortified his open-mindedness about people, as did his need as a politician to appeal for the votes of a wide range of individuals and groups. The fact that until he became President he had not become a member of a social elite helped keep him favorably disposed toward various minorities. Yet his was not a crusading tolerance, for he also gained from the Notch, and from law and politics, the belief that man had to claim his rights and rewards.

Amherst largely bolstered Coolidge's tendencies. What Professors Garman and Morse taught him about idealism, service, and stability augmented and clarified what he had already acquired in the Notch and from his family. The college allowed him to bud, if only as an occasionally droll fellow. By making him something of a scholar and a gentleman, Amherst also made it difficult for him to go home. Indeed, by mixing him with young men from other stations in life the college gave him career goals that could not be satisfied in Plymouth Notch. Northampton became his proving ground, and there he found he could become professionally and politically accepted without the shelter of home or college.

The first twenty-five years of Coolidge's life were important, not only in setting him on the path to the Massachusetts governorship and the White House, but in shaping how he would act when he got there. His hypochondria kept him from being too active, for it was a good excuse to do just the day's work and not to worry about the future. Of course, he was restrained by other things. He probably did possess less stamina than most men. His shyness and taciturnity also kept him in check, and his daydreams siphoned off most of his imaginativeness. These factors fitted in well with his tame 1890s philosophy, and in the absence of any great pressure to reconstruct his thought, he was able to believe that his philosophy and action met the requirements of American life in the 1920s. In fact, not only was there no compelling force to pull Coolidge out of his lassitude, but instead the flattery of his supporters, his ability to disregard his critics (who were far from being astute), and the superficial evidence that everyday in every way things were growing better made it easy for him to hold to a narrow view of his responsibilities as President.

In reputation as well as in fact Coolidge has been a victim of his reserve and of his popularity, for together they restrained him from serious involvement in most of the great problems of the 1920s. He has further suffered from his lack of charm, boldness, and brilliance, qualities for which ambition, dignity, and kind feelings are inadequate substitutes. As it turned out, there was no great achievement with which posterity could identify Coolidge alone. His most vaunted accomplishments, debt and tax-cutting, went for naught with the coming of depression, and the Kellogg-Briand Pact soon became a mockery. The President was also the victim of the suppositions that what he fought against, measures like the McNary-Haugen bill, would have been more beneficial than his policies and that what he ignored, such as adherence to the League of Nations, could have been achieved.

With what, then, is one left in assessing Calvin Coolidge as President? He restored public confidence in the White House, but that drained away during the term of his successor. He was a skillful administrator, but he had little to administer that met the pressing needs of the time. He was a man of considerable courage in not yielding to congressional petulance, but his courage was outweighed by his reluctance to recognize the problems underlying dissidence. When Coolidge acted, he did so forcefully, but his restraint led him to act too seldom. His avoidance of theatrics is a virtue one wishes for in all Presidents and has found in few, but dignity and simplicity of expression are not prime qualities for successful Chief Executives. Coolidge's failure was the failure of a President who does not look ahead and does not fight to head off the problems of the future. Of course, there is little to indicate that he could have succeeded in such a struggle or that there was anyone else available in national politics in the 1920s who could have done substantially better, but the nation would have been morally and intellectually better for the attempt.

ESSAY ON
SELECTED
SOURCES

THE SOURCES OF INFORMATION about the life of Calvin Coolidge
are greatly varied both in character and quality. They are in addition scattered, for there is no backbone source of data.

A great deal of material is found in archives and manuscript
collections. There are four significant collections of papers of Calvin
Coolidge. The largest collection, deposited in the Manuscript Division of the Library of Congress, is disappointing because, on
Coolidge's orders, most of his personal papers were removed and destroyed. The remaining papers, however, cast considerable light on
the operations of, and the pressures on, the Coolidge Administration.
In 1965 a microfilm edition of the Coolidge papers of the Library
of Congress was placed on sale, along with a published index. The
Forbes Library at Northampton, Massachusetts, contains large
amounts of reminiscences, photographs, cartoons, tapes, and me-
mentos, as well as miscellaneous letters and speech copies. Most important in the Forbes Library collection are the transcripts of the
White House press conferences, 1923–29, personal financial records,
general correspondence, 1919–21, and the letters sent from Mrs.
Coolidge to her close friend Mrs. Reuben B. Hills during the 1920s.
Very small but interesting collections of Coolidge letters are found
in the libraries of Amherst and Holy Cross colleges. The Frank W.
Stearns papers at Holy Cross are also significant.

The Library of Congress has a large number of helpful manuscript collections in addition to the Coolidge papers. Especially important for the post-White House years are the papers of Edward T. Clark, who had been one of President Coolidge's secretaries. Illuminating material can be gleaned from the papers of Theodore Roosevelt, Jr., particularly his diary; Elihu Root; James W. Wadsworth; Charles Evans Hughes; James J. Davis; Charles L. McNary; William M. Jardine; Henry T. Rainey; Harry S. New; Wallace H. White; William S. Culbertson; William E. Humphrey; Walter L. Fisher; and, particularly for the 1920 election campaign, George Sutherland. The material relating to Everett Sanders, another of Coolidge's secretaries, is disappointing.

Some reflection of Coolidge's methods of operation as President is found in the National Archives in the general records of the Departments of Agriculture (Record Group 16), Commerce (RG 40), Interior (RG 48), Justice (RG 60), Labor (RG 174), Post Office (RG 28), State (RG 59), Treasury (RG 56), and War (RG 107). Relevant material is contained also in the Protection of the President file of the United States Secret Service (RG 87).

Of limited use are the papers of Warren G. Harding and the R. Baker Harris collection of Harding material in the Ohio State Historical Society and the papers of Arthur Capper in the Kansas State Historical Society.

Other primary sources of value include the reminiscences of John W. Davis, Claude M. Fuess, Albert D. Lasker, and James W. Wadsworth in the Oral History Research Office of Columbia University. Two typescript volumes in the Massachusetts State Library, "Speeches and messages of Calvin Coolidge 1895–July 25, 1924" and "Statements of Calvin Coolidge . . . Jan. 13, 1919–Jan. 5, 1921, some of which are not included in the Official papers," are useful to research on Coolidge's life. A number of newspapers were consulted at strategic points in this study, especially the Boston *Post*, Kansas City *Star*, New York *Times*, and Washington *Post*. Massachusetts' *Manual for the Use of the General Court* (1907–20), the *Congressional Record* (1913–33), the official reports of the proceedings of the Republican National Conventions for 1920, 1924, 1928, and 1932, and the *Papers Relating to the Foreign Relations of the United States* (1923–29), are essential sources of information about Calvin Coolidge. *The Talkative President: The Off-the-Rec-*

ord Press Conferences of Calvin Coolidge (Amherst: University of Massachusetts, 1964) is valuable, not only for the publication of a fine selection of President Coolidge's comments to newsmen, but for the observations of its editors, Howard H. Quint and Robert H. Ferrell. C. Bascom Slemp (ed.), *The Mind of the President* (Garden City: Doubleday, Page, 1926), reveals almost as much about its editor, a former White House secretary, as about its subject.

Studies and reminiscences of Calvin Coolidge's life abound. These include two serious, full-length biographies: Claude M. Fuess' starchy, almost defensive *Calvin Coolidge, The Man from Vermont* (Boston: Little, Brown, 1940) and William Allen White's less accurate, though superbly written, *A Puritan in Babylon, The Story of Calvin Coolidge* (New York: Macmillan, 1938). Caught up in the swirls of depression days, Fuess sees Coolidge as a symbol of sanity and stability, while White views him as a man who misunderstood his times. Less factual, less critical, and less interesting is White's earlier biography, *Calvin Coolidge, The Man Who Is President* (New York: Macmillan, 1925); readable and interesting is Fuess' "Calvin Coolidge—Twenty Years After," *American Antiquarian Society Proceedings*, LXIII (1953), Part 2. Helpful is Ishbel Ross' attractively written *Grace Coolidge and Her Era* (New York: Dodd, Mead, 1962), which is almost as much a biography of the President as of his lady.

A number of books about Coolidge were written while he was still alive. Most useful are Robert M. Washburn's often whimsical *Calvin Coolidge, His First Biography* (Boston: Small, Maynard, 1923) and Ernest C. Carpenter's *The Boyhood Days of President Calvin Coolidge* (Rutland: Tuttle, 1926). Duff Gilfond's *The Rise of Saint Calvin* (New York: Vanguard, 1932) is more readable than reliable. Other contemporaneous biographies include Horace Green, *The Life of Calvin Coolidge* (New York: Duffield, 1924); Thomas T. Johnson, *Have Faith in Calvin Coolidge* (Boston: Christopher, 1925); Cameron Rogers, *The Legend of Calvin Coolidge* (New York: Doubleday, Doran, 1928); Roland D. Sawyer, *Cal Coolidge, President* (Boston: Four Seas, 1924); Edward E. Whiting, *President Coolidge* (Boston: Atlantic Monthly, 1923); and Robert A. Woods, *The Preparation of Calvin Coolidge* (Boston: Houghton Mifflin, 1924).

Books that contain biographical essays and personal estimates of Coolidge include Gamaliel Bradford's crude but fascinating psychograph "The Genius of the Average" in *The Quick and the Dead* (Boston: Houghton Mifflin, 1931); the stimulating chapters in Peter R. Levin, *Seven By Chance: The Accidental Presidents* (New York: Farrar, Straus, 1948) and Walter Lippmann, *Men of Destiny* (New York: Macmillan, 1927); and Alfred P. Dennis' volume of reminiscences, *Gods and Little Fishes* (Indianapolis: Bobbs-Merrill, 1931). Critical of Coolidge's political background is Sherwin L. Cook, *Torchlight Parade, Our Presidential Pageant* (New York: Minton, Balch, 1929); sometimes informative and usually uncritical is Henry L. Stoddard, *As I Knew Them* (New York: Harper, 1927).

A hodgepodge of reminiscences and views is found in Charles J. Adams, "An Early Memory of Calvin Coolidge," *Vermont History*, XXII (October, 1954); Henry T. Brown, "Memories of Calvin Coolidge," *Vermont Quarterly*, XXI (October, 1953); Charles J. Dean, "Mayor Coolidge," *Vermont History*, XXIV (October, 1956); Benjamin F. Felt, "Some Points of View about Calvin Coolidge," *Vermont History*, XXIII (October, 1955); and David C. Mearns' unnecessarily snide "A Neglected Bookman: Calvin Coolidge" in *Largely Lincoln* (New York: St. Martin's, 1961). In a class by itself is John H. McKee's amusing compilation of *Coolidge Wit and Wisdom* (New York: Stokes, 1933).

Coolidge's writings are voluminous and largely unstimulating. Yet if they do not adequately reflect his sense of humor or his intellect, they do mirror his sense of dignity and the simplicity of his principles. This is particularly seen in *The Autobiography of Calvin Coolidge* (New York: Cosmopolitan, 1929) and in his newspaper columns written in 1930–31 and published under the titles of "Calvin Coolidge Says" and "Thinking Things Over with Calvin Coolidge." More interesting are the many articles he wrote in the early 1920s and the early 1930s. See particularly "Whose Country Is This?" *Good Housekeeping*, 72 (February, 1921); "Enemies of the Republic," *Delineator*, XCVIII (June, July, and August, 1921); "Everyman's Property," *Collier's*, 90 (July 23, 1932); and "The Republican Case," *Saturday Evening Post*, 205 (September 10, 1932). A large number of his political and official pronouncements have been published in *Calvin Coolidge, Messages to the General Court, Official Addresses, Proclamations and State Papers* (Boston: The Council, 1920); *Have Faith in Massachusetts* (Boston: Houghton Mifflin, 1919, 1920);

The Price of Freedom (New York: Scribner's, 1924); *America's Need for Education* (Boston: Houghton Mifflin, 1925); and *Foundations of the Republic* (New York: Scribner's, 1926).

Other sources deal with particular aspects of Calvin Coolidge's life. A highly satisfactory genealogy is Emma Downing Coolidge's *Descendants of John and Mary Coolidge of Watertown, Massachusetts, 1630* (Boston: Wright and Potter, 1930). Earle W. Newton's *The Vermont Story, 1749–1949* (Montpelier: Vermont Historical Society, 1949) is a good introduction to Vermont. Helpful in reconstructing Coolidge's relationships with Amherst are Charles E. Garman, *Letters, Lectures and Addresses* (Boston: Houghton Mifflin, 1911); Stanley King, *A History of the Endowment of Amherst College* (Amherst: Amherst College, 1950); and Frank P. Rand, *The Village of Amherst* (Amherst: Amherst Historical Society, 1958). Essential to understanding are Claude M. Fuess' loving history, *Amherst, The Story of a New England College* (Boston: Little, Brown, 1935), and Thomas Le Duc's perceptive book-length essay *Piety and Intellect at Amherst College 1865–1912* (New York: Columbia, 1946). Tercentenary History Committee, *The Northampton Book* (Northampton: The Committee, 1954) contains a great variety of information about Coolidge and the city which nurtured his legal and political careers. Rudolph Marx's *The Health of the Presidents* (New York: Putnam's, 1960) and A.S.W. Rosenbach, "The Libraries of the Presidents of the United States," *American Antiquarian Society Proceedings*, XLIV (1934), are of limited usefulness.

There are many studies in which one can find information and insight about the political and governmental milieu in which Coolidge developed from the 1890s to the 1920s. A cooperative work of uneven quality is Albert Bushnell Hart (ed.), *Commonwealth History of Massachusetts*, 5 vols. (New York: States History, 1930), especially Volume V. Michael E. Hennessy's *Four Decades of Massachusetts Politics 1890–1935* (Norwood: Norwood, 1935) is an engaging brew of perceptiveness and prejudice, fact and folderol. A top-notch study is J. Joseph Huthmacher, *Massachusetts People and Politics, 1919–1933* (Cambridge: Harvard, 1959). Competent works on specialized aspects of Massachusetts public affairs include Arthur Mann, *Yankee Reformers in the Urban Age* (Cambridge: Harvard, 1954); Richard M. Abrams, *Conservatism in a Progressive Era,*

Massachusetts Politics, 1900–1912 (Cambridge: Harvard, 1964); Irston R. Barnes, *Public Utility Control in Massachusetts* (New Haven: Yale, 1930); George C. S. Benson, *The Administration of the Civil Service in Massachusetts* (Cambridge: Harvard, 1935); and Henry Lee Staples and Alpheus T. Mason, *The Fall of a Railroad Empire: Brandeis and the New Haven Merger Battle* (Syracuse: Syracuse University, 1947). Still useful older works are Raymond L. Bridgman, *The Massachusetts Constitutional Convention of 1917* (Boston: the author, 1923); Louis A. Frothingham, *A Brief History of the Constitution and Government of Massachusetts* (Boston: Houghton Mifflin, 1925); and Fitz-Henry Smith, "The New Act Reorganizing the State Departments," *Massachusetts Law Quarterly,* IV (August, 1919).

A number of biographies of Massachusetts political figures are available to the Coolidge biographer. Skimpy in scope and fact are Lawrence B. Evans, *Samuel W. McCall, Governor of Massachusetts* (Boston: Houghton Mifflin, 1916); Solomon B. Griffin, *W. Murray Crane, a Man and a Brother* (Boston: Little, Brown, 1926); and Charles G. Washburn, *Life of John W. Weeks* (Boston: Houghton Mifflin, 1928). Washburn's book boasts an introduction by Calvin Coolidge. Joseph Martin's *My First Fifty Years in Politics* (New York: McGraw-Hill, 1960) is an honest, interesting, but rambling autobiography. Substantial, though overly admiring, is Alpheus T. Mason, *Brandeis, A Free Man's Life* (New York: Viking, 1946). *Joseph B. Eastman, Servant of the People* (New York: Columbia, 1952) is Claude M. Fuess' ablest work. A reliable but too brief volume is John A. Garraty's *Henry Cabot Lodge* (New York: Knopf, 1953). Karl Schriftgiesser's *The Gentleman from Massachusetts: Henry Cabot Lodge* (Boston: Little, Brown, 1944) is far more critical of his subject than of his sources.

A great deal has been written about the Boston Police Strike. Of course, none of Coolidge's biographers failed to write at length about it. Other works that deserve mention include R. L. Lyons' well-balanced "Boston Police Strike of 1919," *New England Quarterly,* XX (June, 1947), and Robert K. Murray's splendid chapter on the strike in *Red Scare* (Minneapolis: University of Minnesota, 1955). Henry Greenleaf Pearson's *Son of New England, James Jackson Storrow, 1864–1926* (Boston: the author, 1932) is quite useful. Francis Russell's ruminations in "Coolidge and the Boston

Police Strike," *Antioch Review*, XVI (Winter, 1956–57), are interesting; his article "The Strike That Made a President," *American Heritage*, XIV (October, 1963), is a skillful, if overdrawn journalistic account.

Wesley M. Bagby's *The Road to Normalcy* (Baltimore: Johns Hopkins, 1962) is an able study of the national election of 1920. Also helpful on post-World War I politics is George H. Mayer's *The Republican Party, 1854–1964* (New York: Oxford University, 1964). One should also consult *The Memoirs of Will H. Hays* (Garden City: Doubleday, 1955); Frank Freidel's splendid *Franklin D. Roosevelt, The Ordeal* (Boston: Little, Brown, 1954); and Andrew Sinclair's provocative *The Available Man, Warren Gamaliel Harding* (New York: Macmillan, 1965).

The number of works treating the decade that followed World War I is huge. Only a few will be mentioned here. Still worthy of attention despite its middle-class, urban, Eastern bias is Frederick Lewis Allen's *Only Yesterday* (New York: Harper, 1931). Although exaggerated and acid in tone, Karl Schriftgiesser, *This Was Normalcy* (Boston: Little, Brown, 1948), is useful to the Coolidge biographer, particularly because of the author's Boston background. Scholarly and more recent works include William E. Leuchtenburg's stimulating essay *The Perils of Prosperity, 1914–32* (Chicago: University of Chicago, 1958) and the provocative articles by Henry F. May, "Shifting Perspectives on the 1920s," *Mississippi Valley Historical Review*, XLIII (December, 1956), and by Arthur S. Link, "What Happened to the Progressive Movement in the 1920s?" *American Historical Review*, LXIV (July, 1959). Filled with facts and apparently oriented from a New Deal standpoint is John D. Hicks' *Republican Ascendancy 1921–1933* (New York: Harper, 1960). More partisan, but also more perceptive, is Arthur M. Schlesinger, Jr.'s *The Crisis of the Old Order, 1919–1933* (Boston: Houghton Mifflin, 1957), the first volume in his *Age of Roosevelt* project.

Many books deal generally with the Senate, the Vice Presidency, and the Presidency. Only those which were most useful in constructing this biography will be cited. Louis C. Hatch and Earl L. Shoup, *A History of the Vice-Presidency of the United States* (New York: American History Society, 1934), despite its frequent superficiality, is still the basic history of that office. More thoughtful, but less full, is Irving G. Williams, *The Rise of the Vice Presidency* (Washington: Public Affairs, 1956). George H. Haynes, *The Senate of the United States*, 2 vols. (Boston: Houghton Mifflin, 1938), is the standard work on the upper house. Joseph P. Harris, *The Advice and Consent of the Senate* (Berkeley: University of California, 1953), is based on an assiduous reading of the printed sources. Edward S. Corwin, *The President, Office and Powers, 1787–1957* (New York: New York University, 1957), sketches boldly and often brilliantly the awesome terrain of his subject. Also useful is W. E. Binkley, *The Powers of the President* (Garden City: Doubleday, Doran, 1937). James E. Pollard, *The Presidents and the Press* (New York: Macmillan, 1947), is as critical of Coolidge's public relations technique as Elmer E. Cornwell, Jr., *Presidential Leadership of Public Opinion* (Bloomington: Indiana University, 1965), is favorable toward it.

A great deal of information and insight can be dredged from the large number of biographies and autobiographies of people who worked for, with, or against Coolidge after 1920. One can start with the people who worked with Coolidge in the White House. Closest to him was Secret Service operative Edmund W. Starling whose delightful memoirs (as told to Thomas Sugrue), *Starling of the White House* (New York: Simon & Schuster, 1946), are highly sympathetic to Coolidge. Of high quality is Guy Hathorn's "The Political Career of C. Bascom Slemp" (Ph.D. dissertation, Duke University, 1950). Elizabeth Jaffray, in *Secrets of the White House* (New York: Cosmopolitan, 1927), writes like a housekeeper scorned, and Irwin H. (Ike) Hoover was egged on to write more than he knew in *Forty-Two Years in the White House* (Boston: Houghton Mifflin, 1934). Of limited value are Everett Sanders' paeans to Coolidge and himself in *Saturday Evening Post*, "The Secretary to the President," 203 (December 6 and 20, 1930, February 28, 1931), and "The Coolidge Character," 205 (June 17, 1933). Of greater usefulness is Sanders' edition of "Last Letters of Calvin Coolidge," *Saturday Evening Post*, 205 (March 25, 1933). Wilson Brown, "Aide to Four Presidents," *American Heritage*, VI (February, 1955), contains an interesting account of Coolidge at sea.

A number of biographical and autobiographical works bearing on Coolidge's relations with the Senate are helpful. Able studies of Senate critics of the President are Harry Barnard, *Independent Man: The Life of Senator James Couzens* (New York: Scribner's, 1958);

J. Leonard Bates, "Senator Walsh of Montana, 1918–1924: A Liberal Under Pressure" (Ph.D. dissertation, University of North Carolina, 1952); Gilbert C. Fite, *Peter Norbeck: Prairie Statesman* (Columbia: University of Missouri, 1948); and Marian C. McKenna, *Borah* (Ann Arbor: University of Michigan, 1961). Views of adversaries are also found in Claudius O. Johnson, *Borah of Idaho* (New York: Longmans, Green, 1936); Walter K. Roberts, "The Political Career of Charles Linza McNary, 1924–1944" (Ph.D. dissertation, University of North Carolina, 1953); the mellowed memoirs of Burton K. Wheeler (written with Paul F. Healy), *Yankee from the West* (Garden City: Doubleday, 1962); and George F. Sparks (ed.), *A Many-Colored Toga, The Diary of Henry Fountain Ashurst* (Tucson: University of Arizona, 1962). Intensely critical of Coolidge are Belle Case La Follette and Fola La Follette, *Robert La Follette*, 2 vols. (New York: Macmillan, 1953); Richard L. Neuberger and Stephen B. Kahn, *Integrity, The Life of George W. Norris* (New York: Vanguard, 1937); and George W. Norris, *Fighting Liberal* (New York: Macmillan, 1945). Views generally sympathetic to Coolidge are contained in Homer E. Socolofsky, *Arthur Capper, Publisher, Politician, and Philanthropist* (Lawrence: University of Kansas, 1962); James E. Watson, *As I Knew Them* (Indianapolis: Bobbs-Merrill, 1936); and in two books by George Wharton Pepper, *Family Quarrels, The President, The Senate, The House* (New York: Baker, Voorhis, 1931), and *Philadelphia Lawyer, An Autobiography* (Philadelphia: Lippincott, 1944).

Relevant published traces of members of the House of Representatives are few. Democrat Sol Bloom, in his *Autobiography* (New York: Putnam's, 1948), and his daughter Vera, in *There's No Place Like Washington* (New York: Putnam's, 1944), write of the Coolidges almost as though no partisan difference existed. Cordell Hull, in his *Memoirs*, 2 vols. (New York: Macmillan, 1948), is almost kind to his opponent in the White House. Among the many things Bascom Timmons neglects, in *Garner of Texas, A Personal History* (New York: Harper, 1948), is Calvin Coolidge. Howard Zinn's splendid *La Guardia in Congress* (Ithaca: Cornell, 1959) is valuable. Less useful on Coolidge is Arthur Mann's tightly focused *La Guardia, A Fighter Against His Times, 1882–1933* (Philadelphia: Lippincott, 1959), the first of three projected volumes on the independent New Yorker.

The memoirs and biographies of the highest echelon of executive officers under Coolidge are plentiful and of considerable value. Paul R. Leach, *That Man Dawes* (Chicago: Reilly & Lee, 1930), is a satisfactory journalistic biography of the Vice President, while Charles G. Dawes, *Notes As Vice President 1928–1929* (Boston: Little, Brown, 1935), reveals almost as much as it obscures about American statecraft in the 1920s. Two perceptive biographical sketches of Coolidge's Secretaries of State are John Chalmers Vinson's "Charles Evans Hughes" and L. Ethan Ellis' "Frank B. Kellogg," which are contained in Norman A. Graebner (ed.), *An Uncertain Tradition: American Secretaries of State in the Twentieth Century* (New York: McGraw-Hill, 1961). Good full-length accounts of the two Cabinet members are Merlo J. Pusey, *Charles Evans Hughes*, 2 vols. (New York: Macmillan, 1951), and David Bryn-Jones, *Frank B. Kellogg* (New York: Putnam's, 1937). Also useful is L. Ethan Ellis, *Frank B. Kellogg and American Foreign Relations, 1925–1929* (New Brunswick: Rutgers, 1961).

Harry M. Daugherty with Thomas Dixon, *The Inside Story of the Harding Tragedy* (New York: Churchill, 1932), is an intriguing lot of special pleading by Coolidge's first Attorney General. Of high quality and abundant detail is Alpheus T. Mason's biography of Daugherty's estimable successor, *Harlan Fiske Stone: Pillar of the Law* (New York: Viking, 1956). Eugene Lyons, *Herbert Hoover* (Garden City: Doubleday, 1964), is overly slick; the discerning reader will find more about the former Secretary of Commerce and Chief Executive in *The Memoirs of Herbert Hoover, The Cabinet and The Presidency, 1920–1933* (New York: Macmillan, 1952). Russell Lord's *The Wallaces of Iowa* (Boston: Houghton Mifflin, 1947) contains an adequate account of Coolidge's first Secretary of Agriculture. Harvey O'Connor's *Mellon's Millions: The Biography of a Fortune* (New York: John Day, 1933) must be used with great care.

Other federal officeholders during Coolidge's Presidency left memoirs or inspired biographies. Outranking them all was William Howard Taft. The standard biography of the former Chief Justice and Chief Executive is Henry F. Pringle, *The Life and Times of William Howard Taft*, 2 vols. (New York: Farrar & Rinehart, 1939). Alpheus T. Mason, *William Howard Taft: Chief Justice* (New York: Simon & Schuster, 1965), of course, concentrates on the 1920s. Of less value, but engrossing reading, is Mark DeWolfe Howe (ed.), *Holmes-Laski Letters, 1916–1935*, 2 vols. (Cambridge: Harvard, 1953). Essential to any study of Coolidge is Harold Nicolson's admirable *Dwight Morrow* (New York: Harcourt, Brace, 1935). In his *Autobiography*, 2 vols. (New York: Farrar & Rinehart, 1935), John Hays Hammond informs, amuses, and pontificates on Coolidge. Hermann Hagedorn's almost adulatory *Leonard Wood* (New York: Harper, 1931) is helpful concerning Wood's governor generalship of the Philippine Islands, although it should be used in conjunction with Garel A. Grunder and William E. Livezey's scholarly *The Philippines and the United States* (Norman: University of Oklahoma, 1951).

Of value is Elting E. Morison's excellent *Turmoil and Tradition: A Study of the Life and Times of Henry L. Stimson* (Boston: Houghton Mifflin, 1960). Reinforcing Morison on Stimson's service in Nicaragua and the Philippines are Richard N. Current, *Secretary Stimson, A Study in Statecraft* (New Brunswick: Rutgers, 1954); Henry L. Stimson, *American Policy in Nicaragua* (New York: Scribner's, 1927); and Henry L. Stimson and McGeorge Bundy, *On Active Service in Peace and War* (New York: Harper, 1948). Important reminiscences of service as ranking career diplomats during the Coolidge Administration are Joseph C. Grew, with Walter Johnson (ed.), *Turbulent Era, A Diplomatic Record of Forty Years, 1904–1945*, 2 vols. (Boston: Houghton Mifflin, 1952), and William Phillips, *Ventures in Diplomacy* (Boston: Beacon, 1952). Too much concerned with their immediate subjects to be of much use to a biographer of Coolidge are Morton Keller's otherwise very good *In Defense of Yesterday, James M. Beck and the Politics of Conservatism 1861–1936* (New York: Coward-McCann, 1958) and T. Bentley Mott's *Myron T. Herrick, Friend of France* (Garden City: Doubleday, Doran, 1929).

A number of other writings of or about people who knew Coolidge are important. Highly personal are the sketches of "The Real Calvin Coolidge," by Mrs. Coolidge and a considerable number of his friends and acquaintances, that appeared in *Good Housekeeping*, C (February, March, April, May, and June, 1935). Willis F. Johnson, *George Harvey, 'A Passionate Patriot'* (Boston: Houghton Mifflin, 1929), is somewhat informative. Studies of two independent Republican leaders are William T. Hutchinson's excellent *Lowden of*

Illinois, 2 vols. (Chicago: University of Chicago, 1957), and M. Nelson McGeary's good but too brief *Gifford Pinchot, Forester, Politician* (Princeton: Princeton, 1960). Among other biographical works worth gleaning are Bernard M. Baruch, *Baruch, The Public Years* (New York: Holt, Rinehart & Winston, 1960); Claude G. Bowers, *Beveridge and The Progressive Era* (New York: Literary Guild, 1932) and *My Life, The Memoirs of Claude Bowers* (New York: Simon & Schuster, 1962); Nicholas Murray Butler, *Across the Busy Years, Recollections and Reflections,* 2 vols. (New York: Scribner's, 1939); Raymond B. Fosdick, *John D. Rockefeller, Jr.— A Portrait* (New York: Harper, 1956); Walter Johnson, *William Allen White's America* (New York: Holt, 1947); Alice Roosevelt Longworth, *Crowded Hours* (New York: Scribner's, 1933); Allan Nevins and Frank E. Hill, *Ford, Expansion and Challenge, 1915– 1933* (New York: Scribner's, 1957); and W. A. Swanberg, *Citizen Hearst* (New York: Scribner's, 1961).

Much of the stuff of America's foreign and military affairs during the Coolidge Administration is found in the myriad of biographies of public officials and in government documents. Yet there are several topical works of importance. A good survey of the operations of the State Department between the two world wars is Dexter Perkins, "The Department of State and American Public Opinion" in Gordon A. Craig and Felix Gilbert (eds.), *The Diplomats, 1919–1939* (Princeton: Princeton, 1953). A penetrating study of the postwar European situation is Hajo Holborn, *The Political Collapse of Europe* (New York: Knopf, 1951). Herbert Feis, *The Diplomacy of the Dollar: First Era, 1919–1932* (Baltimore: Johns Hopkins, 1950), is a challenging guide to the international financial policies of America's government and citizens. George T. Davis, *A Navy Second to None* (New York: Harcourt, Brace, 1940), and Merze Tate, *The United States and Armaments* (Cambridge: Harvard, 1948), contain accounts of armaments questions in America during the 1920s. A fact studded but narrow view of aviation development is Edwin H. Rutkowski, *The Politics of Military Aviation Procurement, 1926–1934* (Columbus: Ohio State University Press). Rodman Paul, *The Abrogation of the Gentlemen's Agreement* (Cambridge: Alpha of Massachusetts, Phi Beta Kappa, 1936), is a balanced account of the fight to incorporate exclusion of Japanese emigrants into the Immigration Act of 1924.

America's interests in Asia during the 1920s are seen through a porthole in Gerald E. Wheeler, *Prelude to Pearl Harbor; the United States Navy and the Far East, 1921–1931* (Columbia: University of Missouri, 1963). Two scholarly works dealing with the Coolidge Administration's policies toward China are Dorothy Borg, *American Policy and the Chinese Revolution* (New York: Macmillan, 1947), and Wesley R. Fishel, *The End of Extraterritoriality in China* (Berkeley: University of California, 1952). Samuel F. Bemis, *The Latin American Policy of the United States* (New York: Harcourt, Brace, 1943), and Alexander DeConde, *Herbert Hoover's Latin-American Policy* (Stanford: Stanford, 1951), provide summaries of the Coolidge Administration's Latin American policies. The tangled history of the Clark Memorandum, America's supposed repudiation of the "right" to meddle in the affairs of Latin American countries, is sketched in Robert H. Ferrell, "Repudiation of a Repudiation," *Journal of American History*, LI (March, 1965). Some useful information can be gleaned on Coolidge and the World Court question from Denna Fleming, *The United States and World Organization* (New York: Columbia, 1938), and Philip C. Jessup, *Elihu Root*, 2 vols. (New York: Dodd, Mead, 1938). Considerably more scholarship and less partiality are found in three works dealing with the background of the Pact of Paris: John E. Stoner's *S. O. Levinson and the Pact of Paris* (Chicago: University of Chicago, 1943); John Chalmers Vinson's *William E. Borah and the Outlawry of War* (Athens: University of Georgia, 1957); and Robert H. Ferrell's splendid *Peace in Their Time, The Origins of the Kellogg-Briand Pact* (New Haven: Yale, 1952).

Topical accounts of the events and politics of the 1920s can contribute to knowledge of Calvin Coolidge. Burl Noggle, *Teapot Dome, Oil and Politics in the 1920's* (Baton Rouge: Louisiana State, 1962), is by far the best study of that episode. The metamorphosis of a regulatory agency into a booster of business is traced in G. Cullom Davis, "The Transformation of the Federal Trade Commission, 1914–1929," *Mississippi Valley Historical Review*, XLIX (December, 1962). James C. Malin's unpublished "A History of the Recent Agricultural Policy of the United States" (1933; a copy is on deposit in the University of Kansas Library) contains a perceptive account of post-World War I farm problems and policies. Other helpful studies are Theodore Saloutos and John D. Hicks, *Agricul-*

tural Discontent in the Middle West, 1900–1939 (Madison: University of Wisconsin, 1951), and James H. Shideler, "Herbert Hoover and the Federal Farm Board Project, 1921–1925," *Mississippi Valley Historical Review*, XLII (March, 1956). There is no sound and balanced investigation of prohibition, although Charles Merz, *The Dry Decade* (Garden City: Doubleday, 1931), and Andrew Sinclair, *Prohibition, the Era of Excess* (Boston: Little, Brown, 1962), are useful and interesting. Of considerable value, despite its partiality, is a book by conservation lobbyist Judson King, *The Conservation Fight* (Washington: Public Affairs, 1959). John Higham, *Strangers in the Land* (New Brunswick: Rutgers, 1955), represents the overly sympathetic approach that characterizes so many American studies of immigration questions. Seldom spotted by tears is Robert A. Divine, *American Immigration Policy, 1924–1952* (New Haven: Yale, 1957). Overinflated but interesting is Robert H. Zieger, "Pinchot and Coolidge: The Politics of the 1923 Anthracite Crisis," *Journal of American History*, LII (December, 1965). Kenneth C. MacKay, *The Progressive Movement of 1924* (New York: Columbia, 1947), is a sound monograph. Two interesting articles that conclude that Coolidge did not want renomination in 1928 are Cyril Clemens and Athern P. Daggett, "Coolidge's 'I do not choose to run': Granite or Putty?" *New England Quarterly*, XVIII (June, 1945), and John L. Blair, "I do not choose to run for President in Nineteen Twenty Eight," *Vermont History*, XXX (July, 1962).

REFERENCES

CHAPTER 1: *Born on the Fourth of July*

1. Claude M. Fuess, *Calvin Coolidge, The Man from Vermont* (Boston, 1940), pp. 10–11.
2. Robert M. Washburn, *Calvin Coolidge, His First Biography* (Boston, 1923), p. 7.
3. Calvin Coolidge, *The Autobiography of Calvin Coolidge* (New York, 1929), p. 12.
4. Mark DeWolfe Howe (ed.), *Holmes-Laski Letters, 1916–1935* (Cambridge, Massachusetts, 1953), I, 673.
5. Washburn, *Calvin Coolidge*, pp. 63–64.
6. Fuess, *Calvin Coolidge*, p. 25.
7. *Ibid.*, p. 30.
8. Ernest C. Carpenter, *The Boyhood Days of President Calvin Coolidge* (Rutland, 1926), p. 25.
9. Fuess, *Calvin Coolidge*, p. 33. Most of the letters written by Coolidge before he was thirty-five and quoted in Fuess' biography are now deposited in the original, or as copies, in the Coolidge Collection of the Forbes Library, Northampton, Massachusetts.
10. *Ibid.*, p. 36.
11. *Ibid.*, p. 38.

CHAPTER 2: *On to Amherst*

1. John Chamberlain, *Farewell to Reform* (reprint of 2nd ed., Gloucester, Massachusetts, 1958), p. 18.
2. Coolidge, *Autobiography*, p. 49.
3. Fuess, *Calvin Coolidge*, p. 48.
4. *Ibid.*, p. 52.
5. Coolidge, *Autobiography*, p. 62.
6. Washburn, *Calvin Coolidge*, pp. 33–34.
7. Coolidge, *Autobiography*, p. 65.
8. Fuess, *Calvin Coolidge*, p. 62.
9. *Ibid.*, p. 69.

CHAPTER 3: *Settling Down in Northampton*

1. Fuess, *Calvin Coolidge*, p. 67.
2. *Daily Hampshire Gazette*, August 5, 1896.
3. Fuess, *Calvin Coolidge*, p. 85.
4. Coolidge, *Autobiography*, p. 91.
5. Fuess, *Calvin Coolidge*, p. 90.
6. William Allen White, *Puritan in Babylon, The Story of Calvin Coolidge* (New York, 1938), p. 60.
7. Alfred P. Dennis, *Gods and Little Fishes* (Indianapolis, 1931), p. 120.
8. Ishbel Ross, *Grace Coolidge and Her Era* (New York, 1962), p. 9.
9. Fuess, *Calvin Coolidge*, p. 88.
10. Ross, *Grace Coolidge*, p. 16.
11. *Ibid.*, p. 17.
12. Coolidge, *Autobiography*, p. 93.

CHAPTER 4: *The Less He Spoke, the More He Heard*

1. Oral History Research Office, Columbia University, Claude M. Fuess transcript, p. 54.
2. Fuess, *Calvin Coolidge*, p. 89.
3. Ross, *Grace Coolidge*, p. 26.
4. White, *Puritan in Babylon*, p. 82.
5. Michael E. Hennessy, *Four Decades of Massachusetts Politics, 1890–1935* (Norwood, Massachusetts, 1935), p. 61.
6. Solomon B. Griffin, *W. Murray Crane, A Man and Brother* (Boston, 1926), p. 104.

7. Hearst picked Hisgen to be the Independence League's candidate for President in 1908, but the Massachusetts man polled only a few thousand votes more nationally than when he had run for governor the previous year.

8. White, *Puritan in Babylon*, p. 85.

9. Massachusetts State Library, Boston, "Speeches and messages of Calvin Coolidge 1895–July 25, 1924" (TS.), especially inaugural speech of January 2, 1911. See also, Coolidge, *Autobiography*, p. 101; Fuess, *Calvin Coolidge*, pp. 106–7; Lawrence E. Wikander, "Calvin Coolidge," in Tercentenary History Commission, *The Northampton Book* (Northampton, 1954), p. 297.

CHAPTER 5: *Senator Coolidge*

1. Hennessy, *Massachusetts Politics*, p. 180.
2. Coolidge, *Autobiography*, p. 104.
3. White, *Puritan in Babylon*, p. 101.
4. *Ibid.*, p. 102.
5. Washburn, *Calvin Coolidge*, p. 59.
6. Ross, *Grace Coolidge*, p. 36.
7. *Ibid.*, and Fuess, *Calvin Coolidge*, p. 478.
8. Coolidge, *Autobiography*, p. 99.
9. *Ibid.*, p. 101.

CHAPTER 6: *Do the Day's Work*

1. Coolidge, *Autobiography*, p. 105.
2. *Ibid.*
3. Calvin Coolidge, *Have Faith in Massachusetts* (Boston, 1919), pp. 3–8.
4. Coolidge, *Autobiography*, p. 108.
5. Washburn, *Calvin Coolidge*, p. 138.
6. Fuess, *Calvin Coolidge*, p. 122.
7. Joseph Martin, *My First Fifty Years in Politics* (New York, 1960), pp. 39–40.
8. Alpheus T. Mason, *Brandeis, A Free Man's Life* (New York, 1946), p. 174.

CHAPTER 7: *Lieutenant Governor*

1. Coolidge, *Autobiography*, p. 111.
2. Perhaps out of esteem for Coolidge, perhaps out of fear of his run-

ning for lieutenant governor, some Democrats and Republicans in 1915 approached Governor Walsh to ask that he appoint the senate president to the public service commission. Coolidge was not considered because the governor was unwilling to put another Republican on the commission. See Coolidge Collection, Forbes Library (hereinafter identified as CFL), David I. Walsh to Frank Buxton, July 29, 1938.

3. Boston *Herald*, July 29, 1920.
4. Coolidge MSS., Amherst College Library (hereinafter identified as CACL), Coolidge to Frank W. Stearns, n.d., 1915.
5. *Ibid.*
6. Hennessy, *Massachusetts Politics*, p. 223.
7. White, *Puritan in Babylon*, p. 123.
8. Coolidge, *Autobiography*, p. 116.
9. CACL, Coolidge to Frank W. Stearns, n.d.
10. Frank W. Stearns MSS., Holy Cross College Library, Stearns to Dwight Morrow, January 8, 1919.
11. John Hays Hammond, *The Autobiography of John Hays Hammond* (New York, 1935), II, 694–95.

CHAPTER 8: *We Must Steadily Advance*

1. Coolidge, *Autobiography*, p. 121.
2. CACL, Coolidge to Frank Stearns, n.d., 1918.
3. Coolidge, *Have Faith in Massachusetts*, pp. 161–63.
4. George C. S. Benson, *The Administration of the Civil Service in Massachusetts* (Cambridge, 1935), p. 36.
5. Coolidge, *Have Faith in Massachusetts*, pp. 256–57.
6. *Ibid.*, pp. 172–73.

CHAPTER 9: *When Firmness Was Needed*

1. Sherwin L. Cook, *Torchlight Parade, Our Presidential Pageant* (New York, 1929), p. 225.
2. Robert K. Murray, *Red Scare* (Minneapolis, 1955), p. 123.
3. *Ibid.*, p. 124.
4. Henry G. Pearson, *Son of New England, James Jackson Storrow* (Boston, 1932), p. 231. For the Storrow Committee's official report, see *Report of Committee Appointed by Mayor Peters to Consider the Police Situation*. City Document 108 (Boston, 1919).
5. Coolidge, *Autobiography*, p. 128.
6. Coolidge, *Have Faith in Massachusetts*, pp. 198, 206.

7. Coolidge, *Autobiography*, p. 128.
8. Pearson, *Son of New England*, pp. 232–33. Francis Russell tells interesting, but questionable story that Monday night, after Cool had conferred with Storrow and Peters, the governor discovered his adjutant general had ordered the only mounted squadron of State Guard to assemble. Coolidge was irate about such orders b given and he went to the Commonwealth Armory to dismiss guardsmen. As the governor was leaving the armory, Mayor P arrived and began accusing him of one thing and another. Coo quacked, "You have no business here," whereupon Peters pun him in the left eye. The governor supposedly wore a shiner the of the week. See "The Strike That Made a President," *Ame Heritage*, XIV (October, 1963), p. 91.
9. White, *Puritan in Babylon*, p. 156.
10. Cook, *Torchlight Parade*, p. 231.
11. Fuess, *Calvin Coolidge*, p. 220. For Commissioner Curtis' o report on the strike, see Boston, Police Commissioner, *Fourt Annual Report*. Public Document 49 (Boston, 1919).
12. Coolidge, *Autobiography*, p. 128.
13. The governor summarized what had been done to contain di in Boston in CFL, Coolidge to Admiral Dunn, September 12, 1c
14. White, *Puritan in Babylon*, p. 164.
15. Coolidge, *Have Faith in Massachusetts*, pp. 219, 221.
16. White, *Puritan in Babylon*, p. 164.
17. It is ironical that years later two of the principals in the strike James J. Storrow and Calvin Coolidge, reversed their origina tions. In 1923 Storrow wrote that he had come to believe that Co by waiting to turn out the Guard, had allowed the public "to understand the issue." Coolidge in 1929, however, wrote, "' always felt that I should have called out the State Guard as s the police left their posts." See Pearson, *Son of New Englan* 234–35; and Coolidge, *Autobiography*, p. 130.
18. New York *Times*, September 12, 1919.
19. *Congressional Record*, 66th Congress, 1st Session, Part 6, p
20. Murray, *Red Scare*, p. 130.
21. Washburn, *Calvin Coolidge*, p. 141.
22. Coolidge, *Have Faith in Massachusetts*, pp. 222–23.

CHAPTER 10: *The Most Popular Figure in the State*

1. Coolidge, *Autobiography*, p. 134.
2. Coolidge, *Have Faith in Massachusetts*, pp. 225–27.

3. *Ibid.*, pp. 243–48.
4. *Ibid.*, p. 263.
5. CFL, Coolidge to Edwin A. Grozier, October 25, 1919.
6. Hennessy, *Massachusetts Politics*, p. 290.
7. On his 1921 income tax statement, Coolidge reported receiving interest and dividends amounting to $1,194, which would indicate, given the probable yield rate of his investments, a fortune of between $25,000 and $30,000. It is unlikely that he was worth more than $15,000 when he was elected governor in 1918. See CFL, Massachusetts State Income Tax Statement of Calvin Coolidge, 1921.
8. Ross, *Grace Coolidge*, p. 51.
9. *Ibid.*, p. 52.
10. Gamaliel Bradford, *The Quick and the Dead* (Boston, 1931), p. 241.
11. White, *Puritan in Babylon*, p. 150.
12. Margaret Long (ed.), *The Journal of John D. Long* (Rindge, New Hampshire, 1956), p. 169. An artifact of Coolidge's brevity is a letter, preserved in the Coolidge Collection of Holy Cross College Library, which he wrote Frank Stearns' daughter-in-law in recognition of her hospitality. In its entirety the letter reads:

April 30 1918

MY DEAR MRS. STEARNS:—
Thank you.

Cordially
CALVIN COOLIDGE

To Mrs. Foster Stearns

CHAPTER 11: *Nomination to Some Other Office?*

1. Stearns MSS., Stearns to Dwight Morrow, January 8, 1919.
2. Stearns MSS., Morrow to Stearns, January 9, 1919.
3. CFL, Coolidge to Morrow, March 10, 1920.
4. Stearns MSS., Stearns to William M. Butler, October 10, 1919.
5. Stearns MSS., Stearns to Dwight Morrow, January 8, 1919.
6. Hermann Hagedorn, *Leonard Wood* (New York, 1931), II, 327.
7. See Henry Cabot Lodge, *Selections from the Correspondence of Theodore Roosevelt and Henry Cabot Lodge, 1884–1918* (New York, 1925), II, 540; and Calvin Coolidge, *Messages to the General Court, Official Addresses, Proclamations and State Papers* (Boston, 1920), p. 38.
8. John A. Garraty, *Henry Cabot Lodge* (New York, 1953), p. 351.

9. Coolidge, *Messages to the General Court*, p. 44.
10. "Joint Debate on the Covenant of Paris," *League of Nations* (April, 1919), II, 49, 64, 90; and Cook, *Torchlight Parade*, p. 235.
11. CFL, Coolidge to Dwight Morrow, April 3, 1919.
12. Garraty, *Lodge*, p. 391.
13. Karl Schriftgiesser, *The Gentleman from Massachusetts: Henry Cabot Lodge* (Boston, 1944), p. 353.
14. Cook, *Torchlight Parade*, p. 234.
15. White, *Puritan in Babylon*, p. 169.
16. William T. Hutchinson, *Lowden of Illinois* (Chicago, 1957), II, 411–12.
17. Fuess, *Calvin Coolidge*, p. 249.
18. Harold Nicolson, *Dwight Morrow* (New York, 1935), pp. 232–33.

CHAPTER 12: *"Coolidge! Coolidge!"*

1. *Official Report of the Proceedings of the Seventeenth Republican National Convention* (New York, 1920), pp. 96–97.
2. Wesley M. Bagby, *The Road to Normalcy* (Baltimore, 1962), p. 81.
3. Massachusetts State Library, "Statements of Calvin Coolidge . . . Jan. 13, 1919–Jan. 5, 1921" (Typescript), pp. 61–62.
4. *Seventeenth Republican National Convention*, p. 150.
5. Bagby, *Road to Normalcy*, p. 85.
6. Coolidge, *Autobiography*, p. 148.
7. Henry L. Stoddard, *As I Knew Them* (New York, 1927), p. 467.
8. *Seventeenth Republican National Convention*, p. 226.
9. See Ross, *Grace Coolidge*, p. 55; White, *Puritan in Babylon*, p. 214; and Fuess, *Calvin Coolidge*, pp. 264–65.

CHAPTER 13: *Something More than a Landslide*

1. Will H. Hays, *The Memoirs of Will H. Hays* (Garden City, New York, 1955), p. 262.
2. Louis C. Hatch and Earl L. Shoup, *A History of the Vice-Presidency of the United States* (New York, 1934), p. 378.
3. *Seventeenth Republican National Convention*, pp. 275–82.
4. Bagby, *Road to Normalcy*, p. 124.
5. Frank Freidel, *Franklin D. Roosevelt, The Ordeal* (Boston, 1954), p. 86.
6. Bagby, *Road to Normalcy*, p. 133.
7. Warren G. Harding MSS., Ohio Historical Society, Coolidge to

Harding, October 5, 1920; and CFL, Coolidge to Will H. Hays, October 5, 1920.

8. Griffin, W. *Murray Crane*, p. 152.
9. Coolidge, *Autobiography*, p. 152.
10. Karl Schriftgiesser, *This Was Normalcy* (Boston, 1948), pp. 59–60.
11. Bagby, *Road to Normalcy*, p. 131.
12. J. Joseph Huthmacher, *Massachusetts People and Politics, 1919–1933* (Cambridge, Massachusetts, 1959), p. 37.
13. Fuess, *Calvin Coolidge*, p. 273.
14. Arthur S. Link, "What Happened to the Progressive Movement in the 1920's?" *American Historical Review*, LXIV (July, 1959), p. 849.

CHAPTER 14: *A Capital Character*

1. Vice President Coolidge was in March, 1921, formally invited to be present at Cabinet sessions. See Harding MSS., Harding to Coolidge, March 7, 1921.
2. *Congressional Record*, 67th Congress, Special Session, Part I, p. 3.
3. Hatch and Shoup, *A History of the Vice-Presidency*, p. 85.
4. Coolidge, *Autobiography*, p. 162.
5. Duff Gilfond, *The Rise of Saint Calvin* (New York, 1932), p. 151.
6. Coolidge, *Autobiography*, p. 162.
7. Russell Lord, *The Wallaces of Iowa* (Boston, 1947), p. 222.
8. *Congressional Record*, 67th Congress, 1st Session, Part 4, p. 3856.
9. White, *Puritan in Babylon*, p. 232.
10. Coolidge, *Autobiography*, p. 164.
11. Harry M. Daugherty with Thomas Dixon, *The Inside Story of the Harding Tragedy* (New York, 1932), p. 278.
12. Merlo J. Pusey, *Charles Evans Hughes* (New York, 1951), II, 426.
13. The present author has found no direct evidence to support Claude M. Fuess' statement on page 288 of his *Calvin Coolidge* that "Harding had great confidence in Coolidge, consulted him frequently, and was influenced by him to a marked degree." In fact, the papers and memoirs of Harding, Coolidge, and other Republican leaders during the early 1920s indicate that the relationship between the Chief Executive and the Vice President, though friendly, was not close.
14. CACL, Grace Coolidge to Frank W. Stearns, March 20, 1921.
15. Fuess, *Calvin Coolidge*, p. 300.
16. Nicholas Murray Butler, *Across the Busy Years, Recollections and Reflections* (New York, 1939), I, 356.
17. CACL, Grace Coolidge to Frank W. Stearns, July 7, 1921.
18. CACL, Grace Coolidge to Frank W. Stearns, May 25, 1921.

19. See CFL, Massachusetts State Income Tax Statements of Calvin Coolidge, 1921 through 1928, and statements of First National Bank, Northampton, and Hampshire County Trust Company to Calvin Coolidge, 1921 and 1922.

CHAPTER 15: *Vice President of What?*

1. Gilfond, *Saint Calvin*, p. 134.
2. Hutchinson, *Frank O. Lowden*, II, 487.
3. CACL, Coolidge to Frank W. Stearns, n.d., 1921.
4. Gilfond, *Saint Calvin*, p. 152.
5. George W. Pepper, *Philadelphia Lawyer, An Autobiography* (Philadelphia, 1944), p. 202.

CHAPTER 16: *To Wake Up a President*

1. Schriftgiesser, *Gentleman from Massachusetts*, p. 359.
2. Fuess, *Calvin Coolidge*, p. 311; Ross, *Grace Coolidge*, p. 81; White, *Puritan in Babylon*, p. 241; and Charles M. Wilson, "Lamplight Inauguration," *American Heritage*, XV (December, 1963), pp. 80–86.
3. Pusey, *Charles Evans Hughes*, II, 563–64.
4. Ross, *Grace Coolidge*, p. 82.
5. Coolidge, *Autobiography*, p. 177.
6. George F. Sparks (ed.), *A Many-Colored Toga, The Diary of Henry Fountain Ashurst* (Tucson, 1962), p. 223.
7. James E. Pollard, *The Presidents and the Press* (New York, 1947), pp. 714–15.
8. Guy B. Hathorn, "The Political Career of C. Bascom Slemp," unpublished Ph.D. dissertation, Duke University, 1950, pp. 194 and 196.
9. Theodore Roosevelt, Jr., MSS., Library of Congress, Diary, August 3, 1923.
10. Pepper, *Autobiography*, p. 196.
11. Willis Fletcher Johnson, *George Harvey, 'A Passionate Patriot'* (Boston, 1929), p. 396.

CHAPTER 17: *Different from the Rest*

1. William Allen White, *Calvin Coolidge, The Man Who Is President* (New York, 1925), p. 6.
2. Earle W. Newton, *The Vermont Story, 1749–1949* (Montpelier, 1949), p. vi.

3. Irwin Hood Hoover, *Forty-Two Years in the White House* (Boston, 1934), p. 251.
4. Coolidge, *Have Faith in Massachusetts*, pp. 200–01.
5. Fuess, *Calvin Coolidge*, p. 358.
6. David Bryn-Jones, *Frank B. Kellogg* (New York, 1937), p. 131.
7. White, *Puritan in Babylon*, p. 247.
8. Alice Roosevelt Longworth, *Crowded Hours* (New York, 1933), pp. 324–25.
9. Washburn, *Calvin Coolidge*, pp. 146–47.
10. Edmund W. Starling as told to Thomas Sugrue, *Starling of the White House* (New York, 1946), p. 208.
11. Fuess, *Calvin Coolidge*, p. 5.
12. Ross, *Grace Coolidge*, p. 65.
13. C. Bascom Slemp, *The Mind of the President* (Garden City, N.Y., 1926), p. 5.
14. Vera Bloom, *There's No Place Like Washington* (New York, 1944), p. 20.
15. Fuess, *Calvin Coolidge*, p. 300.
16. CFL, Grace Coolidge to Mrs. Reuben B. Hills, August 5, 1923.
17. Oral History Research Office, Columbia University, Claude M. Fuess transcript, p. 72; and Fuess, *Calvin Coolidge*, p. 490.
18. Ross, *Grace Coolidge*, p. 65.
19. *Ibid.*, p. 100.
20. Starling, *Starling of the White House*, p. 213.
21. *Ibid.*, p. 208.
22. Hammond, *Autobiography*, II, 694.
23. George H. Mayer, *The Republican Party, 1854–1964* (New York, 1964), p. 390.

CHAPTER 18: *A Man Among Men*

1. Longworth, *Crowded Hours*, p. 337.
2. Pusey, *Charles Evans Hughes*, II, 565.
3. Coolidge MSS., Library of Congress (hereinafter identified as CLC), *e.g.*, Coolidge to W. C. Allen, September 24, 1923.
4. Hammond, *Autobiography*, II, 695.
5. Cordell Hull, *The Memoirs of Cordell Hull* (New York, 1948), I, 127.
6. Coolidge, *Autobiography*, p. 184.
7. Howard H. Quint and Robert H. Ferrell (eds.), *The Talkative President: The Off-the-Record Press Conferences of Calvin Coolidge* (Amherst, 1964), p. 9.

8. Only Secretaries James J. Davis and Andrew W. Mellon and Post-master General Harry S. New remained in the Cabinet throughout Coolidge's years as President. Secretary of State Hughes was succeeded by Frank B. Kellogg in March, 1925. The ailing Secretary of War John W. Weeks was replaced by Dwight F. Davis in October, 1925. Navy Secretary Denby's place was taken by Curtis D. Wilbur in March, 1924. After Harry M. Daugherty was removed in March, 1924, Harlan F. Stone became attorney general until March, 1925, when John Garibaldi Sargent was appointed to the post. Secretary of the Interior Hubert Work was succeeded by Roy O. West in July, 1928. Following the death of Secretary Wallace in October, 1924, Howard M. Gore, until March, 1925, and then William M. Jardine headed the Department of Agriculture. An old Coolidge friend, William F. Whiting, took Herbert Hoover's place as secretary of commerce in August, 1928.

9. Herbert Hoover, *The Memoirs of Herbert Hoover, the Cabinet and the Presidency, 1920–1933* (New York, 1952), p. 55.

10. William M. Jardine MSS., Library of Congress, James J. Davis to Jardine, January 21, 1929.

11. Pusey, *Charles Evans Hughes*, II, 565.

12. Henry F. Pringle, *The Life and Times of William Howard Taft* (New York, 1939), II, 1019.

13. *Ibid.*, p. 1062.

14. See CLC, files 209–209K.

15. Pepper, *Autobiography*, p. 196.

16. M. Nelson McGeary, *Gifford Pinchot, Forester, Politician* (Princeton, 1960), p. 309.

CHAPTER 19: *Man of the World*

1. Hammond, *Autobiography*, II, 752.

2. Quint and Ferrell, *The Talkative President*, p. 228.

3. William Phillips, *Ventures in Diplomacy* (Boston, 1952), p. 119.

4. Quint and Ferrell, *The Talkative President*, p. 255.

5. Burton K. Wheeler with Paul F. Healy, *Yankee from the West* (Garden City, N.Y., 1962), p. 205.

6. Pusey, *Charles Evans Hughes*, II, 527.

7. *Congressional Record*, 68th Congress, 1st Session, Part 1, p. 97.

8. *Papers Relating to the Foreign Relations of the United States, 1923* (Washington, 1938), II, 788. See also CLC, Charles Evans Hughes to Coolidge, December 18, 1923. Secretary Hughes had reports and documents that proved to his satisfaction that Russia, however unsuccessfully, was continuing to foment revolution in the United States.

See *Foreign Relations*, 1923, II, 788–92; CLC, Hughes to Coolidge, August 17, 1923, December 19, 1923; and Theodore Roosevelt, Jr., MSS., Library of Congress, Diary, December 6, 1923.

9. Dexter Perkins, "The Department of State and American Public Opinion," in Gordon A. Craig and Felix Gilbert (eds.), *The Diplomats, 1919–1939* (Princeton, 1953), p. 285.

10. Hull, *Memoirs*, I, 123.

11. See Theodore Roosevelt, Jr., MSS., Library of Congress, Diary, August 7, 1923, and "International Court" Addendum.

12. Phillips, *Ventures in Diplomacy*, p. 119.

13. Quint and Ferrell, *The Talkative President*, p. 151.

14. John E. Stoner, *S. O. Levinson and the Pact of Paris* (Chicago, 1943), p. 124.

15. Quint and Ferrell, *The Talkative President*, p. 176.

16. *Congressional Record*, 68th Congress, 1st Session, Part 1, p. 97.

17. *Ibid.*

18. Joseph C. Grew and Walter Johnson (ed.), *Turbulent Era, A Diplomatic Record of 40 Years, 1904–1945* (Boston, 1952), I, 627.

19. Bryn-Jones, *Frank B. Kellogg*, p. 155.

CHAPTER 20: *A President Approaches Congress*

1. Herbert Hoover, *Memoirs, 1920–1933*, pp. 55–56.

2. W. E. Binkley, *The Powers of the President* (Garden City, N.Y., 1937), p. 244.

3. Quint and Ferrell, *The Talkative President*, pp. 89–90.

4. Irwin Hoover, *Forty-Two Years*, p. 127.

5. Coolidge, *Autobiography*, pp. 228–29.

6. Gilbert C. Fite, *Peter Norbeck: Prairie Statesman* (Columbia, Mo., 1948), pp. 114–15.

7. *Congressional Record*, 68th Congress, 1st Session, Part 1, pp. 96–100.

8. *Ibid.*, pp. 212–14.

CHAPTER 21: *Troubles down the Road*

1. Quint and Ferrell, *The Talkative President*, pp. 55, 59.

2. *Ibid.*, pp. 59–60.

3. *Ibid.*, p. 61.

4. New York *Herald Tribune*, January 27, 1924.

5. *Congressional Record*, 68th Congress, 1st Session, Part 2, p. 1541.

6. New York *Times*, February 9, 1924.
7. Belle Case La Follette and Fola La Follette, *Robert M. La Follette* (New York, 1953), II, 1094.
8. Claudius O. Johnson, *Borah of Idaho* (New York, 1936), p. 287.
9. Slemp, *The Mind of the President*, pp. 86–87.
10. Burl Noggle, *Teapot Dome, Oil and Politics in the 1920's* (Baton Rouge, 1962), p. 117.
11. C. O. Johnson, *Borah of Idaho*, p. 288.
12. Marian C. McKenna, *Borah* (Ann Arbor, 1961), p. 202; and C. O. Johnson, *Borah of Idaho*, p. 289.
13. Pusey, *Charles Evans Hughes*, II, 565.
14. Pringle, *William Howard Taft*, II, 1020.
15. White, *Puritan in Babylon*, pp. 267–68.
16. Wheeler, *Yankee from the West*, p. 218.
17. Noggle, *Teapot Dome*, p. 125.
18. Daugherty, *The Inside Story*, p. 288.
19. *Congressional Record*, 68th Congress, 1st Session, Part 4, p. 3309.
20. CLC, Coolidge to Harry M. Daugherty, March 27, 1924.
21. Hathorn, "C. Bascom Slemp," p. 212.
22. Noggle, *Teapot Dome*, p. 131.
23. *Ibid.*, and *Congressional Record*, 68th Congress, 1st Session, Part 4, p. 3681.
24. Noggle, *Teapot Dome*, p. 132.
25. *Congressional Record*, 68th Congress, 1st Session, Part 4, pp. 3614, 3695.
26. *Ibid.*, p. 3694.

CHAPTER 22: *Frustrated in Congress*

1. Wheeler, *Yankee from the West*, pp. 275–76.
2. Harry Barnard, *Independent Man: The Life of Senator James Couzens* (New York, 1958), p. 162.
3. *Ibid.*, p. 163.
4. *Ibid.*
5. *Congressional Record*, 68th Congress, 1st Session, Part 6, p. 6087.
6. File 44 in the Coolidge Papers in the Library of Congress indicates, though does not prove, that President Coolidge in 1923 had asked Henry Ford not to withdraw his bid for Muscle Shoals.
7. Richard L. Neuberger and Stephen B. Kahn, *Integrity, the Life of George W. Norris* (New York, 1937), p. 209.
8. Rodman W. Paul, *The Abrogation of the Gentlemen's Agreement* (Cambridge, Mass., 1936), pp. 77–78.

9. Quint and Ferrell, *The Talkative President*, p. 92.
10. George H. Haynes, *The Senate of the United States* (Boston, 1938), II, 650.
11. *Congressional Record*, 68th Congress, 1st Session, Part 9, pp. 8660–8661.
12. Ironically, Congress failed to appropriate funds for administration of the Adjusted Compensation Act. Coolidge, feeling obliged to carry out Congress' wishes and perhaps trying not to irk the veterans further, juggled funds from the Veterans Bureau so that the War and Navy departments could process applications for compensation promptly. See CLC, Coolidge to John W. Weeks, June 13, 1924.
13. Fite, *Peter Norbeck*, p. 112.
14. Wheeler, *Yankee from the West*, p. 205.
15. Quint and Ferrell, *The Talkative President*, pp. 119–20.

CHAPTER 23: *Nomination for President*

1. Calvin Coolidge, *Autobiography*, p. 188.
2. Hathorn, "C. Bascom Slemp," p. 197.
3. Hutchinson, *Lowden of Illinois*, II, 534.
4. Fite, *Peter Norbeck*, p. 114.
5. Pusey, *Charles Evans Hughes*, II, 568.
6. Pringle, *William Howard Taft*, II, 1060–61.
7. Theodore Roosevelt, Jr., MSS., Library of Congress, Diary, June 10, 11, 12, 1924.
8. *Official Report of the Proceedings of the Eighteenth Republican National Convention* (New York, 1924), p. 151.
9. William Allen White, *Politics: The Citizen's Business* (New York, 1924), p. 35.
10. Hutchinson, *Lowden of Illinois*, II, 536.
11. Butler, *Across the Busy Years*, p. 282.
12. C. O. Johnson, *Borah of Idaho*, pp. 300–01.
13. Claude G. Bowers, *Beveridge and the Progressive Era* (New York, 1932), p. 539.
14. Hutchinson, *Lowden of Illinois*, II, 539.

CHAPTER 24: *The Campaign of 1924*

1. Kenneth C. MacKay, *The Progressive Movement of 1924* (New York, 1947), p. 16.

2. White, *Politics*, pp. 308–09.
3. White, *Puritan in Babylon*, p. 308.
4. Coolidge, *Autobiography*, p. 190.
5. *Ibid.*
6. Starling, *Starling of the White House*, p. 224.
7. Oswald Garrison Villard, *Fighting Years* (New York, 1939), pp. 497–98.
8. Quint and Ferrell, *The Talkative President*, p. 10.
9. *Ibid.*
10. Pringle, *William Howard Taft*, II, 1061.
11. James W. Wadsworth MSS., Library of Congress, Wadsworth to G. D. B. Hasbrouck, August 20, 1924.
12. Ross, *Grace Coolidge*, pp. 131–32.
13. Charles G. Dawes, *Notes as Vice President, 1928–1929* (Boston, 1935), p. 24.
14. Howard Zinn, *La Guardia in Congress* (Ithaca, 1959), p. 87.
15. Dawes, *Notes*, p. 32.
16. Willis Johnson, *George Harvey*, p. ix.
17. Paul R. Leach, *That Man Dawes* (Chicago, 1930), pp. 232–34.
18. Wheeler, *Yankee from the West*, pp. 254, 263.
19. MacKay, *The Progressive Movement*, p. 162.
20. B. C. and F. La Follette, *Robert M. La Follette*, II, 1120–21.
21. MacKay, *The Progressive Movement*, p. 165.
22. Arthur Garfield Hays, *City Lawyer* (New York, 1942), p. 270.
23. Malcolm Moos (ed.), *A Carnival of Buncombe* (Baltimore, 1956), p. 97.
24. Oral History Research Office, Columbia University, John W. Davis transcript, p. 150.
25. Alpheus T. Mason, *Harlan Fiske Stone: Pillar of the Law* (New York, 1956), p. 163.
26. Harvey O'Connor, *Mellon's Millions: The Biography of a Fortune* (New York, 1933), pp. 162–63.
27. Charles M. Thomas, *Thomas Riley Marshall, Hoosier Statesman* (Oxford, Ohio, 1939), p. 191.
28. Quint and Ferrell, *The Talkative President*, p. 9.
29. Stoddard, *As I Knew Them*, p. 13.
30. Grew, *Turbulent Era*, I, 641.
31. Morton Keller, *In Defense of Yesterday, James M. Beck and the Politics of Conservatism, 1861–1936* (New York, 1958), p. 165.
32. Howe (ed.), *Holmes-Laski Letters*, I, 671.
33. Bowers, *Beveridge*, p. 540.
34. McGeary, *Gifford Pinchot*, p. 315.

CHAPTER 25: *Overture to a Second Term*

1. *Congressional Record,* 69th Congress, Special Session, Part 1, p. 3.
2. Sparks (ed.), *The Diary of Henry Fountain Ashurst,* p. 228.
3. *Congressional Record,* 69th Congress, Special Session, Part 1, p. 7.
4. Pepper, *Autobiography,* p. 168.
5. Elihu Root MSS., Library of Congress, Coolidge to Root, November 12, 1924.
6. Quint and Ferrell, *The Talkative President,* p. 92.
7. Fite, *Peter Norbeck,* p. 117.
8. Sol Bloom, *The Autobiography of Sol Bloom* (New York, 1948), p. 212.
9. George W. Norris, *Fighting Liberal* (New York, 1945), p. 222.
10. Dawes, *Notes,* p. 33.
11. *Congressional Record,* 68th Congress, 2nd Session, Part 4, pp. 3666–68.

CHAPTER 26: *Congress and Administration*

1. Homer E. Socolofsky, *Arthur Capper, Publisher, Politician, and Philanthropist* (Lawrence, Kansas, 1962), p. 154.
2. Mason, *Harlan Fiske Stone,* p. 198.
3. White, *Puritan in Babylon,* p. 321.
4. Joseph P. Harris, *The Advice and Consent of the Senate* (Berkeley, 1953), p. 122.
5. *Ibid.,* p. 260.
6. Quint and Ferrell, *The Talkative President,* p. 94.
7. The progressive Republicans were responsible for frustrating Coolidge's appointment of Warren. Senators Brookhart, Couzens, Frazier, Ladd, McMaster, Norbeck, and Norris voted against confirmation of Warren as attorney general on all three roll calls (La Follette, who was ill, returned to the Senate to join the opposition to Warren on March 18), thereby tipping the scales. *Congressional Record,* 69th Congress, Special Session, Part 1, pp. 101–02, 275.
8. CLC, Coolidge to John Garibaldi Sargent, March 17, 1925.
9. Pusey, *Charles Evans Hughes,* II, 613.
10. CLC, Coolidge to Charles Evans Hughes, January 10, 1925.
11. Bryn-Jones, *Frank B. Kellogg,* pp. 166–67.
12. Quint and Ferrell, *The Talkative President,* p. 11.
13. Starling, *Starling of the White House,* p. 209.
14. Ross, *Grace Coolidge,* p. 214.

15. Pepper, *Autobiography*, p. 202.
16. Henry L. Stimson and McGeorge Bundy, *On Active Service in Peace and War* (New York, 1948), p. 111.

CHAPTER 27: *A Restless Man*

1. Herbert Hoover, *Memoirs, 1920–1933*, p. 55.
2. Starling, *Starling of the White House*, p. 219.
3. Mayer, *The Republican Party*, p. 391.
4. Bradford, *The Quick and the Dead*, p. 223.
5. Claude M. Fuess said in his reminiscences (given in 1962) that Coolidge suffered a heart attack, probably in 1925, while in the White House. Dr. Fuess presented no evidence to support his statement, and the present author has found none. Indeed it might be recalled that in Dr. Fuess' biography of Coolidge he wrote that Dr. Edward Brown, the former President's Northampton physician, found no sign of heart trouble. See Claude M. Fuess transcript, Oral History Research Office, Columbia University, p. 78, and Fuess, *Calvin Coolidge*, p. 458.
6. Moos (ed.), *A Carnival of Buncombe*, pp. 123–24.
7. Russell Lord, *The Wallaces of Iowa*, p. 253.
8. Pepper, *Autobiography*, p. 160.
9. Irwin Hoover, *Forty-Two Years*, p. 322.
10. Nicolson, *Dwight Morrow*, p. 271.
11. White, *Puritan in Babylon*, pp. vi-vii.
12. Ross, *Grace Coolidge*, p. 229.
13. Butler, *Across the Busy Years*, p. 413.
14. Bradford, *The Quick and the Dead*, p. 227.
15. *Ibid.*, p. 228.
16. *Congressional Record*, 69th Congress, 1st Session, Part 4, p. 4372.
17. *Ibid.*, Part 11, p. 13069.
18. Grew, *Turbulent Era*, I, 660.
19. Vera Bloom, *There's No Place Like Washington*, p. 21. Senator James W. Wadsworth identified the lady as his wife. The way the senator told the story, Mrs. Wadsworth told Coolidge at a reception: "Mr. President, that was a splendid speech you made up in the hall of the House of Representatives today. I was so glad to hear it! Indeed, I was so glad to hear it, that I didn't mind standing up during the whole thing." "Yes," said Coolidge, "I stood up myself, how do you do?" James W. Wadsworth transcript, Oral History Research Office, Columbia University, p. 336.
20. Ross, *Grace Coolidge*, p. 156.

21. Claude G. Bowers, *My Life, The Memoirs of Claude G. Bowers* (New York, 1962), pp. 136–37.
22. White, *Puritan in Babylon*, p. x.
23. Starling, *Starling of the White House*, pp. 211–12.
24. Coolidge, *Autobiography*, p. 192.
25. Ross, *Grace Coolidge*, pp. 216–17.
26. Bradford, *The Quick and the Dead*, p. 243.
27. Fuess, *Calvin Coolidge*, p. 373.
28. Record Group 87, United States Secret Service, Protection of the President File, National Archives, Richard Jervis to W. H. Moran, n.d. (late June, 1925).

CHAPTER 28: *Taxes, Airplanes, Farmers, and Elections*

1. *Congressional Record*, 69th Congress, 1st Session, Part 1, p. 457.
2. *Ibid.*, p. 458.
3. Starling, *Starling of the White House*, p. 262.
4. Quint and Ferrell, *The Talkative President*, p. 159.
5. Nicolson, *Dwight Morrow*, p. 281.
6. *Congressional Record*, 69th Congress, 1st Session, Part 1, p. 538.
7. Quint and Ferrell, *The Talkative President*, pp. 96, 104.
8. *Congressional Record*, 69th Congress, 1st Session, Part 1, pp. 461–462.
9. Record Group 16, Department of Agriculture, Secretary's Records, National Archives, Coolidge to R. W. Bingham, November 10, 1923.
10. According to William Allen White, Coolidge is supposed to have said later to Robert A. Cooper: "Well, farmers never have made money. I don't believe that we can do much about it. But of course we will have to seem to be doing something; do the best we can and without much hope." *Puritan in Babylon*, p. 344.
11. *Congressional Record*, 69th Congress, 1st Session, Part 3, p. 2477.
12. Walter K. Roberts, "The Political Career of Charles Linza McNary, 1924–1944" (Unpublished Ph.D. dissertation, University of North Carolina, 1953), p. 62.
13. Quint and Ferrell, *The Talkative President*, pp. 70–71.
14. CLC, Albert Johnson to Coolidge, August 25, 1926.
15. CLC, Irvine L. Lenroot to Coolidge, November 15, 1926.
16. Huthmacher, *Massachusetts People and Politics*, p. 138.

CHAPTER 29: *Coolidge and Business*

1. Coolidge must have known that the McNary-Haugen majority was

composed largely of members of Congress from overrepresented farm areas.

2. Quint and Ferrell, *The Talkative President*, p. 72.
3. Gilbert Seldes, *The Years of the Locust* (Boston, 1933), p. 60.
4. Fuess, *Calvin Coolidge*, p. 11.
5. Quint and Ferrell, *The Talkative President*, pp. 135, 142.
6. *Congressional Record*, 69th Congress, 1st Session, Part 1, p. 5; and 70th Congress, 1st Session, Part 1, p. 747.
7. Schriftgiesser, *This Was Normalcy*, p. 240.
8. White, *Puritan in Babylon*, p. 391.

CHAPTER 30: *Congress and Domestic Issues, 1927–1928*

1. *Congressional Record*, 69th Congress, 2nd Session, Part 1, pp. 29, 35.
2. Leach, *That Man Dawes*, p. 274.
3. Henry T. Rainey Papers, Library of Congress, Rainey to George E. Brennan, February 7, 1927.
4. *Congressional Record*, 69th Congress, 2nd Session, Part 5, pp. 4771–76.
5. Charles L. McNary Papers, Library of Congress, McNary to John H. McNary, March 21, 1928.
6. Roberts, "Charles Linza McNary," p. 86.
7. Lord, *The Wallaces of Iowa*, p. 273.
8. *Ibid.*, p. 272.
9. *Senate Document* No. 141, Misc. II, 70th Congress, 1st Session, pp. 1–7.
10. CLC, files 93, 93A, 93B, and 93C contain valuable material relating to President Coolidge and Negroes.
11. Quint and Ferrell, *The Talkative President*, pp. 81–82.
12. *Ibid.*, p. 82.
13. John D. Hicks, *Republican Ascendancy, 1921–1933* (New York, 1960), p. 126.
14. *Congressional Record*, 70th Congress, 1st Session, Part 1, pp. 103–04.
15. Quint and Ferrell, *The Talkative President*, pp. 111–12.

CHAPTER 31: *Over There*

1. Willis Johnson, *George Harvey*, p. 402.
2. Herbert Feis, *The Diplomacy of the Dollar: First Era, 1919–1932* (Baltimore, 1950), p. 64.
3. Hajo Holborn, *The Political Collapse of Europe* (New York, 1951), p. 136.

4. Wesley R. Fishel, *The End of Extraterritoriality in China* (Berkeley and Los Angeles, 1952), pp. 92–93.
5. *Ibid.*, p. 93.
6. Grew, *Turbulent Era*, I, 659–60.
7. *Foreign Relations, 1925*, I (Washington, 1940), p. 781.
8. Grew, *Turbulent Era*, I, 690.
9. *Congressional Record*, 69th Congress, 2nd Session, Part 4, pp. 4386, 4390.
10. Dorothy Borg, *American Policy and the Chinese Revolution, 1925–1928* (New York, 1947), p. 330.
11. *Ibid.*, p. 431.
12. Stimson and Bundy, *On Active Service*, p. 129.

CHAPTER 32: *Neighbors to the South*

1. James W. Wadsworth, Jr., Papers, Library of Congress, James R. Sheffield to Wadsworth, June 3, 1926.
2. Quint and Ferrell, *The Talkative President*, p. 234.
3. *Ibid.*, pp. 238–39.
4. *Ibid.*, pp. 239–40.
5. Zinn, *La Guardia in Congress*, pp. 113–14.
6. Neuberger and Kahn, *George W. Norris*, pp. 191–92.
7. Elting E. Morison, *Turmoil and Tradition, A Study of the Life and Times of Henry L. Stimson* (Boston, 1960), pp. 271, 273.
8. For pressures on the White House to reach an amicable settlement of Mexican affairs, see the Edward T. Clark Papers, Library of Congress, Mexico file; and CLC, files 146 and 146A, especially Henry L. Doherty to Coolidge, August 18, 1926.
9. L. Ethan Ellis, "Frank B. Kellogg," in Norman A. Graebner (ed.), *An Uncertain Tradition: American Secretaries of State in the Twentieth Century* (New York, 1961), p. 159.
10. Nicolson, *Dwight Morrow*, p. 289.
11. *Ibid.*, pp. 291, 313–14.
12. *Ibid.*, p. 299.
13. For an account of the tortuous history of the Clark Memorandum from 1928–36, see Robert H. Ferrell, "Repudiation of a Repudiation," *Journal of American History*, LI (March, 1965).

CHAPTER 33: *World Court and Arms Limitation*

1. Theodore Roosevelt, Jr., Papers, Library of Congress, Diary, "International Court" Addendum.

2. *Congressional Record*, 68th Congress, 2nd Session, Part 1, p. 55.
3. *Ibid.*, 69th Congress, 1st Session, Part 1, p. 459.
4. Bowers, *Albert Beveridge*, p. 540.
5. John Chalmers Vinson, *William E. Borah and the Outlawry of War* (Athens, Georgia, 1957), p. 105.
6. Franklin L. Burdette, *Filibustering in the Senate* (Princeton, 1940), p. 147.
7. Fite, *Peter Norbeck*, p. 119.
8. Quint and Ferrell, *The Talkative President*, pp. 208–09.
9. *Ibid.*, pp. 209–10.
10. *Ibid.*, p. 168.
11. *Congressional Record*, 68th Congress, 2nd Session, Part 1, p. 55.
12. *Ibid.*, 69th Congress, 2nd Session, Part 3, p. 3401.
13. CLC, Frank B. Kellogg to Coolidge, May 27, 1927.
14. Edward T. Clark Papers, Library of Congress, Clark to Frank W. Stearns, August 1, 1927.
15. *Congressional Record*, 70th Congress, 2nd Session, Part 1, p. 160.

CHAPTER 34: *The Outlawing of War*

1. *Foreign Relations*, 1927, II (Washington, 1942), p. 612.
2. Quint and Ferrell, *The Talkative President*, pp. 211–12.
3. *Foreign Relations*, 1927, II, p. 616.
4. Robert H. Ferrell, *Peace In Their Time, The Origins of the Kellogg-Briand Pact* (New Haven, 1952), p. 98.
5. Bryn-Jones, *Frank B. Kellogg*, p. 231.
6. Stoner, *Levinson and the Pact of Paris*, p. 259.
7. Quint and Ferrell, *The Talkative President*, p. 215.
8. McKenna, *Borah*, p. 244.
9. Bryn-Jones, *Frank B. Kellogg*, p. 232.
10. *Foreign Relations*, 1927, II, p. 627.
11. *The General Pact for the Renunciation of War* (Washington, 1928), pp. 1–3.
12. Ferrell, *Peace In Their Time*, p. 204.
13. *Ibid.*, p. 205.
14. *Ibid.*, p. 225.
15. *Ibid.*, p. 208.
16. Stoner, *Levinson and the Pact of Paris*, p. 327.
17. Quint and Ferrell, *The Talkative President*, p. 218.
18. *Congressional Record*, 70th Congress, 2nd Session, Part 1, p. 21.
19. Bryn-Jones, *Frank B. Kellogg*, p. 249.

20. Dawes, *Notes*, p. 231.
21. *Ibid.*, p. 234.
22. Ferrell, *Peace In Their Time*, p. 254.

CHAPTER 35: *I Do Not Choose To Run*

1. Pringle, *William Howard Taft*, II, 1062.
2. Pusey, *Charles Evans Hughes*, II, 629.
3. Starling, *Starling of the White House*, p. 249.
4. Fite, *Peter Norbeck*, p. 129.
5. Fuess, *Calvin Coolidge*, pp. 392–95; Socolofsky, *Arthur Capper*, pp. 159, 258; Theodore C. Wallen, "Rapid City Statement," New York *Herald Tribune*, August 3, 1927; White, *Puritan in Babylon*, pp. 359–61. All four of the above reports are in conflict. The present account is an attempt to reconcile their differences by emphasizing the testimony of Sanders and Geisser where they were most concerned with the event and Capper's and Wallen's where they were prime witnesses.
6. Holman Hamilton, "Claude Bowers and the Democratic party in the 1920s," paper read before the Mississippi Valley Historical Association, April 21, 1961, Detroit, Michigan.
7. Hutchinson, *Lowden of Illinois*, II, 568.
8. Charles L. McNary Papers, Library of Congress, Carl Smith to McNary, August 17, 1927.
9. Herbert Hoover, *Memoirs, 1920–1933*, p. 190.
10. *Ibid.*, pp. 191, 193.
11. Edward T. Clark Papers, Library of Congress, Clark to Frank W. Stearns, September 14, 1927.
12. *Congressional Record*, 70th Congress, 1st Session, Part 2, p. 2253.
13. Clark Papers, Clark to Frank W. Stearns, December 17, 1927. Clark charged that Hilles was using a Coolidge-for-President movement to gain control of the New York delegation for "his own man," who was left unidentified.
14. *Ibid.*, Clark to Frank W. Stearns, September 14, 1927.
15. White, *Puritan in Babylon*, pp. 361, 366.
16. Lawrence E. Wikander, "Calvin Coolidge," in Tercentenary History Commission, *The Northampton Book* (Northampton, 1954), p. 302. A slightly different quotation is given in Ross, *Grace Coolidge*, p. 226.
17. James E. Watson, *As I Knew Them* (Indianapolis, 1936), pp. 255–256.
18. CACL, Grace Coolidge to Frank W. Stearns, n.d. (probably late June, 1928).

19. White, *Puritan in Babylon*, p. 400.
20. Starling, *Starling of the White House*, p. 269.
21. Quint and Ferrell, *The Talkative President*, pp. 17–18.
22. *Congressional Record*, 70th Congress, 2nd Session, Part 1, p. 20. If Coolidge was pleased with his Administration, Frank W. Stearns was ecstatic about it. At the end of February, 1929, the Boston merchant wrote that, excepting Lincoln's incomparable term, "this is the greatest administration since that of George Washington from the point of view of what it has done for the country." Clark MSS., Stearns to Clark, February 28, 1929.

CHAPTER 36: *Back to Northampton*

1. Dawes, *Notes*, p. 155.
2. Quint and Ferrell, *The Talkative President*, p. 18.
3. Herbert Hoover, *Memoirs, 1920–1933*, p. 211.
4. Quint and Ferrell, *The Talkative President*, p. 18.
5. Mayer, *The Republican Party*, p. 410.
6. Mason, *Harlan Fiske Stone*, p. 263.
7. Quint and Ferrell, *The Talkative President*, pp. 19, 34.
8. Ross, *Grace Coolidge*, p. 255.
9. Fuess, *Calvin Coolidge*, p. 448.
10. W. A. Swanberg, *Citizen Hearst* (New York, 1961), p. 416.
11. James M. Cox, *Journey Through My Years* (New York, 1946), p. 201.
12. Everett Sanders Papers, Library of Congress, Coolidge to Sanders, November 28, 1929.
13. Thanks largely to his writing efforts and his investments, Coolidge at his death left an estate worth about $700,000.
14. Boston *Post*, August 2, 7, 16, November 5, 1930.
15. *Ibid.*, July 3, 1930.
16. *Ibid.*, July 17, 1930.
17. Calvin Coolidge, "The Republican Case," *Saturday Evening Post*, 205 (September 10, 1932), pp. 4, 69, 72,
18. Stanley King, *A History of the Endowment of Amherst College* (Amherst, 1950), p. 154.

CHAPTER 37: *I Know My Work Is Done*

1. CFL, Grace Coolidge to Mrs. Reuben Hills, July 14, 1931.
2. Nicolson, *Dwight Morrow*, p. 353.
3. Huthmacher, *Massachusetts People*, p. 212.

4. Edward T. Clark Papers, Library of Congress, Coolidge to Clark, December 20, 1930.
5. *Ibid.*, Coolidge to Clark, November 10, 1931.
6. *Ibid.*, Coolidge to Clark, March 26, 1932.
7. *Ibid.*, Coolidge to Clark, May 7, 1932.
8. *Ibid.*, Coolidge to Clark, May 28, 1932.
9. *Ibid.*, Coolidge to Clark, June 9, 1932.
10. *Ibid.*, Coolidge to Clark, June 13, 1932.
11. *Ibid.*, Coolidge to Clark, June 17, 1932.
12. *Ibid.*, Coolidge to Clark, July 7, 1932.
13. *Ibid.*, Coolidge to Clark, September 21, 1932. See also similar letter of same date to Everett Sanders, Sanders Papers, Library of Congress.
14. *Ibid.*
15. *Ibid.*, Coolidge to Clark, September 26, 1932.
16. Herbert Hoover and Calvin Coolidge, *Campaign Speeches of 1932* (Garden City, N.Y., 1933), p. 66.
17. Clark Papers, Coolidge to Clark, October 21, 1932.
18. *Ibid.*
19. Hoover and Coolidge, *Campaign Speeches*, pp. 265–67.
20. Clark Papers, Coolidge to Clark, November 16, 1932.
21. Sanders Papers, Coolidge to Sanders, November 25, 1932.
22. Clark Papers, Coolidge to Clark, December 31, 1932.
23. Sanders Papers, Coolidge to Sanders, December 27, 1932.
24. Hathorn, "C. Bascom Slemp," p. 236.
25. Clark Papers, Coolidge to Clark, December 31, 1932.
26. Grace Coolidge and others, "The Real Calvin Coolidge," *Good Housekeeping*, C (June, 1935), p. 209.
27. Starling, *Starling of the White House*, p. 302.

CHAPTER 38: *A President Restrained*

1. Washington *Post*, June 8, 1924.
2. Ashurst, *Diary*, p. 267.
3. Stoddard, *As I Knew Them*, p. 532.
4. Hammond, *Autobiography*, II, 693.
5. *Ibid.*
6. Walter Lippmann, *Men of Destiny* (New York, 1927), p. 15.
7. Peter R. Levin, *Seven By Chance: The Accidental Presidents* (New York, 1948), p. 262.

INDEX